# THE DIARY

OF

# PHILIP HENSLOWE,

FROM 1591 TO 1609

Elibron Classics
www.elibron.com

Elibron Classics series.



ISBN 1-4021-0041-8 (paperback)
ISBN 1-4021-3449-5 (hardcover)

This Elibron Classics Replica Edition is an unabridged facsimile of the edition published in 1845 by the Shakespeare Society, London.

# The Shakespeare Society.

PRESIDENT.

The Most Noble the Marquess of Conyngham.

VICE-PRESIDENTS.

| | |
|---|---|
| The Earl of Powis. | Rt. Hon. Lord Francis Egerton. |
| The Earl of Glengall. | Rt. Hon. Lord Braybrooke. |
| The Earl Howe. | Rt. Hon. Lord Leigh. |

COUNCIL, 1844.

Thomas Amyot, Esq., F.R.S.
William Ayrton, Esq., F.R.S.
Lieut.-Gen. Sir Andrew Barnard, K.C.B.
Beriah Botfield, Esq., M.P.
J. Payne Collier, Esq., F.S.A., Director.
Bolton Corney, Esq.
Peter Cunningham, Esq., Treasurer
The Rev. Alexander Dyce.
Sir Henry Ellis, K.H.
John Forster, Esq

Henry Hallam, Esq., F.R.S.
J. O. Halliwell, Esq., F.R.S.
The Rev. W. Harness.
William C. Macready, Esq.
Samuel Naylor, Esq.
T. J. Pettigrew, Esq., F.R.S.
J R. Planché, Esq., F.S.A.
W. J. Thoms, Esq., F S.A.
F. G Tomlins, Esq., Secretary.
E. V. Utterson, Esq, F.S.A.
Sir F. B Watson, K.C.H.
Thomas Wright, Esq., F.S.A.

---

The Object of the Shakespeare Society is to print and distribute to the Subscribers books illustrative of Shakespeare and of the Literature of his time.

The Advantages derived from the Society are the procuring valuable and interesting works at cost price, which, if published in the usual mode, could not be purchased for three times the amount; and also the preserving and circulating rare works, which, being thus printed, are preserved from total destruction or oblivion. It will be perceived, therefore, that members of this and similar societies receive back more than the pecuniary value of their Subscription. The books are only procurable of the Society by Members.

Admission to the Society, of any respectable person, is made by application to the Agent.

The Subscription is £1 per annum, due on the First of January in each year in advance, on payment of which the Member is entitled to a copy of every book printed by the Society for the year for which the Subscription is made. The Subscription is payable to the London Agent, by cash or through the Country Agent, and must be made for the current year. The Subscribing for any or all of the previous years is optional.

The Affairs of the Society are managed by a Council, consisting of the President, six Vice-Presidents, and twenty-one Members: five of the latter retire every year, and the vacancies are filled up, on the recommendation of the Council, from the general body of the Subscribers, at the Annual General Meeting.

The Council meet on the second Tuesday in every month, to select and superintend the works printed by the Society; and the General Members once a-year, on the 26th of April, to receive a report of the proceedings, and elect the new Councillors.

The Editors and the Council render their services gratuitously to the Society; and every means are adopted to expend as nearly as possible the whole amount of the Subscriptions in producing books; by which course alone so many are rendered for the Subscription.

The Delivery of the Books is made by the London Agent, to whom all communications on the subject should be made. As it is the constant object of the Council to prevent as much as possible useless expenditure, Members are requested to make a clear and permanent arrangement with Mr. Rodd, for the delivery of the books; and it is desirable that, in towns where there is not a Country Agent, a party in London be appointed to receive the publications for the Country Subscribers. The Society deliver gratis to Members within three miles of the Agent's residence, and it is a rule most strictly adhered to, that *No book shall be delivered until the Subscription is paid.*

Contributions to "The Shakespeare Society's Papers" are solicited by the Council—it having been deemed desirable to issue occasional volumes thus formed and entitled, in order to create a medium for preserving and distributing illustrations of the literature, which is the peculiar object of the Society.

# Books issued by the Shakespeare Society.

## FOR 1841.

Memoirs of Alleyn, Founder of Dulwich College. By J. P. Collier, Esq.
Gosson's School of Abuse. With Introduction, &c.
Heywood's Apology for Actors. With Introduction, &c.
The Coventry Mysteries. Edited by J. O. Halliwell, Esq., with Introduction and Notes.
Thynn's Pride and Lowliness. With Introduction, Notes, &c.
Patient Grissell. A Comedy, by Dekker, Chettle, and Haughton. With Introduction and Notes, by J. P. Collier, Esq.

## FOR 1842.

Extracts from the Accounts of the Revels at Court in Elizabeth and James's Reigns. With Introduction and Notes by P. Cunningham, Esq.
Jonson's Conversations with Drummond. Introduction, &c. by D. Laing, Esq.
First Sketch of the Merry Wives of Windsor. The Novels on which it is founded, and an Introduction and Notes by J. O. Halliwell, Esq.
Fools and Jesters; with Armin's Nest of Ninnies, &c. Introduction, &c. by J. P. Collier, Esq.
The Old Play of Timon. Now first printed. Edited by Rev. A. Dyce.
Nash's Pierce Pennilesse. With Introduction, &c. by J. P. Collier, Esq.
Heywood's King Edward the Fourth. Plays. Two Parts. With Introduction and Notes by Barron Field, Esq.

## FOR 1843.

Northbrooke's Treatise. With an Introduction, &c. by J. P. Collier, Esq.
The First Sketches of the Second and Third Parts of Henry the Sixth. With Introduction and Notes by J. O. Halliwell, Esq.
Oberon's Vision Illustrated. By the Rev. A. J. Halpin. In Thre Parts.
The Chester Whitsun Plays —Part I. With Introduction and No es by T Wright, Esq.
The Alleyn Papers, illustrative of the Early English Stage. With Introduction by J. P. Collier, Esq.
Tracts by Forde the Dramatist. With Introduction by J. P. Collier, Esq.

## FOR 1844.

Tarlton's Jests and Tarlton's Newes out of Purgatory. With a Life, &c. by J. O. Halliwell, Esq.
The True Tragedie of Richard the Third, from a unique Copy, and The Latin Play of Richardus Tertius, from a Manuscript. Edited by Barron Field, Esq.
The Ghost of Richard the Third. A Poem. Edited by J. P. Collier, Esq.
Sir Thomas More. A Play. Edited by the Rev. A. Dyce.
VOL. I. of "THE SHAKESPEARE SOCIETY'S PAPERS," being a Miscellany of Contributions Illustrative of the Objects of the Society.
The Taming of *a* Shrew. To which is added, the Woman lapped in Morrel Skin. Edited by Thomas Amyot, Esq.

## FOR 1845.

Illustrations of the Fairy Mythology of Shakespeare. By J. O Halliwell, Esq.
A Reprint of a Unique Contemporary Manuscript, lately discovered, of the First Part and a portion of the Second Part of Shakespeare's Henry the IVth. Edited by J. O Halliwell, Esq.
The Diary of Philip Henslowe, from 1591 to 1609. Printed from the Original Manuscript preserved at Dulwich College. Edited by J. P. Collier, Esq.

## IN THE PRESS.

VOL. II. of "THE SHAKESPEARE SOCIETY'S PAPERS." Consisting of Miscellaneous Contributions.
Part II. of The Chester Whitsun Plays. Edited by T. Wright, Esq.

## PREPARING FOR PRINTING.

Notices of Shakespeare and his Works, from the earliest period to the publication of the "Theatrum Poetarum" in 1675; with memoranda drawn from other sources on his personal and literary history. By Bolton Corney, Esq.
A Selection from Oldys's MS Notes to Langbaine's Dramatic Poets. By P. Cunningham, Esq.
The Fair Maid of The Exchange—A Comedy: and Fortune by Land and Sea—A Play. Both by Thomas Heywood. Editing by Barron Field, Esq.
Funebriæ Floræ. By Thomas Hall. Editing by W. B. D. D. Turnbull, Esq.
Two Masques of Ben Jonson: from the Author's own MSS.
Ralph Roister Doyster, the earliest Comedy, and Ferrex and Porrex, the earliest Tragedy, in the Language. Editing by W. D. Cooper, Esq.

See also Report of Annual Meeting, at the end of Henslowe's Diary.

*June*, 1845.

*** The *early payment* of the Annual Subscription (One Pound, due in advance, on the 1st January in each year), is earnestly requested, as it enables the Council to make suitable arrangements for the year, and otherwise saves expense to the Society. Payable to the Agents only, by Cash or Post-office Order.

N.B. The giving a continuous order on a banker, or compounding by the payment of £10, in addition to the Subscription for the current year, gives the greatest facility for conducting the Society in the simplest and most economical manner.

# THE DIARY

OF

# PHILIP HENSLOWE,

FROM 1591 TO 1609.

PRINTED FROM THE ORIGINAL MANUSCRIPT PRESERVED
AT DULWICH COLLEGE.

EDITED BY

J. PAYNE COLLIER, ESQ., F.S.A.

LONDON:
PRINTED FOR THE SHAKESPEARE SOCIETY.

1845.

FREDERICK SHOBERL, JUNIOR,
PRINTER TO HIS ROYAL HIGHNESS PRINCE ALBERT,
51, RUPERT STREET, HAYMARKET, LONDON.

# COUNCIL

OF

# THE SHAKESPEARE SOCIETY.

---

## President.

THE MOST NOBLE THE MARQUESS OF CONYNGHAM.

## Vice-Presidents.

THE EARL OF POWIS.
THE EARL OF GLENGALL.
THE EARL HOWE.
THE RT. HON. LORD FRANCIS EGERTON.
THE RT. HON. LORD BRAYBROOKE.
THE RT. HON. LORD LEIGH.

THOMAS AMYOT, ESQ., F.R.S., TREAS. S.A.
WILLIAM AYRTON, ESQ., F.R.S., F.S.A.
SIR ANDREW BARNARD, LIEUT. GEN., K.C.B.
BERIAH BOTFIELD, ESQ., M.P.
J. PAYNE COLLIER, ESQ., F.S.A., DIRECTOR.
BOLTON CORNEY, ESQ.
PETER CUNNINGHAM, ESQ., TREASURER.
THE REV. ALEXANDER DYCE.
SIR HENRY ELLIS, K.H., F.R.S., F.S.A.
JOHN FORSTER, ESQ.
HENRY HALLAM, ESQ., F.R.S., V.P.S.A.
J. O. HALLIWELL, ESQ., F.R.S., F.S.A.
THE REV. WILLIAM HARNESS.
WILLIAM C. MACREADY, ESQ.
SAMUEL NAYLOR, ESQ.
T. J. PETTIGREW, ESQ., F.R.S. F.S.A.
J. R. PLANCHÉ, ESQ., F.S.A.
WILLIAM J. THOMS, ESQ., F.S.A.
F. GUEST TOMLINS, ESQ., SECRETARY.
EDWARD V. UTTERSON, ESQ., F.S.A.
SIR FREDERICK BEILBY WATSON, K.C.H, F.R.S.

# INTRODUCTION.

The manuscript from which the present volume has been printed contains minute and valuable information respecting the history and condition of our early drama and stage, from the year 1591 to the year 1609, during the whole of which period Shakespeare was exercising his unequalled powers for the public instruction and amusement. Although his name nowhere occurs in the text of the following pages, the company of players to which he belonged was acting, if not in concert, in the joint occupation of the same theatre for two whole years, viz., from the beginning of June, 1594, to the middle of July, 1596; and it will be seen that in the list of plays performed not a few names occur, either identical with, or very similar to, the titles borne by some of Shakespeare's undoubted productions. Whether they were older pieces on the same subjects, of which our great dramatist subsequently availed himself, or whether some of them may not have been earlier efforts by himself, which he afterwards re-wrote and remodelled, is a point it is not possible to decide, with our present means of information. To this question we shall have occasion again more particularly to advert in speaking of the manner in which the manuscript, directly or incidentally, illustrates the life and works of Shakespeare.

In the first instance, it seems desirable to say something of the origin and history of a volume, which with the greatest liberality was placed, and has been allowed to remain, in our hands for an almost indefinite period. We can hardly rate too highly the obligations of the Shakespeare Society, to the Master, Warden, and Fellows of Dulwich College, in this respect, more especially to the Rev. Mr. Howes, who has charge of the books of the Institution.

The manuscript itself was first discovered by Malone. God's Gift, or Dulwich College was founded by Edward Alleyn; and all the known particulars regarding its construction are detailed in the "Memoirs" of that great actor, and benevolent man, printed by the Shakespeare Society in the year 1841. Into these, therefore, it is not necessary to enter, farther than to state that Alleyn seems to have deposited in the library, or in the archives, all the books and documents of which he was possessed, many of which had devolved into his hands from Philip Henslowe, whose step-daughter he had married, and with whom he was for a long series of years in partnership. The manuscript is mainly in the handwriting of Henslowe, assisted here and there by some clerk or scribe whom he employed: it is a folio volume of considerable bulk, bound in parchment, and it was the depository of memoranda regarding all payments to, or transactions with, dramatists, players, and others, for a period not far short of twenty years. The book itself, from about 1576 to 1586, had been used to record transactions connected with the felling, sale, and consumption of wood in Ashdown Forest, Sussex, for there is reason to believe that Henslowe and his family were of that county; but, as the backs of many leaves were left blank, while upon others there was no writing at all, Henslowe employed most of the unoccupied spaces to register matters connected with undertakings in which he was subsequently personally interested. He appears to have been first concerned with dramatic affairs about the year 1584, when he became joint lessee either of the Rose Theatre on the Bankside, or of the ground on which it stood; but no memorandum is contained in the manuscript before us of so early a date. Regarding Henslowe's transactions of this kind between 1584 and 1591, we have no knowledge.

He married a widow of the name of Woodward, who had a daughter Joan, which Joan, in October 1592, was united to Edward Alleyn: a memorandum of this event is contained in the manuscript (p. 3 of our impression), and it will be observed that two entries immediately preceding it, dated June 1592, relate to the purchase of pieces of plate, which perhaps Henslowe had bought in contemplation of the marriage of the young people, and in order to be presented to them.

Henslowe's original trade seems to have been that of

a dyer (pp. 52, 267); and later in life we find him and his step-daughter's husband, whom he invariably called "son," engaged in a starch manufactory (pp. 233, 262). He also appears to have carried on the business of a pawnbroker, either in his own name or in that of his brother Francis Henslowe (p. 148), and not a few pages of the manuscript are filled with accounts of advances made to various persons, principally among the lower orders, upon pledges of nearly every description. From the earliest date to which this record extends, Philip Henslowe was in partnership with Edward Alleyn in their theatrical speculations, and they continued so until the death of the former in 1616.[1] These speculations seem at first to have been carried on at the Rose Theatre; afterwards Henslowe obtained some interest in the Hope; and in the commencement of the seventeenth century Alleyn and Henslowe removed to the Fortune Theatre, which they had built in Golding Lane, in the parish of Cripplegate. When the company to which they were then attached was playing at the same house, and perhaps in conjunction with the association of which Shakespeare was a member, the performances were at a theatre in Newington Butts,[2] which afterwards fell into disuse. At what precise period Alleyn and Henslowe became tenants of Paris Garden, where bears, bulls, and horses were baited, and which, not long after the accession of James I., was also adapted to the purposes of a playhouse, is not ascertained: they were deputies to Sir Ralph

[1] Memoirs of Edward Alleyn, p. 122.

[2] For an account of the Newington and other early theatres, see Hist. Engl. Dram. Poetry and the Stage, iii., 263.

Bowes, the Master of the Queen's Games, in the spring of 1596 (p. 177), and in April 1602 (p. 267) they stood in the same relation to Sir John Dorrington, who had succeeded to the office, to both of whom they paid a periodical fee: in the latter instance it was £10 per quarter, but in the former the amount is not stated.

Connected with this point, we may here fitly introduce a document not hitherto noticed. It is a privy seal in favour of Henslowe, as "Serjeant of the Bear-garden," to whose care the king committed the custody of "a lion and certain other beasts," which had been sent as a present from the Duke of Savoy in 1613: for keeping and feeding them Henslowe was to be allowed four shillings per day; but, as nothing is said in the instrument regarding Alleyn, we may perhaps conclude that, although Henslowe's partner in the concern, he was not recognized at court in any such capacity. When Stowe, in 1604, calls Alleyn "Master of the Bear Garden," [1] we are to presume that he is speaking of him as one of the two lessees, and not as an officer appointed by the Crown. The instrument is in the following form, as we find it in a manuscript once belonging to Sir Julius Cæsar [2] (Master of the Requests, and subsequently of the Rolls), which was sold among the books of the late Mr. Bright, of Bristol:—

James, by the grace of God, Kinge of England, Scotland, Fraunce, and Ireland, Defendour of the Faith, &c. To our Commissioner for the

[1] Annales, p. 1427. Edit. 1605.

[2] In his Diary, Henslowe mentions having gone in 1597 to wait upon "Mr. Cæsar" at St. Katherine's, of which he was Master.

office of our high Treasurer of England, greeting. Where wee haue committed to the charge of Phillipp Henslow, serieant of the beare garden, a lion and certein other beasts sent vnto vs from the Duke of Savoy, and have agreed to allow vnto him, for the defraying of the charge thereof and of his paines, the somme of fower shillings by the daye. We will and Commaund you, out of our treasure in the receipt of our Exchequer, to paie or cause to be paid vnto the said Phillipp Henslowe, or his Assignes, the said somme of fower shillings by the day. The same to begin from the day of the deliveringe of them into his charge and to continue during our pleasure. And these our letters shall be your sufficient Warrant and discharge in this behalfe. Given vnder our privy Seale at our Pallace of Westminster, the thirtieth day of August in the Eleaventh yeare of our raigne of England, ffrance, and Ireland, and of Scotland, the xliiijth

THO. PACKER.

Notwithstanding the omission of Alleyn's name in the above, there is no doubt that, as early as 1597, he had himself obtained a privy seal for some unexplained purpose, or unascertained office, under which a patent was subsequently made out: Henslowe's Diary (p. 255) contains entries of the payment of forty shillings for them on the 9th June.[1]

It is necessary to remark that this volume, the value of which is at present so well understood, and so justly appreciated, by the authorities of Dulwich College, is not now in the state in which it existed when in the hands of Malone. This fact is established by the circumstance, that Malone made long and curious

[1] On p. 107 will be seen an account dated 1597, which may possibly refer to the same circumstance. Henslowe there calls it "our commission," which was "changed," and regarding which he had to wait upon Sir Julius Cæsar.

quotations from parts of it not now found in the manuscript: these evidently formed a portion of it, when it was for so many years in his hands; and, in order that our work may be as complete as possible, we have added them in the form of an Appendix: as however they have disappeared from the original, of course we are without any means of correction or verification, and we have been obliged to take them as they stand in vol. iii. of Malone's Shakspeare by Boswell.

There is good reason to suppose that, when Henslowe first availed himself of the parchment-covered book for the purpose of entering his theatrical memoranda, leaves and parts of leaves had been cut out; but there can be no doubt that, within perhaps the last fifty years, it has been still farther mutilated, and that many pages have been torn, cut, and otherwise injured, by inconsiderate lovers of the autographs of our old poets and actors. In some instances, the signatures only have disappeared, while in others, the whole of an entry has been removed. This damage must have been done considerably before the time of the present or of the late Master of Dulwich College: ever since it was restored by Malone to its ancient depository, it has been preserved with the care and caution due to the extraordinary curiosity and interest of the relic.

Those who have the patience to travel through its details, with such assistance as our notes may afford, will be aware how importantly, and how authentically, it contributes to our knowledge of particulars connected with the history of our early dramatic literature and performances, and of the theatres then in existence. We shall advert presently to a few of the points thus established; and recollecting that the names of nearly all the other play-poets of the time occur, we cannot but wonder that that of Shakespeare is not met with in any part of the manuscript. The notices of Ben Jonson, Dekker, Chettle, Marston, Wilson, Drayton, Monday, Heywood, Middleton, Porter, Hathway, Rankins, Webster, Day, Rowley, Haughton, &c., are frequent, because they were all writers for Henslowe's theatre; but we must wait, at all events, for the discovery of some other similar record, before we can produce corresponding memoranda regarding Shakespeare and his productions.

It is quite clear that accounts applicable to the Globe and Blackfriars once existed, for John Heminge distinctly speaks of them in his will, dated 9th October 1630, and states that the books he had regularly kept would show how profitable his shares in those two playhouses had been.[1] If these books were at all like that of Henslowe, they would prove, not only the dates when most of Shakespeare's plays were originally brought out, but the very sums he had received for them. More impossible things have happened than the bringing to light even of such sources; and the spirit of inquiry and research generated by the formation and labours of the Shakespeare Society may yet lead to the production even of information, with the existence of which at any former period we are at present unacquainted: we are

[1] Malone's Shaksp. by Boswell, iii., 195.

certain that the account-books of John Heminge, (one of the principal managers of the two theatres in which our great dramatist was interested) must have devolved into the hands of his personal representatives. When Malone found Henslowe's Diary, relating to the Rose, Fortune, and Paris Garden, it came upon him quite by surprise, and late in life; and, though he had it long in his custody, he was by no means accurate in the information he gleaned from it, while, as will be seen hereafter, he left behind him many particulars which we have carefully collected and deposited in the present volume. Our publication is the whole of the manuscript, exactly as it stands, as far as regards the dramatic affairs of the later years of Elizabeth, and the earlier part of the reign of James I.; and in our notes we have pointed out such facts and peculiarities as appeared to deserve or require remark.

Henslowe was an ignorant man, even for the time in which he lived, and for the station he occupied: he wrote a bad hand, adopted any orthography that suited his notions of the sound of words, especially of proper names (necessarily of most frequent occurrence), and he kept his book, as respects dates in particular, in the most disorderly, negligent, and confused, manner. Sometimes, indeed, he observes a sort of system in his entries; but often, when he wished to make a note, he seems to have opened his book at random, and to have written what he wanted in any space he found vacant. He generally used his own pen, but, as we have stated, in some places the hand of a scribe or clerk is visible; and here and there the dramatists and actors themselves wrote the item in which they were concerned, for the sake perhaps of saving the old manager trouble : thus, in various parts of the manuscript, we meet with the handwriting, not merely the signatures, of the following authors—Drayton, Chapman, Dekker, Chettle, Porter, Wilson, Hathway, Day, S. Rowley, Haughton, Rankins, and Wadeson; but, although frequently mentioned, we have no specimen of the handwriting of Nash, Ben Jonson, Middleton, Webster, Marston, or Heywood. Among the players, who sign their own names or introduce memoranda, we find nearly every man that belonged to the company. It should be remarked that Marlowe and Greene died not long after the commencement of the Diary, that Peele certainly did not survive beyond 1598, and that Lodge early diverted his attention from dramatic poetry. It may be doubted whether Fletcher is mentioned in the Diary (p. 78): Beaumont certainly is not; and Massinger, Daborne, Ford, Shirley, &c., became writers for our public theatres too late to be introduced into a manuscript the most modern date in which is 1609.

At various times and for uncertain periods, Henslowe was more or less interested in the receipts obtained by players acting under the names of the Queen, Lord Nottingham, Lord Strange, Lord Sussex, Lord Worcester, and the Lord Chamberlain. The latter was the company of which Shakespeare was a member, either as actor or author, from his first arrival in, until his final retirement from, London; which company, subsequently to the accession of James I., was allowed to assume the distinguishing title of the King's Players.[1]

Malone was not at all aware, when he made extracts from Henslowe's Diary, that it not only shows the number of times different plays were represented, but generally *the very day when they were acted for the first time*. The old manager was in the habit of placing in a particular column, or in the margin of his book, and opposite the title of a new drama, the letters *ne*, the first two letters of the word *new*, which invariably indicate that at that particular date it was brought out. This is often an important and interesting piece of information, and it serves to show more distinctly the comparative popularity each novelty acquired. Towards the commencement of our volume, we could not contrive our printed page exactly to correspond with the page of the manuscript, and we have therefore been obliged in notes to state when *ne* was found affixed to the title of any play, or, in other words, when it was originally performed. As Henslowe proceeded, however, he adopted another course, and placed *ne* in the interval between two columns, and we have been able to follow his example. Thus, by running the eye down this interval, and seeing how often *ne* occurs, it is easy to ascertain how many new plays were produced at Henslowe's Theatre in any given period. On p. 35 begins a highly valuable

[1] It is a new point in stage history, established by Henslowe's Diary, (p. 251) that James I. had granted a license to the players of the Earl of Worcester some days before he conceded it to the association which subsequently acted under the royal name and patronage.

enumeration of all the dramas represented between 3rd June 1594 and 18th July 1596, during the whole of which two years and six weeks the Lord Admiral's Players were jointly occupying, or possibly playing in combination at, the Newington Theatre with the Lord Chamberlain's servants; and here we find, by Henslowe's usual indication, that no fewer than forty new plays were got up and acted.[1] For about ten weeks of the two years, the companies ceased to perform, on account, perhaps, of the heat of the weather, and the occurrence of Lent; so that two years is the utmost upon which a calculation can be made; and the result of it is, that the audiences of that day required a new play upon an average about every eighteen days, including Sundays.[2] The rapidity with which dramas must then have been written is most remarkable, and is testified beyond dispute by later portions of Henslowe's manuscript, where, among other charges, he registers the sums paid, the dates of payment, and the authors who received the money. Nothing was more common than for dramatists to unite their abilities and resources; and, when a piece on any account was to

[1] Against a single memorandum, relating to "Long Meg of Westminster," (p. 49) Henslowe has placed the figure *j*, instead of *ne*; but the meaning is the same, viz., that it was the *first* representation of the drama. Why he varied, in this instance alone, does not appear; and perhaps "j" was added by some other person, to remedy Henslowe's omission of *ne*.

[2] By another list (p. 82), commencing 25th Nov. 1596 and ending 28th July 1597, a period of about eight months, we find that new plays were considered necessary about every seventeen days. The particular parts of the year when novelties were most required is also thus ascertained.

be brought out with peculiar despatch, three, four, five, and perhaps even six poets engaged themselves upon different portions of it. Evidence of this dramatic combination will be found of such frequent occurrence, that it is vain here to point out particular pages where it is to be met with.

Before we advert to other points established by the manuscript, we may be permitted to observe that Malone made some important errors and various omissions in the information he derived from it: he has mistaken dates and misread the titles of several pieces, while he has sometimes assigned to one or more authors the works of others: he has also passed over without notice several plays, the performance of, or the payment for which Henslowe duly records. We only mention this circumstance in order to put our readers on their guard against placing entire confidence in Malone's quotations as printed by Boswell; but, having set these matters right in our notes, it is unnecessary, as well as ungracious, to dwell here upon the defects of a man whose sight failed him towards the end of his career, and who had the merit of being the first to find and to make use of a volume, the thread of which is much entangled, and the handwriting not unfrequently extremely difficult to be deciphered.

We have already spoken of the union of the company to which Shakespeare belonged, and for which he wrote, with that so intimately connected with Philip Henslowe. This union (if such it were, and not merely the joint occupation of the same house, while the Globe was in a course of construction, and for some short time afterwards) lasted for rather more than two years, and, as has been remarked in the Memoirs of Edward Alleyn (p. 22), it is singular that most of the old plays which our great dramatist is supposed more or less to have employed, and of the stories of which he availed himself, are found in Henslowe's list of this period. Here we find a Titus Andronicus, a Lear, a Hamlet, a Henry V., and a Henry VI., a Buckingham, the old Taming of a Shrew, and several others, the titles of which we need not enumerate, because they are inserted in their proper places, precisely as they stand in the manuscript. For aught we know, Shakespeare may originally have had some share in their authorship; or, if he had not, as he probably acted in them, he may have felt himself authorized, as a member of the company, to use them to the extent that answered his purpose. At the same time, Greene could not have referred to this particular circumstance and period, inasmuch as he charged Shakespeare with being "an upstart crow, beautified with our feathers," in 1592 (in September of which year he died) whereas the account to which we advert does not commence until the summer of 1594. Greene must, therefore, allude, in his "Groatsworth of Wit," to some previous transactions of the same kind; but no fact is more clearly made out, and very much by the evidence Henslowe furnishes, than that it was a very common practice for our early dramatists to avail themselves of the materials, whether of plot, character, or language, supplied by their immediate predecessors, and even by their actual contemporaries.

It is remarkable that the first drama in this list, from 1594 to 1596, is upon a sacred subject, "Esther and Ahasuerus:" it was not a new play on 3rd June 1594, and on a previous page (32) we have had a notice of "Abraham and Lot." These may have been modifications of old miracle-plays, traces of which were preserved upon our stage. Incidents from Scripture seem to have been still popular; and it is a circumstance not sufficiently noticed by the historians of our early drama, that even at the time when Shakespeare was in the zenith of his reputation, stories derived from the Bible kept possession of some of our public theatres. Whether such was the case at the Blackfriars and Globe we have no means of knowing, but it is indisputable as regards the Rose and the Fortune; and in the following pages distinct traces may be found of many such performances, beginning with a play in which "a bodice for Eve" (p. 272) was required, and ending with "a jerkin for Caiaphas." A drama entitled "Nebuchadnezzar" was represented in 1596—"Judas" in 1601—"Pontius Pilate" in the same year—"Jephthah," "Tobias," "Samson," and "Joshua" in 1602; and in the same year we meet with a charge for pullies in order to hang Absalom. The number of these sacred representations in 1602 forms a curious feature applicable in particular to that date, and, as far as we know, to Henslowe's and Alleyn's theatres.

In connexion, we may observe, that, although at various periods theatrical performances were forbidden on Sunday, the companies appear to have been permitted to play on Christmas-day; and on 25th Dec. 1595 and 1596, the representations possessed anything but a religious character. Such was probably not the case in 1601, for on the 24th Dec. (p. 205) Samuel Rowley was paid £5 for his "book called Judas;" but "Pontius Pilate," "Jephthah," "Tobias," "Samson," and "Joshua," were brought out in the ordinary course of business, whenever a new play was needed.

Having spoken of old plays acted in 1594, 1595, and 1596, the titles of which resemble some of those of Shakespeare, it may be worth while to observe that Henslowe's Diary indubitably shows that the poets, who wrote for his company at different dates, took up subjects which our great dramatist has also treated: which had the precedence must often be matter of mere speculation; but it will strike everybody as singular that, in 1602, after Richard the Third had been long on the stage, and was so popular, Ben Jonson should have been paid by Henslowe no less a sum than £10, "in earnest of a book called Richard Crookback," and for some "new additions" he was then making to Kyd's Spanish Tragedy (p. 223). It may show that at that period the Earl of Nottingham's players could not venture to represent Shakespeare's Richard the Third, which was in possession of a rival company, or Henslowe would not have given a large sum "in earnest" of a new drama on the same portion of history.[1] The arrest of Thomas Dekker (p. 143)

[1] "The second part of Henry Richmond" reads (p. 159) as if it could not be otherwise than connected with the incidents of the reign of Richard III. A few pages afterwards (p. 163), we meet with a play called Owen Tudor.

by "the Lord Chamberlain's men" in 1598, may very possibly have been connected with some piratical invasion of the rights and property of the association to which Shakespeare belonged; and less than three months afterwards (p. 147) we find Dekker engaged with Chettle upon a play called "Troilus and Cressida." It has never been remarked that in July 1602 Chettle was writing "the Danish Tragedy," (p. 224) which may have been a revival of the old Hamlet under a new name, in order to compete with Shakespeare's Hamlet, then in a course of successful performance at the Globe.[1]

There can be no dispute that Shakespeare's Henry the Eighth, as it has come down to us, was not written until after the accession of James I.; but in June 1601 it appears (p. 189) that Chettle was employed on a drama called "Cardinal Wolsey's Life," and that it became so popular, that, at all events, one, if not two other plays were composed on the same subject. One of these was "the Rising of Cardinal Wolsey," by Chettle, Drayton, and Monday, and the other "the Second Part of Cardinal Wolsey," which may, however, have been meant for "Cardinal Wolsey's Life," which had thus become a second part. Hence it is clear, that other dramatists had availed themselves of that period of our annals before the death of Elizabeth.

[1] Dekker's "Medicine for a Curst Wife" (p. 224) may have been a new play upon the story of the old "Taming of a Shrew," the title of which Shakespeare did not scruple very nearly to adopt, perhaps because Dekker had avoided it. In a note, on p. 230, we have speculated that "Like quits Like" may have been similar to "Measure for Measure."

There are few plays mentioned in the course of our volume that illustrate more strongly than "Cardinal Wolsey's Life" the expense which companies of old did not hesitate to incur, in order that the characters might be splendidly dressed and caparisoned. The charges for scenery were none, and for properties small, so that the actors could afford to spend more money upon velvets, silks, satins, lace, and other personal ornaments. We are to bear in mind that, at the date of which we are speaking, money was of at least five times its present value, and if we find £10 given for a cloak or a suit of apparel, it is to be considered quite equal to £50 of our currency. In the entries respecting Chettle's "Cardinal Wolsey's Life" we find £21 in a single item (p. 197) for "two-pile velvet," at 20*s.* 5*d.* per yard, and for satins and taffaties at 12*s.* and 12*s.* 6*d.* per yard respectively: this alone was equal then to more than £100 now; and the other items, of the same kind and for the same drama, prove that certainly not less than £200 was laid out upon new apparel only. At least as much was spent upon "The Seven Wise Masters" (p. 165). In one instance £19 was given for a single cloak; while the gown of Mrs. Frankford, in Heywood's "Woman Killed with Kindness" (p 248), cost £6 13*s.* 0*d.*, between £30 and £40 of our present money. Taffaty for two women's gowns, in Porter's comedy, "The Two Angry Women of Abingdon," cost more than £45, according to the same calculation.

The contrast between the expense of apparel and the cost of plays is remarkable. Heywood did not receive for the five admirable acts of his "Woman Killed with

Kindness" as much as was given by the company for the gown of the heroine. From Henslowe's Diary we derive very curious and conclusive information respecting the ordinary rewards of dramatists in his day: those rewards seem to have varied sometimes, according to circumstances with which we are not now acquainted. The highest price Henslowe appears, from this manuscript, ever to have given, was for "Page of Plymouth," by Ben Jonson and Dekker, a tragedy founded upon a murder committed by a wife in 1591. For this piece the old manager paid £11 in August 1599: for Dekker's "Medicine for a Curst Wife," he gave £10 0*s.* 0*d.* in September 1602: "Patient Grissill," in December 1599, cost him £9 10*s.* 0*d.*[1]: for "Strange News out of Poland," by W. Haughton, and an otherwise unknown dramatist of the name of Pett, he paid £9 in May 1600: for "Lady Jane Grey" he gave £8 to Dekker, Webster, Heywood, and Smith, in October 1602: "The Unfortunate General" produced £7 to the authors, Hathway, Smith, and Day, in January 1602: Heywood and Chettle obtained £6 10*s.* 0*d.* for their "London Florentine," in the same month, and £6 seems not to have been an unusual sum:

[1] Reprinted by the Shakespeare Society in 1841 from the anonymous edition of 1603. On p. 167 of our present volume will be found an item of the payment of £2 to a printer, not named, as a gift to prevent the appearance of Patient Grissill from the press, companies at that date holding it injurious to their interests that popular dramas should be made legible: they wished them to be only audible and visible. This single fact (and the circumstance is nowhere else more distinctly stated) will explain how it happens that comparatively few old plays have been preserved.

Henslowe gave that price for Drayton's "William Longsword," in January 1598; for "Earl Godwin," in March of the same year; for "Hot Anger soon Cold," in August of the same year; for "the Boast of Billingsgate," in March 1602; for "the Blind eats many a Fly," in January 1602; and for the "Woman Killed with Kindness," in March of the same year. The success of the first part of "the Black Dog of Newgate," for which Henslowe gave £6, seems to have led the authors of the second part, Hathway, Smith, Day, and "another poet," to require an increase of £2 on the cost of the first part, as well as £2 for "additions;" so that, in the whole, they received £10 for it in February 1602. Dramas on sacred history realised about the same amounts; and Henslowe gave £6 for "Samson," and £7 for "Joshua," in July and September 1602. The sum generally paid for putting an old play on the stage, on its revival, with such changes as seemed necessary, was £2, and this sum Edward Alleyn obtained for Tambercam (of which he was not the author, as some have supposed), and for several others (pp. 200, 204, 207, 225); but now and then the expense was considerably more, and Birde and Rowley had £4, in November 1602, for their "additions" to "Faustus."

When a play became unusually popular, and therefore profitable, gratuities were now and then, though rarely, allowed to the authors, by way of encouragement: thus Drayton, Wilson, Monday, and Hathway, received 10*s*. as a gift after the first, and doubtless gratifying, reception of "Sir John Oldcastle," the drama imputed to Shakespeare on the title-page of some copies of the edition of 1600. The same sum was presented to John Day in 1601, when his second part of "the Beggar of Bethnal Green" was performed; and on p. 240 of our volume is recorded a similar stretch of bounty to Dekker: he was paid 10*s.* "over and above the price" of his "Medicine for a Curst Wife." The gift never exceeded this amount. Henslowe appears also to have disbursed small sums to the members of the company to be spent in wine after successful first performances; but on p. 117, as the expense of an entertainment of the kind was 30*s.*, he carefully put it down as a debt. When Drayton, Chettle, and Dekker's "Famous Wars of Henry the First" was read at the Sun in New Fish Street, the old manager expended 5*s.*; and the like sum was laid out in "good cheer" when "Earl Godwin" was accepted.

Notwithstanding the multiplicity of plays written for the association with which Henslowe was connected, it is quite clear, from evidence supplied by the manuscript in our hands, and as well as that obtained from other sources, that the wonderfully prolific dramatists of that day wrote for other companies also: they do not seem in general, like Shakespeare, to have confined themselves necessarily to one theatre, and to one body of actors. It is very possible that our great dramatist was under some express engagement not to compose any play for a rival company; and it is certain, with regard to two of the popular authors in the pay of Henslowe, that such was the case. On 28th February 1698, Henry Porter undertook that Henslowe "should have all the books which he wrote, either himself, or with any other;" and on the 25th March 1602, Henry Chettle sealed a bond with the Earl of Nottingham's Players to write for them only. At these dates there existed a strong competition among different associations; but it must have been still stronger about ten or twelve years afterwards, when Daborne was writing for Henslowe, when the price of new plays had risen considerably, and when he was threatening the old manager with carrying one of his productions to "the King's men," from whose service Shakespeare had very shortly before withdrawn, leaving the company in need of assistance.[1] Henslowe, as we have seen, had never paid more than £11 for any play up to the date to which his manuscript extends; but in a letter dated 25 June, 1613, Daborne asserts that he had been offered £25 for a new tragedy.[2] What connexion this vast and rapid increase in the value of new plays may have had with the removal of Shakespeare from London we have no means of determining, but the fact deserves more notice than it has hitherto received.

Another circumstance, in relation to some of our great dramatist's productions, has been recently, and only recently, adverted to.[3] We allude to the secession of the celebrated comedian, William Kemp, from the company which had always acted Shakespeare's plays.

[1] See The Alleyn Papers (published by the Shakespeare Society), p. 67.

[2] *Ibid*, p. 65. In a note to Henslowe of 3rd June, 1613, Daborne speaks of "the overplus of the second day" as then also due to an author.

[3] See Life of Shakespeare, edit. Whittaker and Co., i., cxxix.

Kemp was a very popular performer as early as 1589, and he unquestionably belonged to the same association as Alleyn prior to 1594: he then seems for a time to have joined the Lord Chamberlain's players; and we know that he was Peter in "Romeo and Juliet," and Dogberry in "Much ado about Nothing." He afterwards quitted that company, and rejoined Henslowe and Alleyn, probably about the time their new theatre, the Fortune, was opened; and in March, August, and September, 1602, Henslowe makes various memoranda of payments to or on account of him. He could not have performed, therefore, in any drama by Shakespeare produced at that period.

It will be found, by those who are inquisitive regarding such matters, that Henslowe's Diary illustrates the origin, state, and progress of our drama, stage, and its professors, in various ways, which we have not thought it necessary here to point out, because they are generally explained in our notes. There is only one more particular to which it may be expedient especially to advert, and it is connected with the office of the Master of the Revels, originally permanently created by Henry VIII. Edmund Tylney was Master of the Revels from 1578 to 1610, consequently, during the whole period to which Henslowe's manuscript applies; and it is curious to see how he gradually augmented his fees from time to time. In 1591 (p. 18), the fee on licensing each play was *5s.;* but in 1597 (p. 118), he had raised it, as far as we know, arbitrarily, to *7s.*: in that year, also, we hear for the first time (p. 79) of a monthly payment to the Master of the Revels of £2 : in one instance (p. 91), Tylney seems to have claimed that sum from Henslowe for permitting his company to act for about three weeks; and in 1599 he had raised his demand to £3 every month the theatre continued open. We may presume pretty safely that he obtained similar payments from other companies; and, supposing only four to be acting at the same time, which no doubt is much under the calculation, his monthly emoluments from this source alone, without reckoning his fees for licensing plays, would exceed, in our present money, £60 per month. As the Master of the Revels was also paid a daily allowance for his duties at Court, his post must have been much more lucrative than it has been hitherto imagined. After Henslowe opened the Fortune Theatre in the year 1601 (the precise date cannot be fixed), he seems to have been obliged to give Tylney a double monthly fee, for the Rose and for his new playhouse: the earliest entry of a payment for the Fortune (p. 213) seems to have been 9th June 1601, and we may infer, perhaps, that it was the first time it had become due.

If the notes are here and there found too numerous, prolix, or minute, the apology of the Editor must be derived from the nature of the manuscript, which is full of confusion and abundant in repetitions.

J. P. C.

Kensington, 21st June, 1845.

# ADDITIONAL NOTES AND CORRECTIONS.

---

Page 5, line 17. This is the only instance in which the name of *John* Towne occurs, and possibly it was written for *Thomas* Towne: John Towne might, however, be related to Thomas Towne.

Page 20, line 16. For "manteltie" read *manteltre.*

Page 22, line 10. The conjecture hazarded in this note has since been confirmed: there was an edition of "The Anatomie of Pope Joane" in 1591. It was printed by Richard Field. 4to. B.L.

Page 25, line 11. Respecting the play of "Jerusalem" see also p. 37, note 1.

Page 32, line 1. In the note upon this play a mistake is committed, when it is stated that Greene's death took place in Sept. 1593: it ought of course to have been Sept. 1592. Greene had probably acted in "The Pinner of Wakefield" shortly before his decease, but certainly not on the occasion referred to.

Page 47, line 5. Towards the conclusion of the Diary, viz., on p. 228, a play called "The *Set* at Tennis" is actually mentioned.

Page 54, line 29. For "*no doubt*" read *probably.*

Page 55, line 19. We have been informed, since this note was written, that Massinger's play of Philenzo and Hippolyto has been recovered in MS., having been found among the Conway Papers.

Page 61, line 7. It was more probably "The Welshman's Prize," enumerated by Henslowe (see p. 276) among "such books as belong to the stock." See also p. 120, note 3.

Page 70, line 29. For "Magelt" read *Magett.*

Page 79, line 16. Add to note 3.—This monthly payment of £2 was subsequently raised to £3: see p. 179.

Page 91, line 12. Among the stock-plays on p. 276, this comedy is called "Friar Pendelton," but *Spendleton*, as in the text, would seem to be the right name.

Page 103, line 27. It seems most likely that this play, "The Cobbler," was what Henslowe elsewhere (p. 276) calls "Cobler quen hive," meaning the Cobbler of Queen Hithe.

Page 119, line 19. Henslowe, not having being able perhaps to make anything out of "Triplicity," calls it in his enumeration of the stock-plays, p. 277, "The *Triangle* of Cuckolds."

Page 119, line 31. For "assigned" read "*correctly* assigned."

Page 127, line 23. "Tasso's picture" is also enumerated in the Inventory of Properties, &c., on p. 273.

Page 127, line 34. A poem, by Robert Greene, on the death of Sir Christopher Hatton, and printed in 1591, may be here noticed. It was omitted by the Rev. Mr. Dyce, in his edition of Greene's Works, as he did not know of its existence. It occupies twenty pages 4to, and is a favourable specimen of the author's abilities and fancy. The intention of the Council of the Shakespeare Society speedily to reprint it renders it unnecessary to insert its full title here.

Page 132, line 8. It seems likely that the play called Vayvode related to the adventures of the Vayvode Michael of Wallachia, in his struggle for independence against the Turks in 1597.

Page 137, line 34. The latest notice of the players of the Earl of Leicester seems to be in 1586. See Hist. Engl. Dram. Poetry and the Stage, i., 264.

Page 140, line 28. For this covenant between Henslowe and Heywood see p. 260.

Page 155, line 9. The following is the title of a unique tract, containing a full account of the murder of Page of Plymouth. "Sundrye strange and inhumaine Murthers lately committed. The first of a Father that hired a man to kill three of his children, neere to Ashford in Kent: The second of Master Page of Plymoth, murthered by the consent of his owne wife: with the strange discoverie of sundrie other murthers. Wherein is described the odiousnesse of murther, with the vengeance which God inflicteth on murtherers. Printed at London by. Thomas Scarlet, 1591." 4to. B.L. There were several contemporary ballads upon the same tragical event.

Page 166, line 22. Yet see a memorandum on p. 250, where it is said that Duke, the actor, in 1602 had been thrown into the Clink for debt.

Page 171, line 7. There is little doubt that "Indes" refers to "the Conquest of the West Indies," afterwards mentioned as a play. The notion that "Judas" was not a fit subject for a drama does not seem to have influenced Henslowe, as appears by subsequent entries.

Page 187, line 30. This prose tract is avowed to be merely a translation, and is dedicated by A. M. to the Lord Mayor, Aldermen, and Sheriffs of London in the year 1601.

Page 205, line 2. There must have been an older play on the story of Hercules than any mentioned in Henslowe's Diary. To this fact we may cite the testimony of Robert Greene in his "Groatsworth of Wit," 1592: a player there says, "The twelve labours of Hercules have I terribly thundered on the Stage, and played three scenes of the Devil in the Highway to Heaven." Here also the player declares that he was "famous for Delphrygus, and the King of the Fairies." Sign. E 2, edit. 1617.

Page 214, line 25. The same fact is mentioned by Gilbert Dugdale in his "Time Triumphant," 1604. 4to. B.L.

Page 225, line 29. See also, regarding "Lust's Dominion" and its real authors, a previous note on p. 165.

Page 230, line 18. It may be disputed whether the title of this play, as Henslowe writes and spells it, were "the bosste of bellengesgate," or "the *bosse* of bellengesgate:" it is more like the former, and so Malone read it; but Stow informs us, "On the north side is Bosse alley, so called of a boss of spring water continually running, which standeth by Billingsgate against this alley, and was sometime made by the executors of Richard Whittington." Page 72, edit. Thoms, 1842.

Page 234, line 27. This Lord Windsor was Henry, the fifth earl, who had been summoned to Parliament eleven years before.

Page 238, line 22. The whole sum paid to Dekker ought to have been stated to be £10, and not £8.

Page 244, line 29. In 1598 Thomas Churchyard printed "A wished

Reformation of Wicked Rebellion," of which only one copy exists, as it was no doubt objected to and suppressed. It refers to the rebellion in Ireland, and to the Earl of Essex.

Page 251, line 27. Nevertheless, it may be the same play which, on 214, Chettle calls "the book of Shore."

Page 271, line 3. All these Inventories, &c., were taken in the spring of 1598-9, and we may presume that they were made out, in order to ascertain the stock of the company of Lord Nottingham's Players in apparel, properties, and plays, before their removal from the Rose on the Bankside to the new theatre, the Fortune, in Golding Lane, Cripplegate.

# THE DIARY

OF

# PHILIP HENSLOWE.

---

*Jonne allen Receved for Rente as folowthe,* 1593.[1]

| | | |
|---|---|---|
| R. of the Duchewoman ther, for mydsomer qrtr. 1593 ........................................ | xv$^{s}$ | viij$^{d}$ |
| R. of the carpenter for mydsomer qrtr 1593...... | xvij$^{s}$ | vj$^{d}$ |
| R. of goody Rowden for mydsomer qrtr 1593 ... | x$^{s}$ | |
| R. of goodman hudson, the 14 of aguste 1593 ... | xv$^{s}$ | |
| R. of goodman glene, the 16 of aguste 1593...... | xxxx$^{s}$ | |
| R. of goody Rowden, the 18 of octobr 1593 ... .. | vij$^{s}$ | x$^{d}$ |

*For tremynge of the Folles head, as foloweth*[2]

| | |
|---|---|
| Item for selynge of the ij chambers, and mendynge of the walles, and whittinge and blackynge the same ........................ | xxx$^{s}$ |

[1] Jonne allen means Joan Alleyn, Edward Alleyn's wife, who received rents during his absence, while playing in the country in 1593, on account of the plague in London. Farther down, on the same page of the Diary, is a statement of money she had paid.

[2] This heading immediately precedes that which follows, but a line is drawn between them. The Fool's Head was probably the sign of a house near the theatre; but "trimming a head" usually meant cutting the hair: here it must be taken for repairing the building.

*A note of what Mrs. Allen hathe payd sence her husband went into the contrey, as foloweth.* 1593.

| | | |
|---|---|---|
| Itm̃ pd for howsse Rente, and for naylles ......... | xx^s | |
| Itm̃ pd unto hime for kepinge of your horsse [1] ... | ix^s | x^d |
| Itm̃ pd unto the Joyner for the beadstead [2] ...... | xv^s | |
| Itm̃ pd for the coshenes .............................. | v^s | |

The 28 of Janeway, 1597, I payd Ja. Fa. [3]

| | | | |
|---|---|---|---|
| Bowght, the 18 of June 1592, a gyllte gyllte [4] goblette, wayinge 17 oz $\frac{1}{2}$ at v^s vj^d q.—the some ............................................ | iiij^li | xix^s | ij^d |
| Bowght the same time j beacker of persell gyllte,[5] wainge viij oz j q^r at vj^s 8^d—some is | | lvj^s | vj^d |

[1] From a passage in a letter quoted in the next note from Henslowe to Alleyn, it appears that by 28 September 1593 Alleyn was tired of the expense of keeping his horse in London, where it could be of no use to him, and accordingly had desired his wife's stepfather to try to sell it. Henslowe says: "We hade a very bade market at Smyth fylld, for no monn would ofer a bove fower pownd for your horsse, and therfor I have not sowld hime, but to save carges, I have sent hime downe into the contrey, that [he] be keapte tell you retorne." This quotation fixes the date of the present account to be prior to 28 September 1593; for it will be observed that at the head of it we have only the year in which the money was paid by Mrs. Alleyn, in the absence of her husband.

[2] In the Memoirs of Edward Alleyn, in a letter from Henslowe to Alleyn, dated 28 September 1593, we read as follows: "Your joyner hath seate up your portowle in the chamber, and hath brothe you a corte cobert, and sayes he will bring the reaste very shortly, and we beare with hime becausse his howsse is visited;" i.e., by the plague: p. 32.

[3] This memorandum stands by itself, and is surrounded by a line to separate it from the rest of the page. It is perhaps impossible to ascertain for whom "Ja. Fa." was intended.

[4] The word "gyllte" is repeated in the MS. The letter *q* in this entry means a farthing, a *quarter* of a penny.

[5] "Persell gyllte" is *parcel*, or partly gilt.

Edward Alen wasse maryed unto Jone Woodward, the 22 of daye of octobr 1592, In the iiij and thirtie yeare of the Quenes Ma[tie] Rayne, elyzabeth, by the grace of god of Ingland france and Iarland, defender of the fayth.[1]

Pearsyvalle Craffte hath geven his worde for the fostchen dier in grobstreat, w[ch] persyvall lifte in Watlynge streate at the syne of the crosse Keayes a crysmas ene last, 1592, for iiij[li].

A. E. D. H.[2]

| | |
|---|---|
| R. of Thomas newman, the 10 of Jenewary 1593, In pte of paymente of a more some, as a pereath upon a bande. I saye Rd by me Phillipe Hensley[3] | xxxx[s] |

The wenscot belowe, in the halle of Edwardes Allenes howsse, is three score and fyve yardes and iij foote, at ij[s] a yarde, w[ch] comes to[4]...........

| | |
|---|---|
| R. of Richarde Waltame, the 27[th] of desembr 1593, in pte of payment of a bande of Thomas new-manes,[5] the some of ............................. | xxxx[s] |

[1] This entry has been quoted in Collier's History of Engl. Dram. Poetry and the Stage, iii., 102. See also the Memoirs of Edward Alleyn, p. 15. The ink in the MS. is different from that of the rest of the page.

[2] Perhaps the initials of witnesses to the fact that Percival Craffte had given his word for the fustian dyer. It would be a waste of time to attempt to assign the initials to any persons elsewhere mentioned in the Diary.

[3] This is not Henslowe's writing, but that of some scribe he employed, whose hand is very commonly found in the MS.

[4] The sum is not filled in.

[5] There was a bookseller of the name of Thomas Newman, for whom Nash (a writer for Henslowe) edited a spurious edition of Sidney's "Astrophel and Stella" in 1591. See Introd. to the Shakespeare Society's reprint of "Pierce Penniless's Supplication," 1592, p. xxi.

*A nott what I have layd owt abowt my playhowsse,*[1] *for payntynge and doinge it abowt w*[th] *ealme bordes, and other Repracyones, as foloweth,* 1595, *in lent.*[2]

| | | |
|---|---|---|
| Itm̃ bowght iij hunderd and a quarter of elmebordes | xxiiij$^s$ | |
| Itm̃ pd the carpenters ther wages | viij$^s$ | |
| Itm̃ geven the paynter in earneste | xx$^s$ | |
| Itm̃ geven the paynter more | x$^s$ | |
| Itm̃ geven more unto the paynter | xx$^s$ | |
| Itm̃ pd unto the paynter [3] | x$^s$ | |
| Itm̃ pd the carpenters ther wages | xvj$^s$ | |
| Itm̃ pd for iij henges | ij$^s$ | |
| Itm̃ pd for a borde | ij$^s$ | ij$^d$ |
| Itm̃ pd for v pownde of spickes | | xv$^d$ |
| Itm̃ pd the carpenters | v$^s$ | iiij$^d$ |
| Itm̃ pd the paynter | v$^s$ | |
| Itm̃ pd for ij bundell of lathes | ij$^s$ | ij$^d$ |
| Itm̃ pd for j lode of sande | | xiiij$^d$ |
| Itm̃ pd for hallfe a thowsen of lathe naylles | | viij$^d$ |
| Itm̃ pd the paynter | vj$^s$ | |

[1] Henslowe was owner of the Rose Theatre, but the ground on which it stood he appears to have rented. See the Memoirs of Edward Alleyn, p. 189, for the particulars respecting the manner in which Henslowe became tenant of the ground on which the Rose, on the Bankside, Southwark, stood: it was built after March 1584, but it is not clear that there had not been a playhouse on the same spot at an earlier period. In 1584 it was called "the little Rose," and it sometimes preserved the name afterwards. This memorandum shows that, like the Globe (and the Fortune on its first construction), the Rose was a wooden building: it was covered with "elm boards" on the outside.

[2] During Lent, theatres of old were usually closed, and on this account Henslowe selected it as the time for repairing the Rose.

[3] This additional sum to the painter, who had already received fifty shillings, is interlined in the MS.

| | | | |
|---|---|---|---|
| Itm̃ pd the paynter ........................ | | iiij$^{s}$ | |
| Itm̃ pd for j lode of lyme ........................ | | | xiiij$^{d}$ |
| Itm̃ pd for wages ........................ | | iiij$^{s}$ | vj$^{d}$ |
| Itm̃ pd the paynter ........................ | | v$^{s}$ | |
| Itm̃ pd the paynter, in fulle ........................ | | xvj$^{s}$ | |
| Itm̃ pd for naylles ........................ | | ij$^{s}$ | iiij$^{d}$ |
| Itm̃ pd the smyth for naylles, in fulle ...... | | xij$^{s}$ | iij$^{d}$ |
| Some is...... | 108$^{li}$ | 19$^{s}$ | 00$^{d}$ |

Itm̃ pd for carpenters worke, and mackinge the throne in the hevenes,[1] the 4 of June 1595 ... } vij$^{li}$ ij$^{s}$

Lent unto frances Henslow, the 3 of maye 1593, to laye downe for his share to the Quenes players, when they broke and went into the contrey to playe,[2] the some of fyften pownd, to be payd unto me at his Retorne owt of the contrey. I saye lent ................................................ } xv$^{li}$

Wittnes, John Towne
Hew Daves
Richard Alleyn.[3]

[1] For some play or plays, perhaps, in which a god or goddess was introduced sitting upon a "throne in the heavens." At an earlier date, and in miracle-plays, the throne might have been for the Deity himself.

[2] The Queen's Players in 1593, like all the other companies, broke up, and "went into the country to play," in consequence of the prevalence of the plague in London. Francis Henslowe was probably one of Philip Henslowe's nephews. Town and Davies, or Daves, who are put down as witnesses, were players, as well as Richard Alleyn, but whether the last was any and what relation to Edward Alleyn is not known. This is the earliest notice of any of them, and it has been quoted in Hist. of Engl. Dram. Poetry and the Stage, i., 318.

[3] These three names are not the signatures of the parties, but of the person who made the entry.

| | | |
|---|---|---|
| 2 of Jenewarye, 1593 | Lent unto Mr Hareye Draper, the second of Jeneway 1593, in Redey money, the some of twenty pownd, to be payd a gayne wthin one moneth next folowinge ...... | xxli |
| | Lent unto Mr Harey Draper, the 4 of aprell 1593, in Redey money the some of ...................... | xvjli |
| | Lent Mrs Draper, the 29 of marche 1594, in Redye money, the some of .................................. | vli |
| | Lent Mr John Sheaperd, the 14 of Desembr 1594, In Redey money, to be payd wth in one monethe after the date herof, the some of fyve pownd. Wittnes........... | vli |

EDWARD ALLEN [1]

E. A.
J. SYNGER
LAME R. JONNES
CHARLES T. TOWNE
ALEN M. SLATER
JUBE
T. DOWTEN
DONSTONE [2]

[1] This and the three preceding items are crossed out in the book. They are not theatrical, as far as we now know; but they are witnessed by Edward Alleyn, although the signature is not in his handwriting.

[2] These seem to have been the names of the principal actors forming the company of the Earl of Nottingham's players about 1595: E. A., at

Lent Richard Hoope, my lord chamberlenes man, the 14 of Jeneway 1595, in Redey money, to be pd at easter next cominge, the some of ....................... } iij[li]

wittnes his owne man,
WILLIAM FERNEY, and
EDWARD ALLEN

Lent unto the master of the Revelles man, W[m] Stonard, the 8 of aprell 1595, the some of seven shillinges, to be pd unto me at his next cominge to london ......... } vij[s]

wittness HEW DAVES, and
JOHN TAYLLER owermaker,[1]
and HEW DAVES his wiffe

Lent unto W[m] Blackwage, my lord camberlenes man, fyve pownd, as a pereth by his Bylle ............ } v[li]

the head of them, are the initials of Edward Alleyn: of "lame Charles Alen" we hear on no other authority, but he was perhaps related to Edward Alleyn. John Singer was an author as well as an actor, (if a piece called "Singer's Voluntary" were written, and not merely acted or sung by him as a Clown's Jig) and so was M. [Martin] Slater, or Slaughter, as his name is usually spelt in the MS. Several of his plays will be mentioned hereafter.

[1] "John Taylor, owermaker," probably means that he was an *oar-maker*. Possibly he was the father of John Taylor, who was subsequently known as "the water-poet," from his having originally followed the occupation of a waterman on the Thames. He is not to be confounded with Joseph Taylor, the actor, who belonged to a company formed by Henslowe at a period subsequent to the last date in this Diary, and who might be the son of "John Taylor, oar-maker."

| | |
|---|---|
| Lent unto M^r Rafe Raye, my lorde chamberlenes man, tenne pownd, as apereth by his bell[1] ........ | $x^{li}$ |

| | |
|---|---|
| Lent unto Frances Henslow, the j of June 1596, in Redey mony, to laye downe for his hallfe share with the company w^ch he dothe playe w^th all, to be payd unto me when he doth receve his mony w^ch he lent to my lord Burle,[2] or when my asyenes dothe demand yt. Wyttnes, I saye nyne pownd ............................ | $ix^{li}$ |

W^M SMYGHT, player
GORGE ATTEWELL, player
ROBARD NYCOWLLES, player.[3]

[1] The servants of the Master of the Revels, the Lord Chamberlain, &c., seem to have not unfrequently borrowed money of Henslowe, which, on various accounts, he might not think it prudent to refuse.

[2] The name is either *Burle*, or *Burte*, perhaps the latter; but it is indistinctly written in the MS. Why Lord Burghley should have borrowed money of Francis Henslowe it is difficult to imagine: possibly it was a false allegation on the part of Francis Henslowe, in order to induce his uncle (if he were so related) to advance the money to him. We shall see afterwards that Francis Henslowe was taken into the domestic service of the Lord Chamberlain, and he might at this time have been in the employ of Lord Burghley, and wages might be due to him. It is not known that Lord Burghley ever had a company of players acting under his name; and by a previous entry, dated three years earlier, viz., on the 3rd of May 1593, it appears that Francis Henslowe became a sharer with the Queen's Players, a distinct body from those of the Lord Chamberlain.

[3] Three actors under Philip Henslowe. "W^m Smyght" no doubt means William Smith, in the irregular spelling of that date. George

Bowght the Jemes is head [1] the 24 of aguste 1595, for........................................................ xxx^li^

and bowghte more as foloweth

| | | | |
|---|---|---|---|
| Itm̃ wanscotte in the halle ......... | xiiij yardes at | 16^d^ | per yd |
| Itm̃ paynted clothe in the halle [2]... | xvj yrdes at | vj^d^ | per yd |
| Itm̃ wanscott setlynge in the parler | x yardes at | xvj^d^ | yd |
| Itm̃ turnde pellers in the parler ... | iij yrdes at | xvj^d^ | yrd |
| Itm̃ a lowd for dores [3] .............. | iiij yrdes at | xvj^d^ | yrd |
| Itm̃ paynted cloth in the parler ... | v yrdes at | vj^d^ | yrdes |

*Layd owt a bowte John Allen adminestracyon* [4] *as folowethe.*

| | | | |
|---|---|---|---|
| 4 of maye | Layd owt a bowt the admenestracyon | xiij^s^ | ij^d^ |
| | pd for her balle .......................... | | xiiij^d^ |
| | pd the sargentes and other charges ... | iij^s^ | |

Attewell was perhaps father to Hugh Attewell, or Atwell, who acted in Ben Jonson's *Epicœne* in 1609 as one of the children of the Revels, who subsequently became one of the players of Prince Charles, and who died on the 25th Sept. 1621. See Hist. Engl. Dram. Poetry and the Stage, i. 423. Respecting Robert Nicholls we have no farther information, and he probably arrived at no distinction.

[1] No doubt the sign of the house—the St. James's Head. It is not likely that the head of King James would have been used as a sign before the death of Elizabeth.

[2] "Painted cloth in the hall" was doubtless tapestry, then often called painted cloth. It is not clear, however, that it was not sometimes canvas painted in oil-colours.

[3] i. e., *Allowed* for doors.

[4] Edward Alleyn's elder brother was named John, and this entry most likely relates to his death, and to the administration under his will: the second item, "pd for her balle," refers to the sureties or *bail* which every person taking out letters of administration is obliged to furnish. The date is 4th May, but no year is mentioned, and John Alleyn did not die until after 1594.—Mem. of Edw. Alleyn, p. 4. The whole of these items is crossed out in the MS.

| | | |
|---|---|---|
| pd for all carges in yeald halle[1] ......... | viij$^{s}$ | j$^{d}$ |
| pd the carman for bringinge the stuffe | iij$^{s}$ | iiij$^{d}$ |
| pd the carman for bringinge the stuffe | ij$^{s}$ | |
| pd going to Stanes by water ........... | v$^{s}$ | |
| and spente in charges for meat and drincke.................................. | xiij$^{s}$ | |
| Itm̃ pd for the Ingrossynge of the Inventory .................................. | x$^{s}$ | vj$^{d}$ |

Jesus. 1592.

*A note of suche carges as I have layd owt a bowte my play howsse,*[2] *in the yeare of our Lord* 1592, *as foloweth.*

| | | | |
|---|---|---|---|
| Itm̃ pd for a barge .............................. | iij$^{li}$ | x$^{s}$ | |
| Itm̃ pd for breakinge up and palynge ...... | | xx$^{s}$ | |
| Itm̃ pd for wharfyng .......... .............. | | viij$^{s}$ | |
| Itm̃ pd for tymber and bryngen by watter | vij$^{li}$ | ix$^{s}$ | |
| Itm̃ pd for lyme .................................. | | ix$^{s}$ | ij$^{d}$ |
| Itm̃ pd for wages .............................. | | xix$^{s}$ | |
| Itm̃ pd for bryngen of dellbordes ........... | | ij$^{s}$ | vj$^{d}$ |
| Itm̃ pd for ij hunderd of lyme .............. | | xj$^{s}$ | |
| Itm̃ pd for iij quarters of a hunderd of deall bordes .......................................... | iij$^{li}$ | | |
| Itm̃ pd for a maste.............................. | | xij$^{s}$ | |
| Itm̃ pd for a some of lathe naylles and hafe[3] | | | |
| Itm̃ pd for wages .............................. | iiij$^{li}$ | x$^{s}$ | |
| Itm̃ pd for iiij hundred of iij peny naylles | | | xij$^{d}$ |

[1] i. e., For all charges in Guild-hall.

[2] It is impossible to decide to which playhouse (for he was concerned in more than one) Henslowe here particularly refers, but it seems, from the items and the length of the account, to have undergone a most thorough repair: perhaps, it was even rebuilt. An account, previously inserted in the MS., for expenses of repairing another theatre, which we have supposed to be the Rose, is dated Lent 1595.

[3] No amount is placed opposite this item and some others lower down.

| | | | |
|---|---|---|---|
| Itm̃ pd for j lode of Rafters .................. | | | |
| Itm̃ pd for j lode of quarters . ................ | | | |
| Itm̃ pd for j thowsen of lathe naylles ...... | | | |
| Itm̃ pd unto the thecher[1] .................... | | vij$^{s}$ | |
| Itm̃ pd for bryngen of stufe .................. | | | vj$^{d}$ |
| Itm̃ pd for j hundred of lyme .............. | | v$^{s}$ | vj$^{d}$ |
| Itm̃ pd for iij dayes for a workman ........ | | iij$^{s}$ | vj$^{d}$ |
| Itm̃ pd for a naler for iiij dayes ........... | | iij$^{s}$ | 4$^{d}$ |
| Itm̃ pd lente the thecher ...................... | | xx$^{s}$ | |
| Itm̃ pd for sande ............................. | | iiij$^{s}$ | vj$^{d}$ |
| Itm̃ j thowsen of lath nayelles ............... | | | |
| Itm̃ pd for xxvj fore powlles .................. | | x$^{s}$ | vj$^{d}$ |
| Itm̃ pd unto my workmen for a weekes wages | vj$^{li}$ | | |
| Itm̃ pd for a hundred of syngell tennes...... | | | x$^{d}$ |
| Itm̃ pd for iiij lode of sande ................ | | iiij$^{s}$ | |
| Itm̃ pd unto the thechers man ........... ... | | iij$^{s}$ | |
| Itm̃ pd for ij hundered of syxpeny naylles | | | xij$^{d}$ |
| Itm̃ pd for hallfe a lode of lathes ......... .. | | | |
| Itm̃ pd for hallfe a some of lathe naylles ... | | | |
| Itm̃ pd for ij hundred and a halffe of dubell tennes ...................................... | | | |
| Itm̃ pd for v hundred of syxpeny naylles ... | | | |
| Itm̃ bowght hallfe a lode of lathes of J. Gryges ................................. | | | |
| Itm̃ pd for iij hundred of syxpeny naylles to Brader .................................. | | | xviij$^{d}$ |
| Itm̃ pd for chake and bryckes .............. | | iij$^{s}$ | 4$^{d}$ |
| Itm̃ pd for j hundred of dubell tennes ...... | | | x$^{d}$ |
| Itm̃ pd for ij hundred of lyme .............. | | xj$^{s}$ | |
| Itm̃ pd unto the thecher...................... | | | |

[1] This and other payments to "the thatcher" show that this theatre, like the Globe before it was burnt in 1613, (owing to the thatch taking fire) was covered, as far as it was roofed-in, with straw or reeds. The only part of the Globe which was thatched was over the stage

| | | | |
|---|---|---|---|
| Itm̃ pd for sande.................................. | | | xij$^{d}$ |
| Itm̃ pd for wages .............................. | | vj$^{s}$ | j$^{d}$ |
| Itm̃ pd for turned ballyesters ij$^{d}$ q$^{r}$ [1] a pece, ij dossen ........................................ | | iiij$^{s}$ | vj$^{d}$ |
| Itm̃ pd for wages ............................ | | iij$^{s}$ | 4$^{d}$ |
| Itm̃ bowght xx fur powell at vj$^{d}$ a pece...... | | x$^{s}$ | |
| Itm̃ pd unto the thecher .................... | | x$^{s}$ | |
| Itm̃ pd for naylles to brader .................. | | ij$^{s}$ | 4$^{d}$ |
| Itm̃ pd the vj of febreary for wages ......... | iiij$^{li}$ | iij$^{s}$ | 4$^{d}$ |
| Itm̃ pd for v hundred of syxpeny naylles ... | | | |
| Itm̃ pd steven coke iij$^{s}$ for his manes wages [2] | | | |
| Itm̃ bowght of J gryges ij C and iij q$^{r}$ and x foote bordes ................................ | | xix$^{s}$ | |
| Itm̃ bowght of J. gryges ij bundell of lathes | | ij$^{s}$ | |
| Itm̃ pd the thecher............................ | | v$^{s}$ | |
| Itm̃ bowght of the Iermonger in Sothwarke ½ C lath naylls ............................ | | | |
| Itm̃ bowght at the fryngpan v hund s. tennes [3] | | ij$^{s}$ | vj$^{d}$ |
| Itm̃ bowght at the fryngpan ij hund. dubl. tennes ........................................ | | iij$^{s}$ | 4$^{d}$ |
| Itm̃ bowght at the fryngpan 7 M of vj$^{d}$ naylles [4] ........................................ | | iiij$^{s}$ | vj$^{d}$ |
| Itm̃ pd for a thowsen of vj$^{d}$ naylles ......... | | | |
| Itm̃ pd for ½ some of ij$^{d}$ naylles.............. | | | |
| Itm̃ bowght j lode of Rafters, and j lode of quarters ........................................ | | | |

'tiring-room, &c. The yard, as the pit was then called, was open to the weather in all public theatres.

[1] i. e., Two-pence *farthing* each for two dozen balusters.

[2] Opposite this item, in the margin, are the words "Reste ij$^{s}$ x$^{d}$."

[3] i. e., He bought at the sign of the Fryingpan five hundred "*single* tennes:" he has previously mentioned "double tennes," and they occur again in the next and other entries.

[4] i. e., Seven *thousand* of sixpenny nails.

| | | | |
|---|---|---|---|
| Itm̃ pd for ij lode of lime and j lode of sande | | iij$^{s}$ | |
| Itm̃ pd for brycklaynge ........................ | | ij$^{s}$ | ij$^{d}$ |
| Itm̃ bowght at the fryingpan ½ some of ij$^{d}$ naylles.................................... | | | |
| Itm̃ pd the laborers wages [1] .................. | | viij$^{s}$ | ix$^{d}$ |
| Itm̃ bowght at the fryinge pan v hundred vj$^{d}$ naylles .................................. | | | |
| Itm̃ bowght at the fryingpan j q$^{r}$ M singell tennes .. ..................................... | | | |
| Itm̃ pd for j hundred of lyme .............. | | v$^{s}$ | vj$^{d}$ |
| Itm̃ bowght iiij hundred of quarter bordes | | xx$^{s}$ | |
| Itm̃ bowght v hunderd of ynche bordes...... | | xx$^{s}$ | |
| Itm̃ bowght halfe a lode of Rafters ......... | | | |
| Itm̃ pd the thecher.............. ............. | | x$^{s}$ | |
| Itm̃ pd for naylles .............. ............. | | | viij$^{d}$ |
| Itm̃ bowght of J gryges halfe a lode of lathes | | xv$^{s}$ | |
| Itm̃ bowght at the fryingpan j q$^{r}$ M dubell tennes ........................... .............. | | | |
| Itm̃ pd unto the carpenters for wages [2]...... | iiij$^{li}$ | x$^{s}$ | |
| Itm̃ pd for carege of tymber .................. | | | vij$^{d}$ |
| Itm̃ pd for iij fort bordes sayed .............. | | iiij$^{s}$ | vj$^{d}$ |
| Itm̃ pd for payntinge my stage [3] ............ | | xj$^{s}$ | |
| Itm̃ pd for v hundred of vj$^{d}$ naylles at fryingpan ......... ......................... | | | |
| Itm̃ pd for a q$^{r}$ of a M of dubell tennes at fryingpad [4] .................................. | | | |
| Itm̃ pd for a q$^{r}$ of a M of syngell tennes fryingpan .................................. | | | |

[1] In the margin, "Smyth had iiij$^{s}$ ij$^{d}$ Joane"—perhaps paid by Henslowe's wife's daughter Joan, afterwards Mrs. Edward Alleyn.

[2] In the margin, "R. of the Smyth 18$^{li}$, and 18$^{li}$, and 15$^{li}$."

[3] "Painting my stage" probably means painting the decorations about the stage, not the boards of which the stage was composed.

[4] *Sic* in MS.

| | | |
|---|---|---|
| Itm̃ bowght of Brader ij hundred of 4$^d$ naylles ........................................ | | viij$^d$ |
| Itm̃ pd for ij dossen of turned ballysters ... | iiij$^s$ | |
| Itm̃ bowght at Braders iij C and ½ iiij$^d$ naylles ........................................ | | |
| Itm̃ bowght at the fryingpan v C vj$^d$ naylles | | |
| Itm̃ bowght at the fryingpan a q$^r$ M dubell tennes ........................................ | | |
| Itm̃ bowght at the fryingpan a q$^r$ M singell tennes ........................................ | | |
| Itm̃ bowght at the fryingpan a q$^r$ M singell tennes ........................................ | | |
| Itm̃ bowght at the fryingpan a M of vj$^d$ naylles ........................................ | | |
| Itm̃ bowght at the fryingpan a q$^r$ of some of lathe naylles .... ........................ | | |
| Itm̃ bowght j lode of syngell quarters ...... | | |
| Itm̃ pd for brynginge of stufe by watter ... | | |
| Itm̃ bowght of Brader v C of 4$^d$ naylles...... | | |
| Itm̃ bowght iij score and ix corsse deall at iij$^d$ ob . ........................................ | xx$^s$ | |
| Itm̃ pd for bryngin them by water ......... | | viij$^d$ |
| Itm̃ pd the thecher ........................................ | v$^s$ | |
| Itm̃ bowght at the fryingpan ½ a q$^r$ M of singell x ........................................ | | |
| Itm̃ bowght at the fryingpan ½ a q$^r$ M dubell x | | |
| Itm̃ bowght at the fryingpan a q$^r$ M vj$^d$ naylles........................................ | | |
| Itm̃ bowght at the fryingpan ½ C of singell x | | xvij$^d$ |
| Itm̃ bowght at the fryingpan j q$^r$ of M singell x ........................................ | | |
| Itm̃ bowght of Brader ij C of 4$^d$ naylles ... | | |
| Itm̃ bowght of J gryges iij C of q$^r$ bordes | xvj$^s$ | |
| Itm̃ bowght at the fryingpan j q$^r$ M singell tenes ........................................ | | xvij$^d$ ob |

Itm̃ bowght at the fryingpan j q$^{r}$ M dubell tennes ..........................................

Itm̃ bowght at the fryingpan j q$^{r}$ M vj$^{d}$ naylles ..........................................

Itm̃ bowght of Brader ij C 4$^{d}$ naylles ......

Itm̃ bowght at the fryingpan j q$^{r}$ M singell tenes .......................................... xvij$^{d}$

Itm̃ bowght at the fryinpan j q$^{r}$ vj$^{d}$ naylles

Itm̃ pd unto the thecher a bondell of lathes xij$^{d}$

Itm̃ bowght of Brader 3 C of vj$^{d}$ naylles[1]...

| | |
|---|---|
| Receaved by me, Jeames Borne,[2] the 2 of March 1591, of M$^{r}$ Phillipe Hinchlie, for the use of Henerie Adames, the some of three pounde, And is in fulle of paymente of a recconneng. I saye Receaved in pay$^{te}$ .. ........... | 3$^{li}$ 8$^{s}$ 0$^{d}$ |
| Pd in fulle paymente, the 7 of March 1591, unto the Iormonger in Sothwarke, at the fryingpan, three pownd and xij$^{s}$. I say Rd..................... | iij$^{li}$ xij$^{s}$ |
| Pd in fulle paymente, the 28 of Marche 1591, unto M$^{r}$ Lee, tymber man, for Rafters, and quarters, and lathes, and bordes, the some of .................. .. | v$^{li}$ xiiij$^{s}$ |

[1] Here the account ends, in consequence of the lower part of the leaf having been torn away. What follows begins on the *verso* of the defective leaf, and we may feel pretty certain that the memorandums relate to the same undertaking as the preceding items.

[2] We hear of two old actors of the names of Borne, or Bird, for they seem to have been known by both,—Theophilus and William. See Hist. Engl. Dram. Poetry and the Stage, i., 307, 381, &c. Perhaps

| | | | |
|---|---|---|---|
| Pd unto my cossen Adren, for money wch I owght him, the 23 of Marche 1591 ........................................ | vijli | | |
| Pd unto the paynters, the 23 of Marche 1591 ........................................ | | xxvjs | |
| Pd unto my cossen Adren, the 13 of aprell 1591 ........................................ | xxijli | xs | |
| 103li 02s 03d [1] | | | |
| Pd for sellynge of the Rome over the tyer-howsse [2] ........................................ | | xs | |
| Pd the wages to the plasterer.............. | | iiijs | |
| Pd for sellinge my lords Rome [3]........... | | xiiijs | |
| Pd for makeinge the penthowsse shed at the tyeringe howsse doore, as fol-oweth, pd for owld tymber ........... | | xs | |
| Pd for bordes and quarters ................. | | xviijs | vjd |
| Pd for bordes ............................. | | xiijs | vjd |
| Pd for naylles, and henges, and bowlltes | | xixs | |
| Pd the carpenters for wages [4] .............. | | ixs | |

James Borne was related to them, and they were in Henslowe's pay. The entry is in the handwriting of James Borne.

[1] This addition of some previous amounts is inserted in the left-hand margin, and not under the sums to which it seems to belong.

[2] This is obviously another part of the same account of money expended by Henslowe on his playhouse in 1592: it is separated only by a blank space. The first item relates to ceiling the 'tiring or *attiring* house, attached to the theatre, where the performers dressed themselves.

[3] The best place in our old theatres was sometimes called "the Lord's room," or box: it was no doubt set apart for the patron of the company and his friends.

[4] Here the account ends, and the rest of the leaf (probably containing some valuable autograph or memorandum) has been torn away.

*A not what mony I haue layd owt of my owne to Frances Henslow, as followeth.* 1593.

| | |
|---|---|
| Lent the 14 of Jeneway 1593 ........... | xxv$^{s}$ |
| Lent the 16 of Jeneway 1593 ........... | xxx$^{s}$ |

*A not what I have layd a bowt the howsse which was Hew Daveses, as foloweth.* 1593. *Looke the next leafe.*[1]

| | | |
|---|---|---|
| Itm̃ pd unto the nayllman for naylles ... | iiij$^{s}$ | |
| Itm̃ pd unto the tyller .................... | | xviij$^{d}$ |
| Itm̃ iiij long peces of tymber .............. | vj$^{s}$ | |
| Itm̃ ij thowssen of lath naylles ....... .... | ij$^{s}$ | viij$^{d}$ |
| Itm̃ pd the tyller and laberer ........... | | xviij$^{d}$ |
| Itm̃ pd for Rege tylles[2] .................... | | xviij$^{d}$ |
| Itm̃ pd for tylle pennes .................... | | ij$^{d}$ |
| Itm̃ pd for a hundered of tylles ........... | | xviij$^{d}$ |
| Itm̃ pd for a hunderd of quarter bordes | vij$^{s}$ | ij$^{d}$ |
| Itm̃ pd for vj syngell quarters ........... | ij$^{s}$ | ij$^{d}$ |
| Itm̃ j longe pece of tymber................. | | xvj$^{d}$ |
| Itm̃ halfe a hunderd of lyme .............. | iij$^{s}$ | |
| Itm̃ pd for heare ............................ | | |
| Itm̃ pd for lome ............................ | | xiiij$^{d}$ |
| Itm̃ j thowsen of lathnaylles .............. | | xvj$^{d}$ |
| Itm̃ pd for iiij quarter bordes...... ........ | iiij$^{s}$ | xj$^{d}$ |
| Itm̃ pd for a payer of henges .............. | | xiij$^{d}$ |
| Itm̃ pd for halfe a thowsend of lathnaylles | | xvj$^{d}$ |
| Itm̃ pd the laborer his wages ............... | | x$^{d}$ |
| Itm̃ pd for bordes and quarters ........... | v$^{s}$ | viij$^{d}$ |
| 16 of october 1595. Itm̃ pd grymes for his wages and his man ......... ............ | vij$^{s}$ | |

[1] The meaning seems to be, that another account for the repair of a house of Hugh Daves in 1595 is contained on the following leaf. Henslowe spent money upon it in 1593 and 1595.

[2] i. e., *Ridge tiles:* the next entry is for *tile-pins.*

Itm̃ j longe pece of tember .................. xvj$^{d}$
Itm̃ pd for a locke .......................... iij$^{s}$ j$^{d}$
Itm̃ pd for j lode of lome ............ ..... xij$^{d}$
Itm̃ pd setyng up the porthole ............ ij$^{s}$ vj$^{d}$
Itm̃ pd the carpenters........... ............ xiij$^{s}$ viij$^{d}$
Itm̃ pd the laborer .......................... v$^{s}$
Itm̃ pd for henges, latches, and bowltes...
Itm̃ pd for a thowsen of lathe naylles ... xvj$^{d}$
Itm̃ pd the smyth for naylles.............. v$^{s}$ j$^{d}$
Itm̃ pd unto the carpenters .............. ij$^{s}$ viij$^{d}$
Itm̃ pd for a ealme bord .................... viij$^{d}$
Itm̃ pd for wages .......................... iij$^{s}$ vj$^{d}$

Receved as foloweth[1]
00 02 00
00 03 00
00 07 00
00 04 04

Itm̃ pd unto M$^{r}$ Tillnes[2] man, the 26 of febreary, 1591 .............................. v$^{s}$
Itm̃ pd unto M$^{r}$ Tyllnes man, the 4 of marche, 1591 .............................. v$^{s}$
Itm̃ pd unto M$^{r}$ Tyllenes man, the 10 of marche, 1591 .............................. v$^{s}$
Itm̃ pd unto M$^{r}$ Tyllnes man, the 17 of marche, 1591 .............................. v$^{s}$
Itm̃ pd unto M$^{r}$ Tyllnes man, the 24 of marche, 1591 .............................. v$^{s}$
Itm̃ pd unto M$^{r}$ Tyllenes man, the 28 of marche, 1591 .............................. v$^{s}$

[1] These small sums are crowded into the margin just above what follows. Whence the money was received is not stated.

[2] Edmond Tylney was Master of the Revels at this date, and for many years afterwards: he was appointed in 1579, and died in 1610.

Itm̃ pd unto M$^{r}$ Tyllnes man, the 7 of aprell, 1591 .............................. v$^{s}$

Itm̃ pd unto M$^{r}$ Tyllnes man, the 19 of aprell, 1591 .............................. v$^{s}$

Itm̃ pd unto M$^{r}$ Tyllnes man, the 27 of aprell, 1591 .............................. v$^{s}$

Itm̃ pd unto M$^{r}$ Tyllnes man, the 28 of aprell 1591 [1] .............................. v$^{s}$

Itm̃ pd unto M$^{r}$ Tyllenes man, the 5 of maye 1592 .............................. v$^{s}$

Itm̃ pd unto M$^{r}$ Tyllnes man, the 10 of maye 1592 .............................. v$^{s}$

Itm̃ pd unto M$^{r}$ Tyllnes man, the 13 of maye, 1592 .............................. xij$^{s}$

Itm̃ pd unto M$^{r}$ Tyllnes man, the 20 of maye, 1592 .............................. vj$^{s}$ 8$^{d}$

Itm̃ pd unto Mr Tyllnes man, the 9 of June, 1592 .............................. vj$^{s}$ 8$^{d}$

Itm̃ pd unto M$^{r}$ Tyllnes man, the 14 of June, 1592 .............................. vj$^{s}$ 8$^{d}$

*Layd owt abowte the howsse which hewe Daves dwelt in laste, in the year* 1595, *as foloweth.* [2]

Itm̃ hallfe a lode of lathes .................. xv$^{s}$ vj$^{d}$

[1] Probably the five last items ought to be 1592, as the new year then began on the 26th of March. Five shillings were paid to the Master of the Revels upon the licensing of every new play; and if these sums were given for licenses in 1591 and 1592, it shews the number of new plays Henslowe bought of their authors between 26 February 1591, and 14 June 1592. Why the sum was 12*s.* and 6*s.* 8*d.* in the later entries of this account it is not easy to explain.

[2] This is what Henslowe refers to, when, at the head of a former account in 1593, he says, "looke the next leafe."

| | | |
|---|---|---|
| Itm̃ elme bordes .............................. | viij$^{s}$ | [illegible]$^{d}$ |
| Itm̃ j hunderd of syngell tennes........... | | x$^{d}$ |
| Itm̃ j Rownd polle .......................... | | xx$^{d}$ |
| Itm̃ j bare of Iorne ........................ | iiij$^{s}$ | viij$^{d}$ |
| Itm̃ j lode of sand ......................... | | xij$^{d}$ |
| Itm̃ ij thowsen of lathe naylles ........... | | xvj$^{d}$ |
| Itm̃ pd the carpenter wages .............. | ij$^{s}$ | vj$^{d}$ |
| Itm̃ pd for fir powles ...................... | v$^{s}$ | |
| Itm̃ j hunderd of vj$^{d}$ naylles .............. | | vj$^{d}$ |
| Itm̃ pd for ij gyrtes to beare the chymne | iiij$^{s}$ | vj$^{d}$ |
| Itm̃ pd for v bundell of lathes ........... | v$^{s}$ | v$^{d}$ |
| Itm̃ j lode of sande for grymes ........... | | xij$^{d}$ |
| Itm̃ geven grymes in mony .............. | xiiij$^{s}$ | |
| Itm̃ pd for ij quarters......................... | | xiiij$^{d}$ |
| Itm̃ j hunderd of lyme .................... | vj$^{s}$ | |
| Itm̃ j manteltie ............................. | | xij$^{d}$ |
| Itm̃ pd to grymes .......................... | vij$^{s}$ | |
| Itm̃ pd to grymes .......................... | | xij$^{d}$ |
| Itm̃ pd for a gutter of leade .............. | xij$^{s}$ | iij$^{d}$ |
| Itm̃ pd the ij carpenters for wages ...... | xv$^{s}$ | vj$^{d}$ |
| Itm̃ pd the laberer ......................... | | vj$^{d}$ |

*In the name of God, Amen,* 1591, *beginge the* 19 *of febreary, my lord Stranges mene, as foloweth.*

1591.[1]

| | | |
|---|---|---|
| Rd at fryer bacone,[2] the 19 of febrary, satterdaye ................................ | xvij$^{s}$ | iij$^{d}$ |

[1] This is the heading of a new page of the Diary, and it means, that "Lord Stranges men," or players, *began* to act on the 19 Feb. 1591, probably at the Rose. Edward Alleyn was at this time one of Lord Strange's men, and played all, or most of the heroes.

[2] This list of plays, acted by Henslowe's company, begins with what was, no doubt, Robert Greene's play of Friar Bacon and Friar Bongay, printed in 1594. See vol. viii. of the last edit. of Dodsley's Old Plays.

| | | |
|---|---|---|
| Rd at mulomorco,[1] the 20 of febreary ... | xxix^s | |
| Rd at orlando,[2] the 21 of febreary......... | xvj^s | vj^d |
| Rd at spanes comodye donne oracoe,[3] the 23 of febreary .............................. | xiij^s | vj^d |
| Rd at syr John mandevell,[4] the 24 of febreary .................................. | xij^s | vj^d |
| Rd at harey of cornwell the 25 of febreary 1591 ...................................... | xxxij^s | |
| Rd at the Jewe of malltuse, the 26 of febrearye 1591............................ | l^s | |
| Rd at clorys and orgasto,[5] the 28 of febreary 1591 ............................ | xviij^s | |
| Rd at mulamulluco, the 29 of febrearye 1591 ....................................... | xxxiiij^s | |

[1] Malone suggests that Mulomorco (elsewhere spelt Mulamulluco, Mulomuloco, Mulamulluco, &c.), was the Battle of Alcazar, printed in 1594, and attributed, probably correctly, to George Peele.

[2] By "Orlando," Henslowe doubtless meant R. Greene's "Historie of Orlando Furioso," first printed, not as Malone says, in 1599, but in 1594: the edit. of 1599 was the second. See Mem. of Edw. Alleyn for an original MS. of the part of Orlando, sustained by Alleyn.

[3] Probably the Spanish Tragedy in which Don Horatio is a principal character; but Henslowe seems to mention "the comedy of Jeronymo" and "Jeronymo" as different productions, and they were certainly sometimes performed on successive days, which is not the case with any other one play. There were two dramas, immediately connected in subject, one called the Spanish Tragedy, printed in, and before, 1599, and the other Jeronymo, printed in 1605. They were most likely intended by Henslowe under the several titles of "Don Oracoe," "the comedy of Jeronymo," and "Jeronymo."

[4] No play with this title, or upon Sir John Mandeville and his travels, has come down to us. The same remark will apply to the next entry.

[5] No such piece is now known: the title does not occur again, and perhaps it was not successful, though Henslowe does not mark it as a new play.

| | | | |
|---|---|---|---|
| Rd at poope Jone,[1] the j of marche 1591 | | xv$^{s}$ | |
| Rd at matchavell[2] the 2 of marche 1591 | | xiiij$^{s}$ | |
| Rd at henery the vj,[3] the 3 of marche 1591 ........................................ | iij$^{li}$ | xvj$^{s}$ | v$^{d}$ |
| Rd at bendo and Richardo,[4] the 4 of marche 1591 ................................ | | xvj$^{s}$ | |
| Rd at iiij playes in one,[5] the 6 of marche 1591 ........................................ | | xxxj$^{s}$ | vj$^{d}$ |
| Rd at hary vj, the 7 of marche 1591 ... | iij$^{li}$ | | |

[1] A drama on the popular story of Pope Joan, we may conclude. In 1624 was published "The Anatomie of Pope Joane," but it was perhaps a reprint of an earlier tract, which had been used as the foundation of a dramatic performance.

[2] At a subsequent date, viz. in 1613, Robert Daiborne was in treaty with Henslowe to write for him a play called Machiavel and the Devil. It might be a revival of the old play with additions and alterations, but the sum agreed upon, £20, was then a large price, even for an entirely new drama. See the Alleyn Papers, p. 56.

[3] This play, whether by Shakespeare or not, was extremely popular and profitable. It produced Henslowe £1 11*s.* 0*d.* for his share on its fourteenth representation. On its performance in 1591, we here see that it brought him £3 16*s.* 5*d.* Malone was of opinion that it was the First Part of Henry the Sixth, included among Shakespeare's works; and it is certain that this entry of 3 March 1591 relates to its original production, as Henslowe has put his mark *ne* in the margin.

[4] No such play is now known.

[5] Four short plays represented on the same night as one play. This was done afterwards, and the Yorkshire Tragedy, attributed to Shakespeare, is a specimen of one of these short plays. We shall find that sometimes "five plays in one" were represented, the object being to afford variety; and they might or might not be connected in subject. In Beaumont and Fletcher's works, we have a piece called "Four Plays in One;" and in Mr. Cunningham's Revels' Accounts, p. 189, is a notice of "five plays in one," and of "three plays in one" at Court, under date of 1584–5.

| | | | |
|---|---|---|---|
| Rd at the lookinglasse,[1] the 8 of marche 1591 ........................ | | vij$^{s}$ | |
| Rd at Senobia, the 9 of marche 1591 ... | | xxij$^{s}$ | vj$^{d}$ |
| Rd at the Jewe of malta,[2] the 10 of marche 1591 ........................ | | lvj$^{s}$ | |
| Rd at hary the vj, the 11 of marche 1591 | | xxxxvij$^{s}$ | vj$^{d}$ |
| Rd at the comodey of done oracio, the 13 of marche 1591 ........................ | | xxviiij$^{s}$ | |
| Rd at Jeronymo, the 14 of marche 1591 | iij$^{li}$ | vj$^{s}$ | |
| Rd at harey,[3] the 16 of marche 1591 ... | | xxxj$^{s}$ | vj$^{d}$ |
| Rd at mulo mullocco, the 17 of marche 1591 ........................ | | xxviij$^{s}$ | vj$^{d}$ |
| Rd at the Jewe of malta, the 18 of marche 1591 ........................ | | xxxix$^{s}$ | |
| Rd at Jeronymo, the 20 of marche 1591 | | xxxviij$^{s}$ | |
| Rd at constantine,[4] the 21 of marche 1591 | | xij$^{s}$ | |
| Rd at Jerusallem, the 22 of marche 1591 | | xviij$^{s}$ | |
| Rd at harey of cornwell, the 23 of marche 1591 ........................ | | xiij$^{s}$ | vj$^{d}$ |
| Rd at fryer bacon, the 25 of marche 1591 | | xv$^{s}$ | vj$^{d}$ |
| Ester. Rd at the lookinglasse, the 27 of marche 1591[5] ........................ | | lv$^{s}$ | |
| Rd at harey the vj, the 28 of marche 1591 | iij$^{li}$ | viij$^{s}$ | |

[1] Malone supposes, with apparent truth, that this was Greene's and Lodge's Looking Glass for London and England, but he was wrong in stating that it was first printed in 1598. There was an edition in 1594.

[2] Previously called by Henslowe the Jew of Malltuse. This was Marlowe's tragedy, not printed until 1633. It is included in Vol. viii. of Dodsley's Old Plays, last edit.

[3] Meaning, no doubt, Harey, or Henry VI.

[4] No such play has reached us. The same may be stated of various other plays to which, for brevity's sake, no notes are attached.

[5] i. e., 1592, even according to the reckoning of that time; but Henslowe goes on to insert 1591, until he comes to the 24th April, when he first writes 1592.

| | | |
|---|---|---|
| Rd at mulo mulucko, the 29 of marche 1591 ........................................ | iij[li] | ij[s] |
| Rd at done oracio, the 30 of marche 1591 | | xxxix[s] |
| Rd at Jeronymo, the 31 of marche 1591 | iij[li] | |
| Rd at mandevell, the 1 of aprell 1591 ... | | xxx[s] |
| Rd at matchevell, the 3 of aprell 1591 ... | | xxij[s] |
| Rd at the Jewe of malta, the 4 of aprell 1591 ........................................ | | xxxxiij[s] |
| Rd at harey the vj, the 5 of aprell 1591 | | xxxxj[s] |
| Rd at brandymer, the 6 of aprell 1591 ... | | xxij[s] |
| Rd at Jeronymo, the 7 of aprell 1591 ... | | xxvj[s] |
| Rd at mulo muloco, the 8 of aprell 1591 | | xxiij[s] |
| Rd at the comodey of Jeronymo, the 10 of aprell 1591 .................................. | | xxviij[s] |
| Rd at tittus and Vespacia,[1] the 11 of aprell 1591 .................................. | iij[li] | iiij[s] |
| Rd at byndo and Richardo,[2] the 12 of aprell 1591 .................................. | | xxiij[s] |
| Rd at henry the vj, the 13 of aprell 1591 | | xxvj[s] |
| Rd at Jeronymo, the 14 of aprell 1591... | | xxxiij[s] |
| Rd at mandevell, the 15 of aprell 1591... | | xxvj[s] |
| Rd at mullo mulluco, the 17 of aprell 1591 ........................................ | | xxx[s] |

[1] Malone prints the name "Titus and Vespasian," when Henslowe gives it "Tittus and Vespacia," excepting in two or three instances, where he has it Titus, but always Vespacia. Malone conjectures, but without apparent reason, that the correct title of the play was "Titus Vespasian:" it perhaps included parts of the reigns of both; but if so, Vespasian ought to precede Titus. Henslowe marks it as a new play by the letters *ne* in the margin, or we might have supposed it the same as is elsewhere called Jerusalem, regarding which a note will be found on the next page.

[2] This play has been previously called Bendo and Richardo: see 4th March 1591. We may perhaps conclude that it was founded upon some Italian romantic story, not now known.

| | | |
|---|---|---|
| Rd at the Jewe of mallta, the 18 of aprell 1591 ........................................ | xxxxviij$^s$ | vj$^d$ |
| Rd at the lockingglasse, the 19 of aprell 1591 ........................................ | xxiiij$^s$ | |
| Rd at tittus and vespacia, the 20 of aprell 1591 ........................................ | lvj$^s$ | |
| Rd at harey the vj, the 21 of aprell 1591 | xxxiij$^s$ | |
| Rd at the comodey Jeronymo, the 22 of aprell 1591 ........................................ | xvij$^s$ | |
| Rd at Jeronymo,[1] the 24 of aprell 1592 | xxviij$^s$ | |
| Rd at Jerusalem,[2] the 25 of aprell 1592 | xxxxvj$^s$ | |
| Rd at fryer bacon, the 26 of aprell 1592 | xxiiij$^s$ | |
| Rd at mulo muloco, the 27 of aprell 1592 | xxvj$^s$ | |
| Rd at the second pte of Tamber came,[3] the 28 of aprell ........ .................. | iij$^{li}$ | iiij$^s$ |

[1] This and the preceding entry seem to show that Henslowe calls either the Spanish Tragedy, or Jeronimo, the comedy of Jeronimo: they are both serious plays, and how either of them could be termed a comedy is not obvious; but the old manager perhaps only wished to distinguish the one from the other. See also note 3, p. 21.

[2] At this repetition of a previous entry, dated 22 March 1591, we may notice Malone's speculation that it was the destruction of Jerusalem, by Dr. Legge; but that, like his *Ricardus Tertius*, (see Mr. B. Field's edition for the Shakespeare Society) was, in all probability, a Latin play. The Jerusalem mentioned by Henslowe may possibly have been an English drama founded upon Dr. Legge's Latin one.

[3] Malone misprints this name "Tamberzanne," when it is usually written by Henslowe "Tamber cam," or "Tamer came." In Shakespeare, by Boswell, iii., 256, is "the plott of the first parte of Tamar Cam." Malone conjectured that it was Marlowe's Tamburlaine the Great; but, about ten years after 1591, Alleyn was paid for producing a piece called Tambercam, and it may have been an alteration of the play in the text which could not have been Marlowe's Tamburlaine, because both parts of that drama were printed in 1590; whereas Henslowe notes that, "the second part of Tamber came" was a new play

| | | |
|---|---|---|
| Rd at harey of cornwell, the 29 of aprell 1592 .......... | | xxvj$^{s}$ |
| Rd at mulo mulloco, the 30 of aprell 1592 | | lviij$^{s}$ |
| Rd at Jeronymo, the 2 of maye 1592 ... | | xxxiiij$^{s}$ |
| Rd at titus and Vespacia, the 3 of maye 1592 .......... | | lvij$^{s}$ |
| Rd at harey the vj, the 4 of maye 1592 | | lvj$^{s}$ |
| Rd at the Jewe of mallta, 5 of maye 1592 | | xxxxj$^{s}$ |
| Rd at fryer bacon, the 6 of maye 1592... | | xiiij$^{s}$ |
| Rd at brandimer, the 8 of maye 1592 ... | | xxiiij$^{s}$ |
| Rd at harey the vj, the 7 of maye 1592 | | xxij$^{s}$ |
| Rd at tittus and vespacia, the 8 of maye 1592 .......... | | xxx$^{s}$ |
| Rd at Jeronymo, the 9 of maye 1592 ... | | xxvj$^{s}$ |
| Rd at the 2 pte of tambercam, the 10 of maye 1592 .......... | | xxxvij$^{s}$ |
| Rd at the Jewe of mallta, the 11 of maye 1592 .......... | | xxxiv$^{s}$ |
| Whittson-tyde. Rd at Jeronymo, the 13 of maye 1592.......... ... | iij$^{li}$ | 4$^{s}$ |
| Rd at harey the vth,[1] the 14 of maye 1592 .......... | | l$^{s}$ |

on 28 April 1592. The probability seems to be that it was a play written for Henslowe on the same story, but it deserves remark that, when Marlowe's Tamburlaine was printed in 1590, the title-page states that it had been "sundrie times shewed upon stages in the Cittie of London, by the right honourable the Lord Admyrall his servants," with whom Henslowe was certainly connected.

[1] Malone takes no notice of this play, which at least was the same in subject as Shakespeare's work. Possibly he read it "Harey the VI.," but it is clearly "Harey the vth." This is the piece to which Nash alluded in his Pierce Penniless, published in 1592; and "The famous Victories of Henry V." was entered at Stationers' Hall to be printed in 1594. Malone was not aware that any such historical drama was mentioned by Henslowe.

| | | | |
|---|---|---|---|
| Rd at tittus and Vespacia, the 15 of maye 1592 .................................... | iij$^{li}$ | | |
| Rd at mandevell, the 16 of maye 1592... | | xxxx$^{s}$ | |
| Rd at mullomuloco, the 17 of maye 1592 | | xxxvj$^{s}$ | vj$^{d}$ |
| Rd at harey of cornwell, the 18 of maye 1592 .................................... | | xxvj$^{s}$ | |
| Rd at harey the vj the 19 of maye 1592 | | xxx$^{s}$ | |
| Rd at the Jewe of mallta, the 20 of maye 1592 .................................... | | liiij$^{s}$ | |
| Rd at the comodey of Jeronymo, the 21 of maye 1592 .......................... | | xxviij$^{s}$ | |
| Rd at Jeronymo,[1] the 22 of maye 1592... | | xxvij$^{s}$ | |
| Rd at the taner of Denmarke,[2] the 23 maye 1592 .............................. | iij$^{li}$ | xiij$^{s}$ | vj$^{d}$ |
| Rd at titus and vespacia, the 24 of maye 1592 .............................. | | xxx$^{s}$ | |
| Rd at harey the vj, the 25 of maye 1592 | | xxiiij$^{s}$ | |
| Rd at tambercame, the 26 of maye 1592 | | xxxvj$^{s}$ | vj$^{d}$ |
| Rd at Jeronymo, the 27 of maye 1592... | | xxiij$^{s}$ | |
| Rd at matchevell, the 29 of maye 1592 | | xxvj$^{s}$ | |
| Rd at the Jewe of malta, the 30 of maye 1592 .................................... | | xxxiij$^{s}$ | |
| Rd at mulemuloco, the 31 of maye 1592 | | xxiiij$^{s}$ | |
| Rd at Bendo and Richardo,[3] the 5 of June 1592.................................... | | xxxij$^{s}$ | |

[1] Here again we see the two plays, the Spanish Tragedy and Jeronimo, distinguished as before, and played on successive days as a continuation of the same subject.

[2] The Tanner of Denmark (although it drew such an audience as gave Henslowe £3 13*s.* 6*d.* for his share) would appear to have been a failure, as we do not find that it was repeated. Henslowe marks it as a new production by the letters *ne* before it.

[3] The company does not appear to have performed between the 31st of May and the 5th of June, or plays would have been recorded in the interval.

| | | |
|---|---|---|
| Rd at tittus and Vespacia, the 6 of June 1592 .......................................... | | xxxxij$^{s}$ |
| Rd at the lookinglasse, the 7 of June 1592... | | xxix$^{s}$ |
| Rd at the tambercame, the 8 of June 1592... | | xxxx$^{s}$ |
| Rd at Jeronymo, the 9 of June 1592 ......... | | xxviij$^{s}$ |
| Rd at a Knacke to Knowe a Knave[1] 1592, 1 day .......................................... | iij$^{li}$ | xij$^{s}$ |
| Rd at harey the vj, the 12 of June 1592...... | | xxxij$^{s}$ |
| Rd at mulemuloco, the 13 of June 1592...... | | xx$^{s}$ |
| Rd at the Jewe of malta, the 14 of June 1592 | | xxxviij$^{s}$ |
| Rd at the Knacke to Knowe a Knave, the 15 of June 1592 .................................. | | lij$^{s}$ |
| Rd at mandevell, the 16 of June 1592......... | | xx$^{s}$ |
| Rd at Jeronymo, the 18 of June 1592......... | | xxiiij$^{s}$ |
| Rd at harey the vj, the 19 of June 1592...... | | xxxj$^{s}$ |
| Rd at the comodey of Jeronymo, the 20 of June 1592 ......................................... | | xv$^{s}$ |
| Rd at tambercame, the 21 of June 1592 ...... | | xxxij$^{s}$ |
| Rd at the Knacke to Knowe a Knave, the 22 of June ........................................ | | xxvij$^{s}$ |

[1] This is a remarkable entry, as Henslowe states that it was the first performance of this celebrated play, which was printed in 1594, and which the Shakespeare Society proposes to reprint. "1 day" is interlined, perhaps, in order to give the information of its original production, but it escaped Malone's notice: *ne* is also in the margin, but Malone did not ascertain the meaning of that note. The previous falling off of the receipts seemed to render some novelty necessary, and on its production "A Knack to know a Knave" put £3 12*s*. 0*d*. into Henslowe's pocket. William Kemp was at this date a member of the company of the Lord Strange's Players, under Henslowe and Alleyn, as he played a principal comic part in the Knack to know a Knave, and introduced into it what are called on the title-page his "applauded merriments." Kemp afterwards became one of the servants of the Lord Chamberlain, then rejoined Henslowe and Alleyn, and finally died a member of the company called the King's Players.

*In the Name of God Amen*, 1592, *begininge the* 29 *of Desember.*[1]

| | | |
|---|---|---|
| Rd at mulomulluco, the 29 of decembr 1592 | iij[li] | x[s] |
| Rd at Jeronymo, the 30 of desembr 1592 ... | iij[li] | viij[s] |
| Rd at the cnacke,[2] the 3 of desembr 1592 ... | | xxx[s] |
| Rd at the Jewe,[3] the 1 of Janewary 1592 ... | | lvj[s] |
| Rd at the cnacke, the 3 of Janewary 1592 ... | | xxix[s] |
| Rd at mandevell, the 4 of Janewarye 1592... | | xij[s] |
| Rd at the gelyous comodey,[4] the 5 of Janewary 1592 ........................................ | | xxxxiv[s] |
| Rd at titus, the 6 of Janewary 1592[5] ......... | | lij[s] |
| Rd at Jeronymo, the 8 of Janewary 1593 ... | | xxij[s] |

[1] Malone observes (Sh. by Bosw. iii., 299), that there was an interruption of theatrical performances in 1593, owing to the prevalence of the plague: in fact, the interruption commenced in the summer of 1592, and in December the companies were allowed to begin again; at least such was the case with the association in which Henslowe was interested. It may be added that Nash's "Summers Last Will and Testament" was performed at this date out of London, in consequence of the plague. See the reprint of it in Dodsley's Old Plays, vol. ix., last edition.

[2] By "cnacke" Henslowe no doubt means the play of the Knack to know a Knave, mentioned in the previous account.

[3] i. e., Marlowe's Jew of Malta.

[4] Malone prints this "the gelyons comedye," whereas the true reading seems to be "the gelyous comodey;" probably a play on some tale of jealousy. Malone's conjecture, that it was founded upon Julian of Brentford's Testament, is very far-fetched: that piece of scurrility and indecency could by no possibility be formed into a play; but by "gelyous" the ignorant old manager may have meant *Julius*. It was a new play, as appears by Henslowe's mark *ne*.

[5] After this entry 1593 is substituted for 1592; but 1593, according to the usual reckoning of that time, did not begin until 26 March. Henslowe is very irregular in his dates.

| | | |
|---|---|---|
| Rd at mulo mulocko, the 9 of Janewary 1592 | | xx$^{s}$ |
| Rd at frier bacon, the 10 of Janewary 1593 | | xxiiij$^{s}$ |
| Rd at the comodey of cosmo,[1] the 12 of Jenewary 1593 ............ .................... | | xxxxvij$^{s}$ |
| Rd at mandevell, the 13 of Janewary 1593... | | ix$^{s}$ |
| Rd at the cnacke, the 14 of Jenewary 1593 | | xxiiij$^{s}$ |
| Rd at tittus,[2] the 15 of Jenewary 1593...... | | xxx$^{s}$ |
| Rd at harey the 6, the 16 of Jenewary 1593 | | xxxxvj$^{s}$ |
| Rd at frer bacon, the 17 of Jenewary 1593... | | xx$^{s}$ |
| Rd at the Jewe, the 18 of Jenewaye 1593 ... | iij$^{li}$ | |
| Rd at tambercam, the 19 of Jenewaye 1593 | | xxxvj$^{s}$ |
| Rd at mulomulco, the 20 of Jeneway 1593... | | xx$^{s}$ |
| Rd at Jeronymo, the 22 of Jeneway 1593 ... | | xx$^{s}$ |
| Rd at cossmo, the 23 of Jenewary 1593 ...... | | xxx$^{s}$ |
| Rd at the Knacke, the 25 of Jenewye 1593... | | xxiiij$^{s}$ |
| Rd at titus, the 29 of Jenewary 1593 ......... | | xxx$^{s}$ |
| Rd at the tragedey of the guyes[3] 30........... | iij$^{s}$ | iiij$^{s}$ |
| Rd at mandevell [not legible][4] | | |
| Rd at frier bacon, the 30 of Jenewary 1593... | | xij$^{s}$ |
| Rd at harey the vj, the 31 of Jenewarye 1593 | | xxvj$^{s}$ |
| Rd at the Jewe of malta, the 1 of Febreary 1593 .......................................... | | xxxv$^{s}$ |

[1] Not marked as a new play, but we have not heard of it before. It perhaps related to the family of the Medici, and dramas upon incidents of Italian history were at this date not uncommon. Not a few of our old poets had visited Italy, and an enumeration of some of them may be seen in Collier's Life of Shakespeare, vol. i., cxxviii.

[2] The play which Henslowe has before called "tittus and vespacia."

[3] In all probability Marlowe's Massacre at Paris, in which the family of Guise play so prominent a part. This entry is valuable, supposing it to apply to Marlowe's tragedy, because it ascertains the day it was first acted, Henslowe having placed *ne* in the margin. It was perhaps Marlowe's last play, as he was killed about six months afterwards.

[4] This memorandum is at the very bottom of the page, and the sum produced by the performance has been worn away.

*In the name of God Amen, beginenge the* 27 *of desember* 1593, *the earle of Susex his men.*[1]

| | | |
|---|---|---|
| Rd at good spede·the plowghe ................. | iij[s] | j[s] |
| Rd at hewen of burdoche,[2] the 28 of desembr 1593 ........................................ | iij[li] | x[s] |
| Rd at gorge a gren, the 29 of desembr 1593 | iij[li] | x[s] |
| Rd at buckingam, the 30 of desembr 1593 ... | | ljx[s] |
| Rd at Richard the confeser,[3] the 31 of desembr 1593 ........................................ | | xxxviij[s] |
| Rd at buckingam, the j of Jenewary 1593 ... | | lviij[s] |
| Rd at gorge a grene, the 2 of Jenewary 1593 | | xviij[s] |
| Rd at hewen of burdokes, the 3 of Jenewary 1593 ........................................ | | xiiij[s] |
| Rd at william the conkrer, the 4 of Jenewary 1593 ........................................ | | xxij[s] |
| Rd at God spead the plowe, the 5 of Jenewary 1593 ........................................ | | xj[s] |
| Rd at frier frances,[4] the 7 of Jenewary 1593 | iij[li] | j[s] |

[1] This account shows that Henslowe was interested in the receipts of the Earl of Sussex's players, at the same time as in those of that association to which the preceding account applies, where no company is mentioned: they were most likely "Lord Strange's men." Excepting the Jew of Malta, always profitable, we meet among the plays with no title that has previously occurred.

[2] i. e., Some play on the romance of Huon de Bordeaux. Henslowe afterwards spells the title differently.

[3] Probably an error, although afterwards repeated, unless it were a play upon a story not historical. It might be in some way connected with the preceding entry of a play called Buckingham, which perhaps was founded upon the rise and fall of that favourite and dupe of Richard III.

[4] See Heywood's Apology for Actors, 1612 (Shakespeare Society's reprint, p. 57), for some account of the plot of this play, and of a "strange accident" at one of the performances of it by the players

| | |
|---|---|
| Rd at the Piner of wiackefelld,[1] the 8 of Jeneware 1593 .................................... | xxiij$^s$ |
| Rd at abrame and lotte,[2] the 9 of Jeneware 1593 ............................................ | liij$^s$ |
| Rd at buckingam, the 10 of Jeneware 1593 | xxij$^s$ |
| Rd at hewen,[3] the 11 of Jeneware 1593...... | v$^s$ |
| Rd at the fayer mayd of ytale,[4] the 12 of Jeneware 1593 ...................................... | x$^s$ |
| Rd at frier frances, the 14 of Jeneware 1593 | xxxvj$^s$ |
| Rd at gorge a grene, the 15 of Jeneware 1593 | xx$^s$ |
| Rd at Richard the confeser, the 16 of Jeneware 1593 ...................................... | xj$^s$ |
| Rd at abrame and lotte, the 17 of Jeneware 1593 ........... ............. .............. | xxx$^s$ |
| Rd at Kinge lude,[5] the 18 of Jenewry 1593 | xxij$^s$ |

of the Earl of Sussex at Lynne, Norfolk. Heywood gives no date, farther than stating that it happened "within these few years" anterior to the publication of his Apology.

[1] The same play as George a-Green, introduced twice before. It was printed in 1599, under the title of George a-Green, the Pinner of Wakefield, and it is attributed to Robert Greene, who is said to have acted the hero himself—possibly in this very company, and on this very occasion. He did not die until September following the date of this entry. Many, if not most, of the dramatists of that time were actors, although there were of course many actors, some of them highly eminent, who were not dramatists.

[2] A Scriptural drama upon the story of Abraham and Lot. It may have been some modification of an old miracle-play.

[3] Hewen must mean Huon of Bordeaux, before spoken of by Henslowe as Hewen of Burdoche, and Hewen of Burdokes.

[4] The Fair Maid of Italy may have been founded upon several novels current at the time, of which fair Italian maids were the heroines.

[5] No doubt King Lud, the supposed restorer of London, or Lud's town, before his time called Troynovant.

| | | |
|---|---|---|
| Rd at frier frances, the 20 of Jenewary 1593 | | xxx^s |
| Rd at the fayer mayd of ytaly, the 21 of Jeneware 1593 ........ | | xxij^s |
| Rd at gorge a grene, the 22 of Jeneware 1593 ........ | | vxv^s |
| Rd at titus and ondronicus,[1] the 23 of Jenewary ........ | iij^li | viij^s |
| Rd at buckengam, the 27 of Jeneware 1593 | | xviij^s |
| Rd at titus and ondronicous, the 28 of Jeneware 1593 ........ | | xxxx^s |
| Rd at abrame and lotte, the 31 of Janeware 1593 ........ | | xij^s |
| Rd at the Jewe of Malta, the 4 of febery 1593 ........ | | l^s |
| Rd at tittus and ondronicus, the 6 of febery 1593 ........ | | xxxx^s |

*In the name of God, Amen, begininge at easter* 1593, *the Quenes men and my lord of Susex to geather.*[2]

| | |
|---|---|
| Rd at frier bacone, the j of Aprell 1593...... | xxxxiij^s |

[1] Elsewhere sometimes spelt "tittus and ondronicus." Malone had no doubt that this was the original Titus Andronicus before Shakespeare touched it. (Shaksp. by Bosw., iii., 300). It may be so, or it may have been a distinct play on the same subject. Whatever it was, it is a novel and material fact that it was a new play on the 23 Jan. 1593: Henslowe placed *ne* in the outer margin to denote it.

[2] These companies were performing, perhaps, in conjunction. In 1590 (See Mr. Cunningham's Revels' Accounts, p. xxxii.) the Queen had two associations of players, one under the Duttons, and the other under Laneham. It is now impossible to ascertain which of the two was acting with the Earl of Sussex's men: the union was of short duration, for the account begins on the 1st and ends on the 8th April, probably 1594, though Henslowe does not so date his memoranda until near the close.

Rd at the Rangers comodey, 2 of Aprell 1593 iij li
Rd at the Jew of malta, the 3 of Aprell 1593 iij li
Rd at the fayer mayd of Italey, the 4 of Aprell 1593 ........................................ xxiij s
Rd at frier bacon, the 5 of aprell 1593......... xx s
Rd at Kinge leare,[1] the 6 of aprell 1593 ...... xxxviij s
Rd at the Jewe of malta, 7 of aprell 1594 ... xxvj s
Rd at Kinge leare, the 8 of aprell 1594 ...... xxvj s

*In the name of God Amen, beginninge the* 14 *of maye* 1594, *by my lord admeralls men.*

Rd at the Jewe of malta, 14 of maye 1594... xxxxviij s
Rd at the Rangers comodey,[2] the 15 of maye 1594 ........................................ xxxiij s
Rd at Cutlacke,[3] the 16 of maye 1594......... xxxxij s

[1] This King Leare was certainly a much older play than Shakespeare's King Lear, and at this date our great dramatist was not one of the Queen's men. The old King Leir, as it is spelt on the title-page, was entered at Stationers' Hall in 1594, but not printed until 1605; at least there is no known copy prior to that date. If orthography go for anything with Henslowe, he spells the name in the same way as Shakespeare spelt it, with the addition of a final *e*.

[2] By a preceding entry, dated 2 April, we have seen that the "Rangers Comedy" had been acted either by the Queen's or the Earl of Sussex's players; yet now we find it in the hands of the "Lord Admiral's men." Rival associations seem at this period to have interfered with each other more than has been generally supposed; and perhaps Henslowe, as the purchaser of the play, communicated his right to act it to any company with which he was concerned.

[3] Cutlack was a part in which Edward Alleyn was famous. E. Guilpin in his "Skialetheia," 1598, Epigr. 43, has this couplet:—

> "Clodius, me thinkes, lookes passing big of late,
> With Dunstan's browes, and Allen's *Cutlack's* gate."

Of the nature of the play we know nothing.

*In the name of God Amen, beginninge at Newington, my Lord Admeralle and my Lorde chamberlen men, as followeth.* 1594:—[1]

| | | |
|---|---|---|
| 3 of June 1594, | Rd at Heaster and asheweros[2] ........ | viij$^s$ |
| 4 of June 1594, | Rd at the Jewe of malta ........ | x$^s$ |
| 5 of June 1594, | Rd at andronicous[3] | xij$^s$ |
| 6 of June 1594, | Rd at cutlacke ... | xj$^s$ |
| 8 of June 1594, *ne* | Rd at bellendon[4] ... | xvij$^s$ |
| 9 of June 1594, | Rd at hamlet[5] ...... | viij$^s$ |

[1] Shakespeare, it is to be borne in mind, was one of the "Lord Chamberlain's men" at this date. Anterior to the 15th of June 1594, Henslowe appears to have been entitled to a much smaller share of the receipts than afterwards: he drew a line in his book when he became entitled to the larger amount.

[2] This is the second play enumerated by Henslowe founded upon Scripture: Abraham and Lott was the first. The Duke of Devonshire has in his collection a unique copy of the drama of Godly Queene Hester, but it is much older than 1594, having been printed in 1561, though it may have served as the foundation of the play subsequently acted.

[3] Henslowe had by this time learned that Andronicus did not begin with the letter *o*, but he transferred it to the end of the word.

[4] Bellendon, as a new play, is marked with *ne*, and we insert it in the place it occupies in the MS.: we know nothing of such a drama.

[5] Malone contends, we think correctly, that this was the old Hamlet, and not Shakespeare's play. Concluding it to be so, our great dramatist might adopt the story, and feel that he had the better right to do so, because the old play had been acted by his friends and fellows, or perhaps with their assistance; for the Lord Chamberlain's players were at this date acting at the Newington theatre with the Lord Admiral's men. The companies may have occupied the house on alternate days, but this is the less likely, because Henslowe received a share of the takings every day. Perhaps they acted twice a day, each company once.

| | | | | |
|---|---|---|---|---|
| 10 of June 1594, | | Rd at heaster ...... | | v$^{s}$ |
| 11 of June 1594, | | Rd at the tamynge of a shrowe[1] ................................ | | ix$^{s}$ |
| 12 of June 1594, | | Rd at andronicous... | | vij$^{s}$ |
| 13 of June 1594, | | Rd at the Jewe[2] ... | | iiij$^{s}$ |
| 15 of June 1594, | | Rd at bellendon ... | iij$^{li}$ | iiij$^{s}$ |
| 17 of June 1594, | | Rd at cutlacke ...... | | xxxv$^{s}$ |
| 18 of June 1594, | | Rd at the Rangers comodey ................................ | | xxij$^{s}$ |
| 19 of June 1594, | | Rd at the Gwies[3]... | | liiij$^{s}$ |
| 20 of June 1594, | | Rd at bellenden ... | | xxx$^{s}$ |
| 22 of June 1594, | | Rd at the Rangers comodey ................................ | | lviiij$^{s}$ |
| 23 of June 1594, | | Rd at the Jewe ... | | xxiij$^{s}$ |
| 24 of June 1594, | | Rd at cutlacke ...... | | xxv$^{s}$ |
| 25 of June 1594, | | Rd at the masacer | | xxxvj$^{s}$ |
| 26 of June 1594, | *ne* | Rd at Galiaso[4]...... | iij$^{li}$ | iiij$^{s}$ |
| 27 of June 1594, | | Rd at cutlacke ...... | | xxxvj$^{s}$ |

[1] No doubt the old Taming of a Shrew, printed in 1594, and recently reprinted by the Shakespeare Society under the care of Mr. Amyot, from the sole existing copy in the library of the Duke of Devonshire.

[2] Under this entry, Henslowe drew a line, apparently to separate the account of his large receipts from his small. For some unexplained reason, he became entitled on 15th June 1594 to a much larger share of the money paid at the doors. When the Jew of Malta was next acted, he received £1 3*s*. 0*d*., instead of only 4*s*.

[3] After this date, the name of "the Guise," for Marlowe's Tragedy, seems dropped, and that of "the Massacre" was adopted in its stead.

[4] A new play: Henslowe wrote *ne*, indicating a first performance, not in the external margin, but between the date and the name of the piece. Such, it will be observed, was the case with Bellendon on the preceding page. Malone has an unhappy conjecture that Galiase, as he prints the name, was intended for Julius Cæsar: that "the *gelyous* comodey" might be meant for it is at least as likely. Henslowe writes it *galiaso*, with unusual uniformity.

| | | | |
|---|---|---|---|
| 30 of June 1594, Rd at the Jew of malta | | xxxj$^s$ | |
| 2 of Julye 1594, Rd at bellendon ... | | xxxxij$^s$ | vj$^d$ |
| 3 of Julye 1594, Rd at the masacer | | xxxj$^s$ | |
| 4 of Julye 1594, Rd at cutlacke ... | | xxiiij$^s$ | |
| 5 of Julye 1594, Rd at the Rangers comodey | | xviij$^s$ | |
| 6 of Julye 1594, Rd at bellendon ... | | xxxiiij$^s$ | |
| 8 of Julye 1594, Rd at the masacer | | xxvij$^s$ | |
| 9 of Julye 1594, Rd at the phillipo and hewpolyto | iij$^{li}$ | ij$^s$ | |
| 10 of Julye 1594, Rd at the Jewe ... | | xxvij$^s$ | |
| 11 of Julye 1594, Rd at bellendon ... | | xxvij$^s$ | |
| 12 of Julye 1594, Rd at galiaso ...... | | xxxxvj$^s$ | |
| 13 of Julye 1594, Rd at phillipo and hewpolyto | | xxxx$^s$ | |
| 15 of Julye 1594, Rd at cutlacke ... | | xxxv$^s$ | |
| 16 of Julye 1594, Rd at masacare ... | | xxxj$^s$ | |
| 17 of Julye 1594, Rd at the Rangers comodey | | xv$^s$ | |
| 18 of Julye 1594, Rd at phillipo and hewpolyto | | xxx$^s$ | |
| 19 of Julye 1594, *ne* Rd at 2 pte of godfrey of bullen [1] | iij$^{li}$ | xj$^s$ | |
| 20 of Julye 1593, Rd at bellendon ... | | xxvij$^s$ | |
| 22 of Julye 1594, Rd at the Jewe of malta | | xxxj$^s$ | |
| 23 of Julye 1594, Rd at galiaso ...... | | xxxj$^s$ | |
| 24 of Julye 1594, Rd at phillipo and hewpolyto | | xxx$^s$ | |

[1] Godfrey of Boulogne is of course intended. No *first* part of the same subject has been mentioned by Henslowe (unless under the name of "Jerusalem") but it was entered at Stationers' Hall 19th June 1594: this "second part" was a new play, according to Henslowe's mark, and a first part must then have been in existence.

| | | | |
|---|---|---|---|
| 25 of Julye 1594, | Rd at bellendon ... | | xlviij$^s$ |
| 26 of Julye 1594, | Rd at godfrey ...... | | xlvij$^s$ |
| 27 of Julye 1594, | Rd at the masacer | | xxij$^s$ |
| 29 of Julye 1594, | Rd at cutlacke ... | | xxix$^s$ |
| 30 of Julye 1594, *ne* | Rd at the marchant of eamden[1] ........ | iij$^{li}$ | viij$^s$ |
| 31 of Julye 1594, | Rd at bellendon, the | | xxvij$^s$ |
| 1 of Aguste 1594, | Rd at the Rangers comodey ........ | | xiij$^s$ vj$^d$ |
| 3 of Aguste 1594, | Rd at phillipo and hewpolito ........ | | xxx$^s$ |
| 4 of Aguste 1594, | Rd at galiaso ...... | | xxiij$^s$ vj$^d$ |
| | Rd at the Jewe of malta[2] ........ | | xxvij$^s$ |

[1] Malone misread this new play "the marchant of candew," and suggested that Candia was perhaps meant: it is very clearly in the MS. *eamden*, or Emden. The Merchant of Emden must have been upon the same incidents as are detailed in a B. L. ballad with the following title, "A most sweet Song of an English Merchant, borne at Chichester." This merchant settled at Emden, and having killed a man in an accidental rencontre, he was tried and condemned to die. He was so handsome that many of the young ladies of the town were in love with him, and did their utmost to obtain his liberation: when brought to the scaffold, several ladies offered to die for him, and one of them hastened to the Governor, and by her tears induced him to pardon the Englishman; we need hardly add that they were afterwards married. It opens thus:—

"A rich merchant man,
That was both grave and wise,
Did kill a man at Emden town,
Through quarrels that did rise."

The whole may be found in Evans's Old Ballads, i., 28, last edition.

[2] There is some error or confusion in dates here, and this representation of the extremely popular play of the Jew of Malta is left without any. Farther on, the 7th and 8th August are repeated.

| | | | | |
|---|---|---|---|---|
| 6 of Aguste 1594, | Rd at seconde pt of godfrey | | xxxvij$^{s}$ | |
| 7 of aguste 1594, | Rd at phillipo and hewpolito | | xxix$^{s}$ | |
| 8 of aguste 1594, | Rd at the masacare | | xxiij$^{s}$ | vj$^{d}$ |
| 7 of aguste 1594, | Rd at the Jewe of malta | | xvij$^{s}$ | vj$^{d}$ |
| 8 of aguste 1594, | Rd at cutlacke ... | | xiij$^{s}$ | vj$^{d}$ |
| 10 of aguste 1594, | Rd at bellendon ... | | xxxiij$^{s}$ | |
| 11 of aguste 1594, *ne* | Rd at tassoes mellencoley [1] | iij$^{li}$ | iiij$^{s}$ | |
| 12 of aguste 1594, | Rd at galliaso...... | | xviij$^{s}$ | |
| 13 of aguste 1594, | Rd at godfrey of bullen | | xxix$^{s}$ | |
| 14 of aguste 1594, | Rd at mahomett [2] | iij$^{li}$ | v$^{s}$ | |
| 15 of aguste 1594, | Rd at phillipo and hewpolyto | | xxj$^{s}$ | |
| 17 of aguste 1594, | Rd at the masaccar | | xx$^{s}$ | |
| 18 of aguste 1594, | Rd at tassoes mallencoley | | xxxxvij$^{s}$ | |

[1] A drama apparently founded upon the later portion of the life of Tasso, who did not die until 1595; and it is singular that any of the incidents of his life should so soon have been presented on the English stage. Perhaps, as our poets at this date were frequent visitors of Italy, they had brought the facts upon which the play was founded from thence. It was acted for the first time on the 11th August 1594.

[2] We have not heard of this play before, but it is not marked by Henslowe as a new one. George Peele wrote a lost drama called the Turkish Mahomet, and Hiren the fair Greek, and this entry possibly relates to its performance. It is mentioned in Peele's Jests, of which the earliest extant edition is dated 1607. Peele was dead in 1598: he was, we have every reason to believe, the son of Stephen Peele, a ballad-writing bookseller, two of whose productions are printed in the earliest publication of the Percy Society. The Rev. Mr. Dyce was not aware of Peele's parentage.

| | | | | |
|---|---|---|---|---|
| 19 of aguste 1594, | Rd at bellendon ... | | xxj$^{s}$ | |
| 20 of aguste 1594, | Rd at the Rangers comodey ... | | xiiij$^{s}$ | vj$^{d}$ |
| 21 of aguste 1594, | Rd at galiaso ...... | | xxj$^{s}$ | vj$^{d}$ |
| 22 of aguste 1594, | Rd at cuttlacke ... | | xxiij$^{s}$ | |
| 24 of aguste 1594, | Rd at phillipo and hewpolyto ... | | xxviij$^{s}$ | |
| 25 of aguste 1594, *ne* | Rd at the Venesyon comodey[1] ... | | l$^{s}$ | vj$^{d}$ |
| 26 of aguste 1594, | Rd at godfrey...... | | xxvij$^{s}$ | vj$^{d}$ |
| 27 of aguste 1594, | Rd at Mahemet... | | xxxx$^{s}$ | |
| 28 of aguste 1594, | Rd at tamberlen[2] | iij$^{li}$ | xj$^{s}$ | |
| 29 of aguste 1594, | Rd at bellendon ... | | xx$^{s}$ | vj$^{d}$ |
| 2 of septembr 1594, | Rd at the Jew of malta ... | | xxiij$^{s}$ | vj$^{d}$ |
| 3 of septembr 1594, | Rd at Tasso ...... | | xxxxvj$^{s}$ | |
| 4 of septembr 1594, | Rd at phillipo and hewpolito ... | | xxij$^{s}$ | |
| 5 of septembr 1594, | Rd at the venesyon comodey ... | | xxxvj$^{s}$ | vj$^{d}$ |
| 6 of septembr 1594, | Rd at cutlacke ... | | xj$^{s}$ | |
| 7 of septembr 1594, | Rd at the masacar ... | | xvij$^{s}$ | vj$^{d}$ |
| 8 of sptembr 1594, | Rd at godfrey ... | | xxxx$^{s}$ | |
| 9 of septembr 1594, | Rd at mahemett... | | xxxv$^{s}$ | |

[1] This was clearly not the play afterwards mentioned as "Venesyon and the love of an Inglishe ladye," because that, as well as "the Venesyon comodey," was a new play, and is so marked by Henslowe. It has been suggested that "the Venesyon comodey" might be a play on the story of the Merchant of Venice; but had it been the Merchant of Venice, Henslowe would probably have called it by that name: we have already had the Merchant of Emden.

[2] This can hardly be the same as Tamercame, before frequently mentioned, and the name approaches much nearer to Marlowe's Tamburlaine: perhaps, it was a revival of it, and the receipt was large.

| | | |
|---|---|---|
| 10 of septembr 1594, | Rd at galiaso ... | xxv$^{s}$ |
| 11 of septembr 1594, | Rd at bellendon | xxiiij$^{s}$ vj$^{d}$ |
| 12 of septembr 1594, | Rd at tamber-len ........................................ | xxxxv$^{s}$ |
| 13 of septembr 1594, | Rd at phillipo and hewpolito ............................ | xx$^{s}$ |
| 15 of septembr 1594, | Rd at the vene-syon comodey ............................ | xxxvj$^{s}$ vj$^{d}$ |
| 16 of septembr 1594, | Rd at the Ran-gers comodey.................................. | xv$^{s}$ |
| 17 of septembr 1594, *ne* | Rd at palamon and arsett[1] ................................ | lj$^{s}$ |
| 18 of septembr 1594, | Rd at tasso...... | xxvij$^{s}$ vj$^{d}$ |
| 19 of septembr 1594, | Rd at phillipo and hewpolyto ............................ | xiiij$^{s}$ vj$^{d}$ |
| 20 of septembr 1594, | Rd at godfrey ... | xxx$^{s}$ |
| 21 of septembr 1594, | Rd at mahemett | xxviij$^{s}$ |
| 22 of septembr 1594, | Rd at the vene-syon comodey ............................ | xxv$^{s}$ |
| 23 of septembr 1594, | Rd at bellendon | xvj$^{s}$ vj$^{d}$ |
| 24 of septembr 1594, *ne* | Rd at venesyon and the love of and Ingleshe lady[2]...... | xxxxvij$^{s}$ |

[1] A play obviously on Chaucer's Palamon and Arcite. This might be an alteration of Edwards's play acted before Queen Elizabeth in 1566, (*Vide* Hist. of Engl. Dram. Poetry and the Stage, i., 191). The Two Noble Kinsmen, in which Shakespeare is stated to have had some concern, is founded on the same incidents. It is very possible that he did something for it when it was acted on the 17th Sept. 1594, by the Lord Chamberlain's Players, (performing with the Lord Admiral's men) and that the alterations and additions he made were employed by Fletcher in the play as it was printed in 1634. On this point see an able Essay by Mr. Spalding, printed at Edinburgh in 1833. 8vo.

[2] This play is here mentioned on its first performance, and afterwards it is styled "Love of and Ingleshe ladey," but no doubt it was the same production. The ballad of the Love of a Spanish Lady for an English-

| | | | |
|---|---|---|---|
| 25 of septembr 1594, | Rd at masacar ... | | xiiij[s] |
| 26 of septembr 1594, | Rd at cuttlacke | | xiij[s] |
| 28 of septembr 1594, | Rd at tamberlen | | xxxj[s] |
| 29 of septembr 1594, | Rd at galiaso... | | xvij[s] |
| 30 of septembr 1594, | Rd at Docter Fostose[1] ........ | iij[li] | xij[s] |
| 2 of octobr 1594, | Rd at the Rangers comodey ........ | | x[s] |
| 3 of octobr 1594, | Rd at the venesyon comodey ........ | | xvij[s] |
| 4 of octobr 1594, | Rd at the love of a gresyan lady[2] ........ | | xxvj[s] |
| 6 of octobr 1594, | Rd at godfrey of bullen ........ | | xx[s] |
| 7 of octobr 1594, | Rd at phillipo and hewpolito ........ | | xij[s] |

man is well known (See Percy's Reliques, ii., 256, edit. 1812), but none of the love of a Venetian for an English lady.

[1] Doubtless, Marlowe's play of the Life and Death of Doctor Faustus, founded upon the old Romance which was first entered on the Stationers' books in 1588, soon after which date the drama, we may conjecture, was written. It now produced a large receipt, but it is not marked by Henslowe as a new play, and such could hardly have been the case, unless it had been posthumous, Marlowe having been killed in 1593. It was not printed until 1604. Alleyn performed the hero, as we learn from the following lines in S. Rowland's Knave of Clubs, 1600:—

"The gull gets on a surplis,
With crosse upon his breast,
Like Allen playing Faustus;
In that manner he was drest."

[2] Malone supposes this to have been Peele's lost play of the Turkish Mahomet and Hiren the fair Greek, but it seems more likely that the Mahomet, several times heretofore introduced by Henslowe, was Peele's drama. See note 2, p. 39. It was not a new play at this date, and the authorship of it is mere matter of speculation.

8 of octobr 1594, Rd at tasso ......... xxvij[s]
9 of octobr 1594, Rd at Docter Fostus ......... xxxxiiij[s]
11 of octobr 1594, Rd at the venesyon comodey ......... xvj[s]
13 of octobr 1594, Rd at bellendon ... xxij[s]
14 of octobr 1594, Rd at mahemett ... xxvj[s]
15 of octobr 1594, Rd at tamberlen ... xxviij[s]
16 of octobr 1594, Rd at palaman and arset ......... xxvij[s]
17 of octobr 1594, Rd at tamberlen ... xxxx[s]
18 of octobr 1594, Rd at the frenshe docter[1] ......... xxij[s]
20 of octobr 1594, Rd at the Jewe of malta, 1594[2] ......... xiij[s]
21 of octobr 1594, Rd at docter Fostus, 1594 ......... xxxiij[s]
22 of octobr 1594, *ne* Rd at the Knacke to know a noneste[3] ......... xxxx[s]
23 of octobr 1594, Rd at tasso ......... xxiij[s]
24 of octobr 1594, Rd at love of and Ingleshe ladey ......... xxiij[s]
25 of octobr 1594, Rd at galleaso ...... xj[s]

[1] Possibly so called from the prominence of the character of a French Doctor in the performance: The Wisdom of Doctor Dodypol was the name of a play printed in 1600.

[2] The popularity of the Jew of Malta, judging from the receipts, seems by this date to have declined considerably; and no wonder, recollecting the frequency of its repetitions.

[3] The Knack to know an Honest [Man] was written, probably, in consequence of the success of the Knack to know a Knave, which we have seen was produced in June 1592. A Knack to know an Honest Man was printed in 1596, and, in the shape in which it has come down to us, it is much inferior to its prototype, both in language and incidents, and indisputably not by the same author.

| | | |
|---|---|---|
| 27 of octobr 1594, Rd at pallaman and harset ................................. | | xxxxvij$^{s}$ |
| 28 of octobr 1594, Rd at the frenshe docter ........................................ | | xv$^{s}$ |
| 29 of octobr 1594, Rd at the Knacke to knowe and oneste man ......... ........ | | xxxxvij$^{s}$ |
| 30 of october 1594, Rd at bullen ... | | xv$^{s}$ |
| 1 of novembr 1594, Rd at the Knacke to knowe and onest man .................. | iij$^{li}$ | iij$^{s}$ |
| 2 of novembr 1594, Rd at bellendon | | vij$^{s}$ |
| 4 of novembr 1594, Rd at tamberlen | | xxxix$^{s}$ |
| 5 of novembr 1594, Rd at Docter Fostes ....................................... | | xxxviij$^{s}$ |
| 6 of novembr 1594, Rd at mahemette | | xv$^{s}$ |
| 7 of novembr 1594, Rd at the knacke[1] | | xxxxiiij$^{s}$ |
| 8 of novembr 1594, *ne* Rd at Seser and pompie[2] .................... ................ | iij$^{li}$ | ij$^{s}$ |
| 9 of novembr 1594, Rd at palamon... | | xij$^{s}$ |
| 11 of novembr 1594, Rd at the Venesyon comodey......... ....................... | | xxj$^{s}$ |
| 12 of novembr 1594, Rd at tasso ...... | | xxv$^{s}$ |
| 13 of novembr 1594, Rd at the gresyan ladye ......................................... | | xv$^{s}$ |
| 14 of novembr 1594, Rd at sesor and pompie ...................................... | | xxx$^{s}$ |

[1] Probably the latest of the two "Knacks" is here intended, but it may have been a revival of the Knack to know a Knave.

[2] This was a new play, and is so marked by Henslowe: two dramas under this title have come down to us, the one by George Chapman, (which, as he himself informs us, was never acted) and the other anonymous. The anonymous Cæsar and Pompey was printed in 1607, but Chapman's "Roman Tragedy" did not come from the press until 1631, although 1607 is the date assigned to it in the Biographia Dramatica. We shall see presently that the success of "Seser and pompie" led to the production of a second part.

| | | |
|---|---|---|
| 15 of novembr 1594, | Rd at bellendon | xij$^{s}$ |
| 16 of novembr 1594, *ne* | Rd at Deoclesyan[1] | liiij$^{s}$ |
| 18 of novembr 1594, Docter | Rd at the Frenshe 189.08.00[2]...... | xxvij$^{s}$ |
| 20 of novembr 1594, | Rd at docter fos- tes ... .................................... .. | xviij$^{s}$ |
| 21 of novembr 1594, | Rd at the Knacke | xx$^{s}$ |
| 22 of novembr 1594, | Rd at deoclesyan | xxxxiij$^{s}$ |
| 23 of novembr 1494, | Rd at the grea- syon comodey[3] ............................ | x$^{s}$ |
| 25 of novembr 1594, | Rd at seser and pompey ..................................... | xxxij$^{s}$ |
| 26 of novembr 1594, | Rd at the vene- cyon comody ............................... | xiij$^{s}$ |
| 27 of novembr 1594, | Rd at tamberlen | xxij$^{s}$ |
| 28 of novmbr 1594, | Rd at warlam- chester[4] ....................................... | xxiij$^{s}$ |
| 29 of novembr 1594, | Rd at the Knacke | xx$^{s}$ |
| 30 of novembr 1594, | Rd at warlam- chester ....................................... | xxxviij$^{s}$ |
| 1 of desembr 1594, | R at the gresyan comody .................................. | iiij$^{s}$ |
| 2 of desembr 1594, *ne* | Rd at the wise man of Chester ......................... | xxxiij$^{s}$ |

[1] This new play of Diocletian may have formed the foundation of Beaumont and Fletcher's Prophetess, or at all events it was a drama on the same part of history.

[2] This sum appears to be Henslowe's adding-up of amounts he had received: it does not tally with any of the receipts previously mentioned, but clearly relates to them.

[3] Possibly the same play as that before called the Love of a Grecian Lady.

[4] This play, which was not a new one, is not to be confounded with "the wise man of Chester," or Westchester, just afterwards inserted in the list, which was a new play on the 2d Dec. 1594.

| | | | |
|---|---|---|---|
| 3 of desembr 1594, | Rd at tasso ...... | | vj[s] |
| 4 of desembr 1594, | Rd at mahemet | | xj[s] |
| 6 of desembr 1594, | Rd at wiseman of westchester ........................ | | xxxiij[s] |
| 8 of desembr 1594, | Rd at Docter fostus .................................. | | xx[s] |
| 9 of desembr 1594, | Rd at the Jew... | | iij[s] |
| 10 of desembr 1594, | Rd at seser ...... | | xij[s] |
| 12 of desembr 1594, | Rd at warlamchester .................................. | | xv[s] |
| 13 of desembr 1594, | Rd at the Knacke | | xij[s] |
| 14 of desembr 1594, *ne* | Rd at the mawe[1] | | xxxxiiij[s] |
| 17 of desembr 1594, | Rd at tamberlen | | xxxj[s] |
| 19 of desembr 1594, | Rd at the 2 pte of tamberlen[2] ........................ | | xxxxvj[s] |
| 20 of desembr 1594, | Rd at Docter fostus...... ......... ......................... | | xviij[s] |
| 25 of desembr 1594, *Cstmes* | Rd at the greasyane comodey[3] ....... ................ | | xxxxvj[s] |
| 26 of desembr 1594, | Rd at the sege of london .................................. | iij[li] | iij[s] |
| 27 of desembr 1594, | Rd at docter fostes .......................................... | | lij[s] |
| 29 of desembr 1594, | Rd at the wissman of westchester ..................... | iij[li] | ij[s] |

[1] Maw was a game at cards, and this play is afterwards called "the seat at mawe:" see note 1, p. 47. It was a new play.

[2] i. e., The second part of Marlowe's Tamburlaine the Great.

[3] It thus appears that, if sometimes prevented on Sundays, companies were allowed to perform on Christmas day, which Henslowe marks, and the difference in his receipts to old plays at this season is very obvious. No new play was deemed necessary until the 11th February, unless "the Siege of London," on 26th Dec. 1594, were new. We have not heard of it before, but Henslowe has no mark against it to show that it was a first performance.

| | | | |
|---|---|---|---|
| 30 of desembr 1594, | Rd at tamberlen | | xxij$^{s}$ |
| 1 of Jeneway 1594, | Rd at the 2 pte of tamberlen ........................... | iij$^{li}$ | ij$^{s}$ |
| 2 of Jeneway 1594, | Rd at the seat at mawe [1] ........................... | | xxiiij$^{s}$ |
| 3 of Jeneway 1594, | Rd at the frenshe docter ........................... | | xxj$^{s}$ |
| 4 of Jeneway 1594, | Rd at velya for [2] | | xj$^{s}$ |
| 7 of Jeneway 1594, | Rd at the Knacke | | xxij$^{s}$ |
| 9 of Jeneway 1594, | Rd at docter fostes ........................... | | xxij$^{s}$ |
| 10 of Jeneway 1595, [3] | Rd at the greasyan comodey ........................... | | xxviij$^{s}$ |
| 11 of Jeneway 1595, | Rd at tasso...... | | xx$^{s}$ |
| 13 of Jeneway 1595, | Rd at the Knacke | | xxxiij$^{s}$ |
| 14 of Jeneway 1594, | Rd at the seage of london ........................... | | xxviij$^{s}$ |
| 16 of Jeneway 1594, | Rd at the wiseman of weaschester ........................... | iij$^{li}$ | |
| 17 of Jeneway 1594, | Rd at the mawe | | xxv$^{s}$ |

[1] No doubt the same play as "the Mawe," produced on the 14th December. Malone (Shaksp. by Boswell, iii., 304) says that this entry is "the seut at mawe," and that it means *suit*, mawe being a game at cards: the latter part is of course true, but the correct reading of the MS. is "the seat at mawe," or *set* at mawe, in the same way that we still talk of a set at tennis and at some other games.

[2] Malone takes no notice of this unintelligible piece: it was perhaps only part of the title "the valya for—" the scribe not knowing the rest. Some months afterwards we meet with Antony and Vallea, and it may have been the drama in question; but here it is not stated to have been a first performance.

[3] In this and the two next entries 1594 has been first written, and then converted into 1595. It was in fact 1595, according to our present reckoning.

| | | |
|---|---|---|
| 18 of Jeneway 1594, Rd at seaser...... | | xxv$^{s}$ |
| 19 of Jeneway 1594, Rd at the Rangers comodey............................... | | xv$^{s}$ |
| 21 of Jeneway 1594, Rd at tasso ...... | | xxxvj$^{s}$ |
| 22 of Jeneway 1594, Rd at the seage of london ................................ | | xxxiij$^{s}$ |
| 23 of Jeneway 1594, Rd at the wiseman of weaschester ...................... | iij$^{li}$ | vj$^{s}$ |
| 24 of Jeneway 1594, Rd at Docter fostes ... ....................................... | | xxiiij$^{s}$ |
| 25 of Jeneway 1594, Rd at the greasyan ........................................ | | xv$^{s}$ |
| 27 of Jeneway 1594, Rd at tamberlen .............................................. | | xxx$^{s}$ |
| 28 of Jeneway 1594, Rd at the mawe | | xxvij$^{s}$ |
| 29 of Jeneway 1594, Rd at the 2 pte of tamberlen .............................. | | xxxxvij$^{s}$ |
| 30 of Jeneway 1594, Rd at the frenshe docter........................................ | | xviij$^{s}$ |
| 31 of Jeneway 1594, Rd at the gresyan comody ............................... | | xxviij$^{s}$ |
| 1 of febreary 1594, Rd at seaser...... | | xxiiij$^{s}$ |
| 3 of febreary 1594, Rd at the sege of london ........................................ | | xxxxv$^{s}$ |
| 4 of febreary 1594, Rd at wyseman of weschester .............................. | iij$^{li}$ | iiij$^{s}$ |
| 5 of febreary 1594, Rd at mahemett | | xxvj$^{s}$ |
| 6 of febreary 1594, Rd at the Knacke | | xxiiij$^{s}$ |
| 7 of febreary 1594, Rd at the frenshe docter........................................ | | xxj$^{s}$ |
| 8 of febreary 1594, Rd at Docter fostes ............................................. | | xviij$^{s}$ |
| 10 of febreary 1594, Rd at the Venesyan .. ...................................... | | xx$^{s}$ |

| | | | | |
|---|---|---|---|---|
| 11 of febreary 1594, | *ne* | Rd at the frenshe Comodey[1] ........ | | l$^{s}$ |
| 12 of febreary 1594, | | Rd at wisman of weschester ........ | | liij$^{s}$ |
| 13 of febreary 1594, | | Rd at the sege of london ........ | | xxix$^{s}$ |
| 14 of febreary 1594, | *j* | Rd at longe mege of westmester[2] ........ | iij$^{li}$ | ix$^{s}$ |
| 15 of febreary 1594, | | Rd at tasso ...... | | xix$^{s}$ |
| 17 of febreary 1594, | | Rd at tamberlen | | xxx$^{s}$ |
| 18 of febreye 1594, | | Rd at the 2 pte of tamberlen ........ | | xxxvj$^{s}$ |
| 19 of febreay 1594, | | Rd at wisman of weschester ........ | | xxxxvj$^{s}$ |
| 20 of febreary 1594, | | Rd at longe mege | | xxxxviij$^{s}$ |
| 21 of febreary 1594, | *ne* | Rd at the macke[3] | iij$^{li}$ | |
| 22 of febreary 1594, | | Rd at the gresyan comodey ........ | | xx$^{s}$ |
| 24 of febreary 1594, | | Rd at the frensh Doctor ........ | | xxxxiiij$^{s}$ |

[1] This new piece is not to be confounded with "the French Doctor," which was a popular and profitable play, much more so than "the French Comedy" ever became.

[2] This was doubtless a new play, though Henslowe has not marked it so in his usual way, but by putting the figure *j* before it to denote that it was its *first* representation. The old tract of Long Meg of Westminster is well-known, and has been reprinted. In N. Field's Amends for Ladies, 1618, but acted earlier by some years, a play called Long Meg is spoken of as in a course of representation at the Fortune theatre, which belonged to Alleyn and Henslowe. It was no doubt the same drama here mentioned, under the date of 14th Feb. 1594. See the suppl. vol. to Dodsley's Old Plays.

[3] Mack was another game at cards, and this new play was perhaps written in consequence of the success of the Maw, already many times represented.

25 of febreary 1594, Rd at the venesyan comodey .............................. xx[s]
26 of febreary 1594, Rd at the Knacke xxiiij[s]
27 of febreary 1594, Rd at the frenshe Comodey .............................. xxxx[s]
28 of febreary 1594, Rd at the wisman of weschester .............................. xxxix[s]
29 of febreary 1594, Rd at lange mege xxxviij[s]
3 of marche 1594, Rd at the sege of london .............................. xxvj[s]
4 of marche 1594, Rd at longe mege on (sraftusdaye)[1] .............................. iij[li]
5 of marche 1594, *ne* Rd at steleo and olempo[2] .............................. iij[li]
6 of marche 1594, Rd at seaser ...... xx[s]
10 of marche 1594, Rd at the Knacke from hence lycensed[3] .............................. xxiiij[s]
11 of marche 1594, Rd at fyrste pt of tamberlen[4] .............................. xxx[s]
12 of marche 1594, Rd at 2 pt of tamberlen .............................. xxij[s]
13 of marche 1594, Rd at longe mege xxviij[s]

[1] What Henslowe, or his scribe, meant by the word they inserted between brackets was doubtless Shrove Tuesday.

[2] Malone gives the name of this new play "Seleo and olempo." It is "Steleo and olempo" in this place; and subsequently the scribe seems to have learned that the first name ought to be Seleo, that Olympo ought to be spelt with a *y*, and that the real name was Olympio.

[3] Are we to suppose from the words "from hence lycensed," which were added afterwards, that until this date the company had been performing without a license, or that "the Knack" had not hitherto been licensed by the Master of the Revels? Possibly the license here spoken of was connected with the prevalence of the plague.

[4] Usually designated only Tamberlen. In this instance, as in several preceding, the second part was acted on the following day.

| | | | |
|---|---|---|---|
| 14 of marche 1594, | Rd at sege of london | | xiiij$^{s}$ |
| Easter mondaye 1595,[1] | easter, Rd at the frenshe Doctor | | liij$^{s}$ |
| 23 of aprell 1595, | Rd at the Knacke | | lv$^{s}$ |
| 24 of aprell 1595, | Rd at the grecian comody | | lj$^{s}$ |
| 25 of aprell 1595, | Rd at the wissman | | lviij$^{s}$ |
| 26 of aprell 1595, | Rd at the wiseman of weschester[2] | iij$^{li}$ | |
| 27 of aprell 1595, | Rd at godfrey of bullen | | xxix$^{s}$ |
| 29 of aprell 1595, | Rd at warlamchester | | xxix$^{s}$ |
| 30 of aprell 1595, | Rd at longe mege... | | xxvij$^{s}$ |
| 31 of aprell 1595, | Rd at fostes | | xxij$^{s}$ |
| 1 of maye 1595, | Rd at longe mege... | | l$^{s}$ |
| 2 of maye 1595, | Rd at seleo and olempo | | l$^{s}$ |
| 3 of maye 1595, | Rd at the frenshe docter | | xj$^{s}$ |
| 5 of maye 1595, | Rd at the Knacke... | | xxiij$^{s}$ |
| 6 of maye 1595, | Rd at the wiseman | | xxxx$^{s}$ |
| 7 of maye 1595, *ne* | Rd at the firste pte of Herculous[3] | iij$^{li}$ | xiij$^{s}$ |

[1] Henslowe draws a line across the page, after the entry of the 14th March, and probably the two companies ceased playing until Easter.

[2] We are perhaps to understand that "the wissman" and "the wiseman of Weschester" were two parts of the same play, acted on two successive days.

[3] A new play. In another part of the Diary it will be found that Martin Slaughter, or Slater, was the author of a drama, in two parts, on the story of Hercules, and this, we apprehend, was one of them. T. Heywood's Brazen Age is on the same subject, but was not written at this early date: it was printed in 1613.

| | | |
|---|---|---|
| 8 of maye 1595, | Rd at the venesyon comodye .................................. | xxx[s] |
| 9 of maye 1595, | Rd at seleo and olympo .................................. | xxvj[s] |
| 10 of maye 1595, | Rd at warlam chester | xxix[s] |
| 12 of maye 1595, | Rd at the frenshe comodye .................................. | xxviij[s] |
| 13 of maye 1595, | Rd at longe mege... | xxviij[s] |
| 14 of maye 1595, | Rd at tasso ........ | xx[s] |
| 15 of maye 1595, | Rd at the wisse man of weschester .................................. | xxxvij[s] |
| 16 of maye 1595, | Rd at the greasyan comodey .................................. | xxxiij[s] |
| 17 of maye 1595, | Rd at godfrey of bullen .................................. | xxij[s] |
| 18 of maye 1595, | Rd at galfrido and Bernardo[1] .................................. | xxxj[s] |

Be[2] yt knowen unto all men by thes presentes, that I John grigges, cyttezin and Butcher of London, do owe unto Phillipe Hinchley, cyttezin and Dyer of London, the some of fyveten poundes of good and lawfull money of England, to be payd unto the sayd Phillipe Hinchley, his ex. adm. and assignes, the

[1] An entry omitted to be noticed by Malone. It relates to a play founded, doubtless, upon the recently-discovered poem by John Drout, entitled "The pityfull Historie of two loving Italians, Gaulfrido and Bernardo le Vayne," printed in 1570 by Henry Binneman. It was formerly supposed (from the entry in the Stationers' Registers, which was all that was known of it) to relate to the incidents of Romeo and Juliet, but such is not the fact. An impression, limited to twenty-five copies, has been recently made from the original.

[2] This memorandum begins a new leaf, and occupies (with some scribbling) the whole of it. A leaf that preceded seems to have been cut out originally. From this document, which appears to be in the handwriting of Griggs, we find that Henslowe was by trade a dyer.

xiijth day of August next ensuienge the datte hereof, unto the which payment I the sayd John grigges do bynd me my heires ex. adm. and assignes by thes presentes. In wyttnes wherof I the sayd John grigges have sette my hand and seale, the xiijth day of July 1592.

ꝑ me JOHN GRIGGES,
[L. S.][1]

| | | | |
|---|---|---|---|
| 19 of maye 1595, | Rd at olimpo ...... | | xxiij$^{s}$ |
| 20 of maye 1595, | Rd at hercolas ...... | iij$^{li}$ | ix$^{s}$ |
| 21 of maye 1595, | Rd at j pt of tamberlen ...... | | xxij$^{s}$ |
| 22 of maye 1595, | Rd at 2 pt of tamberlen ...... | | xxv$^{s}$ |
| 23 of maye 1595, *ne* | Rd at 2 pt of hercolas[2] ...... | iij$^{li}$ | x$^{s}$ |
| 24 of maye 1595, | Rd at frenshe Doctor ...... | | xxij$^{s}$ |
| 26 of maye 1595, | Rd at weschester ... | | xxxj$^{s}$ |
| 27 of maye 1595, | Rd at j pte of hercolas ...... | iij$^{li}$ | |
| 28 of maye 1595, | Rd at 2 pte of hercolas ...... | iij$^{li}$ | ij$^{s}$ |
| 29 of maye 1595, | Rd at olimpo......... | | xxix$^{s}$ |
| 30 of maye 1595, | Rd at warlam chester | | ix$^{s}$ |
| 31 of maye 1595, | Rd at frenshe comodye ...... | | xv$^{s}$ |
| 3 of June 1595, *ne* | Rd at the vij dayes of the weacke[3] ...... | iij$^{li}$ | x$^{s}$ |

[1] The seal has been cut away. After this entry, which, in point of date and on every other account, is much out of its place, the list of plays is regularly continued.

[2] The second part of the play, brought out on the 7th May: see p. 51.

[3] A new play, of which, like many more, we hear on no other authority.

| | | | |
|---|---|---|---|
| 4 of June 1595, | Rd at the wiseman of weschester | | xxijs |
| 5 of June 1595, | Rd at doctor Fostus | | xvijs |
| 6 of June 1595, | Rd at the vij dayes of the weacke | | xxxxiiijs |
| 7 of June 1595, | Rd at olimpio | | xvs |
| 9 of June 1595, *Whittson daie* | Rd at the Knacke | | lvs |
| 10 of June 1595, | Rd at the vij dayes of the wecke | iijli | vjs |
| 11 of June 1595, | Rd at wissman of weschester | | xxxxvijs |
| 12 of June 1595, | Rd at the j pt of herculos | iijli | js |
| 13 of June 1595, | Rd at the 2 pt of herculos | iijli | |
| 14 of June 1595, | Rd at the vij dayes of the wecke | iijli | ixs |
| 16 of June 1595, | Rd at warlamchester | | xxvs |
| 17 of June 1595, | Rd at the frenshe comodey | | xxjs |
| 18 of June 1595, *ne* | Rd at the 2 pte of sesore[1] | | lvs |
| 19 of June 1595, | Rd at longe mege | | xxijs |
| 20 of June[2] [1595, | ]Rd at antonye and vallea | | xxs |

[1] i. e., The second part of the play called, on its first production on the 8th Nov. 1594, "Seser and Pompie." We may add here that the Duke of Devonshire has a copy of the old anonymous play of Cæsar and Pompey, without date, and no doubt earlier than 1607.

[2] The cutting away of Griggs' seal, on the other side of the page, has removed the date of the year from this and the two next entries. "Antonye and vallea" may have been a new play on the 20th of June, but Henslowe's mark to denote the fact has also been cut away, and we have before had "the Valya for" mentioned. See p. 47, note 2. Malone states that it was entered at Stationers' Hall by Humphrey

| | | | |
|---|---|---|---|
| 21 of June [1595, | Rd] at the Knacke... | | xiij$^{s}$ |
| 23 of June [1595, | ]Rd at the vij dayes of the wecke .............................. | iij$^{li}$ | v$^{s}$ |
| 24 of June, mydsomerdaye, | Rd at the frenshe comodey........................... | | xxx$^{s}$ |
| 25 of June 1595, | Rd at the j pte of seaser .................................... | | xxij$^{s}$ |
| 26 of June 1595,[1] | Rd at the 2 pte of seaser .................................... ... | | xx$^{s}$ |
| | | | |
| 25 of aguste 1595, | Rd at the knacke to know a nonest man ........................ | | xvij$^{s}$ |
| 26 of aguste 1595, | Rd at the wiseman of wescheaster ............................. | | xxxix$^{s}$ |
| 27 of aguste 1595, | Rd at the weacke ... | | liij$^{s}$ |
| 28 of aguste 1595, | Rd at longe mege ... | | xvij$^{s}$ |
| 29 of aguste 1595, *ne* | Rd at longe shanke[2] | | xxxx$^{s}$ |

Mosely, the bookseller, on the 29th of June 1660, as the work of Philip Massinger; and, in the list of plays destroyed by Warburton's cook, we meet with one called Antonio and Valia. In the same list is Philenzo and Hippolita, also attributed to Massinger, which may have been the piece repeatedly called by Henslowe Phillipo and Hewpolyto. Massinger, in all probability, revived and altered them from the state in which they were represented in 1594 and 1595: he was of course not old enough to have been their author at that date, having been born in 1584. See Gifford's Massinger, i., li.

[1] The companies probably ceased to act in London between this date and the 25th of August 1595. Perhaps they travelled into the country from want of encouragement, as the receipts had fallen off rapidly, excepting in the instance of the French Comedy.

[2] This could not be G. Peele's historical play of Edward the First, as Malone suggests, unless it was not acted until after it had been printed in 1593. It was most likely a play by some other dramatist upon the same portion of English history: this was its first performance, and is so marked by Henslowe, but Malone did not know that *ne* denoted a first representation. Afterwards it is called "Prince Longshank."

| | | | |
|---|---|---|---|
| 30 of aguste 1595, | Rd at the seage of london ........................................ | | xviij$^{s}$ |
| 1 of septmbr 1595, | Rd at j pte of herculos ........................................ | iij$^{li}$ | iiij$^{s}$ |
| 2 of septmbr 1595, | Rd at 2 pte of herculos ........................................ | iij$^{li}$ | |
| 3 of septmbr 1595, | Rd at the vij dayes of the weacke ........................................ | | lij$^{s}$ |
| 4 of septmbr 1595, | Rd at olempeo and hengenyo[1] ........................................ | | xviij$^{s}$ |
| 5 of septmbr 1595, *ne* | Rd at cracke me this nutte ........................................ | iij$^{li}$ | j$^{s}$ |
| 6 of septmbr 1595, | Rd at valia and antony ........................................ | | xiij$^{s}$ |
| 9 of septmbr 1595, | Rd at the wiseman | | xxxxiiij$^{s}$ |
| 10 of septmbr 1595, | Rd at longshancke | iij$^{li}$ | |
| 11 of septmbr 1595, | Rd at doctor fostes | | xxxvij$^{s}$ |
| 12 of septmbr 1595, | Rd at cracke me this nutte ........................................ | iij$^{li}$ | |
| 13 of septmbr 1595, | Rd at the vij dayes | | xxxvij$^{s}$ |
| | Rd at longe mege[2] | | xvj$^{s}$ |
| 15 of septmbr 1595, | Rd at j pte of tamberlen ........................................ | | xxj$^{s}$ |
| 16 of septmbr 1595, | Rd at godfrey of bullen ........................................ | | xx$^{s}$ |
| 17 of septmbr 1595, *ne* | Rd at the worldes tragedy[3] ........................................ | iij$^{li}$ | v$^{s}$ |

[1] This may possibly be the same play as that before called "Seleo and Olympo," and it is not marked by Henslowe as a new drama. Hengenyo perhaps meant Ingenio; but it is sometimes hardly possible even to guess, on account of Henslowe's ingeniously corrupt spelling.

[2] This entry of Long Meg occurs at the bottom of a page, and without any date.

[3] Also called "the new worldes tragedy" in a subsequent entry: we only know that this was its first performance.

| | | | |
|---|---|---|---|
| 18 of septmbr 1595, | Rd at the Knacke | | xvij$^{s}$ |
| 19 of septmbr 1595, | Rd at the frenshe Doctor | | xvj$^{s}$ |
| 20 of septmbr 1595, | Rd at the sege of london | | xvij$^{s}$ |
| 22 of septmbr 1595,[1] | Rd at the vij dayes | | xxxxiiij$^{s}$ |
| 22 of septmbr 1595, | Rd at j pte of herculos | | xxxj$^{s}$ |
| 23 of septmbr 1595, | Rd at 2 pte of herculos | | xxiij$^{s}$ |
| 24 of septmbr 1595, | Rd at cracke me this nutte | | xxxxij$^{s}$ |
| 25 of septmbr 1595, | Rd at the worldes tragedy | | xxxviij$^{s}$ |
| 26 of septmbr 1595, | Rd at Docter fostes | | xiij$^{s}$ |
| 28 of septmbr 1595, | Rd at crack me this nutte | iij$^{li}$ | vj$^{s}$ |
| 29 of septmbr 1595, | Rd at the wiseman | | xv$^{s}$ |
| 30 of septmbr 1595, | Rd at longe shancke | | xxxij$^{s}$ |
| 2 of octobr 1595, *ne* | Rd at the Desgysses[2] | | xxxxiij$^{s}$ |
| 3 of octobr 1595, | Rd at olempeo[3]... | | xv$^{s}$ |
| 4 of octobr 1595, | Rd at longe mege | | xj$^{s}$ |
| 5 of octobr 1595, | Rd at the vij dayes | | xxxx$^{s}$ |
| 6 of octobr 1595, | Rd at the wiseman | | xvij$^{s}$ |

1 This date ought to be the 21st Sept. 1595, but it stands "22d Sept. 1595."

2 A new play, but whether it had any connexion with the species of dramatic entertainment, at an earlier date called "a disguising," cannot be ascertained. It may have been a piece, like Chapman's Blind Beggar, afterwards introduced, where one actor assumed several characters.

3 Perhaps Olympio and Ingenio, before inserted under date 4th Sept. 1595: it may have been Seleo and Olympo.

| | |
|---|---|
| 7 of octobr 1595, Rd at the worldes tragedy | xxxj[s] |
| 8 of octobr 1595, Rd at cracke me this nutt | xxvj[s] |
| 9 of octobr 1595, Rd at the gresyan comody | x[s] |
| 10 of octobr 1595, Rd at the desgyses | xxix[s] |
| 12 of octobr 1595, Rd at j pte of herculos | xxix[s] |
| 13 of octobr 1595, Rd at 2 pte of herculus | xxv[s] |
| 14 of octobr 1595, Rd at the vij dayes | xvij[s] |
| 15 of octobr 1595, *ne* Rd at the wonder of a woman [1] | liij[s] |
| 16 of octobr 1595, Rd at the desgysses | x[s] |
| 17 of octobr 1595, Rd at the vij dayes | xxviij[s] |
| 19 of octobr 1595, Rd at the wiseman | xvij[s] |
| 20 of octobr 1595, Rd at cracke me this nutte | xxj[s] |
| 21 of octobr 1595, Rd at long shancke | xxx[s] |
| 22 of octobr 1595, Rd at the worldes tragedy | xxxiij[s] |
| 23 of octobr 1595, Rd at the wonder of a woman | xxiij[s] |
| 24 of octobr 1595, Rd at cracke me this nutte | xxiij[s] |
| 25 of octobr 1595, Rd at the j pt of herculos | xxxij[s] |
| 26 of octobr 1595, Rd at Valia and antony | xxvij[s] |

[1] John Marston wrote a play, printed in 1606, called "The Wonder of Women, or Sophonisba her Tragedy;" but Marston does not seem to have been a writer until after this date. W. Rowley, still later, wrote "A new Wonder, a Woman never vexed," printed in 1632.

27 of octobr 1595, Rd at the desgyses xix^s
28 of octobr 1595, *ne* Rd at barnardo and pheameta[1] .................................... xxxxij^s
29 of octobr 1595, Rd at the vij dayes xiij^s
30 of octobr 1595, Rd at the desgysses xxix^s
2 of novmbr 1595, Rd at 2 pt of hercolas .......... .............................. xxviij^s
3 of novmbr 1595, Rd at the new worldes tragedy.............................. xxix^s
4 of novmbr 1595, Rd at the wonder of a woman .................................... xxvij^s
5 of novmbr 1595, Rd at cracke me this nutt .................................... xxiiij^s
6 of novmbr 1595, Rd at barnardo ... xvij^s
Rd at westchester[2] xx^s

Praysed,[3] the 28th of Aprill 1595, thes parsells. A Remnaunt of Black sattin of 7 yardes, and a black Cloke of cloth with owt lyning cape or Lace, both Together att the some of fouer powndes tenn shillings. By us,

the marke of + HUGH DAVIS,
by me,
E ALLEYN.[4]

[1] Afterwards spelt Bernardo and Fiameta. As it was a new play, it had no connexion with Bernardo and Galfrido, before-mentioned on p. 52, unless as a *second* part. The Barnardo, introduced below under date 6th Nov. 1595, might be either one play or the other: as it produced only 17*s*., perhaps it was the older drama.

[2] No date is assigned to the performance of this play, the title of which occurs at the bottom of the page.

[3] This, and the next item of a loan to Jones, the player, occupy the back of the page on which the forty-eight preceding entries are made.

[4] This is Edward Alleyn's own signature, the first time it has occurred in the MS. The body of the memorandum is not by him.

Lent unto M^r^ Jonnes, player, the 17 of novmbr 1599, in Redy mony, fortie shellenges, which is boye Jemes, feched I saye .................................. } xxxx^s^

Wittnes M^rs^ ALLEYN.[1]

| | | |
|---|---|---|
| 9 of novmbr 1595,[2] | Rd at longshancke | xxxiiij^s^ |
| 10 of novmbr 1595, | Rd at desgysses... | xv^s^ |
| 12 of novmbr 1595, | Rd at j pte of tamberlen........................................... | xviij^s^ |
| 13 of novmbr 1595, | Rd at 2 pt of tamberlen........................................... | xxxij^s^ |
| 14 of novmbr 1595, *ne* | Rd at a toye to please my ladey[3] ......................... | lj^s^ |
| 15 of novmbr 1595, | Rd at vij dayes... | xviij^s^ |
| 18 of novmbr 1595, | Rd at cracke me this nutte ..................................... | xxiiij^s^ |
| 19 of novmbr 1595, | Rd at barnardo... | vj^s^ |
| 20 of novmbr 1595, | Rd at wonder of a woman ..................................... | xx^s^ |
| 21 of novmbr 1595, | Rd at a toye to please chaste ladyes ....................... | xxj^s^ |
| 22 of novmbr 1595, | Rd at olempo ... | iiij^s^ vj^d^ |
| 24 of novmbr 1595, | Rd at j herculos | xx^s^ |

[1] It is quite evident that such memoranda as this, to which Alleyn's wife was a witness, were made at subsequent dates in any vacant part of the book: the page where this and the preceding entry are found had been accidentally left blank. We print the MS. exactly in the form in which it has come down to us.

[2] Here, on another leaf, Henslowe continues the long list of plays represented by the Lord Admiral's and the Lord Chamberlain's players at Newington Butts.

[3] By subsequent entries, when the writer was better informed regarding this new play, it appears that the true title was "A Toy to please chaste Ladies."

| | | | | |
|---|---|---|---|---|
| 25 of novmbr 1595, | Rd at 2 pt of herculos | | xvj$^{s}$ | |
| 26 of novmbr 1595, | Rd at longshancke | | xviij$^{s}$ | |
| 27 of novmbr 1595, | Rd at the newes worldes tragedy | | xviij$^{s}$ | |
| 28 of novmbr 1595, *ne* | Rd at harey the v [1] | iij$^{li}$ | vj$^{s}$ | |
| 29 of novmbr 1595, | Rd at the welche man [2] | | vij$^{s}$ | |
| 31 of novmbr 1595, | Rd at the toye to please chaste ladeyes | | xij$^{s}$ | |
| 2 of desembr 1595, | Rd at hary the v | | xxxv$^{s}$ | |
| 3 of desembr 1595, | Rd at barnardo | | vij$^{s}$ | |
| 4 of desembr 1595, | Rd at wonder of a woman | | xiiij$^{s}$ | |
| 6 of desembr 1595, | Rd at Crack me this nutt | | xv$^{s}$ | |
| 8 of desembr 1595, | Rd at hary the v | | xxxxiij$^{s}$ | |
| 10 of desembr 1595, | Rd at prynce Longshanke | | xxx$^{s}$ | |
| 12 of desembr 1595, | Rd at the new worldes tragedy | | xxxj$^{s}$ | vj$^{d}$ |
| 14 of desmbr 1595, | Rd at the vij dayes | | xxiiij$^{s}$ | |
| 16 of desmbr 1595, | Rd at hary the v | | xxix$^{s}$ | |
| 18 of desmbr 1595, | Rd at j pt of herculos | | xiij$^{s}$ | |

[1] This was a new play upon the events of the reign of Henry V. On p. 26, will be seen a notice of the representation of another play, called Henry V., and it may be doubted whether this or that was the drama printed under the title of The famous Victories of Henry V. We apprehend it must have been the former, because it was entered to be printed in 1594, whereas "Harey the v" was not acted until 28th Nov. 1595. It is possible that it was Shakespeare's Henry V., founded upon the Famous Victories of Henry V., and it was unquestionably popular.

[2] This, as Malone supposed, might be Robert Armin's "Valiant Welshman," which was not printed until 1615.

| | | | |
|---|---|---|---|
| 22 of desembr 1595, | Rd at the newe worldes tragedie | | xx[s] |
| 25 of desembr 1595, *Cstmes* | Rd at the wonder of a woman[1] | iij[li] | ij[s] |
| 26 of desembr 1595, | Rd at barnardo | | lviij[s] |
| 28 of desembr 1595, | Rd at harye the v | | lvj[s] |
| 29 of desembr 1595, | Rd at longshancks | | xxxij[s] |
| 30 of desembr 1595, | Rd at the wisman of weschester | | xxij[s] |
| 1 of Jeneway 1595, | Rd at the wecke | | xxxxij[s] |
| 2 of Jeneway 1595, | Rd at cracke me this nutt | | ix[s] |
| 3 of Jeneway 1595, *ne* | Rd at chinone of Ingland[2] | | l[s] |
| 5 of Jeneway 1595, | Rd at harey the v | | xxvj[s] |
| 6 of Jeneway 1595, | Rd at herculos the j pte | iij[li] | |
| 7 of Jeneway 1595, | Rd at knack to know and onest man | | xx[s] |
| 8 of Jeneway 1595, | Rd at new worldes tragedie | | xviij[s] |
| 9 of Jeneway 1595, | Rd at the Jew of malta | | lvj[s] |
| 10 of Jeneway 1595, | Rd at a toye to please chaste ladeys | | xviij[s] |

[1] Immediately before Christmas, the receipts were bad, but the Wonder of a Woman, which on the 4th December had produced Henslowe only 13*s*., on Christmas day brought him £3 2*s*. 0*d*.; Bernardo, which on the 3d December produced only 7*s*., on the 26th of December brought £2 18*s*. 0*d*., so much did the houses improve in the holidays. They, however, very soon fell off again, and a new play became necessary to keep up the public attention.

[2] This drama enjoyed considerable popularity, but the title seems to shew that it was merely fabulous.

| | | | | |
|---|---|---|---|---|
| 12 of Jenewary 1595, | | Rd at chynon of Ingland | | $l^{s}$ |
| 13 of Jenewary 1595, | | Rd at the sege of london | | $xv^{s}$ |
| 14 of Jenewary 1595, | | Rd at cracke me this nutte | | $xxiij^{s}$ |
| 15 of Jenewary 1595, | | Rd at the wonder of a woman | | $xxvij^{s}$ |
| 16 of Jenewary 1595, | *ne* | Rd at Pethageros[1] | $iij^{li}$ | $j^{s}$ |
| | | Rd at wissman of weschester[2] | | $xviij^{s}$ |
| 18 of Jenewary 1595, | | Rd at the Jewe of malta | | $xxxviij^{s}$ |
| 19 of Jenewary, 1595, | | Rd at harey the v | | $xx^{s}$ |
| 20 of Jenewary 1595, | | Rd at barnardo and phiameta | | $xj^{s}$ |
| 21 of Jenewary 1595, | | Rd at chinon of Ingland | | $xxxiij^{s}$ |
| 22 of Jenewary 1595, | *ne* | Rd at the 2 weeke[3] | $iij^{li}$ | |
| 23 of Jenewary 1595, | | Rd at pethagorus | | $xxxvj^{s}$ |
| 25 of Jenewary 1595, | | Rd at the new worldes tragedy | | $xiiij^{s}$ |
| 26 of Jenewary 1595, | | Rd at the 2 weake | | $xxiiij^{s}$ |

[1] It appears, by other parts of Henslowe's Diary, that Martin Slaughter, or Slater, wrote this new play called "Pythagoras."

[2] This performance is without any date opposite to it : there appears to be some little confusion here in this respect.

[3] Malone takes no notice of this new piece, which was doubtless a *second* part to the popular play the Seven Days of the Week, which Henslowe usually abbreviated to "Wecke."

| | | | |
|---|---|---|---|
| 27 of Jeneway 1595, | Rd at chinon ... | | xxj$^{s}$ |
| 28 of Jeneway | Rd at Pethagoros ........................................ | | xxx$^{s}$ |
| 29 of Jeneway 1595, | Rd at the Jew of malta ........................................ | | xxv$^{s}$ |
| 30 of Jeneway 1595, | Rd at the wonder of a woman ................................ | | xj$^{s}$ |
| 2 of febreary 1595, | Rd at the Jew of malta ........................................ | | lvij$^{s}$ |
| 3 of febreary 1595, | Rd at the 1 pt of Forteunatus[1] ............................... | iij$^{li}$ | |
| 4 of febreary 1595, | Rd at wissman of weschester ................................ | | xij$^{s}$ |
| 5 of febreary 1595, | Rd at longshancke | | xiiij$^{s}$ |
| 6 of febreary 1595, | Rd at harey the v | | xviij$^{s}$ |
| 7 of febreary 1595, | Rd at crack me this nutt ..... ............................ | | xix$^{s}$ |
| 9 of febreary 1595, | Rd at pethagores | | xx$^{s}$ |
| 10 of febreary 1595, | Rd at Fortunatus | | xxxx$^{s}$ |
| 11 of febreary 1595, | Rd at chinon of Ingland ................................... | | xxv$^{s}$ |
| 12 of febreary 1595, *ne* | Rd at the blind beger of Elexandria[2] ...................... | iij$^{li}$ | |
| 13 of febreary 1595, | Rd at fosstes...... | | xxv$^{s}$ |

[1] Dekker's play of "Old Fortunatus" was printed in 1600, but it is not called, on the title-page, the *first* part, and we know of no *second.* That there was a second part, arising out of the popularity of the first, is highly probable from this entry. Henslowe does not mark it as a new play on the 3d Feb. 1595, and perhaps it was not so, although this is the earliest mention of it in the Diary, where it is subsequently called "Fortunatus." The sum it produced was as large as if it had been a new play.

[2] George Chapman's "Blind Beggar of Alexandria" was printed in 1598. We learn from Henslowe the day when it was originally brought out. There is a coincidence between a line in it and

| | | | |
|---|---|---|---|
| 15 of febreary 1595, | Rd at pethagores | | xxxv$^{s}$ |
| 16 of febreary 1595, | Rd at the blinde beager ... | iii$^{li}$ | vj$^{s}$ |
| 17 of febreary 1595, | Rd at the Jew of malta ... | | xx$^{s}$ |
| 18 of febreary 1595, | Rd at olempeo ... | | x$^{s}$ |
| 19 of febreary 1595, | Rd at the blind beager ... | | liij$^{s}$ |
| 20 of febreary 1595, | Rd at Fortunatus ... | | xxij$^{s}$ |
| 22 of febreary 1595, *Shrove Monday* | Rd at the blind beager ... | | xxxvj$^{s}$ |
| 23 of febreary 1595, *Shroft tewsd.* | Rd at pethagores | | xxxiiij$^{s}$ |
| 24 of febreary 1595, | Rd at chinone ... | | lvj$^{s}$ |
| 25 of febreary 1595, | Rd at wecke[1] ... | | xx$^{s}$ |
| 26 of febreary 1595, | Rd at the blind beager ... | iij$^{li}$ | |
| 27 of febreary 1595, | Rd at longshanke | | xxx$^{s}$ |

in Marlowe's paraphrase of Hero and Leander. Marlowe's line is correctly cited, with acknowledgment to the "dead Shepherd," by Shakespeare in "As you like it," act iii., sc. 5.

"Who ever lov'd that lov'd not at first sight?"

which Chapman, near the close of his "Blind Beggar of Alexandria," gives thus:

"None ever lov'd but at first sight they lov'd."

The circumstance might have been passed over without notice, if Chapman's play and Marlowe's poem had not been printed in the same year, and if Chapman, at a subsequent date, had not finished the poem which Marlowe left incomplete. Marlowe's portion having been published in 1598, Chapman immediately continued the subject, and the six sestiads appeared together in 1600, not 1606, as stated by Ritson.

[1] There were, as we have seen, two plays called the Seven Days of the Week, but it is not stated whether this was the first or the second part of the same subject.

The master of the Revelles payd untell this time al which I owe hime.[1]

Sowld[2] Mr Richard Jones, player, a manes gowne of peche coler In grayne, the 2 of septmbr 1594, to be payd by fyve shellenges a weeke imediatly folowinge, and beginynge as fowloweth.

Rd of Mr Jones, the 7 of septembr 1594 .................. vs
Rd of Mr Jones, the 13 of septembr ......................... vs
Rd of Mr Jones, the 20 of septembr 1594 ... .............. vs
Rd of Mr Jones, the 4 of octobr 1594 ...................... vs
Rd of Mr Jones, the 11 of octobr 1594 ......... .......... vs
Rd of Mr Jones, the 18 of octobr 1594 ...................... vs
Rd of Mr Jones, the 24 of octobr 1594 ...................... vs
Rd of Mr Jones, the 2 of novembr 1594 ................. vs
Rd of Mr Jonnes, the 9 of novmbr 1594 .................. .. vs
Rd of Mr Jonnes, the 16 of novmbr 1594 ................. vs
Rd of Mr Jones, the 23 of novmbr 1594 ..................... vs
Rd of Mr Jonnes, In full payment, the 30 of novmbr 1594 vs

Sowld unto William Sley,[3] the 11 of octobr 1594, a Jewell of gowld, seat with a whitte safer, for viijs to be payd after xijd a weacke as followeth.

Rd of Wm Sley, the 18 of octobr 1594 .............. vjd
Rd of Wm sley, the 24 of octobr 1594 .............. vjd

[1] The meaning of this note at the end of the list of plays most likely is, that the Master of the Revels had been paid all that Henslowe owed him for licensing new plays at *5s.* each. Here and there he seems to have inserted such memoranda as "Master paid," &c., in order to prove the date when a new account began.

[2] This account with its title is crossed out in the MS.

[3] There was a player of the name of John Slee, or Slye, in the reign of Henry VIII., (Hist. of Engl. Dram. Poetry and the Stage, i., 118), and William Sley, or Sly, Shakespeare's fellow-actor, was possibly de-

| | |
|---|---|
| Rd of W$^{m}$ sleye, the 2 of novembr 1594.............. | vj$^{d}$ |
| Rd of W$^{m}$ sleye, the 9 of novmbr 1594 .............. | vj$^{d}$ |
| Rd of W$^{m}$ sley, the 16 of novembr 1594 ........... | vj$^{d}$ |
| Rd of W$^{m}$ sley, the 30 of novmbr 1594 .............. | xij$^{d}$ |
| Rd of W$^{m}$ sley the 14 of Desembr 1594.............. | xij$^{d}$ |
| Rd o$^{r}$ W$^{m}$ sley, the 17 of Jeneway 1594 ........... | ij$^{s}$ |

1596,[1]

| | | |
|---|---|---|
| 12 of aprelle, ester munday, Rd at barnardo and fiameta ......................... | | xxx$^{s}$ |
| 13 of aprell 1596, | Rd at toye to please chaste ladeys ................................ | xxxix$^{s}$ |
| 14 of aprell 1596, | Rd at fortunatus ... | xviij$^{s}$ |
| 15 of aprell 1596, | Rd at the blynd beger .......................................... | xxxx$^{s}$ |
| 16 of aprell 1596, | Rd at the Knacke | xj$^{s}$ |
| 17 of aprell 1596, | Rd at the wisman of weschester .................................. | xxx$^{s}$ |
| 19 of aprell 1596, | Rd at Doctor fostes | xij$^{s}$ |
| 20 of aprell 1596, | Rd at the Jewe ... | xx$^{s}$ |
| 21 of aprell 1596, | Rd at longshancke | xiiij$^{s}$ |
| 22 of aprell 1596, | Rd at pethagorus ... | xviij$^{s}$ |
| 23 of aprell 1596, | Rd at chinon ...... | xx$^{s}$ |

scended from him. This account, for some stage-jewel probably, furnishes the earliest notice of him, and we may infer that he was not very rich in 1594; but in 1596 we find him petitioning the Lords of the Council as one of the "owners and players" of the Blackfriars' Theatre (Ibid. i., 298). His name occurs seventh in the Patent of James I. in 1603. It is very possible that he filled the part of Christopher Sly in "The Taming of the Shrew," when acted by the King's Players, or in the older "Taming of a Shrew," when represented by Henslowe's company.

[1] This looks like a continuation of the former account, but it begins at the top of a separate page, and there is an interval between the 27th February 1595-6 and the 10th April 1596.

24 of aprell 1596, Rd at Hary the v... xvs
26 of aprell 1596, Rd at the blind beger xxxxs
27 of aprell 1596, Rd at new worldes tragedy ........................................ xxixs
28 of aprell 1596, Rd at longshancke xxs
29 of aprell 1596, *ne* Rd at Julian the apostata[1] ...... .............................. xxxxvijs
30 of aprell 1596, Rd at wisman ...... xs
Maye daye 1596, Rd at wonder of a woman ........................................ xxijs
2 of maye 1596, Rd at chinon ...... xxs
3 of maye 1596, Rd at the blinde beger ........................................ xxxvs
4 of maye 1596, Rd at pethagorus ... xxs
5 of maye 1596, Rd at Docter Fostes xxs
6 of maye 1596, *ne* Rd at tambercame[2] xxxxvijs
7 of maye 1596, Rd at cracke me this nutte ........................................ xviijs
10 of maye 1596, Rd at Julian apostata ........................................ xxvjs
11 of maye 1596, Rd at fortunatus ... xviijs
12 of maye 1596, Rd at tambercame... xxxxvs
13 of maye 1596, Rd at blind beger ... xxxxs
14 of maye 1596, Rd at the Jew of malta ........................................ xxiiijs
16 of maye 1596, Rd at chynone ...... xxxiijs
17 of maye 1596, Rd at tambercame... xxxxvjs

[1] The smallness of the receipts, excepting to Chapman's Blind Beggar of Alexandria, rendered the production of this new drama expedient.

[2] Edward Alleyn had some concern in preparing and bringing out this new play, called for by the difficulty of keeping up the receipts, although Julian the Apostate had been produced only seven days before. It must have been a different Tambercame to that recorded on p. 25, and how to reconcile the identity of the titles we know not. It may have been a blunder by Henslowe.

| | | |
|---|---|---|
| 18 of maye 1596, | Rd at beger ......... | xxxxix$^s$ |
| 19 of maye 1596, *ne* | Rd at tragedie of Focasse[1] ......... | xxxxv$^s$ |
| 20 of maye 1596, | Rd at Julyan apostata ......... | xiiij$^s$ |
| 22 of maye 1596, | Rd at pethageros ... | xxvij$^s$ |
| 23 of maye 1596, | Rd at tragedie of Focasse ......... | xxxix$^s$ |
| 24 of maye 1596, | Rd at Fortunatus... | xiiij$^s$ |
| 25 of maye 1596, | Rd at tambercame | xx$^s$ |
| 26 of maye 1596, | Rd at hary the v ... | xxiij$^s$ |
| 27 of maye 1596, | Rd at chinone[2] ...... | ix$^s$ |

| | |
|---|---|
| Sowld unto Jeames Donstall, player, the 27 of aguste 1595, a manes gown of purpell coller cloth, faced with conney and layd on the sleves with buttens, for xxxxiij$^s$ iiij$^d$, to be payd xx$^s$ in hand, and xxiij$^s$ iiij$^d$ at mychellmaste next cominge after the datte a bove written. I saye for ......... | xxxxiij$^s$ iiij$^d$ |
| Rd in pte payment, the same daye, beinge the 27 of aguste 1595, of Jemes Donstall the some of......... | x$^s$ |
| Rd in pte of payment, the 28 of aguste 1595, In monye of Jemes Donstall the some of ......... | x$^s$ |

Reste to paye 23$^s$ iiij$^d$.

[1] In this play, represented for the first time, Martin Slater, or Slaughter, had some interest, perhaps as one of its joint authors. Elsewhere it is spelt Phocas, and perhaps we ought to read Phocus, who revenged the death of his father Phocion.

[2] Here this account ends, but we shall find it resumed on p. 73, under date of 31 May 1596.

Sowld unto Steven Magett,[1] the 20 of Jeneway 1595, a dublet of fuschen playne, and a payer of Venesyones of brade cloth, with ij laces of belement, for xvj$^{s}$, to be payd by xij$^{d}$ a wecke, begenynge the 23 of Jeneway 1595, beinge saturdaye and so forth. Receved as foloweth.

| | | |
|---|---|---|
| Rd the 23 of Jeneway 1595 ........................ | | xij$^{d}$ |
| Rd the 30 of Jeneway 1595 ........................ | | xij$^{d}$ |
| Rd the 7 of febreary 1595.............................. | | xij$^{d}$ |
| Rd the 13 of febreary 1595 .................. ....... | | xij$^{d}$ |
| Rd the 20 of febreary 1595 ........................... | | xij$^{d}$ |
| Rd the 27 of febreary 1595 ........................... | | xij$^{d}$ |
| Rd of maye daye 1596 ..................................... | iiij$^{s}$ | |
| Rd 6 of maye 1596 .......................................... | iiij$^{s}$ | |
| Rd in full payment, the 3 of maye 1596[2] ........ | ij$^{s}$ | |

[Here follow, among scribblings and calculations of nativities, various medical receipts and charms: among them:—

"To know where a thinge is that is stolen—Take vergine waxe and write upon yt Jasper, + Melchiser + Balthasar + and put yt under his head to whom the good partayneth, and he shall knowe in his sleape where the thinge is become.

"Wryte these wordes in virgins parchement with the blood of a batt uppon tewesday morning, betwixt v or vj in the morning, or at nighte, Halia J. K. turbutzi, and tye yt about thy left arme, and aske what ye will have.

"To cleanes a hurte wounde and heale yt—Mixe valencia scuger with freashe butter, for beinge layd to yt plaster wysse yt consumeth the superflueshe fleashe, or evell corupted mater; yt healleth yt allso: moste exsilent proved."]

[1] Stephen Magelt seems to have been the 'Tireman of the Company, and to have had charge of the apparel, &c. He is sometimes called Stephen, sometimes "Stephen the 'Tireman," and sometimes "the 'Tireman."

[2] The account is therefore crossed out. In the margin opposite the heading are the words "some is xvj$^{s}$ to paye."

M^m^. that I Thomas Chaloner do owe unto Mr. Philipe Hensley vij^li^ x^s^, to be payed unto P. the laste daye of June 1592.

By me THOMAS CHALONER.[1]

Witnes WILL^M^. HENSLYE.

Lent W^m^. Atkynsone, leather dreaser, the 6 of Jenewary 1597, in Readey money fortishillinges, to be payd me agayne the 17 day of the same moneth: in wittnes of the lendinge of this money is

E. ALLEYN.[2] pd

Lent Mr. Jonnes, player, the 8 of Jenewary 1597, upon iiij Rynges, j gemer of gowld, j sparke of a dimond, j Ringe with v sparkes of Rewbes, j small sell Rynge of gowld, the some of forty shillinges. I say xxxx^s^.

Lent unto Mr. Jonnes, player, the 21 of aprell 1598, in Redey money tenne shillinges, which Williame Cartwrighte, I say, lent x^s^.

Pd unto Thomas Dickers, the 20 of Desembr 1597, for adycÿons to Fostus twentie shellinges, and fyve shellenges for a prolog to Marloes Tamberlen, so in all I saye payde twentye fyve shellinges.

Rd by me of Mr. Phillipp Hynsley, for my M^r^ the Master of the Revells, this second daie of Januarye 1594, in full payement of a bonde of one hundreth powndes, the somme of tenn powndes, and in full payement of what soever is due from the daie above wrytten, untill Ashwednesdaie nexte

[1] See the Mem. of Edw. Alleyn, p. 63, where a person calling himself Francis Challoner would have borrowed £10 of Mrs. Alleyn in 1603. This memorandum is written wrong side upwards in the MS., as if scribbled in anywhere in haste.

[2] This memorandum is subscribed by Alleyn in his own handwriting, but not written by him.

ensuinge after the date hereof. In wittness whereof I have put to my hande.

ꝑ me THO. STONNARD.[1]

*A notte of what carges my soger peter hath stode me in this yeare*, 1596.[2]

| | | |
|---|---|---|
| Itm̃ pd for iiij dayes traynynge........................ | v$^{s}$ | 4$^{d}$ |
| Itm̃ fownd hime viij$^{li}$ of powder ............... ... | vj$^{s}$ | 8$^{d}$ |
| Itm̃ pd for his lyvery, and mony in his pursse ... | xiij$^{s}$ | 8$^{d}$ |
| Itm̃ fownd a head pece which coste ................. | vij$^{s}$ | |
| Itm̃ fownd a sorde and a dager.............. ........ | vij$^{s}$ | |
| Itm̃ fownd a bealt and a geardell .................... | | xij$^{d}$ |
| Itm̃ geven at his goinge a waye for powder, and to drycke by the waye.................................. | v$^{s}$ | |
| Itm̃ pd for featchenge of my head pece from graves end ............................................ | ij$^{s}$ | iiij$^{d}$ |

Lade owt for my soger this laste traynynge, the seamsters husband

| | | |
|---|---|---|
| Itm̃ pd for j dayes traynge, and halfe of a j$^{li}$ of powder .............................................. | | xviij$^{d}$ |

| | |
|---|---|
| Rd for ij weekes paye, which was dew unto the M$^{r}$ of the Revelles, frome the 12 of aprell 1596 unto the 26 of the same moneth, xx$^{s}$. I say Rd ............................................ | xx$^{s}$ |

MICHEL · M. B. BLUENSONS
MARKE

DOWNTON.[3]

[1] This entry is in the handwriting of Stonnard.

[2] Part of this account for Henslowe's soldier, Peter, is repeated a few pages afterwards.

[3] Downton's name has been added as a witness, but without his Christian name, Thomas; and it is not his own handwriting.

| | |
|---|---|
| Lent unto John tomsone, player, the 22 of desembr 1598, in Redey money the some of.............. | v$^{s}$ |

Thomas Downton, the 25 of Jenewary 1599, did hire as his covenante servante [1]            for ij yers, to begyne at shrofe tewesday next, and he to geve him viij$^{s}$ a wecke as longe as they playe, and after they lye stylle one fortnyght, then to geve hime hallfe wages. Wittness P. H. and edward browne and charlles massey.

*Lent unto Roger Evanes, grome of the Queenes chamber*, 1598, *as folowth in Redy money.*

| | |
|---|---|
| Lent hime the 28 of marche 1598.......................... | viij$^{s}$ |
| Lent hime the 16 of aprell 1598 .......................... | vj$^{s}$ |
| Lent hime the 8 of June 1598 ............................ | iij$^{s}$ |
| Lent hime the 6 of Jenewary 1598 ..................... | vij$^{s}$ |
| Lent hime the 9 of Jenewary 1598 ....................... | vj$^{s}$ |

1596 [2]

| | | | |
|---|---|---|---|
| 31 of maye whittsen munday, | Rd at pathagoras | iij$^{li}$ | |
| 1 of June 1596, | Rd at chinone of Ingland | | iij$^{s}$ [3] |
| 2 of June 1596, | Rd at longshancke......... | iij$^{li}$ | |
| 3 of June 1596, | Rd at the blinde beager... | | xxxxj$^{s}$ |
| 4 of June 1596, | Rd at the tragedie of focas | | xxxj$^{s}$ |
| 5 of June 1596, | Rd at tambercame......... | | xxviij$^{s}$ |
| 7 of June 1596, | Rd at cracke me this nutte | | xxviij$^{s}$ |

[1] A blank is left for the name of the "covenant servant," so hired by Downton.

[2] This is evidently a continuation of a former account, which ends (see p. 69) on 27th May 1596. Preceding it is an erased repetition of the account of Henslowe's substitute, "soldier Peter," and some other matters not theatrical.

[3] Most likely miswritten for iij$^{li}$, as there is no other entry of so low a receipt in the account.

| | | | | |
|---|---|---|---|---|
| 8 of June 1596, | | Rd at wisman of weschester | | xx$^{s}$ |
| 9 of June 1596, | | Rd at the chaste ladye | | xviij$^{s}$ |
| 10 of June 1596, | | Rd at tambercame | | xxviij$^{s}$ |
| 11 of June 1596, | *ne* | Rd at the 2 pte of tambercame[1] | iij$^{li}$ | |
| 12 of June 1596, | | Rd at Docter fostes | | xvij$^{s}$ |
| 14 of June 1596, | | Rd at sege of london | | xxx$^{s}$ |
| 15 of June 1596, | | Rd at pethagores | | xxiij$^{s}$ |
| 16 of June 1596, | | Rd at Focase | | xx$^{s}$ |
| 17 of June 1596, | | Rd at hary the v. | | xxvij$^{s}$ |
| 19 of June 1596, | | Rd at j pte of tambercame | | xxxvj$^{s}$ |
| 20 of June 1596, | | Rd at 2 pte of tambercame | | xxxv$^{s}$ |
| 21 of June 1596, | | Rd at the Jew of malta | | xiij$^{s}$ |
| 22 of June 1596, | | Rd at focas | | l$^{s}$ |
| 23 of June 1596, | *ne* | Rd at troye[2] | iij$^{li}$ | ix$^{s}$ |
| 24 of June 1596, | | Rd at cracke me this nutt | | xij$^{s}$ |
| 25 of June 1596, | | Rd at the beager | | xix$^{s}$ |
| 26 of June 1596, | | Rd at j pte of tambercame | | xxx$^{s}$ |
| 27 of June 1596, | | Rd at 2 pte of tambercame | | xx$^{s}$ |
| 1 of Juley 1596, | *ne* | Rd at the paradox[3] | | xxxxv$^{s}$ |

[1] This was, as is clear from Henslowe's mark, the first performance of the second part of Tambercame, which had been written in consequence of the popularity of the first part. Here the difficulty recurs, arising from the identity of title. See p. 68, note 2.

[2] A new piece founded upon the Siege of Troy. T. Heywood's Iron Age embraced this portion of history, and was perhaps in part derived from this older play called Troy. The Iron Age was not printed until 1632.

[3] The name of this new play does not occur again, and perhaps it was condemned.

2 of Julye 1596, Rd at troye .............. $xxiiij^s$
3 of July 1596, Rd at fostes .............. $xiiij^s$
5 of July 1596, Rd at focasse .............. $xxij^s$
6 of July 1596, Rd at sege of london ...... $xv^s$
7 of July 1596, Rd at wisman of weschester .............................................. $xvj^s$
8 of July 1596, Rd at j pte of tambercame .............................................. $xiiij^s$
9 of July 1596, Rd at longshancke ......... $xv^s$
10 of July 1596, Rd at harye the v.......... $xiiij^s$
11 of July 1596, Rd at bellendon ........... $xxxv^s$
12 of July 1596, Rd at the toye ........... $x^s$
13 of July 1596, Rd at pethagores ......... $xxij^s$
15 of July 1596, Rd at hary v............... $xxij^s$
16 of July 1596, Rd at troye................. $xxj^s$
17 of July 1596, Rd at focas.................. $xxix^s$
18 of July 1596, *ne* Rd at the tyncker of totnes[1] .............................................. $iij^{li}$

Lent unto marten Slather, the 22 of June 1596, the some of $viij^{li}$ of good and lafulle mony of Ingland, to be payd the same daye moneth folowinge, or els to forfete for not payinge of the same $xvj^{li}$, wher upon he hath bownd hime selfe by tackynge of a $j^d$ upon and a sumsett. wittnes to this edward alleyn and his wiffe.

Sowld unto Mr. Jonnes, player, the 27 of maye 1596, ij yardes and iij quarters of brode clothe for eyghtene shelynges, to be payd by $iiij^s$ a weacke as foloweth.

Rd the 5 of June of M^r^ Jonnes .......................... $iiij^s$
Rd the 12 of June of M^r^ Jonnes .......................... $iiij^s$
Rd the 19 of June of M^r^ Jonnes .......................... $iiij^s$

[1] A new play, possibly on a similar story to that of "the Tinker's Good Fortune."

Rd the 23 of June of M$^{r}$ Jonnes .......................... ij$^{s}$
Rd in full payement the 7 of Julye 96 .................... iij$^{s}$

Delivered unto the company,[1] the 23 of marche, beinge good frydaye, 1597, the some of fyve pownd and fortenshelyngs, w$^{ch}$ mackes up the some of thirtye powndes, as her under writen maye be sene, w$^{ch}$ they owe unto me, I say.........xxx$^{li}$
wittnes edward allen.

*Lente unto my lord admerall players at severall tymes in Redey money as foloweth.* 1596.

| | | |
|---|---|---|
| Lent unto Jeames Donstall for to by thinges for the playe of Valteger[2] .................... | v$^{li}$ | |
| Lent unto marten slater, to bye coper lace and frenge for the playe of valteger, the 28 of novembr 1596 .............................. | | xxxx$^{s}$ |
| Lent unto marten slather, the 29 of novembr 1596, to by for the play of valteger lace and other thinges.................................... | | xxv$^{s}$ |
| Dd unto Steven, the tyerman, for to delyver unto the company, for to by a headtier and a Rebato and other thinges, the 3 of Desembr 1596... | iij$^{li}$ | x$^{s}$ |
| Lent unto my sonne, to by the saten dublet with sylver lace[3] ...................................... | iiij$^{li}$ | |

Some xv$^{li}$ xv$^{s}$: the wholl some of this and the other syde is 22$^{li}$ 15$^{s}$ 00$^{d}$

[1] The company of the Lord Admiral's players, mentioned in the next entry; which, as well as the three previous memoranda, are crossed out in the MS.

[2] Perhaps a play on the story of Vortigern. It was acted, as we shall see hereafter, for the first time on the 4th December 1596, when it was still called Valteger by Henslowe.

[3] "My son" was E. Alleyn, the husband of Henslowe's step-daughter. Both in the Diary and in Henslowe's letters he is so designated, and relationships were not then accurately distinguished.

| | | |
|---|---|---|
| Lente more, the 8 of desembr 1596, for Stewtleyes[1] hosse ........................................ | iij$^{li}$ | |
| Lent Donston and marten,[2] the 11 of desembr 1596 ........................................ | | xxxx$^{s}$ |
| Lent marten, the 14 of desembr 1596 ......... | | xx$^{s}$ |
| Dd unto M$^{r}$ Porter,[3] the 16 of desembr 1596 | v$^{li}$ | |
| Payd unto the carmen for fetcheng your wagen[4] | | ij$^{s}$ |
| Lent unto M$^{r}$ Porter, the 7 of march 1597 ... | iiij$^{li}$ | |
| Dd unto my sonne, for to by sylcke and other thinges for Guido[5] the 14 of marche ......... | iiij$^{li}$ | ix$^{s}$ |

| | | |
|---|---|---|
| Sowld unto steven maget, the 27 of maye 1596, a clocke of sade grene, to be payde by xij$^{d}$ a weacke, which clocke is sowld for ........... | | xviij$^{s}$ |
| Receved as foloweth— | | |
| Rd the 5 of June of steven......................... | | xij$^{d}$ |
| Rd the 12 of June of steven ..................... | | xij$^{d}$ |
| Rd the 20 of June of steven ..................... | | xij$^{d}$ |
| Rd the 26 of June of steven ..................... | ij$^{s}$ | |
| Rd the 12 of July of steven ..................... | | xij$^{d}$ |
| Rd the 22 of septmbr of steven .................. | vij$^{s}$ | |

[1] The company was getting up a play upon the story of Captain Stutely, or Stukeley, and the "hose" must have been expensive to cost £3. See an account of Stukely, and a ballad upon his adventures, in "Old Ballads," printed for the Percy Society in 1841. There is another ballad on the history of the same adventurer in Evans's Coll., iii., 148, edit. 1810. The play of "Stewtley" was brought out on 11th December 1596; and it is to be borne in mind that in the Battle of Alcazar, attributed to G. Peele, Stukely plays a prominent part; but see p. 21, note 1.

[2] By "marten" Henslowe must have meant Martin Slater, or Slaughter.

[3] i.e., Henry Porter, a dramatic poet, whose name will afterwards frequently occur.

[4] i.e., perhaps the waggon of the company, for conveying properties, &c.

[5] The title of a play in preparation. It was not brought out until 19th March 1597.

*A note of suche money as I have lent unto thes menne, whose names folow, at severall tymes; Edward Alleyn, Martyne Slather, Jeames Donstall, and Jewby.* 1596.

All this lent sence the 14 of octobr.

| | |
|---|---|
| Lent unto martyne to feache Fleacher[1] ... | vjs |
| Lent unto theme to feache Browne ........ | xs |
| Lent unto my sonne for Thomas Honte... | vjs 8d |
| Lent unto them for Hawodes booke[2] ...... | xxxs |
| Lent unto them at a nother tyme ......... | ls |
| Lent unto marteyn at a nother tyme ...... | xxxs |
| Lent unto the tayllor for the stocke ...... | xxxs |
| Lent them to by a boocke ................. | xxxxxs |
| Lent the company to geve Fleatcher, and the[y] have promysed me payment: who promysed me is marten, Donson, and Jewby .................................... | xxs |

| | |
|---|---|
| Rd in pt of payment, the 29 of octobr 1596 | xxs |
| Rd in pt of payment of all holanday 1596 | xxs |
| Rd in pt of payment, the 13 of desembr 1596[3] ....................................... | xxxxs |

Tottalles ........... 31li 15s 00d

Some ixli

[1] This has been supposed by Malone to mean John Fletcher the poet, but there was also Lawrence Fletcher an actor, whose name stands first in the Patent granted by King James on the 17th May 1603, and a few years afterwards we hear of Laz. Fletcher. Browne, mentioned in the next entry, was a player, but why they were to be "fetched," and from whence, does not appear. The entry lower down, "Lent the company to geve Fleatcher," &c., looks as if it were money advanced by Henslowe to enable the company to purchase a play.

[2] No doubt some play (or "book," as it was then often called) written by Thomas Heywood, which was purchased for the company.

[3] This memorandum is struck out in the MS.

| | | |
|---|---|---|
| Rd at the second time of playinge, that wilbe,[1] the 4 of Jenewary 1597, the some of ........................................ | | xxxx$^{s}$ |
| Rd at Jeronymo, the 7 of Janeway 1597, in pte of payment.............................. | vij$^{li}$ | |
| Rd at elexsander and lodwicke,[2] the 14 of Janewarye, the fyrste tyme yt wasse playde, 1597, in pte....................... | v$^{li}$ | |
| Rd at a womon hard to please, the 27 of Janewary 97................................ . | iiij$^{li}$ | |

*Ultimo die maij, Anno regni Dne Nre Regine Tricessimo nono.*

| | |
|---|---|
| Received the daie and yeare above written, by me Robert Johnson, to the use of the M$^{r}$ of the Revells, of Phillippe Henslaye, the fulle and whole some of fortie shillinges, dew for this presente monthe aforesaide[3]....................... | xl$^{s}$ |

xxvij$^{th}$ of June 1597.

| | |
|---|---|
| Received, the daie and yeare above written, by me Robert Johnson, to the use of the M$^{r}$ of the Revells, of Phillip Henchley, the full and whole some of fortie shillings of lawfull English monney, dew for this present monthe aforesaide | xl$^{s}$ |

[1] i.e., a play called That will be Shall be, or What will be Shall be, the date of the production of which is duly noted on January 3, 1597.

[2] We shall again meet with the name of this play and a Woman hard to Please, under their proper dates.

[3] From this and other following entries it appears that Henslowe (and probably other managers did the same) was in the habit of paying the Master of the Revels a monthly fee of 40*s*., beyond the sum he received for granting licenses for new plays. As there were many companies of actors at this period, he would thus derive a considerable income from his office; and such emoluments do not seem to have been contemplated at the creation of the office.

Receaved, this xix[th] of July 1597, of M[r] Henchley, the some of fortie shillings, and is to the use of the M[r] of the revells, as appeareth by a quittans which M[r] blewinsone hath in keapinge. I say Rd the some of ........................................ } xl[s]

ꝑ me W[M] HATTO.

Octobris xij[o] 1598.

Receaved, the daie and yeare above written, by me Robert Johnson, of M[r] Henchley the full and whole some of vj[li], to the use of the M[r] of the Revells, for iij monethes endinge the daie aforesaide, after xl[s] a monethe ............................ } vj[li]

This agremente and bargen Betweene edward alleyn and M[r] Arthour langworth, as foloweth, was made the 5 daye of July 1596. Yt was agreed upon that M[r] Langworth shold geve unto edward alleyn for the leasse of the parsonage of Furlle iij thowsen powndes of lafful mony of England, to be payd in xx yeares in maner folowinge, by a hundred and fiftie powndes a yeare, and to be gine payment at our ladey daye next folowing, and so to paye every halfe yeare the hallfe of the hundreth and fiftie powndes, or within one moneth after, beinge xxviij dayes; and for the performence of this xx yeares payment hath promesed to putte hime in suche a suerence, as by his learned cownsell he shall devise at his next cominge to towne after the daye above written: in wittnes where of to this I have seate my hand,

PHILLIPPE HENSLOW.[1]

Rd of Bengemenes Johnsones share as foloweth. 1597.[2]

Rd the 28 of July 1597 ................................ iij[s] ix[d]

[1] The signature is by Henslowe, but the body of the agreement is by the scribe he usually employed.

[2] This entry is crossed out, as if the account were ended, and Henslowe had received no more than the 3*s.* 9*d.* of Ben Jonson's share.

Sowld unto Thomas Towne, player,[1] a Blacke clothe clocke, layd with sylke lace for xxvj$^{s}$ viij$^{d}$, to be payd by xij$^{d}$ a wecke, and to be gyne payment the 2 of Jenewary 1597, and so to contenew weckelye payment, as

Lent unto Thomas towne, the 20 of marche 1598, Redy mony ........................................ ....... } xij$^{d}$

Lent unto thomas Towne upon a skarffe ........... v$^{s}$

Sent my horsse to grasse, the 9 daye of Aprelle, beinge tewsdaye, 1600, to M$^{r}$ Kellocke at redreffe, for xx$^{d}$ a weeke.[2]

Lent unto charlles Massey,[3] the 3 of desember 1600, in Redy mony, to be payd a gayne at crysmas next, the some of........................................ } x$^{s}$

Md that the xxix$^{th}$ daye of september 1596, beinge Mihelmas Daye, the some of one hundred and xxvj$^{li}$ was tendered, and redye to be payd yn the house of M$^{r}$ Phillipe Henslowe, the daye and yeare aforesayd, which sayd some was to be payd by Edwarde Allene, as aforesayd, before the settinge of the sunne of the same daye, yn the presentes of thos whose names ar herunder wryten, unto Arthure Langworthe gent.[4]

[1] Regarding Thomas Towne, we shall find more in other parts of the Diary. His name has already occurred on p. 6.

[2] Crossed out. There are three other entries on the same page respecting Henslowe's horse at grass with "Mr. Woodcocke of Rotherhithe," which are not erased. Excepting the change of name and dates, they are in the same words.

[3] This entry, respecting Massey, is inserted on a blank space among others of an earlier date: we shall hear of him again hereafter. See also Memoirs of E. Alleyn, p. 109.

[4] Perhaps this memorandum related to some other pecuniary transactions between Alleyn and Langworth, besides the purchase and sale of the parsonage of Firle. The sum does not correspond with the entry on the preceding page.

*In the name of God Amen: begynynge one simone and Jewdes daye, my lord Admeralles men, as foloweth:*
1596.[1]

| | | |
|---|---|---|
| 27 of October 1596, | Rd at Chynon..... | lij$^s$ |
| 28 of October 1596, | Rd at Doctore fostes ........................................... | xxvij$^s$ |
| 29 of October 1596, | Rd at the frenshe Docter ........................................ | xv$^s$ |
| 1 of novembr 1596, | Rd at longe Meage, Alholandaye .................................. | xxxxvij$^s$ |
| 2 of novembr 1596, | Rd at Chinone of Jngland ........................................ | xvij$^s$ |
| 3 of novembr 1596, | Rd at the cnacke to knowe ....................................... | xv$^s$ |
| 4 of novembr 1596, | Rd at Doctor fostes | xvij$^s$ |
| 5 of novembr 1596, | Rd at longe Meage | v$^s$ |
| 6 of novembr 1596, | Rd at the beager ... | xxx$^s$ |
| 8 of novembr 1596, | Rd at the toye...... | xiij$^s$ |
| 9 of novembr 1596, | Rd at the frenshe Docter ........................................ | xiiij$^s$ |
| 10 of novembr 1596, | Rd at chinon ..... | x$^s$ |
| 11 of novembr 1596, | Rd at the vij dayes | xxxv$^s$ |
| 12 of novembr 1596, | Rd at the beager... | xvj$^s$ |
| 13 of novembr 1596, | Rd at tambercame | xvij$^s$ |
| 15 of novembr 1596, | Rd at the vij Dayes | xij$^s$ |

*In the name of god, Amen: beginninge the* 25 *of November* 1596, *as foloweth; the lord admerall players.*

| | | |
|---|---|---|
| 25 of novembr 1596, | Rd at long meage | xj$^s$ |

[1] No new plays are included in this brief list; and, excepting on the 1st Nov. (All Saints' Day), and one or two others, the receipts were comparatively small—so small, that no plays appear to have been acted between 15th and the 25th Nov., when a fresh account was opened.

| | | | | |
|---|---|---|---|---|
| 26 of novembr 1596, | | Rd at weake ...... | | xvij$^{s}$ |
| 27 of novembr 1596, | | Rd at the toye ... | | xj$^{s}$ |
| 2 of Desembr 1596, | | Rd at the beager... | | xx$^{s}$ |
| 4 of Desembr. 1596, | *ne* | Rd at Valteger [1] ... | | l$^{s}$ |
| 5 of Desembr 1596, | | Rd at Valteger ... | | xxxv$^{s}$ |
| 10 of Desembr 1596, | | Rd at the beager... | | x$^{s}$ |
| 11 of Desembr 1596, | *ne* | Rd at Stewtley [2] ... | | xxxx$^{s}$ |
| 12 of Desembr 1596, | | Rd at the vij Dayes | | ix$^{s}$ |
| 14 of Desembr 1596, | | Rd at stewtley ... | | xxxx$^{s}$ |
| 16 of Desembr 1596, | | Rd at Valteger ... | | xxxv$^{s}$ |
| 17 of Desembr 1596, | | Rd at docter fostes | | ix$^{s}$ |
| 19 of Desembr 1596, | *ne* | Rd at Nabucadoni-nizer, [3] ........................................ | | xxx$^{s}$ |
| 21 of Desembr 1596, | | Rd at Valteger ... | | xxv$^{s}$ |
| 22 of Desembr 1596, | | Rd at nabucadonizer | | xxvj$^{s}$ |
| 23 of Desembr 1596, | | Rd at the beager... | | iij$^{s}$ |
| 24 of Desembr 1596, | | Rd at valteger...... | | xij$^{s}$ |
| 27 of Desembr 1596, | *Xmas day* | Rd at nabucadoni-zer [4] ........................................ | iij$^{li}$ | viij$^{s}$ |
| 28 of Desembr 1596, | | Rd at Stewtley ... | iij$^{li}$ | iiij$^{s}$ |
| 29 of Desembr 1596, | | Rd at Valteger ... | | xxij$^{s}$ |

[1] This play has been already mentioned (p. 76) as in preparation by the company. It was now acted for the first time, and the state of the treasury seemed to render a new piece necessary.

[2] The new plays at this period were frequent, as the old stock-pieces do not seem to have been attractive. "Stewtley," or Stutely, has been spoken of as in preparation on p. 77. A drama was printed in 1605 under the title of "The Life and Death of Captain Thomas Stukeley," and it was perhaps the piece here mentioned by Henslowe.

[3] A new play adapted to Christmas; no doubt, founded upon the scriptural story of Nebuchadnezzar.

[4] The figures opposite this and the following entry have been altered: they were originally 25th and 27th December. The receipt was unusually large on both occasions. It would seem as if Christmas day had been kept on the 27th, and that no play was acted on the 25th December.

| | | | | |
|---|---|---|---|---|
| 30 of Desembr 1596, | *ne* | Rd at that wilbe shalbe[1] ........ | | ls |
| 31 of Desembr 1596, | | Rd at vij dayes ... | | vjs |
| 1 of Jenewary 1597, | | Rd at Valteger ... | | xxxxvs |
| 3 of Jenewary 1597, | | Rd at that wilbe shalbe........ | | xxxxijs |
| 4 of Jenewary 1597, | | Rd at nabucadonizer ........ | | xvjs |
| 5 of Jenewary 1597, | | Rd at docter Fostes | | vs |
| 6 of Jenewary 1597, | | Rd at that wilbe shalbe ........ | | xxxxijs |
| 7 of Jenewary 1597, | | Rd at Joronymo[2] | iijli | |
| 8 of Jenewary 1597, | | Rd at Valteger ... | | xijs |
| 10 of Jenewary 1597, | | Rd at stewtley ... | | xxviijs |
| 11 of Jenewary 1597, | | Rd at Joranymo... | | xxxxs |
| 12 of Jenewary 1597, | | Rd at nabycadnazer | | xiijs |
| 13 of Jenewary 1597, | | Rd at that wilbe shalbe........ | | xxijs |
| 14 of Jenewary 1597, | *ne* | Rd at Alexsander and Lodwicke[3] ........ | | lvs |
| 15 of Jenewary 1597, | | Rd at the blinde beager ........ | | ixs |
| 17 of Jenewary 1597, | | Rd at Joronymo... | | xxs |
| 18 of Jenewary 1597, | | Rd at that wilbe shalbe........ | | xvs |
| 19 of Jenewary 1597, | | Rd at nabucadonyzer ........ | | xs |
| 20 of Jenewary 1597, | | Rd at stewtley ... | | xjs |
| 21 of Jenewary 1597, | | Rd at Valteger ... | | xijs |
| 22 of Jenewary 1597, | | Rd at Joronymo... | | xixs |

[1] A new play, of which we know nothing more. Malone prints it "*What* will be shall be," and so it is sometimes written in the MS.

[2] Probably a revival of the popular play called the Spanish Tragedy.

[3] A new play, founded on the ballad of the two friends, Alexander and Lodowick, unless the ballad were founded upon it.

| | | | | | | | | |
|---|---|---|---|---|---|---|---|---|
| Janewary 1597 | 24 | | Rd at that wilbe shalbe[1] ...... | 0 | 17 | 00 | 19 | 07 |
| | 25 | | Rd at the blinde beager ......... | 0 | 19 | 03 | 08 | 00 |
| | 26 | | Rd at Nabucadonizer ........... | 0 | 09 | 02 | 00 | 03 |
| | 27 | *ne* | Rd at womon hard to please[2]... | 2 | 11 | 06 | 07 | 08 |
| | 28 | | Rd at longmege ................ | 0 | 07 | 01 | 30 | 00 |
| | 29 | | Rd at womon hard to please ... | 2 | 03 | 04 | 14 | 11 |
| | 31 | | Rd at Joronymo ................ | 01 | 04 | 01 | 15 | 06 |
| Febreary 1597 | 1 | | Rd at womones hard to pleasse | 01 | 05 | 02 | 11 | 02 |
| Candelmast day | 2 | | Rd at what wilbe shalbe......... | 01 | 18 | 01 | 03 | 00 |
| | 3 | | Rd at Oserycke ................ | 01 | 09 | 03 | 12 | 01 |
| | 4 | | Rd at womon hard to please ... | 01 | 08 | 04 | 07 | 00 |
| | 5 | | Rd at valteger.................. | 01 | 09 | 05 | 13 | 09 |
| Shrove munday | 7 | | Rd at oserycke ................ | 00 | 14 | 07 | 16 | 00 |
| Shrove tewesday | 8 | | Rd at womon hard to please ... | 01 | 09 | 01 | 02 | 01 |
| | 9 | | Rd at Joronymo.................. | 00 | 17 | 04 | 15 | 02 |
| | 10 | | Rd at stewtley ................ | 00 | 18 | 01 | 01 | 00 |
| | 11 | | Rd at elexsander and lodwicke | 03 | 05 | 00 | 17 | 00 |
| | 12 | | Rd at alexsander and lodwicke | 01 | 14 | 09 | 13 | 00 |
| Begynyng in leant | 3[3] | | Rd at what wilbe shalbe ...... | 00 | 09 | 00 | 16 | 00 |
| | 5 | | Rd at elexsander and lodwicke | 01 | 15 | 00 | 13 | 00 |
| Marche 1597 | 7 | | Rd at a Womon hard to please | 01 | 05 | 06 | 02 | 01 |
| | 8 | | Rd at Joronymo.................. | 01 | 01 | 00 | 03 | 04 |

[1] It is not easy to understand what was meant by some of the divisions of the page, now adopted in the MS. The first column clearly gives the month and year with observations; the second the day of the month; the third shows whether the piece was new or old; the fourth and fifth probably contained, in pounds and shillings, expressed in Arabic figures, the sum Henslowe received as his share; but the sixth column must remain matter of conjecture.

[2] This, like other new pieces, was marked in the usual way. See p. 79.

[3] The company seem to have ceased playing from the 12th February to 3d March, when they began again in Lent.

| | | | | | | | | |
|---|---|---|---|---|---|---|---|---|
| | 9 | | Rd at Lodwicke ... .............. | 01 | 16 | 07 | 04 | 00 |
| | 12 | | Rd at valteger..................... | 00 | 18 | 09 | 01 | 04 |
| | 14 | | Rd at the beager.................. | 00 | 18 | 03 | 00 | 00 |
| | 15 | | Rd at stewtley .................. | 01 | 05 | 00 | 00 | 00 |
| | 19 | ne | Rd at Guido [1] .................... | 02 | 00 | 00 | 13 | 01 |
| | 20 | | Rd at elexsander and Lodwicke | 00 | 17 | 00 | 09 | 02 |
| | 21 | | Rd at nabucadnazer ........... | 00 | 05 | 00 | 00 | 03 |
| | 22 | | Rd at guido........................ | 01 | 04 | 00 | 03 | 00 |
| Easter Munday | 28 | | Rd at a womon hard to please... | 01 | 11 | 00 | 00 | 10 |
| tewsday | 29 | | Rd at Elexsander and lodwicke | 02 | 01 | 00 | 04 | 03 |
| wensday | 30 | | Rd at guido ..................... | 02 | 17 | 00 | 00 | 00 |
| Mr pd [2] | 31 | | Rd at belendon .................. | 01 | 15 | 00 | 04 | 03 |
| Aprelle | 1 | | Rd at blinde beger .............. | 00 | 05 | 03 | 00 | 00 |
| 1597 | 2 | | Rd at valteger..................... | 00 | 04 | 01 | 01 | 00 |
| | 4 | | Rd at Guido ..................... | 01 | 08 | 00 | 04 | 03 |
| | 5 | | Rd at elexsander and lodwicke | 01 | 02 | 00 | 03 | 05 |
| | 6 | | Rd at what wilbe shalbe........ | 00 | 07 | 03 | 00 | 08 |
| | 7 | ne | Rd at v playes in one [3] ......... | 02 | 01 | 00 | 18 | 01 |
| | 8 | | Rd at womon hard to please ... | 00 | 05 | 03 | 00 | 00 |
| | 11 | | Rd at belendon ................. | 01 | 00 | 00 | 04 | 00 |
| | 12 | | Rd at eleyxsander and lodwicke | 00 | 14 | 03 | 00 | 01 |
| | 13 | | Rd at times triumphe and Foztus [4] | 01 | 05 | 01 | 00 | 03 |
| | 14 | | Rd at Stewtley ................. | 00 | 17 | 00 | 12 | 00 |
| | 15 | | Rd at v playes in one ......... .. | 01 | 08 | 02 | 00 | 00 |

[1] A new and now unknown play.

[2] The meaning seems to be that the Master of the Revels had been paid up to this date.

[3] Probably five new short plays, each, like the Yorkshire Tragedy, in one act, represented on the same day, and given as one play. See p. 22.

[4] This entry reads as if two different pieces had been performed on the same day. There is a passage in N. Field's Amends for Ladies (Suppl. Vol. to Dodsley's Old Plays, p. 27), from which we may infer that two dramas were sometimes so given. Time's Triumph seems a new title, but it is not marked by Henslowe as a new piece.

| | | | | | | | | |
|---|---|---|---|---|---|---|---|---|
| | 18 | *ne* | Rd at a frenshe comodey [1] ...... | 02 | 00 | 01 | 01 | 03 |
| | 19 | | Rd at belendon .................. | 00 | 09 | 02 | 00 | 00 |
| | 20 | | Rd at v playes in one ............ | 00 | 19 | 00 | 07 | 11 |
| | 21 | | Rd at Jeronymo .................. | 00 | 17 | 00 | 03 | 04 |
| | 22 | | Rd at frenshe comodey ......... | 01 | 02 | 00 | 17 | 01 |
| | 23 | | Rd at Guido ..................... | 00 | 16 | 01 | 11 | 00 |
| | 25 | | Rd at v playes in one ........... | 01 | 13 | 01 | 00 | 00 |
| | 26 | | Rd at frenshe comodey ......... | 01 | 02 | 00 | 17 | 00 |
| | 27 | | Rd at elexsander and lodwick... | 01 | 02 | 00 | 00 | 00 |
| | 28 | Mr pd | Rd at bellendon ................ | 01 | 00 | 00 | 13 | 00 |
| | 29 | *ne* | Rd at Uterpendragon [2] ......... | 02 | 14 | 01 | 01 | 03 |
| | 30 | | Rd at what wilbe shalbe......... | 00 | 14 | 00 | 17 | 08 |
| Maye | 2 | | Rd at frenshe comodey ......... | 01 | 01 | 00 | 09 | 03 |
| 1597 | 3 | | Rd at uterpendragon ............ | 01 | 03 | 00 | 01 | 00 |
| | 4 | | Rd at Jeronymo .................. | 00 | 11 | 07 | 14 | 00 |
| | 5 | | Rd at frenshe comodey ......... | 01 | 07 | 01 | 00 | 00 |
| | 6 | | Rd at v playes in one ......... .. | 00 | 16 | 00 | 03 | 00 |
| | 7 | | Rd at Pendragon ............... | 00 | 14 | 00 | 04 | 00 |
| | 9 | | Rd at Lodwicke and elexsander | 00 | 14 | 00 | 00 | 00 |
| | 10 | | Rd at womon hard to plesse ... | 00 | 17 | 07 | 10 | 00 |
| | 11 | *ne* | Rd at the comodey of Umers [3]... | 02 | 03 | 00 | 13 | 00 |

[1] This was a new play, but we have had the title before: see p. 49. It might be a comedy on a French story.

[2] Uther Pendragon was the father of King Arthur. This new play (also called Pendragon) was doubtless founded on the early chronicles.

[3] Malone was of opinion that this piece was Ben Jonson's Every Man in his Humour: if so, we see that it was played by the Lord Admiral's men for the first time on the 11th May 1597, whereas, in the folio edit. of 1616, Ben Jonson informs us expressly that his comedy was "first acted" by the Lord Chamberlain's servants in 1598; therefore, it is nearly certain to have been some other production, and in Henslowe's Diary it is sometimes called merely "Umers," i.e., "Humours." See Collier's Life of Shakespeare, p. clxv., where this point is considered, and reasons are assigned for supposing that our great dramatist was instrumental in the introduction of Ben Jonson to the company, and in the original production of his first play.

| | | | | | | | | |
|---|---|---|---|---|---|---|---|---|
| | 12 | | Rd at pendragon .................. | 0 | 17 | 00 | 00 | 00 |
| | 14 | | Rd at v playes in one ............ | 00 | 07 | 00 | 00 | 00 |
| Whittsone | 16 | | Rd at pendragon .................. | 02 | 19 | 00 | 14 | 00 |
| munday. | 17 | | Rd at elexsander and lodwicke | 03 | 00 | 00 | 03 | 04 |
| | 18 | | Rd at stewtley.................... | 01 | 12 | 01 | 17 | 00 |
| | 19 | | Rd at the comody of Umers ... | 02 | 15 | 00 | 00 | 00 |
| | 20 | | Rd at bellendon .................. | 00 | 10 | 00 | 00 | 00 |
| | 21 | | Rd at frenshe comodey ......... | 00 | 14 | 00 | 03 | 06 |
| | 23 | | Rd at v playes in one ............ | 01 | 00 | 07 | 00 | 01 |
| | 24 | | Rd at comodey of Umers ...... | 02 | 18 | 00 | 03 | 02 |
| | 25 | | Rd at Joronymo .................. | 00 | 19 | 00 | 14 | 06 |
| | 26 | *ne* | Rd at Harey the firste life and deth[1] .......................... | 02 | 10 | 01 | 03 | 09 |
| | 27 | | Rd at womon hard to pleasse ... | 00 | 05 | 00 | 00 | 00 |
| | 28 | Mr pd | Rd at elexsander and lodwicke | 00 | 13 | 01 | 10 | 00 |
| | 30 | | Rd Harey the fyrste life and deth | 00 | 19 | 06 | 00 | 00 |
| | 31 | | Rd at the Umers.................. | 03 | 04 | 01 | 03 | 00 |
| June 1597. | 1 | | Rd at frenshe comodey ......... | 00 | 13 | 00 | 04 | 06 |
| | 2 | | Rd at pendragon ................ | 00 | 16 | 00 | 04 | 06 |
| | 3 | *ne* | Rd at Frederycke and basellia[2] | 02 | 02 | 01 | 13 | 04 |
| | 4 | | Rd at the comodey of Umers... | 03 | 06 | 02 | 14 | 06 |
| | 6 | | Rd at what wilbe shalbe ......... | 00 | 10 | 00 | 16 | 00 |
| | 7 | | Rd at the comodey of Umers... | 03 | 10 | 00 | 00 | 00 |
| | 8 | | Rd at Harey the firste liffe and death ......................... | 00 | 12 | 06 | 00 | 00 |

[1] Malone puzzled himself (Shakesp. by Boswell, iii., 307), by misreading "Harey the *fifte*" for "Harey the *firste*," as it undoubtedly stands in the MS. It occurs six times after this note of its earliest performance, and is invariably "Harey the firste," generally with the addition of "life and death." Had it been "Harey the *fifte*," it would have been Henslowe's third play on that reign. See p. 61, note 1.

[2] No doubt the same piece as that of which "the plott" once existed at Dulwich, and is printed in Malone's Shakesp. by Boswell, iii., 356. The precise nature of the representation it is now perhaps impossible to ascertain. Malone prints this title erroneously "Frederycke and Basellers."

| | | | | | | | | |
|---|---|---|---|---|---|---|---|---|
| | 9 | | Rd at fredericke and baselia ... | 01 | 00 | 00 | 00 | 00 |
| | 10 | | Rd at v playes in one ........... | 00 | 11 | 03 | 01 | 00 |
| | 11 | | Rd at the Umers.................. | 02 | 18 | 00 | 00 | 00 |
| | 13 | | Rd at pendragon ................. | 01 | 00 | 00 | 00 | 00 |
| | 14 | | Rd at Harey the fyrste life and death ........................ | 00 | 14 | 00 | 00 | 00 |
| | 15 | | Rd at Bellendon ................. | 00 | 13 | 00 | 00 | 00 |
| | 16 | | Rd at frenshe comodey ......... | 00 | 07 | 00 | 13 | 06 |
| | 17 | | Rd at comodey of Umers ...... | 02 | 10 | 01 | 04 | 01 |
| | 18 | | Rd at fredericke and basilia ... | 00 | 11 | 00 | 14 | 06 |
| | 20 | | Rd at Joronemo ........ ......... | 00 | 14 | 00 | 00 | 00 |
| midsomer | 21 | | Rd at the comodey of Umers... | 03 | 00 | 00 | 00 | 00 |
| daye. | 22 | | Rd at Henges[1] ................. | 00 | 06 | 00 | 11 | 06 |
| | 23 | | Rd at frenshe comodey ......... | 00 | 08 | 00 | 00 | 00 |
| | 24 | | Rd at harey the firste........... | 00 | 14 | 00 | 00 | 00 |
| | 25 | Mr pd | Rd at bellendon .................. | 00 | 07 | 00 | 00 | 00 |
| | 27 | | Rd at stewtley..................... | 00 | 14 | 00 | 01 | 06 |
| | 28 | | Rd at v playes in one ........... | 01 | 00 | 00 | 13 | 11 |
| S. Petters | 29 | | Rd at elexsander and lodwick... | 01 | 02 | 00 | 14 | 00 |
| daye. | 30 | *ne* | Rd at liffe and death of Marten Swarte[2] ...................... | 02 | 08 | 01 | 11 | 09 |

[1] The title of this play has not occurred before, but it is not marked as a new one, and the sum received by Henslowe, 6*s*., does not look like it. It may have been an old play, introduced in this part of the MS. under a new name. The proper title was probably "Hengist," and there is an existing MS. play called Hengist King of Kent.

[2] A new play on the adventures of Martin Swart, who was sent over in 1486 by Margaret, Duchess of Burgundy, to assist the insurrection headed by Lord Lovell. "Martin Swart and all his merry men" are mentioned by Skelton in his poem "Agaynste a comely Coystrowne," &c.; and again in an early morality called "The longer thou livest the more Foole thou art," by W. Wager. The fate of Martin Swart is well known. There were early ballads upon his adventures, which perhaps served as the foundation for this drama, or, at all events, rendered the subject popular.

| | | | | | | | | |
|---|---|---|---|---|---|---|---|---|
| July 1597. | 1 | | Rd at Harey the firste ......... | 00 | 06 | 01 | 12 | 11 |
| | 2 | | Rd at frenshe commodey ...... | 00 | 04 | 02 | 00 | 13 |
| | 4 | | Rd at fredericke and baselia .. | 01 | 00 | 01 | 14 | 06 |
| | 5 | | Rd at what wilbe shalbe......... | 00 | 10 | 02 | 00 | 00 |
| | 6 | | Rd at life and deth of marten Swarte........................... | 02 | 10 | 01 | 13 | 09 |
| | 7 | | Rd at Comodey of Umers ...... | 01 | 18 | 02 | 17 | 01 |
| | 8 | | Rd at wiseman of Weschester | 01 | 00 | 01 | 00 | 03 |
| | 9 | | Rd at life and death of marten Swarte........................... | 01 | 13 | 02 | 13 | 01 |
| | 12 | | Rd at wismane of weschester... | 00 | 18 | 00 | 01 | 00 |
| | 13 | | Rd at comodey of Umers ...... | 01 | 10 | 01 | 11 | 01 |
| | 14 | | Rd at the wiche of Islyngton[1] | 01 | 07 | 02 | 00 | 00 |
| | 15 | | Rd at elexsander and lodwicke | 00 | 08 | 00 | 13 | 00 |
| MartenSla- | 16 | Mr pd | Rd at frenshe comodey ...... .. | 00 | 09 | 00 | 14 | 00 |
| ther went | 18 | | Rd at wisman ..................... | 01 | 10 | 00 | 00 | 00 |
| for the com- | 19 | | Rd at Jeronemo ................. | 01 | 00 | 01 | 13 | 01 |
| pany of my | 20 | | | | | | | |
| lord adme- | 27 | | Rd at v playes in one........... | 00 | 14 | 03 | 14 | 00 |
| ralls men, | 28 | | Rd at the wiche of Islyngton... | 01 | 18 | 00 | 13 | 00 |
| the 18 of | | | | | | | | |
| July 1597[2] | | | | | | | | |

[1] The title of this play has not occurred before in the MS., but there is no other reason to think it was a new production. It may have been a stock piece, brought out before the date when the Diary commences.

[2] It is not easy to explain the meaning of this memorandum, because Henslowe is recording the performances of the Lord Admiral's men. Possibly we ought to read "for" *from;* and understand that, at this date, and for a time, Martin Slater, Slaughter, or Slather, went *from* the company. On the other hand, as it is recorded at the same date that the Master of the Revels was paid, it is not unlikely that Henslowe thus registered that Martin Slater had gone to him for the purpose, on behalf of the association. We do not learn elsewhere that he ceased to be one of the Lord Admiral's men, and he seems to have been much too useful to have been readily parted with by Henslowe.

| | | | | | | | | |
|---|---|---|---|---|---|---|---|---|
| *October 1597. In the name of God, amen.* | 11 | | Rd at Jeroneymo[1] .............. | 02 | 00 | 01 | 13 | 00 |
| | | | Rd at the comodey of Umers... | 02 | 00 | 00 | 19 | 00 |
| the xj of | | | Rd at Docter fostes.............. | 0 | | | | |
| october be- | | | Rd at [2] | | | | | |
| gane my | | | Rd at | | | | | |
| lord adme- | 19 | | Rd at | | | | | |
| rals and my | | | Rd at Hardacute[3] .............. | 00 | 16 | 00 | 00 | 10 |
| lord of Pem- | 31 | *ne* | Rd at fryer spendelton[4] ......... | 02 | 00 | 01 | 14 | 00 |
| brockes | | 2 | Rd at Burbon ...................... | 00 | 16 | 30 | 12 | 00 |
| men, to | | 3 | Rd at Knewtus .................. | 00 | 10 | 00 | 14 | 00 |
| playe at my | | 4 | Rd at Umers ...................... | 00 | 16 | 03 | 00 | 01 |
| howsse, | | 5 | Rd at fryer spendelton ........ | 00 | 14 | 01 | 14 | 01 |
| 1597. | | | | | | | | |

The Mr payde the 2 of novembr 1597
for iij weekes, the some of xxxxs.[5]

[1] The entries here become irregular, and what ought to have been the heading of the account is inserted in the margin.

[2] If any plays were performed at this date by the Lord Admiral's and Lord Pembroke's players, both the titles and sums are wanting in the MS. "My house," in the margin, probably meant the Rose; but Henslowe seems to have had some concern with the Hope theatre.

[3] Ought we not to read *Hardiknute?* Afterwards we have Knewtus for *Canutus*, meaning, no doubt, the same drama.

[4] This new play is mentioned in a Medley Ballad of the time of Queen Elizabeth, but the subject of it is not known: the words of the ballad (pr. by E. Allde without date) are—

> "Friar Spendleton, the play,
> Carried it away;"

which serves to show that it was popular.

[5] Another proof of the monthly payment of 40s. to the Master of the Revels. The house had been open rather more than three weeks.

Lent unto my felow, Mr Vallantyne Haris,[1] one of the gromes of her Matis chamber, the 8 of aguste 1598, in Redey money, the some of three powndes, to be payd me agayne at his Retorn owt of the contrey. I say lent ........ ..... ................ } iijli

Wittnes Hareys brother in lawe.

Lent unto phillipe Yearen, the 4 of Jenewary 1599, in Redy money, the some of I say...... } xxs

Pd xs. PHILLIP HERNE.[2]

Lent unto Thomas Towne, the 3 of march 1600, pd upon a gowld Ringe with a grene stone in it, the some of ............. ............................... } xxs

Lent unto Thomas towne, by my wiffe, the 13 of marche 1601, upon a payre of sylcke stockens, tenne shellens, wch stockens he fetched agayne and payd us not; so oweth us stylle.............. } xs

1599.

Received of Mr Henselowe, in earnest of the tragedie of Merie, the some of xxs, the 27 of novbr.

W. HAUGHTON. J. D.[3]

[1] Several entries precede this, of money advanced to Mr. Arthur Langworth, and to two persons not named, which appear to have no connexion with theatrical affairs. We are to understand that Valentine Harris was Henslowe's "fellow," not as an actor, which Henslowe seems never to have been, but as a fellow-groom of the chamber.

[2] Philip Herne, or Hearn, was an actor who never attained much celebrity. The sum advanced to him was struck through with a pen in the MS., probably after it was repaid.

[3] This entry is in the handwriting of Haughton, who also added the initials of John Day. "The tragedy of Merie" (afterwards called "the tragedy of Thomas Merrye") may have been upon the same incidents as one of the plots of Yarrington's "Two Tragedies in One," (printed in

Received of M$^{r}$ Henselow, in earnest of the Orphanes Tragedy, the somme of x$^{s}$, the 27$^{th}$ of november.

Rec$^{d}$ of M$^{r}$ Hinchloe more, in ernest of the Tragedy of Thomas Merrye, 20$^{s}$.

JOH. DAY.
W. HAUGHTON.

Rec$^{d}$ more of M$^{r}$ Hinchloe, upon the same booke, 10$^{s}$.

By JOHN DAY.[1]

Lent unto harey Chettell, the 27 of novmbr 1599, in earneste of a Boocke called the orphenes tragedie, the some of x$^{s}$, as may apeare above by his hand crossed: some of........................ x$^{s}$

Lent unto W$^{m}$ Harton,[2] the 2 of febreary 1599, the some of ............................................ v$^{s}$

Lent unto M$^{r}$ Jonnes, the 4 of aguste 1601, in Redy mony, the some of twenty shellenges, w$^{ch}$ he leant unto Richard Weabe .................... xx$^{s}$

Received in pt of paiment of Damon and Pythias, this 16 of February 1599 ......................... xx$^{s}$

By me, HENRY CHETTLE.[3]

1601), which relates to the murder of a person of the name of Beech by his servant Thomas Merry, and to the killing of the children in the wood. This double story is strangely interwoven.

[1] This, and the preceding entry, are in the handwriting of John Day; but the first is signed by Haughton.

[2] Of course the same dramatist whose name is usually spelt Haughton, as, indeed, he writes it himself.

[3] Other entries, preceding and following this (which is in Chettle's handwriting), are crossed out, and part has been cut away.

Lent the 14 may 1597, to Jubie, uppon a notte from Nashe, twentie shellinges more, for the Jylle of dogges, w^ch^ he is wrytinge for the company [1] ..........................................

| | |
|---|---|
| Lent Harey Porter, the 11 of aprill 1599, the some of | ij^s^ vj^d^ |
| Lent Harey Porter, the 16 of aprell 1599, the some of | xij^d^ |
| Lent Harey Porter, the 5 of may 1599, the some of | ij^s^ vj^d^ |
| Lent Harey Porter, the 15 of maye 1599, the some of | ij^s^ vj^d^ |

HENRY PORTER.

Be it knowne unto all men, that I, Henry Porter, do owe unto Phillip Henchlowe the some of x^s^, of lawfull money of England, w^ch^ I did borrowe of hym the 26 of maye, a^o^ dom. 1599.

HENRY PORTER.[2]

Receved of M^r^ Phillip Hinchlow, the som of six shillinges. I say receved six shillinges for my selfe...... .................. .......................... } vj^s^

By me, THOMAS DOWNTON.[3]

[1] At this date, 14th May 1597, Nash was writing his play of the Isle of Dogs for Henslowe. A subsequent memorandum, dated 23d August 1597, shows that he was then in confinement in the Fleet for having composed such a piece, which had been acted. Gabriel Harvey in his "Trimming of Thomas Nash," (published in the name of Litchfield) 4to, 1597, inserts a wood-cut representing him in fetters, and a fac-simile of it may be seen in the Bridgewater Cat., p. 213.

[2] The whole of this acknowledgment is in Porter's handwriting. He affixed only his signature to the preceding entries. He was the author of the Two Angry Women of Abingdon, 1599, 4to., which, together with its second part (which has not survived), will be found hereafter mentioned.

[3] This actor's name is sometimes spelt Dowton, but he here gives it himself Downton. On p. 72 it is also Downton.

Lent unto John Daye, the 4 of Jenewary 1599, in Redy mony, the some of ........................ } v[s]
wittnes EDWARD ALLEYN.[1]

Received by me, william Haughton, for the use of Thomas Dickers, on the 30 of Januarie, the some of ................................................ } 20[s]
In parte paymente for the booke of truths supplication to candle light.[2]

I received forty shillinges of M[r] Phillip Hinslowe, in part of vj[li], for the playe of Willm Longsword, to be delivered present[ly], with[in] 2 or three dayes, the xxj[th] of January 1598 ................. } xxxx[s]
MIC. DRAYTON.[3]

The 1 of novembr 1599.

W. Haughton received of M[r] Hinslowe, in parte of payement of the tragedie of John Cox, the some of ........... 20[s]

Willyam Haughtonn receyved of M[r] Hinchloe, in part of paymente of the Tragedy of Cox of Collumpton, the some of ................................................................ 20[s]

pd and quite[4] JOHN DAYE.

[1] This is not signed by Alleyn, but Henslowe's scribe made a memorandum that Alleyn had seen the money paid to Day.

[2] Thomas Dickers is, of course, Thomas Dekker, whose name, like others at that date, was variously spelt. No such play as Truth's Supplication to Candle-light (like many others included in this Diary) is now known.

[3] The whole entry was written, or rather scribbled, by Drayton, who was in such haste that he wrote "present" for *presently*, and "with" for *within*, near the end of it.

[4] These words, "pd and quite," were added by Henslowe's scribe. The first of the two entries, regarding the tragedy of John Cox of Collompton, was written by Haughton, and the second by Day.

Received, in earnest of patient Grissell, by us, Tho Dekker, Hen Chettle, and Willm Hawton, the summe of $3^{li}$ of good and lawfull money, by a note sent from M$^{r}$ Robt Shaa, the 19 of december 1599 .......................................... } iij$^{li}$

By me, HENRY CHETTLE.
W. HAUGHTON.
THOMAS DEKKER.[1]

Lent unto John Pallmer, grome of the Queenes Chamber, the 5 of febreary 1598, the some of twentie shillinges, in Redy money, and wittnes to the lendinge of the same ...................... } xx$^{s}$

Lent unto John Pallmer, the 8 of July 1599, when he playd a[t] shove groate[2] at the cort. Redy mony ...................................... .......... } v$^{s}$

M$^{r}$ GRIFFIN, at the hachette.
M$^{r}$ DRAYTON.
HAREY CHETTELLE.[3]

[1] This memorandum ascertains that the "pleasant Comodie of Patient Grissill" was the authorship of Chettle, Haughton, and Dekker: it has been reprinted by the Shakespeare Society, and the entry is quoted in the Introduction. Robert Shaa, or Shaw, was an actor under Henslowe, and sometimes appears to have managed matters relating to the company. The only other printed specimen of Haughton's abilities is a comedy of considerable humour called Englishmen for my Money, printed in 1616, 1626, and 1631.

[2] Shove-groat was the name of a game, probably similar to what was called shovel-board. The three witnesses were perhaps present at the Court on the occasion.

[3] These names were written by Henslowe's scribe, as witnesses to the transaction: the witnesses to the preceding loan on 5 Feb. 1598, if indeed there were any, are omitted. The words, "at the hachette," must mean that the hatchet was the sign of the house at which Griffin resided.

Lent unto John Pallmer, grome of the Quenes chamber, the 7 of aprell 1599, the some of fortye shellinges. I say ........................................ xxxx^s

Wittnes Hewe Daves.

As maye a pere by his Bande.[1]

John Pallmer owith me more, the some of w^ch was my wages, w^ch he tocke up and spent at his wiffes linge in[2] ........................................ lv^s

Receaved by us, Richard Hathway and William Rankins, in pt of payment for the playe of Hanniball and Scipio, the summe of forty shillynges, we say receaved the 3 daye of Januarye 1600 ........................................ xxxx^s

By us Ri. Hathwaye.

W. Rankins.[3]

Rd of W^m Birde at severalle times, as foloweth, begininge the 17 of June 1598.

[1] Palmer having given his bond to Henslowe for the money.

[2] Wages were due to Henslowe, as one of the grooms of the chamber, which Palmer seems to have borrowed, and spent at the lying-in of his wife.

[3] William Rankins pursued a course directly opposite to that of Stephen Gosson: Stephen Gosson wrote plays, then repented, and produced violent attacks upon the stage: Rankins printed his "Mirror for Monsters" in 1587, an invective against theatrical representations, and we subsequently find him, as is shewn by this entry, joining Richard Hathway in the composition of Hannibal and Scipio. Thomas Nabbes wrote a tragedy called Hannibal and Scipio, which was printed in 1637; and he may have been indebted to the older play by Hathway and Rankins. This memorandum is followed by a detailed account of the expenses Henslowe had incurred "for bylldinge of my howsse upon the bancksyde, which was goodman Deres, 1599." It contains nothing theatrical; but Street, the builder of the Globe and Fortune, was the carpenter employed.

Rd the 17 of June 1598 [1] .................................... $v^s$

Pd this 23 of aguste 1597, to harey Porter, to carye to T. Nashe, nowe at this time in the Flete, for wrytinge of the eylle of Dogges, ten shellinges, to be paid agen to me when he canne. I saye ten shellinges [2] ...... } $x^s$

Rd of gabrell Spenser,[3] at severall tymes, of his share in the gallereyes, as foloweth, be gynynge the 6 of aprell 1598.

Rd the 6 of aprell 1598 .................................. $v^s$ $vj^d$
Rd the 14 of maye 1598 .................................. $vij^s$
Rd the 27 of maye 1598 .................................. $iiij^s$
Rd the 17 of June 1598 .................................. $v^s$
Rd the 24 of June 1598 .................................. $iiij^s$

Lent unto $M^r$ Jones, Robart Shawe, Thomas Dowton, $W^m$ Birde, the same time they pd $M^r$ Langleyes his money for the agreement, and fechéd home the Riche clocke frome pane, which the stocke is not to paye, but thes meane: I saye lent in Readey money the some of $ij^{li}$, the 4 of octobr 1598 ........................................................ $iij^{li}$

wittnes JEWBY.
JOHN SYNGER. [4]
THOMAS TOWNE.

[1] This is the only entry under the preceding head.

[2] Respecting Nash's play, the Isle of Dogs, see Hist. Engl. Dram. Poetry and the Stage, i., 307; and Collier's Shakespeare, i., clxx.

[3] This is the player whom Ben Jonson killed in a duel in Hoxton Fields, according to Henslowe's letter in the Memoirs of Edward Alleyn, p. 51. His name occurs several times before, but never after the date of Henslowe's letter, 26 Sept. 1598. If there were originally any more items in this account, they have been cut away.

[4] This is not Singer's signature, nor that of Jewby, or Towne, but of Henslowe's scribe. The words, "frome pane," mean from *pawn*, the

| | |
|---|---|
| Lent unto Antoney Jeaffes,[1] the 11 of Aprell 1599, in Redey money, to by divers thinges ageanst sente gorges daye, the some of .................... wittnes BEATTRES. | xx^s |

| | |
|---|---|
| Pd unto M^r Blunsones, the M^r of the Revelles man, this 27 of aguste 1597, ten shellinges, for newes of the restraynte beinge recaled by the lordes of the Queenes counsel[2] ............................ | x^s |

*A Juste acownte of all suche money as I dooe Receve for Umfrey Jeaffes and antoney Jeaffes, begenynge the* 29 *of Aprell* 1598, *as foloweth of the companey:*

| | |
|---|---|
| Rd the 29 of aprell 1598.................................... | ij^s vj^d |
| Rd the 7 of aprell[3] 1598 .................................. | ij^s vj^d |
| Rd the 14 of maye 1598........ ........................... | ij^s vj^d |
| Rd the 20 of maye 1598.................................... | ij^s vj^d |
| Rd the 27 of maye 1598..................... ........... | ij^s vj^d |

rich cloak having been pledged, and Henslowe registering that the money was not to be paid out of the stock of the company, but by "these men:" viz., Jones, Shawe, Dowton or Downton, and Birde. This memorandum and the next are crossed out in the MS.

[1] There were two actors of the name of Jeffes, and perhaps they were related to Abel Jeffes, the printer of the first *authorized* edition of Nash's "Pierce Penniless's Supplication." See Shakespeare Society's reprint, Introd., p. xiii. The name of Humphrey Jeffes, perhaps brother to Anthony, occurs in the next account.

[2] The restraint upon the company, in consequence of the offensive performance of Nash's Isle of Dogs, had by this date been recalled, and Henslowe paid Blunson ten shillings for bringing the welcome news.

[3] This date ought obviously to be the 7th of May 1598, but Henslowe's scribe sometimes commits such errors, where they occasion more confusion than in the present instance. Still lower down in this account, and elsewhere, he makes June have thirty-one days.

Rd the 3 of June 1598 .................................... v^s
Rd the 10 of June 1598 .................................... ij^s vj^d
Rd the 17 of June 1598 .................................... ij^s vj^d
Rd the 24 of June 1598 .................................... ij^s vj^d
Rd the 31 of June 1598 .................................... ij^s vj^d
Rd the 8 of July 1598 .................................... ij^s vj^d
Rd the 14 of July 1598 .................................... ij^s vj^d
Rd the 21 of July 1598 .................................... ij^s vj^d

Lente unto humfrey Jeaffes, the 6 of aprell 1598, in Redy money, xx^s

Lent unto Umfrey Jeaffes, the 5 of Septemb 1598, to by a payer of silke stockenes .................. } xv^s

pd and quite. Lent unto Umfrey Jeffes, the 12 desembr 1599, the some of ...... } x^s

Lent unto M^r Richard Jonnes,[1] player, the 2 of June 1599, to be payd me agayne by x^s a wecke, the some of fyve pownds, to be gene at the daye above written: I saye lent Redy mony ......... } v^li

pd and quite.[2]

*Rd of M^r Jonnes, player, of this* v^li *above written as foloweth*
1599.

Rd the 7 of June 1599 .................................... x^s
Rd the 14 of June 1599 .................................... x^s
Rd the 21 of June 1599 .................................... x^s
Rd the 28 of June 1599 .................................... x^s

[1] Richard Jones may also have been the bookseller, or related to the bookseller, who published the *unauthorized* impression of Nash's "Pierce Penniless's Supplication" in 1592. In the Alleyn Papers, p. 19, will be seen a letter from Richard Jones to Alleyn.

[2] i.e., Paid and quit, according to the account which succeeds, which, as well as this memorandum, is crossed out in the MS.

| | |
|---|---|
| Rd the 6 of July 1599 .................................... | x$^{s}$ |
| Rd the 13 of July 1599 .................................... | x$^{s}$ |
| Rd the 20 of July 1599 .................................... | x$^{s}$ |
| Rd the 27 of July 1599 .................................... | x$^{s}$ |
| Rd the 5 of aguste 1599 .................................... | x$^{s}$ |
| Rd the 15 of septembr 1599 .................................... | x$^{s}$ |

pd and quite.

Receved as folowethe of the company of my lorde Admeralls mean, from the 2 of aprell 1598, at divers tymes, as foloweth.

| | | | |
|---|---|---|---|
| Rd the 2 of Aprell 1598 ........................ | | xxvj$^{s}$ | |
| Rd the 9 of Aprell 1598 ........................ | iij$^{li}$ | vij$^{s}$ | vj$^{d}$ |
| Rd the 14 of Aprell 1598........................ | | lvij$^{s}$ | |
| Rd the 22 of Aprell 1598........................ | vj$^{li}$ | iij$^{s}$ | vj$^{d}$ |
| Rd the 29 of Aprell 1598........................ | | lij$^{s}$ | vj$^{d}$ |
| Rd the 6 of aprell[1] 1598 ........................ | iiij$^{li}$ | ij$^{s}$ | vj$^{d}$ |
| Rd the 14 of maye 1598 ........................ | v$^{li}$ | ij$^{s}$ | |
| Rd the 20 of maye 1598 ........................ | iiij$^{li}$ | vj$^{s}$ | |
| Rd the 27 of maye 1598 ........................ | iij$^{li}$ | iiij$^{s}$ | vj$^{d}$ |
| Rd the 3 of June 1598 :........................ | | lij$^{s}$ | vj$^{d}$ |
| Rd the 10 of June 1598 ........................ | v$^{li}$ | xvj$^{s}$ | vij$^{d}$ |
| Rd the 17 of June 1598 ........................ | iij$^{li}$ | xvj$^{s}$ | |
| Rd the 24 of June 1598 ........................ | v$^{li}$ | vij$^{s}$ | |
| Rd the 31 of June 1598 ........................ | v$^{li}$ | xviij$^{s}$ | iij$^{d}$ |
| Rd the 8 of July 1598[2]........................ | | lj$^{s}$ | vij$^{d}$ |

Lent unto thomas towne, the 26 of aprell 1600, in Redy mony, the some of.............. } x$^{s}$

Borrowed of Mr. phyllip Henslowe, the xj$^{th}$ of november

[1] Meaning, of course, the 6th May 1598. Lower down we again have "31st of June."

[2] The addition of these payments, inserted in the margin, is not legible, but it is of no importance.

1597, the some of xl$^{s}$, to be payd on the x$^{th}$ of December next ensuinge

By me ROBT SHAA.[1]

*A Juste acownte of the money which I have Receved of Humfreye Jeaffes hallfe sheare,*[2] *beginynge the* 14 *of Jenewary* 1597, *as foloweth*:—

| | | |
|---|---|---|
| Rd the 21 of Jenewary 1597 ......................... | viij$^{s}$ | |
| Rd the 28 of Jenewary 1598[3] ......................... | iij$^{s}$ | 4$^{d}$ |
| Rd the 4 of febreary 1598 ......................... | xj$^{s}$ | vij$^{s}$ |
| Rd the 11 of febreary 1598 ......................... | vj$^{s}$ | vij$^{d}$ |
| Rd the 18 of febreary 1598 ......................... | viij$^{s}$ | |
| Rd the 25 of febreary 1598 ......................... | x$^{s}$ | |
| Rd the 4 of marche 1598 ......................... | xiij$^{s}$ | |

This some was payd backe agayne unto the companey of my lord admeralles players, the 8 of marche 1598, and they shared y$^{t}$ a mongste them: I saye pd backe agayne the some of iij$^{li}$.

*A Juste acownte of all suche monye as I have Receved of my lord admeralles and my lord of penbrocke men,*[4] *as foloweth, begynynge the* 21 *of octobr* 1597:—

| | | | |
|---|---|---|---|
| Rd the 21 of octobr 1597 .................. | v$^{li}$ | j$^{s}$ | vj$^{d}$ |
| Rd the 28 of octobr 1597 .................. | iij$^{li}$ | xj$^{s}$ | x$^{d}$ |
| Rd the 30 of octobr 1597 .................. | iij$^{li}$ | | |

[1] This memorandum is entirely in Shaw's handwriting.

[2] Hence we see that Humphrey Jeffes, whatever might be the case with Anthony, was only a half-sharer in the company.

[3] In this account Henslowe makes the 21st January fall in 1597, and the 28th of the same month in 1598: the error of course arose from the confusion in the time of commencing the new year. For new-year gifts, &c., the year began at this date on the 1st January, but for other purposes generally on the 26th March.

[4] Probably the Lord Admiral's and Lord Pembroke's players had been acting in conjunction. See an entry on the next page.

| | | | |
|---|---|---|---|
| Rd the 5 of novmbr 1597 .................. | | $\text{liij}^{s}$ | $\text{x}^{d}$ |
| Rd the 12 of novmbr 1597.................. | | $\text{xxxxvij}^{s}$ | |
| Rd the 19 of novmbr 1597.................. | | $\text{xxxxviij}^{s}$ | $\text{viij}^{d}$ |
| Rd the 26 of novmbr 1597.................. | | $\text{xxxxiiij}^{s}$ | |
| Rd the 3 of desembr 1597.................. | | $\text{xxxxiiij}^{s}$ | |
| Rd the 10 of desembr 1597.................. | | $\text{xxvj}^{s}$ | |
| Rd the 17 of desembr 1597.................. | | $\text{xxxxix}^{s}$ | |
| Rd the 30 of desembr 1597, beinge crysmas weacke [1] .............................. | $\text{vij}^{li}$ | $\text{xvj}^{s}$ | |
| Rd the 7 of Janewary 1597.............. | | $\text{xxx}^{s}$ | |
| Rd the 14 of Janewary 1597 ........... | | $\text{l}^{s}$ | |
| Rd the 21 of Jenewary 1597 ........... | $\text{iij}^{li}$ | $\text{ix}^{s}$ | |
| Rd the 28 of Janewary 1598 ........... | | $\text{xxviij}^{s}$ | $\text{ix}^{d}$ |
| Rd the 4 of febreary 1598 .............. | $\text{v}^{li}$ | | |
| Rd the 11 of febreary 1598 .............. | | $\text{lvj}^{s}$ | $4^{d}$ |
| Rd the 18 of febreary 1598 .............. | $\text{iij}^{li}$ | $\text{ix}^{s}$ | |
| Rd the 25 of febreary 1598 .............. | $\text{iiij}^{li}$ | $\text{xv}^{s}$ | |
| Rd the 4 of marche 1598................. | $\text{v}^{li}$ | $\text{xj}^{s}$ | $\text{iij}^{d}$ |

Lent unto Thomas Dowton, the 25 of aprell 1598, in Redy mony, the some of } $\text{v}^{s}$

looke the 4 leaffe forwarde [2]

Lent unto Robarte shawe, the 23 of octobr 1597, to by a boocke for the company of my lorde admeralls men, and my lord of penbrockes, the some of...... } $\text{xxxx}^{s}$

called the cobler [3] wittnes

E. ALLEYN.

[1] Shewing the greater receipts during the holidays.

[2] *Sic* in MS.; but nothing referable to the subject is to be found on the fourth leaf either way: on the page immediately following are several memoranda of money advanced to Dowton, or Downton.

[3] This play could not have been "the Coblers Prophesie," by R. Wilson, which was printed in 1594, and written considerably earlier,

| | |
|---|---|
| Lent unto Robart shawe, the 5 of novmbr 1597, to by a boocke of yonge Horton,[1] for the company of my lord admeralles men, and my lord of pen-brockes, the some of ...................... | x$^s$ |
| wittnes | E. Alleyn. |

| | |
|---|---|
| Lent unto Robart Shawe, the 26 of novembr 1597, to by viij yds of clothe of gowld, the some of fower powndes: I saye lent for the usse of the company... | iiij$^{li}$ |

| | |
|---|---|
| Lent unto Robart shawe, to geve to the tayller to bye tensell for Bornes womones gowne,[2] the j of desembr 1597........... | ix$^s$ |

| | |
|---|---|
| Lent Thomas Dowton, the 12 of no-vembr 1597, in Redy money, the some of .......................................... | x$^s$ |
| Lent Thomas Dowton, the 16 of no-vmbr 1597, in Redy money, the some of | v$^s$ |
| Lent Thomas Dowton, the 20 of no-vmbr 1597, in Redy money, the some of | v$^s$ |
| Lent unto Thomas Dowton, the 24 of novmbr 1597, in Redy money, w$^{ch}$ Robart shawe gave his worde for y$^t$ to be payd me agayne with in one fort-nyght next folowinge, wittnes to the same Edward Alleyn ..................... | xxxx$^s$ |

unless it were some revival of the piece, with additions and alterations, in 1597, to give it novelty. This and the entry following are witnessed by E. Alleyn, in his own handwriting.

[1] William Haughton, at this date a young dramatist.

[2] Hence we may infer that William Borne (whose proper name seems to have been Birde) played female characters in the company.

| | | |
|---|---|---|
| Lent thomas Dowton, to fee a cownseller, the 12 of desember................. | | x^s^ |
| Lent Thomas Dowton, to featche ij clockes owt of pane, the 2 of novmbr 1597, the some of xij^li^ x^s^; for w^ch^ money thes ij clockes were leafte unto me in pane: the one wasse and embrodered clocke of ashe colerd vellvet, the other a blacke vellvett clocke layd with sylke laces abowt. I saye lent unto hime in Redy money ................................ | xij^li^ | x^s^ |

| | |
|---|---|
| Rd of the companey of my lorde admeralles men, in pte of payment, the firste of desember 1597, of Robarte shawe, the some of.......................... | xx^s^ |
| Layd owt for the company of my lord admeralls men, for to by tafetie and tynsell to macke a payer of bodeyes for a womones gowne, to playe allece perce,[1] for w^ch^ I dellyvered unto the littell tayllor in Redey money, the 8 of desembr 1597, the some of .......................... | xx^s^ |

wittnes E. ALLEYN.

| | |
|---|---|
| Layd owt mor the same tyme for makynge and a payer of yeare sleavfe, of the bodeyes of Pages gowne[2] ......... | vj^s^ vij^d^ |

[1] The play of Alice Pierce was not actually brought out until some time afterwards. It nowhere appears in the Diary by whom it was written.

[2] i.e., *Hair sleeves* for the play founded upon the story of the murder of Page, at Plymouth. Several ballads were written upon the subject at this date, and have come down to us; but Malone, not being acquainted with them, calls the tragedy "*Peg* of Plymouth," and sometimes *Pyg*.

| | |
|---|---|
| Lent unto Bengemen Johnsone, the 3 of desembr 1597, upon a Booke $w^{ch}$ he was to writte for us befor crysmas next after the date herof, $w^{ch}$ he showed the plotte unto the company: I saye lente in Redy money unto hime the some of[1] .......... .......................... | $xx^s$ |
| Lente unto Robarte shawe, for to by copper lace of sylver, to lace a payer of hosse for alles perce, the 10 of desembr 1597, the some of .............. .......... | $xvj^s$ |

Wittnes $W^M$ BORNE, JUBE and GABRELL SPENCER.

| | |
|---|---|
| Layd owt for ij gyges, for Shawe and his companye,[2] to ij yonge men, the 12 of desembr 1597, the some of ........... | $vj^s$ $8^d$ |
| Layde owt, the 22 of desembr 1597, for a boocke called mother Redcape, to antony monday and $M^r$ Drayton......... | $iij^{li}$ |

[1] Quoted by Malone, in Shakespeare, by Boswell, iii., 333. Ben Jonson was to finish the play between Dec. 3 and Christmas; but he had proceeded so far as to have shown the plot of it to the company, and no doubt had written much of it. It will be observed that the date of this transaction is about three-quarters of a year before "Benjamin Jonson, bricklayer," as Henslowe calls him in his letter (Mem. of E. Alleyn, p. 51), killed Gabriel Spenser (whose name occurs just below) in Hoxton Fields. See also p. 80, for a still earlier memorandum of the connexion between Ben Jonson and Henslowe.

[2] This entry looks as if Shawe were at the head of the company at this date, and his name is often prominent. What was meant by "ij gyges" must be matter of speculation—probably "jigs," a species of comic performance by clowns, regarding which see Hist. Engl. Dram. Poetry and the Stage, iii., 376.

| | |
|---|---|
| Layd owt the 28 of desembr 1597, to antoney monday toward his boocke, which I delyvered to thomas Dowton[1] | v[s] |

*Ano Do.* 1595, *the* xxviij*th* *of november.*

Resesed of M[r] Henslow, the day and yeare above written, the Som of syx poundes of curant mony of England, and is in part of a mor som by twyxt the sayd Phillyp Henslow and me consarning a bargen of the bear-garden. I say Reseved........................................................ vj[li]

By me JOHN MAULTHOUSE.[2]

Wittnes I E. ALLEYN.

*Layd owt at sundrey tymes, of my owne Readey money, abowt the changinge of our comysion, as foloweth,* 1597 :—

| | | |
|---|---|---|
| Layd owt for goinge to the corte, to the M[r] of the Requeastes .................................. | | xij[d] |
| Layd owt for goinge to corte ij ..................... | ij[s] | |
| Geven unto the clarcke of the senetes[3] man, Edward .............................................. | v[s] | |
| Layd owt for goinge to the corte to the senet ... | | xij[d] |
| Itm̃ pd for goinge up and downe to the corte to grenwiche .......................................... | | viij[d] |

[1] This memorandum and the one which precedes it, no doubt, had reference to the same play, viz., Mother Redcap, by Anthony Munday, and Michael Drayton. Henslowe's Diary is the only source of information respecting any such piece.

[2] The nature of this bargain, about the Bear-garden, where Henslowe and Alleyn acted as deputies to Dorington, the Master of the Games, nowhere appears. It seems unlikely, from the date, that the items under the next head relate to the same transaction, although "our commission" must have meant the power under which they baited bears, bulls, and horses, for public amusement.

[3] "Clarcke of the senetes man" is, of course, *Clerk of the Signets' man.*

Itm̃ pd for goinge up and downe to caylleng crosse to the clarke [1] .............................. vj^d

Itm̃ pd unto the clarke of the senette ........... xxxx^s

Itm̃ pd unto the clarkes mane .................... v^s

Itm̃ pd for goinge up and downe to sencaterens, M^r Seser [2] .. ......... ........................ ... iiij^d

Lent unto W^m Borne, the 12 of desembr 1597, in Redey money, to be pd unto me agayne at crysmas eve next comynge, the some of twenty shyllynges: I saye lent............................ } xx^s

Wittnes ROBART SHAWE
THOMAS DOWTON
and E. ALLEYN.

Lent unto W^m Borne, the 19 of desembr 1597, in Redey money, to be payd me agayen at crystmas eve next comynge, the some of thirtene shillinges: I saye lent .......................................... } xiij^s

wittnes THOMAS DOWTON biger boye,[3] whome fetched y^t fore hime.

Layd owt for a wascotte, wraght with sylke, for W^m Borne, the 24 of febreary 1598, the some of } xx^s

looke the next leaffe folowinge.[4]

[1] Probably *Charing Cross* is meant by "Caylleng crosse," but we meet nowhere else in the Diary with the same specimen of ignorance.

[2] Mr. Cæsar, afterwards Sir Julius Cæsar, who lived at St. Catherine's, and was Master of the Requests.

[3] The players engaged boys as a species of apprentices, and Thomas Downton had two, one of them being distinguished as his "bigger boy." The same actor's "biger boye" is again mentioned afterwards in a repetition of this item.

[4] This note refers to entries on the next leaf, some of which are erased repetitions of what are here found. In one instance, "Borne, *alias* Bird," is charged 13*s.* 4*d.*, for what, on a preceding page, is only stated at 6*s.* 8*d.*,

Rd, the 31 of october 1597, of Mr. Phillip Henchlowe, the Summe of xiiij[s] ij[d], for one quarters rent, due at Michaelmas last past, and is to the use of Harry Weadover. I say Rd .............. } xiiij[s] ij[d]

p̲ me RA. CARTER.[1]

Pd unto Thomas Whittle, the 2 of Jenewary 1597, the some of xxxx[s], which was dewe unto the M[r] of the Revelles for one monethe playinge, which was dewe unto hime the 28 of Desembr 1597. I saye pd .................................. } xxxx[s]

Pd unto Thomas Whittle, the 22 of Jenewary 1598, the some of xxxx[s], w[ch] was dewe unto the M[r] of the Revelles for one moneth playinge, w[ch] was dewe unto hime the 21 of Jenewary 1598. I saye pd.......................................... } xxxx[s]

Pd unto John Carnab, the 23 of febreary 1598, the some of xxxx[s], which [was] dew unto the M[r] of the Revells for one moneth playinge. I saye pd .......................................... } xxxx[s]

*W[m] Borne, alles Birde*, 1598, *deatte as foloweth.*

Lent W[m] Borne, the 29 of marche 1598, to discarge the areaste betwext Langleye and hime ... } vj[s] viij[d]

Lent W[m] Borne, by my wiffe, the 3 of aguste 1598 .............................................. } v[s]

Lent W[m] Borne, to folowe the sute agenste Thomas Poope,[2] the 30 of aguste 1598, by my wiffe } x[s]

viz., when he was discharged from Langleye's arrest. He is also made debtor twice over for 20*s*., lent to buy him a pair of silk stockings.

[1] This memorandum is in Carter's handwriting. The "rent" might be the ground-rent of the Rose.

[2] Thomas Pope was a comic actor of great eminence, and in 1596 was one of the company at the Blackfriars. No explanation is found in any part of the MS. respecting this law "suit" between him and Borne.

| | |
|---|---|
| Lent unto Wm Borne, the 9 of aguste 1598, the some of viijs, which thomas towne feched for hime: I saye .................... .................... | viijs |
| Lent Wm Borne, the 27 of septmbr 1598, when he roade to Croyden, to ther lorde,[1] when the quene came thether ......................... .............. | vs |
| Lent Wm Birde, ales Borne, the 27 of novembr, to bye a payer of sylke stockens, to playe the Gwisse in ............................................. | xxs |
| Lent Wm Borne, to bye his stockens for the gwisse[2] ................................................. | xxs |

*Wm Bornes, alles birde, Recknynge, player: at severall times lent as foloweth*, 1597.

| | |
|---|---|
| Lent Wm Borne, the 12 of desembr 1597, in Redy moneye, to be payde me agayne at crysmas eve next comynge, the sume of twenty shyllynges. wittnes Robart shawe, Thomas Dowton, and E. Alleyn .............................................. | xxs |
| Lent Wm borne, the 19 of desembr 1597, in Redey money, to be payd me agayne at crysmas eve next comynge, thirten shillinges. Wittines Thomas Dowtons biger boye, whome feched yt for hime ................................................ | xiijs |
| Layd owt for a wraght wascotte for Wm Borne, the 24 of febreary 1598, the some of .. ............... | xxs |

[1] "Ther Lorde" probably means the Lord Admiral, whom the Queen was at this date visiting, and when the attendance of his company of players was required for her Majesty's entertainment.

[2] "The Gwisse" has been supposed to be "The Guise," i.e., Marlowe's play of "the Massacre at Paris." (See p. 30.) This was possibly some revival of the older drama, with additions and alterations; but John Webster, at a subsequent date, was the author of a play, which he himself calls "The Guise." See the Ded. to his "Devil's Law Case," 1623.

| | |
|---|---|
| Lent unto W$^{m}$ borne, Thomas Dowton, and gabrell Spencer, abowt the sewt be twext marten and them,[1] the 8 of marche 1598, in Redy money, the some of ............................ | xxx$^{s}$ |
| Lent unto W$^{m}$ Borne, the 25 of marche 1598, in Redey money, at ij paymentes, the some of ...... | v$^{s}$ |
| Lent W$^{m}$ borne, to discarge the areaste of Langleyes, 29 marche 1598 ............................ | xiij$^{s}$ 4$^{d}$ |

W$^{m}$ Borne. *A Just Recknynge what I have Receved of W$^{m}$ Borne for xx$^{s}$, w$^{ch}$ I lent hime to by a wraght wascotte, as foloweth*, 1598.

| | |
|---|---|
| Rd the 25 of febreary 1598 ............................ | ij$^{s}$ vj$^{d}$ |
| Rd the 27 of febreary 1598 ............................ | ij$^{s}$ vj$^{d}$ |
| Rd the 1 of marche 1598 ............................ | ij$^{s}$ vj$^{d}$ |
| Rd the 4 of marche 1598 ............................ | ij$^{s}$ vj$^{d}$ |

Borrowde of M$^{r}$ Phillip Hinchlow, the 3 of apriell 1598, the some of 3 powndes, in redye monye, to be payd att what time he shall call. By me, WILLIAM BIRDE.[2] I say borrowed iij$^{li}$

Be it knowen unto all men, by thes presentes, that I, gabrell Spencer, dothe aknowledge my sealfe to owe and stande fermly in deated unto phillipe Hensley the some of fower powndes, of good and lafull money of Inglande. Looke iij leaves further.[3]

[1] "Marten" is probably Martin Slaughter or Slater, with whom Borne, Dowton, and Gabriel Spenser had had some dispute at law. This fact may confirm the supposition that Slaughter had temporarily quitted the company. The 8th March 1598 must mean 8th March 1597-8.

[2] Here we see that "Borne, alias Birde," as Henslowe calls him, signs his name William Birde. The whole memorandum is of his writing. How he obtained the name of Borne does not appear.

[3] The entry was not complete on this page, and it is repeated, with additions, two (not three) leaves farther on in the MS.

*Gabrell Spencer.*

| | |
|---|---|
| Lent unto gabrell spencer, the 10 of marche 1598, in Redey money, the some of $x^s$. I saye lent... | $x^s$ |
| Lent unto gabrell spencer, the 20 of marche 1598, in Redy money, upon a Jewell .................... | $vj^s$ |
| Md, that I, gabrell spencer, the 5 of aprell 1598, have borowed of Phillipe Henslow the some of thirtie shellynges, in Redy money, to be payed unto hime agayne when he shalle demande yt: I saye borowed ................. ....................... | $xxx^s$ |

GABRIELL SPENSER.[1]

| | |
|---|---|
| Lent M^r Richard Fuller, my attorney, the 29 of aguste, in Ready money, to be payd me agayne at mihellmasse tearme next cōminge after the datte herof, 1594, above written, and witneses to the leandynge herof ................................ | $xx^s$ |

M^r SHEALDEN, player,[2]
and M^r Fullers man.

The ij chelldren of Edmond Hensley, mary and nanne, came up to London to me to keppe, the 27 of febreary, and in the yeare of our lord 1595.[3]

[1] The signature only is by Gabriel Spenser, who was killed in September following the date of this item. He subscribed the memorandum twice, but erased it in the second instance.

[2] We meet with the name of Sheldon as a player nowhere else.

[3] There is a family account on the preceding page, thus headed, "A note of all such carges as I, phillipe Hensley, have layd owt of my owne money, in be hallfe of the Cheldren of Edmond Hensley, desesed, 1592, as foloweth." The meaning seems to be that, Edmond Henslowe having died in 1592, his children came to live with Philip Henslowe in London, in 1595. There is nothing theatrical in any of the items.

borowed of M^r hinchlow, the xx^th of marche 1598, the som of 40 shillings, I say xxxx^s

p̱ me THOMAS DOWNTON.[1]

| | |
|---|---|
| Lent unto Robarte shawe, player, the 20 of marche 1598, in Redey money, the some of .............. | v^s |
| Lent unto Thomas Dowton, the 25 of aprell 1598, in Redy money, the some of ...................... | v^s |
| Lent unto W^m Birde, the 23 of october 1598, upon a longe taney clocke of clothe of his owe, the some of thirti shillinges: I saye lent unto hime | xxx^s |
| Lent unto W^m Borne, the 19 of novembr, 1598, upon a longe taney clocke of clothe, the some of xij^s, w^ch he sayd yt was to Imbrader his hatte for the Gwisse[2] ....... ............................ | xij^s |
| Lent unto W^m Birde, ales borne, the 22 of desembr 1598, when the widow came to M^rs Reves to super, in Redey money, the some of.............. | x^s |
| Dd unto W^m Birde, ales borne, ij gewells of gowld, w^ch he layd to me to pane for x^s, w^ch I dd to hime agayne withowt money, w^ch he owes me ... | x^s |

Be yt knowne unto all men by this presents, that I, Wil-liame Birde, and gabrell spencer, and Thomas Dowton dothe aknowlege our seallves to owe and stande fermly in deatted unto phillipe Henslow the some of syxe powndes, of good and lafulle money of England, we borowed of hime, and to be payd unto the sayd phillipe his heires, exec^rs, or assignes, at St. Jhon Baptist next ensuing the date here of, at his howse;

[1] This entry is in the handwriting of, and is subscribed by Downton, whom Henslowe usually calls Dowton.

[2] It seems likely that William Birde had a female character in "the Guise," and that he wore an embroidered hat, for the purpose of

the wich payment wee bind us or heirs executors and assignes, by these present: in witnes whereof we have to this bill sett or hands, the ix$^{th}$ of Aprill 1598. I say vj$^{li}$.

WILLIAM BIRDE.
GABRIELL SPENSER.
THOMAS DOWNTON.[1]

Be it knowne unto all men by thes presentes, that I, gabrell spencer, of london, player, doe aknowlege my sealffe to owe and stand fermly in deated unto Phillipe Hensley, the some of fower powndes, of good and lafulle money of Inglande; and for the trewe payment herof I bynde me, my eares, executors, and adminystrators, by this presente. In wittness here to I have seatte my hande, the 20 of aprell 1598: ageanste sent gorges day.

GABRIELL SPENSER.[2]

| | |
|---|---|
| Lent unto gabrell spencer, the 24 of aprell 1598 ... | x$^s$ |
| Lent unto gabrell spencer, the 19 of maye 1598, to bye a plume of feathers, w$^{ch}$ his mane bradshawe feched of me, x$^s$. I saie lente .................. .. | x$^s$ |
| Lent W$^m$ Birde, alles Borne, the 22 of aprell 1599, in redey money, which his mane, William Felle, Rd yt of me for hime, the some of forti shillinges. I say .......................................... | xxxx$^s$ |

Wittnes E. ALLEYN.

decorating which, he pawned to Henslowe his long tawny cloth cloak. On p. 110, it appears that he borrowed 20*s*. to buy a pair of silk stockings for the same part.

[1] The signatures are those of the three players, but the memorandum is partly in the handwriting of Henslowe and partly in that of Downton.

[2] The signature only is by Spenser, and the rest of the memorandum by Henslowe, who spelt "heirs" *eares*, though in the entry immediately preceding it is in the proper orthography.

| | |
|---|---|
| Lent unto Mrs Birde, alles Borne, the 26 of novembr 1600, in Redye monye, to descarge her husband owt of the Kynges benche, when he laye upon my lorde Jeffe Justes warant[1] for hurtinge of a felowe which browght his wiffe a leatter: some of three powndes I saye ................ | iijli |

*A not of all suche goods I haue Bowght for playinge, sence my my sonne edward Allen leafte playinge*, 1597.[2]

| | |
|---|---|
| Bowght, the 29 of desembr 1597, j shorte veallvett clocke, ymbradered with bugells, and a hood cape | iijli |
| bowght, the 18 of aprell 1598, xvj ownces of coper-lace, brad with sylver and gowld, coper at viijd ownce ........................................ | xs viijd |
| Itm̃ for makynge of the gercken of threed ........ | iijs iiijd |
| Bowght, the 8 of novmbr 1598, xiiij ownces of coper lace, wraght with opene worcke, for xiiijd and ownce ............ ... ...... ........................ | xvjs |

*A Juste acownt of all suche money as I have layd owt for my lord admeralles players, begynyng the xj of octobr, whose names ar as foloweth: Borne, Gabrell, Shaw, Jonnes, Dowten, Jube, Towne, Synger, and the ij Jeffes.* 1597.[3]

| | |
|---|---|
| Layd owt unto Robarte Shawe, to by a boocke for the companey, the 21 of octobr 1597, the some of | xxxxs |

Called the cobler.[4] Wittnes

E. ALLEYN.

[1] i.e., The Lord Chief Justice's warrant.

[2] This account establishes that Alleyn had temporarily seceded from the stage prior to the 29th of December 1597.

[3] Hence we learn that Alleyn was not a member of the Lord Admiral's company even in October 1597. At the same time, he witnesses several payments, so that he had not quitted London.

[4] This item and some others appear to be repetitions, with variation and addition, of entries already inserted on p. 103, &c.

Lent unto Robarte Shaw, to by a boocke of yonge Harton, the 5 of novembr 1597, the some of ... } x^s^

Wittnes

E. Alleyn.

Lent unto Robarte Shaw, for the companey, to bye viij yardes of clothe of gowlde for the womones gowne in Branhowlte,[1] the 26 of novembr 1597, the some of ............................................ } iiij^li^

Lent unto Robarte Shawe, to geve the tayller to by tynsell for Bornes gowne, the j of desembr 1597 } ix^s^

Layd owt for the company to by tafetye and tynsell for the bodeyes of a womones gowne to playe allce perce,[2] w^ch^ I dd unto the littell tayller, the 8 of desembr 1597 ........................................ } xx^s^

Wittnes E. Alleyn.

Layd owt for mackynge allce perces bodeyes, and a payer of yeare sleaves, the some of .............. } vj^s^ vij^d^

Lent unto Bengemen Johnson, the 3 of desembr 1597, upon a boocke w^ch^ he showed the plotte unto the company, which he promysed to dd unto the companye at cryssmas next, the some of[3] ........................................ } xx^s^

Lent unto Robarte Shawe, to by coper lace of sylver for a payer of hosse in alls Perce, the 10 of desembr 1597 ........................................ } xvj^s^

Wittnes W^m^ Borne, Jube, and gabrell Spenser.

Layd owt for ij gyges for the companey, to ij yonge men, the 12 of desembr 1597, the some of } vj^s^ 8^d^

[1] Possibly Brennoralt, a subject treated by Sir John Suckling about the year 1639.

[2] Alice Pierce, the mistress to Edward III.

[3] Compare the memorandum on p. 106, which is of the same date and nearly in the same terms.

| | |
|---|---|
| Layd owt, the 22 of desembr 1597, for a boocke called mother Readcape, to Antony Monday and Drayton ........................................... | iij$^{li}$ |
| Layd owt, the 28 of desembr 1597, for the boocke called mother Readcape, to antoney mondaye ... | v$^{s}$ |
| Lent the company, to bye a flame coler satten dublett, the 5 of Janewary 1597, the some of[1] ...... | xxxxv$^{s}$ |

*Layd owt for my lord Admeralles meane, as foloweth*, 1597.

| | |
|---|---|
| Pd unto Antony Mondaye and Drayton, for the laste payment of the Boocke of mother Readcape, the 3 of Jenewary 1597, the some of[2] ........... | lv$^{s}$ |
| Layd owte for coper lace for the littell boye, for a valle for the boye, ageanste the playe of Dido and Eneus,[3] the 3 of Jenewary 1597 ................. | xxix$^{s}$ |
| Lent unto thomas Dowton, the 8 of Jenewary 1597, twenty shillinges, to by a bookes of M$^{r}$ Dickers. Lent ....... ........................................ | xx$^{s}$ |
| Lent unto the company, when they fyrst played Dido at nyght,[4] the some of thirty shillynges, w$^{ch}$ wasse the 8 of Jenewary 1597. I saye..... | xxx$^{s}$ |

[1] This note is crossed out in the MS.

[2] Making in the whole £6 to Monday and Drayton for their play of Mother Redcap. See also p. 106 and 107.

[3] Perhaps some alteration and revival of Marlowe and Nash's "Dido, Queen of Carthage," printed in 1594: it might, however, be a new production on the same subject, and hereafter we shall meet with a play called "Æneas' Revenge." The boy who was to be furnished with "a veil" was perhaps to act the part of the heroine.

[4] The performances were in the day-time, and here we are not to understand that Dido was "played at night." Probably the 30*s.* was for some entertainment to the company at night (at the Sun in Fish Street, mentioned afterwards), on the successful performance of the play for the first time.

| | |
|---|---|
| Lent unto the company, the 15 of Jenewary 1597, to bye a boocke of Mr Dicker, called fayeton,[1] fower pownde. I saye lent ........................ | iiijli |
| Lent unto Thomas Dowton, for the company to paye to the Mr of the Revells for lysensynge of ij boockes, xiiijs: abated to Dowton vs, so reaste[2] .................................................... | ixs |
| Lent unto Thomas dowton, for the company to bye a sewte for phayeton, and ij rebates, and j fardengalle, the 26 of Jenewary 1598, the some of three pownde. I saye lent ...................... | iijli |
| Lent unto Thomas Dowton, the 28 of Jenewary 1598, to bye a whitte satten dublette for phayeton, forty shyllenges. I saye lent .............. | xxxxs |
| Lent unto the companey, the 4 of febreary 1598, to disecharge Mr Dicker owt of the cownter in the powltrey, the some of fortie shillinges. I saye dd to thomas Dowton ............................ | xxxxs |
| Layd owt unto antony monday, the 15 of febreary 1598, for a playe boocke, called the firste parte of Robyne hoode[3] .................................. | vli |

[1] This "book of Mr Dekker, called Phaeton," may have been the production to which Ford afterwards contributed, and which was printed as his work and Dekker's, under the title of "The Sun's Darling, a Moral Masque," in 1657. See Gifford's Ford's Works, ii., 360.

[2] This entry, and others to be met with hereafter, show that the fee of the Master of the Revels on licensing a play was now 7*s*. According to memoranda on pp. 18 and 19, the fee in 1591 and 1592 was only 5*s*. for each play. It may have been raised arbitrarily by Tylney.

[3] This excellent play was printed anonymously in 1601, under the title of "The Downfal of Robert, Earl of Huntington, afterward called Robin Hood of merrie Shirwood," &c. The "second part," as Henslowe, farther on, calls it, came from the press in the same year, with the title of "The death of Robert, Earl of Huntington." Both are reprinted in the supplementary vol. to Dodsley's Old Plays.

| | |
|---|---|
| Lent unto Robarte Shawe, the 18 of febreary 1598, to paye unto Harton for a comodey called a Womon will have her will,[1] the some of ........ | xx$^{s}$ |
| Lent unto thomas Dowton, the 20 of febreary 1598, to lende unto antony mondaye, upon his seconde parte of the Downefall of earlle Huntyngton, surnamed Roben hoode. I saye lent the some of .............................................. | x$^{s}$ |
| Layd owt unto Robarte Lee, the 22 of febreary 1598, for a boocke called the Myller, some of ... | xx$^{s}$ |
| Lent unto thomas Dowton, the 25 of febreary 1598, to geve unto chettell, in part of paymente of the seconde parte of Robart hoode, I saye lent [2]...... | xx$^{s}$ |
| Lent unto Antony Mondaye, the 28 of febreary 1598, in parte paymente of the second parte of Roben Hoode ........................................ | v$^{s}$ |
| Lent unto Thomas Dowton, and Robart Shaw, and Edwarde Jeweby, the 1 of marche 1598, to bye a boocke of M$^{r}$ Dickers, called the treplesetie of cockowlles,[3] the some of fyve powndes. I say lent ......................... ...................... | v$^{li}$ |

[1] It was not printed until 1616, when the name here given was made the second title, "Englishmen for my money, or a Woman will have her Will." It was several times reprinted, and is an extremely good comedy, but it was not given to any author until the discovery of the MS. before us. In the last old edition, 4to, 1631, the printer dropped the first part of the title, and reverted to the name it bears in Henslowe's Diary.

[2] Hence we find that Henry Chettle was Monday's coadjutor, at least in the Death of Robert Earl of Huntington. In the supplementary vol. to Dodsley's Old Plays, upon the authority of Henslowe's Diary, "The Downfal of Robert Earl of Huntington" has been assigned to Monday alone, and "The Death of Robert Earl of Huntington" to Monday and Chettle.

[3] The title, no doubt, was "The Triplicity of Cuckolds," but Henslowe and his scribe contrived to misspell names with great ingenuity. We have no other intelligence regarding this comedy.

| | |
|---|---|
| Lent unto Robart Shawe, the 8 of marche 1598, in full paymente of the seconde parte of the boocke called the Downfall of Roben Hoode, the some of ........................................ | iij^li^ |

J SYNGER

p me, THOMAS DOWNTON.

p me, WILLIAM BIRDE.

ROBT SHAA. RICHARD JONES.

GABRIELL SPENSER. CHARLES MASSYE.

THOMAS TOWNE. SAMUELL ROWLYE.[1]

HUMFREY JEFFES.

Thes men dothe acknowlege this deat to be dewe by them by seatynge ther handes to ytte.[2]

| | |
|---|---|
| Lent unto Drayton and Cheattell, the 13 of marche 1598, in pte paymente of a boocke, wher in is a pte of a weallche man written,[3] which they have promysed to delyver by the xx daye next folowinge. I say lent R. money | xxxx^s^ |
| Lent unto the company, to paye Drayton and Dyckers and Chetell ther full payment for the boocke called the famos wares of Henry the fyrste and the prynce of Walles,[4] the some of ........................................ | iiij^li^ v^s^ |

[1] These are the original signatures of the ten members of the company, arranged as we have given them. Alleyn does not seem to have been an actor at this date, or Henslowe did not consider him his debtor.

[2] Henslowe's note, who has summed up the amount in the margin, viz., £46 *7s.* *3d.*

[3] Malone (Shakespeare by Boswell, iii., 318) conjectures that this was "The Valiant Welchman," by R. Armin, printed in 1615; but we have already had a play called The Welshman under date of 29th November 1595, which is more likely to have been Armin's drama.

[4] R. Davenport wrote a play upon this portion of English history, licensed in 1624, and attributed to him and Shakespeare in the Stationers'

| | |
|---|---|
| Lent at that tyme unto the company for to spend at the Readynge of that boocke, at the sonne in new fysh streate ...................... | vs |
| Pd unto the carman for caryinge and bryngyn of the stufe backe agayne when they played in fleat-streat, pryvat, and then owr stufe was loste [1] ........................................ | iijs |
| Layd owt for the company, to bye a boocke of Mr Drayton, and Mr Dickers, Mr chettell, and Mr Willsone, which is called Goodwine and iij sones,[2] fower powndes in pte of payment, the 25 of marche 1598, in Redey mony: I saye ........................................ | iiijli |
| Layd owt the same tyme at the tavarne in fysh-streate for good cheare, the some of ........... | vs |
| Layd owt, the 28 of marche 1598, for the licensynge of ij booke to the Mr of the Revelles, called the ij ptes of Robarte hoode ........... | xiiijs |
| Lent unto the companye, the 30 of marche 1598, in full paymente for the boocke of Goodwine and his iij sonnes. I saye lent .............. | xxxxs |
| Lent unto the company to geve Mr Willsone, Dickers, Drayton, and cheattell, in parte payment of a boocke called Perce of Exstone,[3] the some of.................................... | xxxxs |

Registers, under date of 9 Sept. 1653. Perhaps Davenport only revived and altered this piece, which Henslowe assigns to Drayton, Dekker, and Chettle.

[1] The company had performed at some private entertainment in Fleet Street, where we must conclude that part of the "stuff," meaning dresses, properties, &c., was lost.

[2] The correct title probably was "Earl Godwin and his three Sons." Earl Goodwin is again mentioned afterwards.

[3] Sir Pierce of Exton killed Richard II., and this play was most likely connected with that historical incident.

Lent unto the company to by a Damask casocke, garded with vellvett, the 7 of aprell 1598, the some .......................................... xx$^{s}$

Lent unto thomas Dowton, the 11 of aprell 1598, to bye tafitie, to macke a Rochet for the beshoppe, in Earlle goodwine ................. xxiiij$^{s}$

Lent unto the company, the 12 of aprell 1598, to paye M$^{r}$ Hathwaye, in fulle payment for his boocke of Kynge Arthore,[1] the some of fower pownde. I saye .............................. iiij$^{li}$

Lent unto the companey, the 29 of aprell 1598, to bye a bugell doblett and a payer of paned hoose, of bugell panes drane owt with clothe of sylver, and canyoms[2] of the same........... xxxxvj$^{s}$ viij$^{d}$

Lent unto Thomas Dowton, 2 of maye 1598, to bye a Robe for the playe of the lyfe of Arthure in money, the some of ......................... iij$^{li}$ pd

Lent unto Cheattell, upon the playe called black batmone of the northe,[3] the some of Wittnes THOMAS DOWNTON .................... xx$^{s}$

Lent unto Downton, to paye unto Horton, in pte of paymente of his boocke called a Womon will have her wille.................................... xx$^{s}$

[1] On p. 87, a play of Utherpendragon, the father of King Arthur, has been introduced. It does not seem that Hathway had any coadjutors in his drama, afterwards called the Life of Arthur, King of England. In 1587 had been printed a play entitled "The Misfortunes of Arthur," which was principally composed by Thomas Hughes. It is reprinted in the supplementary vol. to Dodsley's Old Plays.

[2] What "canyoms of the same" may be, it is not easy to determine; but see p. 144: "paned hose" were breeches, composed of small squares, or *panes*, the figures in this instance being defined by bugles.

[3] It appears lower down that Wilson, Drayton, and Dekker, were joint authors with Chettle in Black Batman of the North. The B. L. ballad of Bateman's Tragedy probably relates to the same events.

Lent unto Mr Cheattell and Mr Dickers, the 6 of aprell 1598, upon ther boocke of Goodwine, the 2 pte,[1] the some of.................................. xxs

Lent unto the companey, the 9 of maye 1598, to bye a dublett and a payer of hoosse, layd thick with gowld lace, the some of .................... vijli

Lent unto Mr Chapmane,[2] the 16 of maye 1598, in earneste of a boocke for the companye. Wittnes, Wm BIRDE ............................ xxxxs

Lente unto the company, the 16 of maye 1598, to bye v boockes of martine Slather, called ij ptes of Hercolus, and focas, and pethagoras, and elyxander and lodicke,[3] which laste boocke he hath not yet delyvered, the some of........ vijli

The xith of Aprell.

Rd of Phillipp Hinchlow, twenty shillings, in earnest of a booke cald the Lyfe of Artur King of England, to be delivered one thursday next following after the datte hereof. I say Rd xxs by me.................. ................ xxs

RI. HATHWAYE.[4]

[1] Malone (iii., 319) represents that Drayton alone was the author of this second part of Earl Godwin, and does not mention the names of Chettle and Dekker in connexion with it. Wilson was also a coadjutor.

[2] Chapman had written for Henslowe at least as early as 1595-6, for his Blind Beggar of Alexandria was played for the first time on 12 Feb. of that year. See p. 64.

[3] These pieces have all been mentioned before at earlier dates (see pp. 51, 53, 63, 69, and 84), when they were severally performed for the first time. At the date of this memorandum, Martin Slather, or Slaughter, must again have had them in his hands, perhaps for alteration and addition, and received £7 for his pains. On 16 May, 1597, he had not re-delivered Alexander and Lodowick, as amended, to Henslowe.

[4] The whole of this memorandum is in Hathwaye's handwriting.

| | | |
|---|---|---|
| Bowght of Mr Willsones, Drayton, and Dickers, and cheattell, for the companey, a boocke, called blacke Battmane of the northe, the 22 of maye 1598, which coste sixe powndes.[1] I saye layd owt for them ........................ | vj li | |
| Lent unto Wm Birde, the 23 of maye 1598, which he lent unto Mr Chappman, upon his boocke, which he promised us........................ | | xx s |
| Lent unto the company, the 30 of maye 1598, to bye a boocke called love prevented, the some of fower powndes, dd to THOMAS DOWTON. Mr. Porter[2] ........................ | iiij li | |
| Lent unto Thomas Dowton, the 6 of June 1598, to leand unto Drayton. I saye leante ........ for the 2 pt of goodwine. | | x s |
| Lent unto the companey, the 10 of June 1598, to lend unto Mr Chapman ........................ | | x s |
| Lent unto the company, the 10 of June 1598, to paye unto Mr Drayton, Willson, Dickers, and cheattell, in full paymente of the second pte of Goodwine, ls, as foloweth: Drayton 30s, and Willson xs, and cheattell xs.[3] Some is ..... | | l s |
| Lent unto Mr Willsone, the 13 of June 1598, upon a bocke called Richard Cordelion funeralle[4] ........................ | | v s |

[1] We have already seen, on p. 122, that Chettle had separately received 20*s*. on account of this play.

[2] The name "Mr. Porter" was doubtless added here, in a different hand, to indicate that Love Prevented was by him.

[3] Dekker seems to have been omitted in the division of the money. Perhaps Drayton received 30*s*. for himself and Dekker.

[4] Chettle, Monday, and Drayton, were also concerned in the authorship of Richard Cordelion's Funeral, as we afterwards find by other notices.

| | |
|---|---|
| Lent unto thomas Dowton, the 13 of June 1598, to bye divers thinges for blacke batmane of the northe, the some of fyve pownd. I saye lent .................... | $v^{li}$ |
| Lent unto Thomas Dowton, the 14 of June 1598, to bye divers thinges for blacke batmane of the northe, the some.................... | $iij^{li}$ |
| Lent unto Cheattell, the 14 of June 1598, in earneste of a boocke called Richard cordeliones funerall .................... | $v^s$ |
| Lent unto Robart Shawe and Edward Jube, the 15 of June 1598, to geve M^r^ Chapman, in earneste of his boocke called the Wylle of a Womon[1].................... | $xx^s$ |
| Lent unto Cheattell, the 15 of June 1598, in earneste of ther boocke called the funerall of Richard cordelion .................... | $v^s$ |
| Lent unto Cheattell, Willsone, and Mondaye, the 17 of June 1598, upon earneste of ther boocke called the funerall of Richard cordelion........... | $xv^s$ |
| Lent unto M^r^ cheattell, the 21 of June 1598, in earneste of a boocke called the funerall of Richard cordelion, the some of .................... I saye $xxv^s$: wittness W^m^ BIRDE .................... | $xxv^s$ |
| Lent unto Anthony Munday, the 23 of June 1598, in earneaste of a boocke called the funerall of Richard cordelion, the some of .................... | $xx^s$ |
| Lent unto M^r^ Drayton, the 24 of June 1598, in earneste of a boocke called the funerall of Richard cordelion, the some of .................... | $xxx^s$ |

[1] This may not have been a separate play, but the same called on pp. 119 and 122, A Woman will have her Will, where it is imputed to William Haughton alone: Chapman may have added to it, or assisted him in it. It seems unlikely that two plays, so resembling in title, would have been produced at the same time.

Lent unto M^r cheattell, the 24 of June 1598, the some of x^s. I saye ............................... x^s

All his pte of boockes to this place are payde which weare dew unto hime, and he reastes, be syddes, in my deatte the some of xxx^s [1]....................

Lent unto M^r Willson, the 26 of June 1598, the some of xx^s, which is in full paymente of his pte of the boocke called Richard cordelion funerall: and so M^r Willson reasteth in my deate, albeinge payde .................................... xx^s

Lent unto Thomas Dowton, the 26 of June 1598, to by satten to macke ij dublettes, for the 2 pte of goodwine, the some of ........................ v^li

Lent unto Cheattell, the 26 of June 1598, in earneste of a boocke called the 2 pte of blacke Battman of the north; and M^r Harey Porter hath geven me his worde for the performance of the same, and allso for my money .................... xx^s

Lent unto Thomas Dowton, the 27 of June 1598, to bye divers thinges for the 2 pte of Goodwin... xxx^s

Lent nnto M^r Willson, M^r Drayton, and M^r Dickers, the 31 of June 1598, in earneste of a boocke called the made manes mores, [2] the some of...... iij^li

Lent unto M^r Cheattell, the 8 of July 1598, upon a Boocke called the 2 pte of Blacke Battman, the some of ........................................... iij^li

[1] Chettle would appear to have been poor, and to have always required small advances, as the work proceeded. At this date, besides having been paid for all his "books," he was 30*s.* in debt to Henslowe. Just below, it will be seen that the old manager would make no more advances to him, unless a brother author (Porter) would engage his word for the delivery of the second part of Black Bateman of the North, in which he, as well as Wilson, might be aiding Chettle.

[2] The Mad Man's Morris seems to have been the real name of the piece: nothing more is known of it.

| | |
|---|---|
| Lent unto Mr Drayton, the 9th of July 1598, upon a Boocke called the mad manes mores, the some of .................................................. | xxs |
| Pd unto Mr Willsone and Mr Dickers, in full payment of a boocke called the mad manes moris, the 10 of July 1598, the some of ................. | xxxxs |
| Lent unto Mr Willsones, the 13 of July 1598, in pt payment of a boocke called the 2 pt of blacke battman, the some of ................................ | xs |
| Lent unto Mr Wilsone, the 14 of July 1598, in pt payment of a boocke called the 2 pt of blacke battman, the some of ................................ | xvs |
| Pd unto Mr cheattell, the 14 of July 1598, in full payment of a boocke called the 2 pt of blacke battmane, the some of ........ ................... | xvs |
| Lent unto Harey Cheattell, the 14 of July 1598, upon a boocke called the playe of A womon Tragedye, the some of vli, which Robart shawe willed me to delyver hime. I saye ........................ | vli |

Eather to dd the playe, or els to paye the mony within one forthnyght.

| | |
|---|---|
| Lent unto Wm Borne, the 14 of July 1598, for to geve the paynter in earneste of his pictor,[1] the some of ................................................ | vs |
| Lent unto Thomas Dowton, the 16 of July 1598, for to bye a Robe to playe Hercolas in,[2] the some of................................................... | xxxxs |
| Lent unto Mr Willsone, the 17 of July 1598, in earneste of a comodye called Haneballe and hermes, the some of ................................ | xs |

[1] This entry might look as if scenery had been employed; but it was payment for a portrait used in the course of a play: in another hand, in the margin, we read "Tassoes Picture."

[2] i e., On the revival of the play. R. Greene speaks of a play on "the twelve labours of Hercules:" see his Groatsworth of Wit, in 1592.

| | |
|---|---|
| Pd unto Marteyne Slawghter, the 18 of July, for a boocke called elexsander and lodwicke,[1] the some of ........................................................ | xx$^{s}$ |
| Lent unto M$^{r}$ Willson, M$^{r}$ Drayton, and M$^{r}$ Dickers, the 17 of July 1598, for a Boocke called Haneballe and hermes, the some of .............. | iij$^{li}$ |
| Lent unto Robart shawe and Jewby, the 19 of July 1598, for a Boocke called Vallentyne and orsen,[2] in full paymente, the some of v$^{li}$, to paye hathwaye and mondaye ............................ | v$^{li}$ |
| Pd unto the M$^{r}$ of the Revelles man, for the licensynge of iij boockes, the 24 of July 1598, the some of ........................................ | xxj$^{s}$ |
| Lent unto W$^{m}$ borne, the 25 of July 1598, to by a sewte of satten for the playe of the made mannes moris, the some of......................... | iiij$^{li}$ xiij$^{s}$ 4$^{d}$ |
| Lent unto M$^{r}$ Willsone, the 26 of July 1598, upon a Boocke called Haneballe and Hermes, the some of ........................................... | xx$^{s}$ |
| Lent unto M$^{r}$ Drayton and M$^{r}$ Dickers, the 27 of July 1598, in pt of a Boocke called Haneballe and Hermes, the some of ........................ | xxx$^{s}$ |
| Lent unto the company, the 28 of July 1598, to by a payer of sceartes of whitte satten,[3] for a womons gowne layd with whitte lace, the some of......... | xxxiij$^{s}$ 4$^{d}$ |
| Pd unto M$^{r}$ Drayton and M$^{r}$ Deckers, the 18 of July 1598, in full payment of a boocke called haneball and hermes, other wisse called worsse feared then hurte ................................ | x$^{s}$ |

[1] See p. 123, where it is stated that this altered play had not been delivered on 16th May 1598.

[2] In various shapes this famous romance has ever since kept possession of the stage, last as an admirable burlesque.

[3] i.e., *Skirts* of white satin.

| | |
|---|---|
| Lent unto Mr Deckers, the same time, upon ther next boocke,[1] called Perce of Winchester ........ | xs |

120li 15s 4d

*Here I Begyne to Receve the wholle gallerys from this daye, beinge the* 29 *of July* 1598.[2]

| | | |
|---|---|---|
| Rd the 29 of July 1598 .............................. | xli | xiiijs |
| Rd the 6 of aguste 1598 .............................. | vijli | xs |
| Rd the 13 of aguste 1598 .............................. | ixli | ixs |
| Rd the 19 of aguste 1598 .............................. | viijli | xijs |
| Rd the 26 of aguste 1598 .............................. | viijli | ijs |
| Rd the 2 of septmbr 1598 .............................. | viijli | xiiijs |
| Rd the 10 of septmbr 1598 .............................. | ixli | iijs |
| Rd the 17 of septmbr 1598 .............................. | vjli | xviijs |
| Rd the 24 of septmbr 1598 .............................. | viijli | ijs |
| Rd the 29 of septembr 1598 .............................. | vli | xiiijs |
| Rd the 7 of octobr 1598 .............................. | vjli | iijs |
| Rd the 14 of octobr 1598 .............................. | vijli | xvs |
| Rd the 21 of octobr 1598 .............................. | xli | xiiijs |
| Rd the 28 of octobr 1598 .............................. | vli | xixs |
| Rd the 5 of novmbr 1598 .............................. | viijli | ijs |
| Rd the 12 of novmbr 1598 .............................. | vli | iijs |
| Rd the 19 of novmbr 1598 .............................. | vjli | xvjs |
| Rd the 24 of novmbr 1598 .............................. | iiijli | xvjs |

[1] Drayton and Wilson joined Dekker in this new play, as we shall find hereafter.

[2] The receipts upon this account are weekly, and they are of very irregular amounts, the highest being £16 12*s.* 0*d.*, on the 3rd June 1599, and the lowest £2 on the 13th October, 1599, when the statement closes, perhaps by reason of the smallness of the sum taken at the doors: it is interposed between the memoranda of advances to authors and actors. To what theatre it refers is not stated, but it was probably the Rose, shortly before the Fortune was constructed by Henslowe and Alleyn.

| | | |
|---|---|---|
| Rd the 2 of desembr 1598 | $vj^{li}$ | $xvj^{s}$ |
| Rd the 9 of desembr 1598 | $vij^{li}$ | $xvj^{s}$ |
| Rd the 16 of desembr 1598 | $iiij^{li}$ | $iij^{s}$ |
| Rd the 23 of desembr 1598 | $iiij^{li}$ | $v^{s}$ |
| Rd the 30 of desembr 1598 | $xij^{li}$ | $x^{s}$ |
| Rd the 7 of Janewary 1598 | $vij^{li}$ | $xvij^{s}$ |
| Rd the 14 of Janewary 1598 | $viij^{li}$ | $xj^{s}$ |
| Rd the 21 of Janewary 1598 | $viij^{li}$ | $xiij^{s}$ |
| Rd the 28 of Janewary 1598 | $vij^{li}$ | $vj^{s}$ |
| Rd the 4 of Febreary 1598 | $x^{li}$ | $xvij^{s}$ |
| Rd the 11 of Febreary 1598 | $vij^{li}$ | $x^{s}$ |
| Rd the 18 of Febreary 1598 | $vij^{li}$ | $x^{s}$ |
| Rd the 29 of Febreary 1598 | $xv^{li}$ | $iij^{s}$ |
| Dew $233^{li}$ $17^{s}$ $7^{d}$ | | |
| Rd the 26 of marche 1598 | $iij^{li}$ | $xviij^{s}$ |
| Rd the j of Aprell 1598 | $ij^{li}$ | $ij^{s}$ |
| Rd the 8 of Aprell 1598 | $iij^{li}$ | $viij^{s}$ |
| Rd the 15 of Aprell 1599 [1] | $xiij^{li}$ | $vij^{s}$ |
| Rd the 22 of Aprell 1599 | $xiij^{li}$ | $xvj^{s}$ |
| Rd the 29 of Aprell 1599 | $xj^{li}$ | $v^{s}$ |
| Rd the 6 of maye 1599 | $viij^{li}$ | $x^{s}$ |
| Rd the 13 of maye 1599 | $ix^{li}$ | |
| Rd the 20 of maye 1599 | $xj^{li}$ | $xj^{s}$ |
| Rd the 27 of maye 1599 | $x^{li}$ | $viij^{s}$ |
| Rd the 3 of June 1599 | $xvj^{li}$ | $xij^{s}$ |
| Rd the 6 of octobr 1599 | $v^{li}$ | $iij^{s}$ |
| Rd the 13 of octobr 1599 | $ij^{li}$ | |

Receved with the company of my Lord of notingame men to this place, beinge the 13 of octobr 1599; and yt doth apere that I have Received of the deate which they owe unto me iij hundred fiftie and eyght powndes.[2]

[1] The three last items ought also to have been 1599, reckoning the new year to begin on the 26th March.

[2] The whole amount of the debt of the Lord Admiral's players to Henslowe is nowhere stated in the MS.

Lent the company,[1] the 30 of July 1598, to bye a Boocke of John Daye, called the conqueste of Brute with the first fyndinge of the Bathe, the some of.......................................... xxxx^s

Lent unto the company, the 8 of aguste 1598, to paye M^r Drayton, Willsone, and Dickers, in pte of payment of a boocke called perce of winschester, the some of......................... l^s

Lent unto antonye Monday, the 9 of aguste 1598, in earneste of a comodey for the corte,[2] called —— the some of.................................. x^s

M^r Drayton hath geven his worde for the boocke to be done with in one fortnight. Witness THOMAS DOWTON ...... .........................

Lent unto the company, the 10 of aguste 1598, to paye M^r Drayton, Willsone, and Dickers, in fulle payment for a boocke called perce of winschester, the some of......................... l^s

Lent unto the company, the 18 of aguste 1598, to bye a Boocke called hoote anger sone cowld,[3] of M^r porter, M^r cheattell, and bengemen Johnson, in fulle payment, the some of... vj^li

[1] A leaf has been cut out of the MS. before this account of disbursements is renewed, but such may have been the state of the book when Henslowe made the entries. The last date was 18th July 1598, a payment in full to Drayton and Dekker for Hannibal and Hermes; and the renewed account begins 30th July 1598, leaving an interval of twelve days, to which the missing leaf may have applied.

[2] Either Henslowe or his scribe was ignorant of the name of the play, and a blank was left for it: this and the next item were subsequently crossed out.

[3] "Hot Anger soon cold" was the name of the play, rather strangely distorted in the orthography. The date of this memorandum is, as nearly as may be, a month before "Benjamin Jonson, bricklayer," (to use Henslowe's words) killed Gabriel Spenser.

| | |
|---|---|
| Lent unto the company, the 19 of aguste 1598, to paye unto Mr Willson, monday, and Deckers, in pte of payment of a boocke called chance medley, the some of iiijli vs, in this maner— Willson, xxxs, cheattell, xxxs, [1] mondye, xxvs, I say ............... ........................... | iiijli vs |
| Lent unto Thomas Dowton, the 21 of aguste 1598, to bye a sewte and a gowne for Vayvode,[2] the some of tene pownde. I saye lent......... | xli |

wittnes Mr WILLSONE.

| | |
|---|---|
| Lent Mr Willsone, the 21 of aguste 1598, in earnest of a Boocke called cattelyne,[3] some of......................................... | xs |
| Lent unto Thomas Dowton, the 22 of aguste 1598, to by divers thinges for vayvode, the some of ......................................... | xxxxvjs |
| Lent unto Thomas Dowton, the 24 of aguste 1598, to bye divers thinges for vayvode, the some of ................................ .......... | xiiijs |
| Pd unto Mr Drayton, the 24 of aguste 1598, in fulle payment of a Boocke called chance medley, some of ................................ | xxxvs |

[1] There is evidently some mistake here, for, according to the first part of the entry, Dekker ought to have been paid, and not Chettle, for "Chance Medley." Drayton was afterwards paid 35*s*. as one of the authors of Chance Medley.

[2] Malone (Shakesp. by Boswell, iii., 320) attributes "Vayvode" to Thomas Downton, the actor, as if he were the author of it, when it is obvious that £10 was only advanced to him "to buy a suit, and a gown" for the play. See Painter's "Pal. of Pleasure," ii., fo. 140, &c., respecting "Vayvode."

[3] The same piece afterwards called "Cateline's Conspiracy:" it was by Wilson and Chettle. It was one of the oldest subjects on our stage, as Gosson had written a tragedy called "Cateline's Conspiracies" before 1579: see Shakesp. Soc. reprint of the School of Abuse, p. 30. Ben Jonson's "Cateline his Conspiracy" was not printed until 1611.

| | | |
|---|---|---|
| Lent unto Robart shaw, the 25 of aguste 1598, to paye the lace manes byll, ij$^{li}$ xvj$^{s}$ vj$^{d}$; and the tayllers byll, xxviij$^{s}$ vj$^{d}$: some is .............. for Vayvode.................... | iiij$^{li}$ | v$^{s}$ |
| Lent unto Harey cheattell, the 26 of aguste 1598, in earneste of a Boocke called cattelanes con-speresey, the some ................................ | | v$^{s}$ |
| Lent unto hary cheattell, the 29 of aguste 1598, at the apoyntment of thomas Dowton, for his playe of Vayvode, the some of ................. | | xx$^{s}$ |
| Lent unto M$^{r}$ Willsone, the 29 of aguste 1598, at the request of hary cheattell, in earneste of cattelyne, the some of............................. | | x$^{s}$ |
| Lent unto the company, the 30 of aguste 1598, to geve in earneste of boocke called worse afeard then hurte,[1] unto M$^{r}$ Drayton and Dickers, the some of ........................... | | l$^{s}$ |
| Lent unto the company, the 4 of aguste 1598, to paye in fulle payment for a Boocke called worse Afeared then hurte, unto M$^{r}$ Drayton and M$^{r}$ Dickers, the some of.................... | | l$^{s}$ |
| Lent unto hary Cheattell, the 8 of aguste 1598, in earneste of a boocke called Brute,[2] the some of ........................................... | | ix$^{s}$ |

[1] Malone (Shakesp. by Boswell, iii., 321) makes this a distinct play, but reference to an entry already inserted on p. 128 shows that "Worse afeard then hurte" was only the second title of Hannibal and Hermes, by Drayton, Dekker, and Wilson. Perhaps the first title was subsequently dropped, and the second title considered more intelligible and attractive.

[2] By a preceding entry, on p. 131, we learn that John Day was Chettle's co-partner in the composition of this drama, which is there called "the Conquest of Brute, with the first Finding of the Bath." Malone mistakenly supposed that John Singer was also a joint author of it, but it only appears that a certain sum was paid to Chettle at his appointment as an actor, but not to Singer as an author.

Lent unto hary cheattell, the 9 of septmbr 1598, in earneste of a Boocke called Brute, at the Apoyntment of Johne Synger, the some of... } xx$^{s}$

Lent unto hary cheattell, the 16 of septembr 1598, in earneste of a Boocke called Brute ... } v$^{s}$

Hary cheattell untell this place owes us viij$^{li}$ ix$^{s}$ dew, all his boockes and Recknynges payd.[1]

Lent unto the company, the 19 of septmbr 1598, in Redy money, a bowt the agrement betwext Langly and them,[2] the some of................. } xxxv$^{li}$

Lent unto the company, the 23 of septmbr 1598, to bye divers thinges for perce of winchester, the some of x$^{li}$, dd unto thomas Dowton. I saye } x$^{li}$

Lent unto thomas Dowton, the 28 of septmbr 1598, to bye divers thinges, for pearce of winchester, the some of........................ } xxxx$^{s}$

Lent unto thomas Dowton, the 29 of septmbr 1598, to bye divers thinges for perce of winchester[3] ........................................ } xij$^{li}$

Lent unto the company, the 29 of septmbr 1598, to bye a boocke of M$^{r}$ Drayton and M$^{r}$ Dickers, called the firste syvell wares in fraunce[4] ...... } vj$^{li}$

[1] By this date Chettle had become still more deeply indebted to "us," meaning, perhaps, Henslowe and Alleyn in partnership: the word "us" may, however, apply to the company generally. By a note on p. 126 it appears that Chettle's debt was then only 30*s*.

[2] The nature of this agreement between Langley and the company is not explained: we have previously been informed (p. 109) that William Birde, or Borne, had been arrested by Langley.

[3] The words, "to fetche home a riche clocke which they had of M$^{r}$ Langley," are erased with the pen in this entry, and the other words substituted. Possibly Langley had agreed to furnish the company with certain apparel, and an entry on the next page refers to the same subject.

[4] Meaning, of course, the First Civil Wars in France.

| | | |
|---|---|---|
| Lent unto the company, the 31 of septmbr 1598, to bye a Boocke of M$^{r}$ Chapman, called the founte of new facianes :[1] pd in pte.............. | iij$^{li}$ | |
| Bowght of M$^{r}$ Jewby, the 28 of septmbr 1598, a blacke vellvet gercken, and a payer of harcoler clothe of sylver hoosse, for....................... | iiij$^{li}$ | |
| Bowght for the company, the 1 of octobr 1598, a whitte satten womanes dublett, and a blacke tynsell valle, for .................................. | | xx$^{s}$ |
| Lent unto the company, the 3 of octobr 1598, to by a boocke of M$^{r}$ Ranckenes,[2] called mulmutius Donwallow, the some of................. | iij$^{li}$ | |
| Lent unto the company, the 4 of octobr 1598, to by a Riche clocke of M$^{r}$ langley, which they had at ther agrement,[3] the some of ........... | xix$^{li}$ | |

[1] Malone (Sh. by Bosw., iii., 321) calls this play "the *Fountain* of new Fashions," and in a subsequent entry Henslowe gives it that name.

[2] At this date Rankins was writing and printing satires, as well as plays, and in 1598 came out a small 8vo., of only 27 leaves, with the following title: "Seaven Satyres, applyed to the weeke, including the worlds ridiculous follyes. True felicity described in the Phœnix. *Maulgre.* Whereunto is annexed the wandring Satyre. By W. Rankins, Gent. Imprinted at London by Edw. Allde, &c. 1598." There was a rage for satire-writing and satire-reading at the time, which led to the productions in this class of Donne, Lodge, Hall, Marston, Rankins, &c. Rankins may be considered inferior to all his rivals, and the most remarkable feature about his satires is, that they are in seven-line stanzas. "True felicity described in the Phœnix" is a pious poem, headed, *Sola felicitas: Christus mihi Phœnix.*

[3] This sum of £19 for even a "rich cloak" seems a large price, recollecting that it was then equal to nearly £100 of our present money. The next entry is also large, but that was for two cloaks: the cost to which the companies sometimes went for apparel in dressing their plays was enormous. See also upon this point the Alleyn Papers, printed by the Shakespeare Society, pp. 11 and 12.

| | | |
|---|---|---|
| Lent unto Thomas Dowton, to feache ij clockes owt of pane, the 2 of novmbr 1597, the some of xij$^{li}$ x$^{s}$: the one clocke was and ashe colerd vellvet embradered with gowld, the other a longe black vellvet clocke layd with sylke lace, which they exsepted into the stock, the 28 of septembr 1598: some .............. | xij$^{li}$ | x$^{s}$ |
| Lent unto thomas Dowton, the 8 of octobr 1598, to bye divers thinges for the playe called the firste sevelle warres of france, the some of ... | vj$^{li}$ | |
| Lent unto Thomas Dowton, the 11 of octobr 1598, to bye divers thinges for the play called the first syvell wares of france, the some of ...... | iiij$^{li}$ | |
| Lent unto the company, the 12 of octobr 1598, to paye unto M$^{r}$ Chapmane, in fulle payment, for his playe called the Fowntayne of new facions .......................................... | | xx$^{s}$ |
| Lent unto the companey, the 12 of octobr 1598, to geve harey cheattell, in pte of payment for his playe called Brutte, some of................. | | x$^{s}$ |
| Payd for the company, the 12 of octobr 1598, unto the lace man, for the playe of Perce of winchester, the some of ......................... | v$^{li}$ | ij$^{s}$ |
| Payd unto M$^{r}$ Drayton and M$^{r}$ Dickers, the 16 of octobr 1598, in pt payment for a Boocke called Connan prince of cornwell,[1] some of ... | | xxx$^{s}$ |
| Pd unto Bradshaw,[2] at the requeste of M$^{r}$ Drayton and M$^{r}$ Dickers, in pte of payment of ther boocke called the Connan prince cornwell, some of ... | | x$^{s}$ |

[1] Malone (Shakesp. by Boswell, iii., 321) gives the date of September 1598 to this play, but we now hear of it first.

[2] Bradshaw was not concerned in the authorship of the play: he was either the messenger who conveyed the money to Drayton and Dekker, or this might be a mode taken by the two poets of paying a private debt.

| | | |
|---|---|---|
| Layde owt for the company, the 18 of octobr 1598, for a Boocke called Brutte, the some of To Harey chettell ................................ | iij$^{li}$ | |
| Layd owt for the companey, the 20 of octobr 1598, unto M$^{r}$ Drayton and M$^{r}$ Dickers, for a Boocke called connan prince of Cornwell, the some of ............................................ | iiij$^{li}$ | |
| Lent unto the company, the 22 of octobr 1598, to paye harey cheattell for his boocke called Brute, in fulle payment, the some of ........ | | l$^{s}$ |
| Lent unto Robart shaw and Jewby, the 23 of octobr 1598, to lend unto M$^{r}$ Chapman one his playe boocke, and ij ectes of a tragedie of bengemens plotte,[1] the some of................. | iij$^{li}$ | |
| Layd owt for the company, the 3 of novmbr 1598, to M$^{r}$ Drayton and M$^{r}$ Dickers, for a Boocke called the second pte of the syvell wares of fraunce,[2] the some of................ | vj$^{li}$ | |

[In the margin, and crossed out, we read as follows:—" Lent H. Cett. v$^{s}$ and ij$^{s}$ and ij$^{s}$ and v$^{s}$ ij$^{d}$ and ij$^{s}$ vj$^{d}$, for to areste one with lord Lester. Lent H. Cet. j$^{s}$ 8$^{d}$."][3]

[1] We possess no farther information respecting this "tragedy of Benjamin's plot." Malone concludes that Benjamin Jonson was intended, and we know of no other person with that Christian name who was connected with the company. We have already seen, under date of 3 Dec., 1597, pp. 106 and 116, that Ben Jonson had shown the plot of a new play to the company; but we may perhaps conclude, from the terms used, that he was to have no coadjutor in it.

[2] This drama must have been the second part of the First Civil Wars of France, which, we have seen, p. 134, was complete on 29th September.

[3] Possibly "H. Cett" means Henry Chettle, and that for some cause or other he had arrested one of the players of the Earl of Leicester, though we hear of no company acting in 1598 under the name of that nobleman. The earldom became extinct ten years before.

| | |
|---|---|
| Lent unto Jube and Thomas Dowton, the 8 of novmbr 1598, to bye divers thinges for the playe called the fownte of new faciones, some | v$^{li}$ |
| Lent unto Thomas Dowton, the 10 of novmbr 1598, to bye a sackbute of marke antoney for[1] | xxxx$^{s}$ |
| Lent unto Robart shawe, the 13 of novmbr 1598, to bye wemenes gownd, and other thinges for the fowntayne of newe faciones, the some of... | vij$^{li}$ |
| Lent unto thomas Dowton, the 14 of novmbr 1598, to bye divers thinges for the playe called the fowntayne of newe faciones, the some of... | v$^{li}$ |
| Lent unto Robart shaw and Thomas Dowton, the 15 of novmbr 1598, to lend to M$^{r}$ Haslett,[2] the some of xx$^{s}$, which W$^{m}$ Whitte hathe geven his word for yt ................................ | xx$^{s}$ |
| Lent unto Robert shaw and Thomas Dowton, the 16 of novmbr 1598, to lend to M$^{r}$ Haslette, agaynest his valtinge, w$^{ch}$ W$^{m}$ Whitte hath geven his word for yt, the some of ........... | xx$^{s}$ |
| Jemes Cranwigge, the 4 of novmbr 1598, playd his callenge in my howsse, and I sholde have hade for my pte xxxx$^{s}$, which the company Rd and oweth yt to me[3] ...................... | xxxx$^{s}$ |

[1] Was "Mark Antony" a nickname for a player who had represented the part, or was the sackbut to be purchased *for* Mark Antony, as a property necessary in the performance of the character? Henslowe affords elsewhere no means of answering the question.

[2] Haslett, as we learn from the next and other entries, was a tumbler, or vaulter, who exhibited at Henslowe's theatre.

[3] Respecting James Cranwidge, some curious information may be found in Mr. Halliwell's Introduction to the Shakespeare Society's reprint of "Tarlton's Jests." He was a fencer, who had put out bills challenging all comers, and had agreed to pay a certain sum for the use of the theatre, 40*s.* of which ought to have gone to Henslowe; but it seems that the company had taken possession of his share as well as of their own.

| | |
|---|---|
| Lent unto Robarte shawe, the 18 of novmbr 1598, to lend unto Mr Dickers, in earneste of a boocke called the 3 pte of the syvell wares of france,[1] some .................................. | xxs |
| Lent unto Robarte shawe, the 18 of novmbr 1598, to lend unto Mr Cheattell, upon the mendynge of the firste pt of Robarte hoode,[2] the some of..... .......... ....................... | xs |
| Lent unto Robert shaw and Jewby, the 19 of novmbr 1598, to bye divers thinges for the playe called the 2 pte of the syvelle wares of france[3]......................... .................. | xli |
| Lent unto Jewby, the 24 of novmbr 1598, to bye divers thinges for the playe called the 2 pte of the syvell wares of france, the some of......... | xli |
| Lente unto Harey Chettell, at the Requeste of Robart Shawe, the 25 of novmbr 1598, in earneste of his comodey called tys no deseayt to deseve the desever—for mendinge of Roben hood for the corte[4].................. ........... | xs |

[1] The succession of new pieces must at this date have been rapid: we have heard of the *second* part of this subject only on the 3rd November, and now we learn, on the 18th of November, that a *third* part of the Civil Wars of France was in preparation.

[2] "The mending of the first part of Robin Hood" means making additions and improvements: the piece so mended was, in all probability, "the Downfal of Robert Earl of Huntington." By another entry, lower down, it appears that the play was one of those which had been selected by the Master of the Revels, &c., for performance before the Queen at Court, and on this account it was to be refurbished, and perhaps provided with a new prologue and epilogue.

[3] So that at this date the *second* part had probably not been acted, though Henslowe had paid money in hand for the *third* part.

[4] These words, "for mending of Robin hood for the Court," are interlined.

| | |
|---|---|
| Lent unto Robart shawe, the 27 of novmbr 1598, to bye a dublett and a payer of hosse of clothe of gowld, layd thick with blacke sylke lace, some of ........................................ | lviij^s |
| Sowld unto the company, the 28 of novmbr 1598, a shorte vellvett clocke, wraght with bugell, and a gearcken of vellvet layd with brade coper sylver lace, for .................. | iiij^li |
| Lent unto the company, the 28 of novmbr 1598, to geve harey cheattell, in earneste of his boocke called tis no desayt to deseave the desever,[1] the some .. .............................. | xx^s |
| Lent unto Robart shawe, the 1 of novmbr 1598,[2] to lend unto M^r Chapman, the some of......... | x^s |
| Lent unto Robarte Shawe, the 6 of desembr 1598, to bye a boocke called ware with owt blowes and love with owt sewte, of Thomas Hawodes,[3] some of ........................................ | iij^li |

[1] Chettle seems to have had no co-partner in the composition of 'Tis no Deceit to deceive the Deceiver, which is first mentioned on the preceding page.

[2] This is an obvious error for 1st December 1598. There is an addition of £88 10*s.* 0*d.* under this item, probably due from the company, but it must refer farther back than the page at the bottom of which it is found, as the sums on that page amount only to £32 8*s.* 0*d.*

[3] We shall see elsewhere that Thomas Heywood became "a covenant servant" to Henslowe for two years, to play only at his house, on 25th March, 1598. He had been a writer for Henslowe a year and a half before he seems to have adopted the profession of an actor, if, under date 14 October 1596, p. 78, we are to understand "Hawode's boocke" to mean a play by him, which is highly probable. Hereafter we shall meet with frequent mention of him. An account of Heywood and his writings, dramatic and undramatic, as far as materials exist, is prefixed to the Shakespeare Society's reprint of his "Apology for Actors," 1612, 4to.

| | | |
|---|---|---|
| Lent unto Same Rowley, the 12 of Desembr 1598, to bye divers thinges for to macke cottes for gyantes[1] in Brutte, the some of ........... | | xxiiij^s |
| Lent unto Richard Jonnes, the 22 of desembr 1598, to bye a basse viall and other instrementes for the companey[2] ...................... | | xxxx^s |
| Lent unto thomas Dowton, the 22 of desembr 1598, to bye a boocke of harey Poorter called the 2 pte of the 2 angrey wemen of abengton[3] | v^li | |
| Pd unto M^r Drayton and M^r Dickers, the 30 of desembr 1598, for a boocke called the 3 pte of the syvell wares of france, the some of...... | v^li | |
| Lent unto M^r Chapman, the 4 of Jenewary 1598, upon iij actes of a tragedie, w^ch thomas Dowton bad me dd hime, the some of, —— called...... | iij^li | |
| Lent unto Robart shawe, the 8 of Jenewary 1598, to paye M^r Chapman in fulle payment for his tragedie,[4] the some of, —— called...... | iij^li | |
| Lent unto Thomas Downton, the xvij of Janewary 1598, to lend unto harey chettell, to paye his charges in the marshallsey,[5] the some of ........................................ | | xxx^s |

[1] Chettle's play, in which, as we learn from this memorandum, giants were introduced. "Same Rowley" was of course Samuel Rowley, the dramatist and actor, a member of the company of the Lord Admiral's players, whose name has already occurred on p. 120.

[2] For music probably between the acts.

[3] Henry Porter had written the comedy of "the Two Angry Women of Abingdon" (printed twice in 1599); and we here see that he followed it up by a second part of the same subject.

[4] Henslowe did not know the name of this tragedy by Chapman: it was doubtless the same piece as that for which he had received £3 for three acts four days before.

[5] Chettle's necessities had, by this date, driven him into the Marshalsea prison, in Southwark, not far from Henslowe's theatre.

Lent unto Thomas Downton, the 20 of Janewary 1598, to lend unto M^r Drayton, in earneste of his playe called W^m longberd,[1] the some of.......................... ................ } iij^li

Lent unto W^m Jube,[2] the 20 of Janewary 1598, to lend M^r Dickers, in earneste of his playe called the first Introducyon of the syvell wares of france,[3] the some of.......................... } iij^li

Pd unto my sonne, Edward Alleyn, the 21 of Janeway, for the playe of Vay vod,[4] for the company, the some of xxxx^s. I saye pd 1598 } xxxx^s

[1] Malone (Shakesp. by Boswell, iii., 320) misread this entry, and called the play William Longsword, instead of "William Longbeard:" he also assigns a wrong date to it. Nevertheless, it is quite clear, on Drayton's own evidence, that he had written a drama called William Lonsword: see p. 95. From the correspondence of dates it may perhaps be set down as Henslowe's error; but Thomas Lodge had printed a novel, in 1593, on the story of William Longbeard, and this play by Drayton might be founded upon it. Lodge's tract bears this title: "The Life and Death of William Long beard, the most famous and witty English Traitor, borne in the City of London. Accompanied with manye other most pleasant and prettie histories: by T. L. of Lincolns Inne, Gent. *Et nugæ seria ducunt.* Printed at London by Rychard Yardley and Peter Short, &c. 1593." 4to, B.L. It is in prose, but interspersed with much poetry; and it contains so many materials adapted to stage representation, that it may appear strange that, in their eagerness to find subjects, it had not yet been taken up by Lodge himself, or some other dramatists of that day.

[2] Probably this Christian name should be Edward, not William: Edward Juby has been frequently spoken of.

[3] The civil wars of France had already, as has been shown (see pp. 134, 137, and 139) furnished three plays to Henslowe's company, and this seems to have been a fourth, in which Dekker took up the story anterior to its commencement by his fellow dramatists.

[4] Alleyn was perhaps the medium of conveying the money to the author of Vayvode.

| | | |
|---|---|---|
| Lent unto Thomas Downton, the 22 of Janewary 1598, to leand unto M$^{r}$ Chapman, in earneste of a boocke called the world rones a whelles,[1] the some of.............................. | iij$^{li}$ | |
| Lent unto Robart Shawe, the 26 of Janewary 1598, to paye Thomas Hawode in full payment for his boocke called Ware without blowes and love withowt stryfe,[2] the some of ........ | | xxxx$^{s}$ |
| Lent unto thomas Downton, the 26 of Janewary 1598, to bye the skyrtes of a womoans gowne of sylver chamlett, the some of ................. | | lv$^{s}$ |
| Lent unto Thomas Downton, the 30 of Jenewary 1598, to descarge Thomas Dickers frome the areaste of my lord Chamberlens men.[3] I saye lent .......... .................................. | iij$^{li}$ | x$^{s}$ |
| Lent unto Thomas Dowton, the 31 of Janewary 1598, to bye tafetie for ij womones gownes, for the ij angrey wemen of abengton,[4] the some of | ix$^{li}$ | |

[1] Malone erroneously places this comedy, "the World runs on Wheels," by George Chapman, under the date of Jan. 1597-8, but it in fact belongs to Jan. 1598-9. The expression was proverbial, and John Taylor published a tract, in 1623, entitled "The World runs on Wheels."

[2] In an earlier entry, on p. 140, this piece, by Thomas Heywood, is called "War without blows, and Love without *suit*."

[3] It is impossible now to ascertain why Dekker had been arrested by the Lord Chamberlain's men — the company to which Shakespeare belonged. Possibly he had received money from them in earnest for a play which he had neglected to write, or, when written, had carried it to Henslowe's theatre. Only ten days before this date he received £3 from Henslowe on account of his First Introduction of the Civil Wars of France.

[4] This must have been the *second* part of the play, already noticed, although not so marked in Henslowe's Diary. See also two memoranda, dated only twelve days afterwards, in both of which the *second* part of the Two Angry Women of Abingdon is referred to.

| | | |
|---|---|---|
| Layd owt for the company, the 1 of febreare 1598, to bye a blacke vellvett gercken, layd thicke with black sylke lace, and a payer of rownd hosse of paynes of sylke, layd with sylver lace, and caneyanes[1] of clothe of sylver, at the requeste of Robarte shawe, the some of ............................................ | iiij li | x s |
| Lent unto harey Porter, the 17 of Janewary 1598, at the request of Richard Alleyn[2] and Wm Birde, the some of ......................... | | xx s |
| Lent unto Thomas Dowton, the 10 of febreary 1598, to bye a boocke of Mr Hewode, called Jonne as good as my ladey,[3] the some of...... | iij li | |
| Lent unto Thomas Dowton and Samwell Redley,[4] the 10 of febreary 1598, to bye a boocke called fryer Fox and gyllen of Branforde, the some of | v li | x s |

[1] See also the word "canyoms," on p. 122, which seems meant for the same part of dress.

[2] Richard Alleyn is not to be confounded with Edward Alleyn, as Steevens confounded them in his note to "the plott of Frederick and Basilea," in Malone's Shakesp. by Boswell, iii., 356.

[3] i.e., "Joan as good as my Lady:" on p. 1, Henslowe spelt Joan *Jonne*. He inserted the name of the comedy after he had made the memorandum of the advance, and partly in the margin of the MS.

[4] "Samuell Redley" is most likely an error for Samuel Rowley. We know of no person of the name of Samuel Redley in connexion with the stage; yet the wonder is how even Henslowe, having often had occasion to mention Samuel Rowley, could make the blunder. The piece here spoken of was some comic performance, in which Friar Fox and the celebrated Julian of Brentford figured. The lady is alluded to by many writers, and a very coarse piece in verse, called "Jyl of Brainfort's Testament," was written by R. Copland, and printed by W. Copland not very long before this date; but, as we have elsewhere remarked (p. 29), the incidents of that drama must have been entirely different from those of the tract, although Julian of Brentford was a character in it.

| | |
|---|---|
| Lent unto Thomas Downton, the 12 of febreary 1598, to paye Mr Hawode, in fulle payment for his boocke called Jonne as good as my Ladey, the some of............................... | ij$^{li}$ |
| Lent unto Thomas Downton, the 12 of febreary 1598, to paye Mr Poorter, in fulle payment for his boocke called the 2 pte of the angry wemen of abington,[1] the some of ........................ | ij$^{li}$ |
| Lent unto Thomas Downton, the 12 of febreary 1598, to bye divers thinges for the playe called the 2 pte of the angrey wemen of abington ... | ij$^{li}$ |
| Lent unto Mr Chapman, the 13 of febreary 1598, in pt of payment of his boocke called the world ronnes on whelles .............................. | xx$^{s}$ |
| Lent unto Samwell Rowley, the 16 of febreary 1598, to lend in pte of payment unto Hary Chettell, upon his boocke of polefemus ......... | xx$^{s}$ |
| Lent unto Thomas Downton, the 27 of febreary 1598, to paye unto harey cheattell, in fulle payment for a playe called Troyes Revenge,[2] with the tragedy of polefeme, the sume of fiftye shellenges; and strocken of his deatte, which he owes unto the company, fiftye shellinges more ........................................ ............. | l$^{s}$ |

[1] In reference to this play, and its first part, Malone made an extract from a subsequent part of Henslowe's Diary, (see the next page) but he misquoted the date by eight years, making it 28th Feb. 1590 instead of 28th Feb. 1598, which in fact, according to our present reckoning, was the spring of 1599. See Malone's Shaksp. by Bosw. iii., 322. Henry Porter is not mentioned by Henslowe until 1597.

[2] Malone (Shaksp. by Bosw., iii., 322), read this entry "*Æneas* Revenge," but is a clear mistake, and probably was the same play as Polyphemus, mentioned in the preceding entry. Chettle was paid 50*s.* in hand, and 50*s.* more were struck off the debt he owed to the company, he having been, as we have before seen, over-paid for plays.

| | | |
|---|---|---|
| Lent unto harey porter, at the Requeste of the company, in earneste of his boocke called ij mery wemen of abenton,[1] the sume of forty shellings; and for the Resayte of that money he gave me his faythfull promysse that I shold have all the boockes which he writte, ether him selfe or with any other, which some was dd the 28 of febreary, 1598. I saye THOMAS DOWNTON, ROBART SHAWE. ......... | | xxxx^s |
| Lent unto Thomas Downton, the 8 of marche 1598, to paye unto the M^r of the Revelles, for the lycensinge of ij playes, the some........... | | xiiij^s |
| Lent unto Harey cheattell, the 4 of marche 1598, in earneste of his boocke, which harey Porter and he is a writinge, the some of, —— called the Spencers[2] ....................... | | x^s |
| Pd unto the M^r of the Revelles, the 18 of marche 1598, for the lysensynge of ij boockes, some of ............................................ | | xiiij^s |
| Pd unto the M^r of the Revelles man, for the lysensynge of a boocke called the 4 Kynges... | | vij^s |
| Lent unto Robart Shawe, the 22 of marche 1598, to paye unto M^r porter, in full paymente of his playe called the Spensers the some of... | v^li | x^s |

[1] "The two merry Women of Abingdon" was probably another name for the second part of "the two angry Women of Abingdon." The conclusion of the entry shows that Henry Porter was in request as a dramatist, and that at this time there existed strong rivalry among the companies acting in London and its vicinity. The arrest of Dekker, at the instance of the Lord Chamberlain's players, p. 143, may perhaps be considered a proof to the same effect.

[2] Malone attributes this play, on the story of the Despencers, to Henry Porter alone, but Henry Chettle was concerned with him in writing it. Marlowe's Edward the Second was printed in 1598, perhaps owing to the success of Porter's and Chettle's play.

Pd unto the Mr of the Revelles man, for the lysenynge of a boocke called Brute grenshillde,[1] the some of .......................................... } vijs

Some 84li. 16s. 00d.[2]

Lent hary chettell the 27 of marche 1598, the some of vs ............... }

Lent unto Jewbe, the 31 of marche 1598, to bye divers thinges for elexander and lodewicke[3] the some of ........................ ........... } vli

Lent unto Harey Porter, at the apoyntment of Thomas Downton, the 7 of aprell 1599, the some of .......................................... } xxs

Lent unto Thomas Downton, to lende unto Mr Dickers and harey cheattell, in earneste of ther boocke called Troyeles and creasse daye,[4] the some of, —— aprell 7 daye 1599 ......... } iijli

Lent unto Thomas Towne and Richard Alleyn, to go to the Corte upon ester even,[5] the some of, —— Aprell 7 daye 1599..................... } xs

[1] It may be doubted whether "Brute Grenshillde" is the same play as the "Brute," previously introduced on p. 133.

[2] This is Henslowe's addition of his advances at the bottom of the page, where the loan of *5s.* to Chettle is thrust into the corner.

[3] On a revival of the play, for it had been produced (see p. 84) on the 14th January 1597.

[4] Malone quotes this remarkable entry (showing that Dekker and Chettle were engaged in April 1599 on a play with the name, and on the subject, adopted by our great dramatist) in Shaksp. by Boswell, iii., 331. Henslowe gets a little nearer the proper spelling of the title in a subsequent memorandum. It seems probable (Shakesp. by Collier, vi., 4) that Shakespeare's Troilus and Cressida was not acted until 1609, and that the entry in the Stationers' Registers of a play with that title, dated 7th Feb. 1602, applies to Dekker's and Chettle's drama.

[5] When, perhaps, there were theatrical performances at Court.

| | | |
|---|---|---|
| Lent unto Thomas Downton, the 9 of Aprell 1599, to bye dyvers thinges, as 4 clothe clockes, and macke up a womones gowne, the some of—For the Spencers .................... | $x^{li}$ | |
| Lent unto the companye, the 11 of aprell 1599, to bye a frenche hoode, the some of ........... | | $x^{s}$ |
| Lent unto Thomas Downton, the 14 of Aprell 1599, to macke divers thinges for the playe of the Spencers, the some of .............. ........ | $xv^{li}$ | |
| Lent unto harey cheattell and Mr Dickers, in pte of payment of ther boocke called Troyelles and cresseda, the 16 of Aprell 1599[1] ......... | | $xx^{s}$ |
| Lent unto the company, the 17 of aprell 1599, to lend unto Edward, my lordes pagge,[2] which was dd unto Robart Shawe, the some of ...... | | $xxx^{s}$ |
| Delyvered unto Thomas Downton boye, Thomas parsones, to bye divers thinges for the playe of the Spencers, the 16 of aprell 1599, the some of[3] ........................................ | $v^{li}$ | |

[1] Malone (Shaksp. by Bosw., iii., 331) by an important error of the press, in connexion with Shakespeare's Troilus and Cressida, misdates this memorandum 16th April 1592.

[2] Meaning, the page of the Earl of Nottingham, Lord Admiral.

[3] After this entry, several leaves have been cut out, and the next ten pages relate to loans to various persons, either to or through Francis Henslowe, upon pledges of every description—plate, jewels, apparel, furniture, &c. The dates are between 16 January, and 11 October 1593. They are in no respect illustrative of the stage or drama of the time, and no poets or actors are named; and the following may be given as sufficient specimens of this portion of the MS.:—

"Lent unto Francis, the 9 of Aprill 1593, upon a remnant of brod clothe, which the Quene gave a mandy Thursday to a poore womon dwellinge in theveng lane, for $x^{s}$.

"Lent unto Francis, the 9 of Aprell 1593, upon a sade greene cloke of goodwiffe Allen, which [she] lyfte in the rome of a remnant of clothe brode,

Hary Cheattell hath strocken of his deate as foloweth, 1598, with the companye.

Pd of his deate in his boocke of polefeme[1] .................. l^s
Pd of his deate in his boocke of the spencers.............. x^s
Pd of his deate in his boocke of plasidas[2] .................. x^s

Antony Jeaffes and the company doth owe unto me for my boye, Jeames Bristo, wages, from the 23 of Aprell 1600; w^ch Robart shawe hath geven his word for the paymente.

Wittnes RICHARD JONNES.
THOMAS TOWNE.

Troyeles and creasseday.[3]

Receved by me, thomas bristo,[4] scietison and uphoulder, the xxix of Januarie 1594, in fulpemente of richarde vickers, the some of iiij^li x^s. I say receved by mee, THOMAS BRISTO.

which the Quene gave on Mandy Thursday to a poore womon dwellinge in theven lane, x^s.

"Lent unto Francis, the 11 of October 1593, upon iiij gowld Ringes, 1 pancey, j mayes, j ringe of a whitte stone, j hoope ringe, for xx^s.

"Lent unto Francis, the 18 of July 1593, upon and owld carpett of turkey worcke, very thicke, for x^s.

"Lent unto Francis, the 10 of Desembr 1593, upon a footmanes cotte of vellvet, with the colysenes [cognisances?] upon them of sylver, xx^s."

[1] This is a confirmation of the memorandum on p. 145, that Chettle had struck 50^s off his debt to the company.

[2] Malone takes no notice of this entry, which shows that Chettle had contrived to make a play out of the dull incidents of the legend of Sir Placidas, upon which John Partridge had written and printed a poem in 1566, 8vo. It is mentioned again afterwards.

[3] This title stands by itself at the top of a page, as if something had been intended to be added which was omitted.

[4] Thomas Bristo, the writer of this note, was perhaps the father of Henslowe's boy, James Bristo, mentioned in the preceding entry.

Lent unto John Haslett, valter, the 27 of marche 1598, in Redey money, the some of tenne shillinges. I saye .................................. } xs

Wittnes PIGGE,[1] and JEMES.

Lent John Haslette, valter, to bye a gearte for his horsse when he tombled[2] .................. } vjd

Lent unto John Haslette, valter, the 7 of Aprell 1599, the some of .................................. } xs

wittnes E. ALLEYN.

Lent unto cheattell, for Sir plasidas, the 9 of Aprell 1599, the some of ........................ } xs

Be it knowen to all men by these presents, that I, Henry Chettle, of London, Stationer,[3] doo ow unto Phelip Hinslow, of the parish of St Saviours, the somme of ixli ixs, on this 22d of october 1598. In witnes whereof I have here under seat my hand.

HENRY CHETTLE.

Wytnesse ROBT. SHAA.

[1] Apparently the nickname of some actor, introduced also into the plot of Frederick and Basilea. Malone conjectured that Pigge, and Pyge, and Pygge, might mean *Psyche*, (Shaksp. by Boswell, iii., 310, 313, 315), which, as Steevens remarked, was not a very happy guess. "Jemes," the other witness to this loan, was most likely Henslowe's boy.

[2] Haslett, who has been before mentioned on p. 138, was no doubt to vault over the horse.

[3] This entry is entirely written by Chettle, who in it calls himself "Stationer:" he had been, at one time, a printer, and writing to Thomas Nash, in 1596, subscribes himself "your old compositor." See "Have with you to Saffron Walden," sign. v, 2 *b*. One work with Chettle's name at the bottom of the title-page is known: it bears date in 1591, and he was then in partnership with W. Hoskins and J. Danter. In 1592 he edited Greene's Groat'sworth of Wit, and followed it by his own Kind-heart's Dream; but neither of them was printed by or for him.

Borrowed of phillip Henchlowe, xx$^{s}$, the vij$^{th}$ of Aprill, anno. dom. 1599.

HENRY PORTER.[1]

| | |
|---|---|
| Lent Thomas Dickers and harey chettell, the 2 of maye 1599, to descarge harey chettell of his A reste from Ingrome,[2] the some of twenty shellyngs, in Redy money: I saye lent xx$^{s}$ ................ | xx$^{s}$ |
| Lent more the same time unto M$^{r}$ Dickers, in earneste of a Boocke called orestes fures[3] ........... | v$^{s}$ |
| Lent unto Frances Henslow, the 15 of desembr 1597, when he went to tack his howsse one the bancksyde, called the uper grown,[4] the some of vj$^{li}$ I saye leant.. ................................ | vj$^{li}$ |

*Heare I begane to Receve the gallereys agayne, which they Receved, begynynge at myhellmas wecke, beinge the* 6 *of octobr* 1599, *as foloweth:*[5]

| | | |
|---|---|---|
| Rd the 6 of octobr 1599 ............................ | v$^{li}$ | iij$^{s}$ |
| Rd the 20 of octobr 1599...................... ...... | iiij$^{li}$ | iij$^{s}$ |

[1] This memorandum is in the handwriting of Henry Porter.

[2] Henry Chettle being again in difficulties, and under arrest, his friend Dekker seems to have interfered with Henslowe in his behalf.

[3] Dekker does not appear to have had any coadjutor in Orestes' Furies.

[4] The Upper Pike Garden is mentioned in the Alleyn Papers, p. 49: perhaps "the upper ground" was near it.

[5] This erased account occupies the whole page, and extends to the 13th July 1600. The company seems not to have performed between the 10th Feb. and the 9th March 1599-1600. Henslowe is very careless in his dates, and makes the 30th March belong to the year 1599, when in fact the year 1600 began five days earlier. See on p. 129 what appears to be the commencement of the same account, but here one item is repeated, and another omitted: here, as there, it is impossible now to ascertain why the receipts were so irregular.

Rd the 27 of octobr 1599 ........ iij$^{li}$ xiiij$^{s}$
Rd the 3 of novmbr 1599 ........ viij$^{li}$ xvj$^{s}$
Rd the 10 of novmbr 1599 ........ vj$^{li}$ ix$^{s}$
Rd the 18 of novmbr 1599 ........ ij$^{li}$ xvij$^{s}$
Rd the 25 of novmbr 1599 ........ vij$^{li}$ iiij$^{s}$
Rd the 1 of Desembr 1599 ........ v$^{li}$ xiij$^{s}$
Rd the 8 of Desembr 1599 ........ iiij$^{li}$
Rd the 16 of Desembr 1599 ........ ij$^{li}$ xvij$^{s}$
Rd the 23 of Desembr 1599 ........ iij$^{li}$ iij$^{s}$
Rd the 30 of Desembr 1599 ........ x$^{li}$ viij$^{s}$
Rd the 6 of Jenewary 1599 ........ ix$^{li}$ ix$^{s}$
Rd the 13 of Janewary 1599 ........ vj$^{li}$ xvj$^{s}$
Rd the 20 of Janewary 1599 ........ iij$^{li}$ ij$^{s}$
Rd the 27 of Janewary 1599 ........ j$^{li}$ xvj$^{s}$
Rd the 3 of febreary 1599 ........ vij$^{li}$ xiiij$^{s}$
Rd the 10 of febreary 1599 ........ vij$^{li}$ xiij$^{s}$
Rd the 9 of marche 1599 ........ iij$^{li}$ xiij$^{s}$
Rd the 16 of marche 1599 ........ vj$^{li}$
Rd the 23 of marche 1599 ........ iiij$^{li}$ xvij$^{s}$
Rd the 30 of marche 1599 ........ xj$^{li}$ xiiij$^{s}$
Rd the 6 of Aprell 1600 ........ vj$^{li}$ ij$^{s}$
Rd the 14 of Aprell 1600 ........ v$^{li}$ x$^{s}$
Rd the 21 of aprell 1600 ........ vj$^{li}$ xiiij$^{s}$
Rd the 29 of aprell 1600 ........ iiij$^{li}$ x$^{s}$
Rd the 4 of maye 1600 ........ iiij$^{li}$ vij$^{s}$
Rd the 11 of maye 1600 ........ iiij$^{li}$ xvj$^{s}$
Rd the 18 of maye 1600 ........ xij$^{li}$ iiij$^{s}$
Rd the 25 of maye 1600 ........ iiij$^{li}$ vij$^{s}$
Rd the 1 of June 1600 ........ iiij$^{li}$ xvij$^{s}$
Rd the 8 of June 1600 ........ vj$^{li}$ xj$^{s}$
Rd the 15 of June 1600 ........ iij$^{li}$ xiij$^{s}$
Rd the 22 of June 1600 ........ vij$^{li}$ ij$^{s}$
Rd the j of Julye 1600 ........ v$^{li}$ viij$^{s}$
Rd the 6 of Julye 1600 ........ iiij$^{li}$ xij$^{s}$
Rd the 13 of Julye 1600 ........ iiij$^{li}$ vj$^{s}$

*Layde owt for the company of my lord of Notingame men, frome the* 26 *of maye* 1599, *as foloweth:* 1599 *:* [1]

| | | |
|---|---|---|
| Pd unto the lace man, at the apoyntment of the company, the 26 of maye 1599, in pte of payment to hime for lace, the some of ........... | v$^{li}$ | |
| Lent unto M$^{r}$ Dickers and M$^{r}$ Chettell, the 26 of maye 1599, in earneste of a Boocke called the tragedie of Agamemnon,[2] the some of ... | | xxx$^{s}$ |
| Lent unto Robarte Shawe, the 30 of maye, 1599, in full paymente of the Boocke called the tragedie of Agamemnone, the some of to M$^{r}$ Dickers and harey chettell .............. | iij$^{li}$ | v$^{s}$ |
| Pd unto the M$^{r}$ of the Revelles man, for lycensynge of a Boocke called the tragedie of agamemnon, the 3 of June 1599[3].............. | | vij$^{s}$ |
| Pd unto the lace man, the 2 of June 1599, in pte of payment to hime for coper lace, the some of............................................ .. | v$^{li}$ | |
| Lent unto Robart shawe, the 2 of June 1599, to paye unto M$^{r}$ Chapman, for his Boocke called the worlde runes a whelles, some of ........... | | xx$^{s}$ |
| Pd unto the lace man, the 8 of June 1599, at the apoyntment of the company, in pt of payment to hime for coper lace, some of ........ | v$^{li}$ | |
| Lent unto W$^{m}$ Borne and Jewby, the 21 of June 1599, to lend unto M$^{r}$ Chapman upon his Boocke called the world ronnes a whelles, the some of ............................................ | | xxxx$^{s}$ |

[1] It will be seen on p. 148 that the last account of this kind terminated on 16 April 1599, leaving therefore an interval of more than a month.

[2] This title is interlined over the words "Troylles and creseda."

[3] We may perhaps conclude that the tragedy was represented for the first time very soon after it had been so licensed.

| | |
|---|---|
| Lent unto thomas Dowton, the 2 of July 1599, to paye Mr Chapman, in full paymente for his boocke called the world rones a whelles, and now all foolles, but the foolle,[1] some of......... | xxxs |
| Lent thomas Dowton, the 5 of Julye 1599, to bye coper lace, the some of .................... | xijs 4d |
| Lent unto Thomas Downton, the 13 of July 1599, to bye enstrumentes[2] for the company, the some of .................................. | xxxs |
| Lent unto Samewell Rowley and Thomas Downton, the 15 of Julye 1599, to bye a Boocke of Thomas Dickers, called the gentle Craft,[3] the some of ......... ................................ ...... | iijli |
| Lent unto Thomas Downton, the 17 of Julye 1599, to lend unto Mr Chapman, in earneste of a pastrall tragedie,[4] the some of ........... | xxxxs |
| Lent unto Thomas Deckyers, the 24 of July 1599, at the Requeste of Samuell Rowly and Thomas Downton, in earneste of a Boocke called stepmothers tragedy[5] ................................ | xs |

[1] In this memorandum, we seem to have a notice of three separate works by Chapman; the World runs on Wheels, All Fools, and The Fool. Of the two last, no mention is made by Malone, but All Fools was printed in 1605, and is reprinted in Dodsley's Old Plays, last edit., vol. iv., p. 102. It may be doubted whether Henslowe does not mean that the title of All Fools was substituted for the World runs on Wheels.

[2] Musical instruments. We have had money advanced for the same purpose before: see p. 141.

[3] This play was first printed anonymously in 1600, under the title of The Shoemaker's Holiday, or The Gentle Craft. Henslowe interlined the title, not knowing it when he first made the memorandum of the payment of the money.

[4] Malone overlooked this entry regarding Chapman's Pastoral Tragedy.

[5] Dekker and Chettle were joint authors of this play, but Malone, vol. iii., p. 323, erroneously assigns it to Chettle only.

| | |
|---|---|
| Lent unto Robart Shawe, the 1 of aguste 1599, to paye M^r^ Deckers for a boocke called beare a braine,[1] the some of xxxx^s^, in fulle payment: lent unto M^r^ Deckers, at that time, xx^s^, so all is ........ | iij^li^ |
| Lent unto W^m^ Borne, alles birde, the 10 of aguste 1599, to lend unto Bengemyne Johnsone and thomas Deckers, in earneste of ther boocke they are a writtinge, called pagge of plimothe,[2] the some ........ | xxxx^s^ |
| Lent unto Thomas Downton, the 20 of aguste 1599, to lend unto Hawghton, in earnest of a Boocke called the poore manes paradice, the some of ........ | xiij^s^ |
| Lent unto Harey Chettell and Th. D.[3] the 23 of aguste 1599, in earneste of his playe called the stepmothers tragedie, the some of ........ | xx^s^ |
| Lent unto Thomas Downton, the 25 of aguste 1599, to pay Thomas Hawton[4] for his Boocke called the poore manes paradice, the some of | xvij^s^ |
| Lent unto W^m^ Birde, Thomas Downton, and Jewbey, the 25 of aguste 1599, to paye harye Chettell for his Boocke called the stepmothers tragedie, some ........ ........ | xx^s^ |

[1] Interlined above "Better latte then never," which is struck through.

[2] Malone calls this piece Peg of Plymouth, and (vol. iii., p. 323), assigns the authorship of it to Bird, Downton, and Juby, who were only actors in it: elsewhere, however, (p. 334) he informs us that Ben Jonson was concerned in it with Dekker. On p. 105 will be seen an entry of Dec. 1597, regarding a drama on the same subject.

[3] Th. D. no doubt stands for Thomas Dekker. For "his play" we should of course read *their* play.

[4] This author's name was William, and not Thomas Haughton: it is interlined, Henslowe having first written H. Chettle. In the next item but one Henslowe calls Edward Juby William Jube.

| | |
|---|---|
| Lent unto W[m] Birde, Thomas Dowton, W[m] Jube, the 2 of Septembr 1599, to paye in fulle payment for a Boocke called the lamentable tragedy of Pagge of plemoth, the some of......... | vj[li] |
| Lent unto Thomas Downton, the 3 of septmbr 1599, to lend unto Thomas Deckers, Bengemen Johnson, hary Chettell, and other Jentellman, in earneste of a playe calld Robart the second, Kinge of Scottes tragedie,[1] the some of.............................................. | xxxx[s] |
| Lent unto Jewbey and thomas towne, the 12 of septmbr 1599, to bye wemen gownes for Page of plemoth, the some of.......................... | x[li] |
| Lent unto Samwell Rowley and Robart shawe, the 15 of septmbr 1599, to lend in earneste of a Boocke called the Scottes tragedi, unto Thomas Dickers and Harey chettell, the some of.............................................. | xx[s] |
| Lent hary chettell, the 16 of septmbr 1599, in earneste of a Boocke called the scottes tragedie, the some of.......................................... | x[s] |
| Lent unto W[m] Borne, the 27 of Septmbr 1599, to lend unto Bengemen Johnsone, in earneste of a Boocke called the scottes tragedie, the some of ........................................ | xx[s] |
| Lent unto W[m] Borne, the 28 of septembr 1599, to lend unto M[r] maxton, the new poete (M[r] Mastone),[2] in earneste of a Boocke called ——, the some of ............................. | xxxx[s] |

[1] Malone quotes this item (Shaksp. by Boswell, iii., 334), but he puts "gentleman" in the plural, as if four poets were not enough for one tragedy. Henslowe did not know the name of the "other gentleman" concerned with Dekker, Jonson, and Chettle.

[2] The name, "Mr. Mastone," is interlined in a different hand, in order to correct the misspelling of "Maxton;" but neither was right, "the

Lent unto the littell tayller, the 4 of octobr 1599, to bye divers for the play of polefeme, the some of.......................................... } viij$^s$

The 13$^{th}$ of october 1599, Lent unto Thomas Downton, for the Booke of Trystram de Lyons[1] .......................................... } 3$^{li}$

Reckned with the company of my lorde the Earlle of notingames men to this place, and I have layd owt for them the some of vj hunderd and thirtie two powndes, and they have payd unto me of this deatte iij hunderd and fiftie and eyghte powndes, to this daye, being the 13 of octobr 1599.

Lent H. chettell, some of v$^s$
Lent H chettell, some v$^s$
Lent H chettell, some v$^s$
Lent iij$^s$ Lent ij$^s$.[2]

This 14$^{th}$ o October 1599.

Receaved by me Robt Shaa, of phillip Henslowe, to paye H. Chettle, in full paiment of a booke called the stepmothers tragedy, for the use of the company, iiij$^{li}$ I say Receaved[3] ........ } 4$^{li}$

new poet" being, no doubt, the celebrated John Marston. The name of his contribution to Henslowe's company is nowhere mentioned: his Antonio and Mellida and Antonio's Revenge were printed in 1602, and it might be one of them. As far as we know, he commenced his career in 1598, when his "Metamorphosis of Pigmalion's Image and certain Satyres" came out: his "Scourge of Villany" appeared in the same year, and both were so popular that they were twice reprinted in 1599. This last fact is not generally known.

[1] Malone takes no notice of this play of Tristram de Lyons: the note is entirely in Downton's handwriting.

[2] This entry of small advances to Chettle is inserted in the margin of the MS., and is without date.

[3] This memorandum is in Shaw's handwriting.

This 16 of october 99

| | |
|---|---|
| Receved by me, Thomas Downton, of phillip Henslow, to pay Mr Monday, Mr Drayton, and Mr Wilson and Hathway, for the first pte of the lyfe of Sr Jhon Ouldcasstell, and in earnest of the second pte,[1] for the use of the compayny, ten pownd, I say receved ........ | 10li |
| Receved by me, Samuell Rowlye, of phyllyp Henchloe, for Harrye chettell, in earneste of the playe of patient Gryssell, for the use of the comepanye[2]..... .................................. | xxs |
| Lent unto Robart shaw, the 1 of novmbr 1599, to lent unto Mr Willsones, the some of........ | xs |
| Lent unto Robart shaw, the 1 of novmbr 1599, to lend unto Wm Harton, in earneste of a Boocke called the tragedie of John Cox, some of. ............................................ | xxs |
| Receved of Mr Hinchloe, for Mr Mundaye and the Reste of the poets, at the playnge of Sr John Oldcastell, the ferste tyme. As a gefte[3]...... | xs |

[1] This entry (which is quoted by Malone, iii. 329, in proof that Shakespeare had nothing to do with the piece as printed in 1600) is entirely in the handwriting of Downton, the actor, who received the money for Monday, Drayton, Wilson, and Hathway. At a subsequent date, we shall find that Dekker was paid for "additions to Oldcastle." It deserves remark that there are copies of the play, printed in 1600, with and without the name of Shakespeare on the title-page.

[2] In the handwriting of Rowley. Haughton and Dekker were also (as appears by other memoranda) concerned in it: it was printed anonymously in 1603, and has been reprinted by the Shakespeare Society.

[3] Although this entry (by Samuel Rowley) is without date, yet, placed where it is, there can be little doubt that the first part of Sir John Oldcastle was played for the first time between the 1st and the 8th of Nov. 1599. The success seems to have been so great as to induce the old careful manager to make the four poets a present of half-a-crown each.

Receaved of Mr Ph. Hinchlow, by a note under the hand of Mr Rob. Shaw, in full payment, for the second pt of Henrye Richmond,[1] sold to him and his Companye, the some of eight pownds current money, the viijth daye of november 1599 .................................. viijli

By me R. WILSON.

Lent unto Wm Harton and John Daye, at the Apoyntment of Thomas Dowton, in earnest of a Boocke called the tragedie of Cox of collinster, the some of ................. ........ xxs

The ix of november.

Receved of Phillipp Hinchlow, to pay Thomas Deckker, in earnest of a booke cald the hole history of Fortunatus,[2] xxxxs: by me Thomas Downton.......................................... xxxxs

Lent unto Thomas Dowton, the 10 of novmbr 1599, to lend unto harey chettell, in earneste of his boocke called ——, the some of tenne shellenges. I saye.................................. xs

The xiiijth of november 1599.

Receved of Mr Phillipp Hinchlow, to pay to William hauton and Jhon Day, for the tragedy of Cox of Collomton,[3] the som of three pownd.—received in full ................. iijli

[1] We know nothing of any *first part* of Henry Richmond.

[2] This play must have been some new version of the story of Fortunatus, for we have already seen (p. 64) that the first part of a play, with that title, had been acted in 1595. Possibly the earlier drama was not by Dekker, as we have supposed, or that this "whole history of Fortunatus" is to be considered the *second* part of the former play. It appears that Dekker received £6 for the play, and afterwards £3 more for altering it, to adapt it for performance at Court. It was printed in 1600.

[3] Malone calls this play "John Cox of Colmiston," and just above we see the place spelt Collinster, but the true title of it was "John Cox of

| | | |
|---|---|---|
| Lent unto W^m Harton, the 21 of novmbr, in earneste of his boocke called Merrie,[1] the some of ........................................... | | x^s |
| Lent unto Thomas Dickers, the 24 of novmbr 1599, in earneste of his Boocke called the wholle historye of fortewnatus, the some of... | iij^li | |
| Wittnes JOHN SHAA.[2] | | |
| Lent unto W^m Harton and John Daye, the 27 of novmbr 1599, in earneste of a tragedie called Mereie, the some of .................... | | xx^s |
| as may apere. | | |
| Lent unto harey chettell, the 27 of novmbr 1599, in earneste of a Boocke, called the tragedie of orphenes,[3] the some of ——, as may apere ... | | x^s |
| Receaved of M^r Henslowe, this xxx^th of novembr 1599, to pay M^r Deckers, in fulle payment for his booke of fortunatus ........................ | | xx^s |
| By me ROBT. SHAA.[4] | | |
| Receaved of M^r Henshlow, this xxxi^st of novem 1599, for the use of the Com., ten pownd for wemens gowns.............................. ...... | x^li | |
| By me THOMAS DOWNTON. | | |

Collumpton," and it related to a murder committed there. It has been already introduced on p. 95, under date of 1 Nov. 1599.

[1] Afterwards called "the Tragedy of Merry." See also pp. 92 and 93.

[2] Probably related to Robert Shaa, or Shaw, whose name has frequently occurred. The signature only was written by John Shaa.

[3] "The tragedy of Orphans" is inserted by Malone, in his extracts from Henslowe's Diary, under the date of Sept. 1601, but this is an error. It has been before noticed on p. 93, and possibly it was founded on the popular story of the Children in the Wood.

[4] In this part of the MS. the entries were not unfrequently made by the actors themselves, and not by Henslowe or the scribe he sometimes employed: such is the case in the present instance.

| | | |
|---|---|---|
| Lent unto Thomas Dickers, at the apoyntment of Robart shawe, the 31 of novmbr 1599, which I borowed of M$^r$ greffen,[1] for the altrenge of the boocke of the wholl history of fortewnatus, the some of........................ | | xx$^s$ |
| Lent unto W$^m$ Hawton and John Day, the 5 of Desembr 1599, in earneste of ther boocke called Mereye, at the apoyntment of Robart shawe, the some of——, as may apere......... | | xx$^s$ |
| Lent unto John Daye, the 6 of desembr 1599, in earneste of a boocke called merye, as may apere ............................................. | | x$^s$ |
| Pd unto W$^m$ Hawghton and John Daye, the 6 of Desembr 1599, in full payment of ther boocke called the tragedie of merie, the some of...... | | xxxx$^s$ |
| Receved of M$^r$ Hinchlow, for the use of the companye, x$^{li}$, for to by things for Fortunatus ............................................... | x$^{li}$ | |

By me THOMAS DOWNTON.

| | |
|---|---|
| Pd unto M$^r$ Deckers, the 12 of Desembr 1599, for the eande of Fortewnatus, for the corte, at the apoyntment of Robarte shaw, the some of | xxxx$^s$ |
| Lent unto harey chettell and W$^m$ Harton, the 13 of Desembr 1599, in earneste of his Boocke called arceadian virgen,[2] the some of........... | x$^s$ |
| Lent unto harey chettell and W$^m$ Harton, the 17 of Desembr 1599, in earneste of ther boocke called arkedian virgen, the some of ........... | v$^s$ |

[1] We might infer from this entry that there had been so considerable a drain upon Henslowe's purse, that he was obliged to borrow £1, to be paid to Dekker for *altering* Fortunatus: "the whole history" may therefore have been an improvement of the old play of 1595.

[2] Henslowe no doubt meant some piece called The Arcadian Virgin, of which we hear on no other authority.

| | | |
|---|---|---|
| Lent unto thomas Dickkers, harey chettell, W^m^ harton, in earneste of a Boocke called patient Grissell, at the apointment of Robart shawe, by his letter, the some of three powads, the 19 of desembr 1599 .............................. | iij^li^ | |
| Receaved of M^r^ Henshlowe, to pay the taylor xxv^s^, and to the M^r^ of the Revells man xiiij^s^ for the lycensynge of 2 bookes .................. | | xxxix^s^ |

by me ROBT SHAA.

| | |
|---|---|
| Receved of M^r^ Henchlow, for the use of the company, to pay M^r^ Drayton for the second pte of S^r^ Jhon Ouldcasell, foure pownd: I say receved ............. ............................ .. | iiij^li^ |

ꝑ me THOMAS DOWNTON.[1]

| | |
|---|---|
| Receaved of M^r^ Henshlowe, the 26^th^ of decembr 1599, to pay Tho. Deckers, H. Chettle, and Will Hawton, for pacient Grissill, vj^li^ I say Receaved | vj^li^ |

by me ROBT SHAA.[2]

| | | |
|---|---|---|
| Lent unto thomas Deckers, the 28 of desembr 1599, in earneste of a playe called pacyent gresell, the some of........ ...................... | | v^s^ |
| Lent unto W^m^ Harton, the 29 of Desembr 1599, in earneste of patient Gresell, some of........ | | v^s^ |
| Receaved this 19^th^ of January 1599, in behalfe of the Company, to pay the Laceman v^li^: I say Receaved ...................................... | v^li^ | |

ROBT. SHAA.

[1] Quoted by Malone in Shakesp. by Boswell, iii., 329. On the 16th October 1599 (p. 158), we have had a previous entry of money paid upon account for this second part of Sir John Oldcastle.

[2] In the whole, it seems that Henslowe paid the unusually large sum of £10 10*s*. 0*d*. for Patient Grissil.

| | |
|---|---|
| Lent unto John Daye, the 10 of Jeneware 1599, in earneste of his boocke called the etalyan tragedie of[1] the some of .............. | xxxxˢ |
| At the apoyntment of Robarte shawe. | |
| Lent unto mihell Drayton, antony mondaye, Mʳ Hathwaye, and Mʳ Willsone, at the apoyntment of Thomas Downton, in earneste of a playe Boocke called Owen teder,[2] the some of | iiijˡⁱ |
| Pd unto the Mʳ of the Revells man, for lycensynge of a Boocke called Beches tragedie,[3] the some of.................................. | vijˢ |
| Lent unto Thomas towne, the 18 of Janewary 1599, to lend Thomas Dickers, in earneste of a playe Boocke called trewghts suplication to candelighte,[4] some of, as may apere ........... | xxˢ |
| Receaved of Mʳ Henshlowe, the 26ᵗʰ of January 1599, xxˢ, to geve unto the tayler to buy a grey gowne for gryssell,[5] I say Receaved...... | xxˢ |
| by me ROBT. SHAA. | |

[1] A blank was left by Henslowe for the name of this Italian tragedy, which he did not afterwards fill up.

[2] No doubt Owen Tudor, as Malone prints the title.

[3] Beches, or Beech's tragedy must have been the same as the tragedy of Thomas Merry, previously introduced. Beech was a London merchant, who was murdered by his servant Merry.

[4] Henslowe means "Truth's Supplication to Candle-light." See another entry on p. 95, where the title is properly spelt.

[5] The gown in which she was dressed in the earlier scenes of the play, and in which the Marquis, before she is sent back to her father, has her re-clad:—

> "Disrobe her of these rich habiliments;
> Take down her hat, her pitcher, and her gown,
> And as she came to me in beggary,
> So drive her to her father's" &c.
>
> *Patient Grissil, Shakesp. Soc. repr. p.* 55.

| | |
|---|---|
| Pd unto the Lace man, the 28 of Janewary 1599, at the apoyntment of Robart shawe and Thomas Downton, the some of ........... | iij[li] |
| Lent unto Thomas Dickers, at the apoyntment of the company, the 30 of Janewary 1599, in erneste of a Boocke called trewth suplication to candelithe ........................................ | xx[s] |

Rd by W[m] Harton for hime.

| | |
|---|---|
| Lent unto the company, the 6 of febreary 1599, for to bye a drome, to go into the countrye[1] ........................................ | vj[s] vj[d] |
| Receaved of M[r] Henshlowe, this 7[th] of febreary 1599, the some of xxij[s], to buy 2 trumpettes ... ........................ ................ | xxij[s] |

ROBT. SHAA.

| | |
|---|---|
| Pd unto the laceman, the 9 of febreary 1599, at the apoyntment of the company, the some of.......................................... | iij[li] |
| Lent unto the company, the 9 of Febreary 1599, to paye the cootchman, Symes, the some of ........................................ | iij[li] |
| Lent unto me, W. Birde, the 9 of februarye, to paye for a new booke, to Will Boyle,[2] cald Jugurth, xxx[s], w[ch] if you dislike Ile repaye it backe ........................................ | xxx[s] |

[1] Probably, the company made an expedition into the provinces, and for this purpose required a drum, and the two trumpets mentioned in the next entry, which were often beaten and blown to give notice of their arrival in any town where they intended to perform. Lower down, there is a payment of £3 on the 9th Feb. to a coachman.

[2] The name of William Boyle has not occurred before; and as it is not afterwards mentioned by Henslowe, we may perhaps infer that he "disliked" the piece, and that W. Birde (who wrote the entry) was obliged to refund the money.

| | | |
|---|---|---|
| Lent unto Thomas Dowton, 10 of febrearye 1599, for the companye to geve unto father ogell, and other thinges ................................ | | x[s] |
| Sence we left playinge.—Layd owt for the company, the 13 of febrearye 1599, for a boocke called the Spaneshe Mores tragedie,[1] unto Thomas Deckers, W[m] Harton, John Daye, in pte of payment, the some of .................... | iij[li] | |
| Layd owt for the company, the 16 of febrearye 1599, in earnest of a Boocke called Damon and Pethyus,[2] as may apere: some is ........ to hary chettell. | | xx[s] |
| Receavd of M[r] Hinchlow, the 1 of march, to paye to Harry chettell, Thomas Decker, William hawton, and Jhon Daye, for a boocke calld the 7 wise M[rs],[3] the some of.................... | | xl[s] |

W. BIRDE.

[1] i.e., "The Spanish Moors Tragedy," which Malone miscals "the Spanish Morris." (Shaksp. by Bosw., iii., 324.) The error is the more important as it is most likely the very piece of which a Spanish Moor is the hero, and which was printed in 1657 under the title of "Lust's Dominion," and then falsely attributed to Marlowe. *Vide* Hist. Engl. Dram. Poetry and the Stage, iii., 96; and Dodsley's Old Plays, ii., 311, last edition. The historical events in Spain to which Lust's Dominion relates did not happen until some years after the death of Marlowe, and this fact was pointed out as long since as the year 1825; but it has nevertheless been absurdly included in the collected editions of the works of Marlowe. See Collier's Shakespeare, iv., 98.

[2] Richard Edwards wrote a play on the story of Damon and Pythias, which was printed in 1582, if not earlier, and included in Dodsley's Old Plays, i., 177, last edit. This might be a new piece, by Henry Chettle, on the same incidents, or an alteration of the older play.

[3] By subsequent entries (not, like the present, in Birde's handwriting), it will be seen that Henslowe advanced no less than £38 for taffaty, satin, &c., for producing the play of the Seven Wise Masters. This sum was equal to not much less than £200 of our present money.

| | |
|---|---|
| Lent unto Samewell Rowley, the 8 of marche 1599, to paye unto Harey chettell and John Daye, in fulle payment of a boocke called the vij wisse masters, the some of ................. | l^s |

SAMUELL ROWLYE.

| | |
|---|---|
| Lent unto hary chettell, the 2 of marche 1599, in earneste of a boocke called the 7 wisse masters, the some of ............................ | xxx^s |
| Lent unto W^m Birde, the 10 of marche 1599, to geve harey chettell, in earneste of his Boocke called Damon and pethias, the some of | xxvj^s |
| Lent unto Robarte shaw, the 10 of marche 1599, to lend W^m Harton, to releace hime owt of the clyncke,[1] the some of ...................... | x^s |
| Dd unto the littell tayller, at the apoyntment of Robart Shawe, the 12 of marche 1599, to macke thinges for the 2 pte of owld castell,[2] some of | xxx^s |
| Lent unto W^m Harton, the 18 of marche 1599, in earneste of a Booke called ferex and porex,[3] the some of.......................................... | xx^s |

[1] At this date, William Haughton was confined in the Clink prison, Southwark. He had most likely got into some scrape, as the Clink was not a prison for debtors, but, to use Stow's words (Survey., Edit. Thoms, p. 151), "for such as should brabble, fray or break the peace" on the Bankside. The Rose theatre was situated in what was called the Liberty of the Clink, and Henslowe and Alleyn (until the removal of the latter to Dulwich) resided in the same district.

[2] i.e., The second part of the play of Sir John Oldcastle. See pp. 158, 162.

[3] Here we see Haughton resorting to old plays. Lord Buckhurst and Thomas Norton, as is well known, were the authors of an early drama under the title of Ferrex and Porrex, which was called the Tragedy of Gorboduc in the first edition of 1565. From this very rare impression it is about to be reprinted by the Shakespeare Society.

Lent unto Robart Shaw, the 18 of marche 1599, to geve unto the printer, to staye the printing of patient gresell,[1] the some of.................. } xxxx^s

by me, ROBT. SHAA.

Lent unto W^m Harton, the 25 of marche 1599, in earneste of his Boocke called ferex and porexe, the some of ............................. } v^s

Receaved of M^r Henslowe, to lay out for the play of the 7 wise M^rs, in taffataes and sattyns, the some of........................................ } xx^li

In behalfe of the Companey: by me, ROBT. SHAA.

Receaved more of M^r Henshlowe, to lay out for the play of the 7 wise Maisters, in behalfe of the Companey .................................... } x^li

Receaved more of M^r Henshlowe, to lay out for the play of the 7 wyse Maisters, in behalfe of the Company ....................................... } viij^li

By me, ROBT. SHAA.

Lent unto Robart Shaw, the 2 of aprell 1600, for to by a Robe for Tyme,[2] some of ......... } xxxx^s

[1] No doubt it was thought that the printing of Patient Grissill would be injurious to the receipts of the theatre: a printer, who had obtained a copy of it, in March 1599, was therefore to be induced to relinquish the design of publishing the play by a present of 40*s*. His name is not given; but when the comedy came out in 1603 it was "imprinted for Henry Rocket." See the Shakesp. Soc. reprint. This single fact, without adverting to others, will account for the very few plays that have come down to us in a printed form, compared with the immense number written and irretrievably lost.

[2] Time had therefore been introduced upon the stage (perhaps as the Chorus) by some author anterior to Shakespeare, supposing the Winter's Tale to be one of his later plays, as there is little doubt it was.

| | | |
|---|---|---|
| Lent W[m] Harton, at the apoyntment of Robarte shawe, the 3 of marche 1600, in earneste of a boocke called ferex and porex, the some of ... | | vij[s] |
| Receaved of M[r] Henshlowe, in behalfe of the Company, to pay Will Haulton, in full payment of his play of Ferrex and Porrex, iij[li] iij[s] By me, ROBT SHAA ........................... | iij[li] | iij[s] |
| Receaved of M[r] Henshlowe, to pay for x lb of Copper lace, in behalfe of the Company. By me, ROBT SHAA[1] ........................... | | xxxx[s] |
| Pd unto the sylke man, the 13 of aprell 1600, at the apoyntment of Robart shawe, forty shellings. I say lent ........................... | | xxxx[s] |
| Lent unto W[m] Harton, the 16 of aprell 1600, in earneste of a boocke called the Ingleshe fegetives, the some of ........................... | | x[s] |

W. HAUGHTON.

| | | |
|---|---|---|
| Item, received more of M[r] Henchelowe, in earnest of the englishe fugitives, on the 24[th] of Aprill, by me received ........................... | | 20[s] |

W. HAUGHTON.[2]

| | | |
|---|---|---|
| Lent unto harey chettell, the 26 of aprell 1600, in pte payment of a Boocke called Damon and pethias, at the apoyntment of Robart Shawe, the some of........................... | | xxx[s] |

HENRY CHETTLE.[3]

[1] The memoranda signed by Shaw are always in his handwriting in this part of the MS.

[2] This entry is in Haughton's handwriting, and that above is signed by him. We may guess that the play was on the story of the Duchess of Suffolk, afterwards dramatised by Drue, and printed in 1631: it was also the subject of a well-known ballad.

[3] Chettle's own signature, but the entry is by Henslowe.

| | |
|---|---|
| Lent unto the Company, to goo to Winswarth,[1] to the installinge, the 27 of aprell 1600 ...... | l[s] |
| Receaved of M[r] Henshlowe, in behalfe of the Company, to geve Tho. Deckers and Jhon Day, in earnest of a booke called The golden Ass, and Cupid and Psiches[2] ................. | xxx[s] |

By me, ROBT SHAA.

| | |
|---|---|
| Pd to Harry Chettle, in full payment of vj[li] for his booke of Damon and Pithias, xxxxiiij[s] ... | xxxxiiij[s] |
| Receaved by me, Henry Chettle, of M[r] Henshlowe, in earnest of a booke called the Wooinge of Death[3] ........................................ | xx[s] |

By me, HENRY CHETTLE.

| | |
|---|---|
| Pd, at the apoyntment of Robart Shawe, to one for coper lace, the 6 of maye 1600, some of ... | viij[s] |
| Lent unto Richard Alleyne, the 6 of maye 1600, to lende unto hary cheattell, the some of...... | v[s] |
| Lent unto W[m] Harton, the 6 of marche 1600, in earneste of a Boocke which he wold calle the Devell and his dame[4] ...................... | v[s] |
| Pd for lycencynge of a Boocke to the M[r] of the Revelles, called ferex and porex .............. | vij[s] |

[1] No doubt Henslowe's scribe, who wrote this memorandum, meant Windsor, by Winswarth, and that the company had been called upon to perform there during an installation.

[2] "The xj Bookes of the Golden Asse" of Apuleius had been translated as early as 1566 by W. Adlington, and often reprinted.

[3] This note regarding the Wooing of Death was written by Shaw and signed by Chettle.

[4] This entry has been struck out, but is still legible. Possibly Haughton never meant to write any piece under the title of the Devil and his Dam, but, by pretending that he did, he persuaded Henslowe to lend him *5s*.

Lent, at the apoyntment of Robart shawe, to thomas Deckers, and John Daye, and harye chetell, the 10 of maye 1600, in pte payment of a Booke called the gowlden asse, cupid and siches,[1] some of.................................. } iij^li

By JOHN DAY, to the use of TH. DEKKER, HARRY CHETTLE, and himselfe.[2]

Pd at the apoyntment of Robart Shawe, the 14 daye of maye 1600, in fulle payment of a Boocke called the gowlden asse, cuped and siches, to thomas Deckers, and hary chettell, and John Daye, some of ...................... } xxx^s

Pd unto the M^r of the Revelles man, for lycensynge of a Boocke called Damon and pethias, the 16 of maye 1600, some of[3]................. } vij^s

Receaved of M^r Henshlowe, the 17th of maye 1600, in behalfe of the Company, to paye Will Haulton and M^r Pett, in full payment of a play called straunge newes out of Poland[4] } vj^li

[1] This play of "The Golden Asse, Cupid and Psyche," introduced in a previous entry without date, was perhaps a modernization of an older drama, mentioned about 1581 by Stephen Gosson in his "Plays confuted in five Actions," as having been performed by "the children of Pauls," as they were called. The same author, in the same work, speaks of "Cæsar and Pompey," "The Fabii," "The Blacksmith's Daughter," "The Jew," and "Ptolemy," as popular and commendable performances. —Vide Hist. of Engl. Dram. Poetry and the Stage, ii., 418, and iii., 274.

[2] This addition, after the signature of Day, was made by Dekker.

[3] Above we had, paid 7*s*. for licensing Ferrex and Porrex. We may presume that plays so authorised were brought out soon afterwards, but we have no means of fixing the precise date.

[4] We have no other notice of "M^r Pett" as a dramatic poet. The play of "Strange News out of Poland" was probably founded on some popular tract of the time not now known.

| | | |
|---|---|---|
| Receaved of M$^{r}$ Henshlowe, the 26$^{th}$ of May 1600, in behalfe of the Companye, to pay H. Chettle and John Day, in full payment of a booke called the blynd Begger of bednall greene,[1] the some of ........................... | $v^{li}$ | $x^{s}$ |
| Lent unto W$^{m}$ Harton, the 27 of maye 1600, in earneste of a Boocke called Indes, the some... W. HAUGHTON.[2] | | $x^{s}$ |
| Dd unto the littell tayller, at the apoyntment of Robart Shaw, the 25 of maye 1600, for to macke sewts for the play called strange newes out of powland .................................. | $iij^{li}$ | |
| Receaved of M$^{r}$ Henshlowe, thys 3$^{d}$ of June 1600, in behalfe of the Company, to An. Munday and the reste,[3] in pte of payment for a booke called the fayre Constance of Roome, the some of ........................... ............. | $iij^{li}$ | $v^{s}$ |
| Lent unto Thomas Dowton, the 5 of June 1600, to bye a sewt for his boye in the playe of cuped and siches, the some of .................. | | $xxxx^{s}$ |
| Pd unto Drayton, Hathway, Monday, and Deckers, at the apoyntment of Robart Shawe, in full payment of a boocke called the fayre constance of Rome, the 14 of June 1600, some of ......................................... | | $xxxxiiij^{s}$ |

[1] The play was printed in 1659, as by John Day only, under the title of "The Blind Beggar of Bethnall Green, with the merry Humours of Tom Strowd, the Norfolk Yeoman." It was founded upon the older ballad, and seems to have been very popular.

[2] The entry was written by Henslowe, and the name may be read either "Indes," as we have printed it, or *Judas*: it is more like the last, but Judas would hardly have been a fit subject for a drama at this date.

[3] i.e., Drayton, Hathway, and Dekker, as appears by the next entry but one.

Lent to W^m^ Hawton, ij^s^: more ij^s^

| | |
|---|---|
| Dd unto Robart shawe, the 19 of June 1600, for to lend unto harey chettell and J. Daye, in earnest of a boocke called [1] .................. | x^s^ |
| Lent unto Robart shawe, the 20 of June 1600, to lend them, Hathway, in earneste of the second pte of Constance of Rome,[2] the some of | xx^s^ |
| Payd to M^r^ Allen, by M^r^ Henshlowe, in behalfe of the Company, the some of xj^li^, which is the remainder of a debt of l^li^, for the payment of which we stood bound in a C^li^................. | xj^li^ |
| So that the full some of all the debtes which we owe M^r^ Henshlowe, this x^th^ of July 1600, cometh to just the some of three hundred powndes ............................................ | ccc^li^ |

Which some of three hundred poundes, we whose names are hereunder written doe acknowledge our dewe debt, and doe promyse payment.

| | |
|---|---|
| J SINGGER.[3] | ROBT SHAA. |
| THOMAS DOWNTON. | THOMAS TOWNE. |
| HUMFRY JEFFES. | W. BIRDE |
| ANTHONY JEFFES | RICHARD JONES. |
| CHARLES MASSYE. | EDWARD JUBYE. |
| SAMUELL ROWLYE. | |

| | |
|---|---|
| Lent unto Robart shawe, the 14 of aguste 1600, to bye a dublett and hosse of sewater grene satten, some of .................................. | iij^li^ |

[1] A blank is left for the name of the play.

[2] We have only heard of the *first* part on 3 June, and in the interval it had probably been acted.

[3] These are the original signatures of the eleven players being sharers of the company, exclusive of hirelings, who were paid a weekly stipend, and boys, employed under the principal actors. Just above we have had a notice of Downton's boy, who played in "Cupid and Psyche."

| | | |
|---|---|---|
| Pd at the apoyntment of the company, the 16 of aguste 1600, for viij yards of mury satten, the some of.......... | iij[li] | xij[s] |
| Lent unto Robart Shawe, the 29 of aguste 1600, the some of fower powndes. I saye........... | iiij[li] | |
| Pd unto Robart shawe, the 2 of aguste 1600, the some of.......... | | viij[s] |
| Lent unto Robarte Shawe, the 6 of septmbr 1600, to paye unto Thomas Deckers, for the boocke called the forteion tenes,[1] some of...... | | xx[s] |
| Lent unto Robart Shawe, the 12 of septembr 1600, the some of three powndes, I saye...... | iij[li] | |
| Lent unto the companye, the 11 of novmbr 1600, to paye unto my sonne, E. Alleyn, abowt ther composicion,[2] the some of fower powndes. I saye lent.......... | iiij[li] | |
| Pd unto my sonne, Alleyn, for the firste weckes playe, the xj parte of xvij[li] ix[s], which came to therti and ij shellenges. I saye pd ........... | | xxxij[s] |
| Lent unto Samwell Rowley, the 14 of desembr 1600, to geve unto Thomas Dickers, for his paynes in fayeton,[3] some of .......... | | x[s] |

[1] It is not easy to make anything out of the name given by Henslowe to this play by Dekker: Malone passes it over without notice. It may possibly have been some farther alteration of Fortunatus.

[2] What is meant here by the "composition" on the part of the company it is difficult to decide. It was perhaps connected with the next entry, from which we may gather that the profits upon the week being £17 9*s*., Alleyn became entitled to an eleventh share, or £1 12*s*. It appears from the acknowledgment on the preceding page, that Alleyn was either not an acting member of the company in the summer of 1600, or that he was not considered one of the parties who owed Henslowe £300.

[3] Dekker's "Phaeton" was at this date represented at Court, as the entries almost immediately following shew, and the author was called upon to make some alterations in it to suit the occasion.

| | |
|---|---|
| Lent unto Samwell Rowley, the 20 of desembr 1600, to lend unto W^m^ Harton, in earneste of a Boocke called Roben hoodes penerthes[1] ... | xx^s^ |
| Pd unto the littell tayller, at the apoyntment of the companye, the 20 of desembr 1600, some .......................................... | xx^s^ |
| Lent unto Samwell Rowley, the 22 of desembr 1600, to geve unto Thomas Deckers, for alterynge of fayton for the corte .............. | xxx^s^ |
| Pd at the apoyntment of the company, unto the littell tayller, in full payment upon his bille, some of xix^s^, the 23 of desembr 1600. I saye pd ............... .................................... | xix^s^ |
| Lent unto William Hawghton, the 27 of desembr 1600, in earneste of his Boocke called Roben hoodes penerthes......... ................. | x^s^ |
| Lent unto W^m^ Bird, the 2 of Janewary 1600, for divers thinges abowte the playe of Fayeton, for the corte, some of .......................... | xx^s^ |
| Lent unto M^r^ Ranckens and hathwaye, in earnest of a Boocke called Hanyball and Sepius,[2] the 3 of Janewary 1600, some of ... | xxxx^s^ |
| Lent unto W^m^ Haughton, the 4 of Jenewary 1600, in pt payment of a Boocke called Roben hoodes penerths, some of ...................... | x^s^ |
| Lent unto M^r^ hathway and Ranckens, the 11 of Janewary 1600, in pt of payment of a play called Haneball and sepius........ ............... | v^s^ |

[1] "Robin Hood's Pennyworth's" was probably the title, but what was meant by it is now hardly intelligible. It was doubtless in some way connected with the Downfal and Death of Robinhood, two much applauded plays by Anthony Monday and Henry Chettle already mentioned. See pp. 118 and 119.

[2] Of course Hannibal and Scipio. Afterwards, Henslowe gets a little nearer the name of Scipio.

| | | |
|---|---|---|
| Pd unto M$^r$ Ranckene and M$^r$ Hathwaye, the 12 of Janewary 1600, in fulle payment of a boocke called Haneball and sepios, some of ... | iij$^{li}$ | xv$^s$ |
| Pd at the apoyntment of W$^m$ Birde unto M$^r$ Harton, for his playe of Roben hoodes penerthe, the 13 of Janewary 1600 ........... | | xxxx$^s$ |
| Lent unto M$^r$ Hathwaye and Rancken, the 23 of Janewary 1600, in earneste of a Boocke, wherein is skogen and scellton,[1] some of ...... | | x$^s$ |

Wittnes E. ALLEYN.

*Lent unto my sonne edwarde Allen, as foloweth, for the company*, 1596.[2]

| | | | |
|---|---|---|---|
| Itm̃ lent the 2 of maye 1596 ................. | xj$^{li}$ | | |
| Itm̃ lent the 10 of maye 1596 ................. | | liij$^s$ | iiij$^d$ |
| Itm̃ lent the 13 of maye 1596 ................. | iij$^{li}$ | | |
| Itm̃ lent the 15 of maye 1596 ................. | | xxx$^s$ | |
| Itm̃ lent the 16 of maye 1596 ................. | | xxxx$^s$ | |
| Itm̃ lent the 25 of maye, to paye marcum[3] ... | | xxx$^s$ | |
| | 21 | 13 | 04 |

[1] Malone (Shaksp. by Boswell, iii. 324) calls this piece "Scogan and Skelton," as if that had been the name of the play, whereas it was a "book" in which Scogan, or Scoggin, and Skelton, (a jester and a jester-poet of the reign of Henry VIII.,) were characters: it is mentioned frequently afterwards in the same terms. The Rev. Mr. Dyce, in his Account of Skelton and his Writings, takes no notice of the manner in which he was thus brought on the stage near the end of the reign of Elizabeth.

[2] This account commences a new page: it proves how irregularly, in point of date, Henslowe kept his Diary; but of this fact we have already had abundant evidence.

[3] Probably the name of a person; but, as Henslowe and his scribe used capitals and other letters merely capriciously, it is impossible to judge from that circumstance.

| | | |
|---|---|---|
| Lent unto my sonne, for the company, to bye a newe sewte of a parell………………… | vij$^{li}$ | x$^{s}$ |
| Lent unto my sonne, to feneshe up the blacke velvet gowne ………………… | iij$^{li}$ | |
| Turned over from my sonne, the some of……… | vij$^{li}$ vj$^{s}$ viij$^{d}$ | |

E. A.[1]

*Receved agayne of my sonne E. A. of this deate above written, as foloweth.*

| | | |
|---|---|---|
| Rd the 10 of maye 1596……………………… | | xxx$^{s}$ |
| Rd the 11 of maye 1596……………………… | | xx$^{s}$ |
| Rd the 12 of maye 1596……………………… | | xxxxvj$^{s}$ |
| Rd the 13 of maye 1596……………………… | | xxxxvj$^{s}$ |
| Rd the 14 of maye 1596……………………… | | xxvj$^{s}$ |
| Rd the 15 of maye 1596……………………… | | xxiiij$^{s}$ |
| Rd the 16 of maye 1596……………………… | | xxxvj$^{s}$ |
| Rd the 17 of maye 1596……………………… | | l$^{s}$ |
| Rd the 18 of maye 1596……………………… | | liij$^{s}$ |
| Rd the 22 of maye 1596……………………… | | xxviij$^{s}$ |
| Rd the 23 of maye 1596……………………… | | xxxx$^{s}$ |
| Rd the 24 of maye 1596……………………… | | xxij$^{s}$ |
| Rd the 25 of maye 1596……………………… | | xxv$^{s}$ |
| Rd the 11 of June 1596……………………… | iij$^{li}$ | iiij$^{s}$ |
| Rd the 23 of June 1596……………………… | iij$^{li}$ | xiij$^{s}$ |
| Rd the 25 of June 1596……………………… | | xxj$^{s}$ |
| Rd the 26 of June 1596……………………… | | xxx$^{s}$ |
| Rd the 27 of June 1596……………………… | | xxj$^{s}$ |
| Rd the 1 of Julye 1596……………………… | | xxxxvij$^{s}$ |
| Rd the 2 of Julye 1596……………………… | | xxv$^{s}$ |
| Rd the 5 of Julye 1596……………………… | | xxiij$^{s}$ |
| Rd the 6 of Julye 1596……………………… | | xvij$^{s}$ |
| Rd the 8 of Julye 1596……………………… | | xxij$^{s}$ |

[1] The initials of Edward Alleyn, which were added by Henslowe: the whole amount is not summed up in the MS.

Mr. VAHAN.[1]—I have often seante unto you to leat you understand, that I have ben therepened to be sued by one Edward Phillipes, consernynge the state which I have of a platte of grownd and barnes and stables, belongine unto the howsse ther, called the corner howsse, which I have in the behallfe of the children of Edmond hensley, I being exsexor to the sayde Edmonde. The trewth is the sayd Phillipes hath mad a Reentry, and beinge with stoode hath brothe yt to a exsegente: therfor I desyer you to locke unto yt, and forther more wolde advise you, because you stand bownd to conferme the state to be good; yf not upon your perell be it, for I promes you yf I be forced to spende aney money for the sute of yt, which I speack unto youe abowt you are to looke unto and to conferme, I wishe you to acknowlege your sealffe that I have geven you to understand of yt, and that you will conferme me the state quietly, and defend me from sute and trubell abowt yt, or I promes youe, yf I sustayne aney damages by the sute of yt, I will put your band in sute, and this asure your seallfe: and this I reast, comitinge you to God. from London the ix of febreary 1593.

Yours as you use hime,
PHILLIPE HENSLOWE.

This is a trew copeye of a leater seant downe in to Susex unto the partie abowffe named: witnesses to the same

WILLIAM HENSLEY
EDWARDE ALLEYN.[2]

S[r]—I praye you cause such monye as is dewe unto me for my quarters fee dew to be payd at our ladye daye laste, to be

[1] This copy of a letter is inserted in the midst of matters of account with which it has no connection.

[2] These are not original signatures: the handwriting is the same as that of several letters preserved at Dulwich.

delyvered unto this bearer, and this shalbe your suficyante discarge. frome grenweche this xvij of aprell 1596

RAFFE BOWES.[1]

To our lovinge frende
Mr William Kelegraye esquier.

Memorandum, that I, the said phillipe Henslow, did demand of widow Valle, the 8 daye of July 1597, her hallfe yeares reant, which was dew unto me by my leasse from the quene, under the great sealle of Ingland, bowght of Mrs Keyes, which rente wasse to be payd at midsumer in this yeare 1597, or with in xiiij dayes after. This Rent wasse by me lafulye demanded at the quarter, and at the 14 daye after, which was the laste daye, and not payd nor tendered, for which cause I saye heare leasse is forfette. wytnesse to the demand

HEWE DAVIS.[2]

Md., that I, Robert Wilson,[3] do owe unto Mr Phillippe Hensloe the some of twentie shillinges, current moneye of England, to be payde unto hym, his executors and assignes, att hys or theyr will and pleasure. Wyttnes my hand, the second daye of June 1598, Ao Regni Reginæ nunc quadragesimo. By me,

R. WILSON.[4]

[1] This appears to be only a copy of the order by Sir Ralph Bowes, then Master of the Queen's games.

[2] If this were the original writing and signature of Hugh Davis, (as it would seem to be,) it shews that he was the scribe or clerk Henslowe sometimes employed in keeping his books and writing his letters. However, by an entry on p. 59 it seems that Hugh Davis was only a marksman.

[3] Previous to this memorandum, the account of loans upon pledges to, or through, Francis Henslowe is renewed, and continues for seventeen pages without affording any information on the history of the stage. The dates are from 10th Dec. 1593, to the 22nd Jan. 1594.

[4] The whole of this memorandum is in the handwriting of R. Wilson.

xxv$^{th}$ daie of October 1599

Rec. the daie aforesaid, for the use of my M$^{r}$ Edmond Tylney Esquier, of M$^{r}$ Henslowe, the some of........................................ } iij$^{li}$

ꝑ me, RICH. VEALE.[1]

xx$^{o}$ die Novembr 1599

Rec. the daie aforesaid, for the use of my M$^{r}$ Edmond Tylney Esquier, of M$^{r}$ Henslowe, the some of........................................ } iij$^{li}$

ꝑ me, RICH. VEALE.

the ix$^{th}$ daye of Januarye 1600

Rec. the daye aforesayde, for the use of my M$^{r}$ Edmond Tyllney, Esquire, M$^{r}$ of the revells, of M$^{r}$ Henslowe, the some of.......... ......... } iij$^{li}$

ꝑ mei, WILLM PLAYSTOW

the ix$^{th}$ daye of Februarye 1600.

Rec. the daye and yeare abovewritten, for the use of my M$^{r}$, Edmond Tyllney, M$^{r}$ of the revelles of M$^{r}$ Henslowe, the some of ........ } iij$^{li}$

ꝑ me, WILLM PLAYSTOWE.

ROBERT JOHNSON, of letherhed,
in Sury, M$^{r}$ Revells man.[2]

[1] These and other entries of the same kind shew, that at least Henslowe's company at this date made a heavy monthly contribution to the Master of the Revels, besides the payment of seven shillings on the licensing of every new play. By pp. 79, 91, and 109, it appears that the monthly payment had been 40*s*., but here and afterwards we see that it was raised in 1599 to £3, equal to at least £15 of our money; and it is probably to be looked upon as a gratuity to secure the favour of the Master of the Revels.

[2] This note stands by itself at the top of a page in the MS.

the xxviij[th] of Aprill 1600.

Receaved the daye and yeare above written, for the use of my M[r], Edmond Tylney, esquire, of phillip Hinslowe, the som of iij[li], of good and lawefull money of England: I say the som̃ of } iij[li]

ꝑ mei, WILLM PLAYSTOWE.

the xxiiij[th] of maye, ano 1600.

Receaved the daye and yeare above written, for the use of my M[r], Edmonde Tyllneye, esquire, of Phillip Hynslowe, the som of three poundes, of good and lawfull monye of England: I say Rd ........................................................ } iij[li]

ꝑ mei, WILLM PLAYSTOWE.

Received of M[r] Henchlowe, in ernest of the second parte of the blind begger of Bednall Greene, the sum of .............. .............. } 40[s]

29 of January 1600

W. HAUGHTON.
J. DAY.[1]

Lent unto Nicolas Bickers,[2] the 10 of June 1601, at the Request of the lorde of Notengams players, the some of thirtie shillenges, to be payd me agayne by ij[s] a week, begenenge at the daye above written. I saye lent ...... } xxx[s]

[1] See p. 171 for a memorandum, dated some months before the present, regarding what was probably the *first* part of this play. It shews that the first part was the production of Chettle as well as Day, and here we see that Haughton was Day's coadjutor in the *second* part. We shall soon find that a *third* part on the same subject was written.

[2] We are without any other information respecting Nicholas Bickers, (or more probably Vicars,) but he was doubtless an inferior actor of the company.

| | |
|---|---|
| Rd the 24 of June 1601, in pte | ij$^{s}$ |
| Rd the 28 of June 1601, in pte | ij$^{s}$ |
| Rd the 11 of Julye 1601, in pte | ij$^{s}$ |
| Rd the 18 of Julye 1601, in pte | ij$^{s}$ |
| Rd the 8 of aguste 1601, in pte | ij$^{s}$ |
| Rd the 15 of aguste 1601, in pte | ij$^{s}$ |
| Rd the 22 of aguste 1601, in pte | ij$^{s}$ |
| Rd the 3 of septembr 1601, in pte | ij$^{s}$ |
| Rd the 10 of septembr 1601, in pte | ij$^{s}$ |
| Rd the 17 of septembr 1601, in pte | ij$^{s}$ |

*I begine to Receve of antony Jeaffes, for the weackes which he is behind and owes unto me for my boye Jeames wages, which begines the* 8 *of aguste* 1600, *as foloweth :*

| | |
|---|---|
| Rd the 8 of aguste, of antony Jeffes | iij$^{s}$ |
| Rd the 16 of aguste, of antonye Jeffes | iij$^{s}$ |

*My lord of Penbrockes men begane to playe at the Rosse, the* 18 *of octobr* 1600, *as foloweth :*[1]

| | | |
|---|---|---|
| Octbr 28 | Rd at the licke unto licke [2] | xj$^{s}$ |
| 29 | Rd at Rodericke | v$^{s}$ |

[1] This account is headed, and continued, as far as it goes, in Henslowe's handwriting. Probably it is so short because the experiment did not answer, and the receipts did not make it worth while for the company to persevere in their performances: shortly afterwards they removed to the Fortune Theatre, recently erected by Henslowe and Alleyn in Cripplegate parish.

[2] Possibly some adaptation of Ulpian Fulwell's comic interlude, or moral-play, printed in 1568 under the title of "Like will to Like, quod the Devil to the Collier:" the word "Devell" was first written, and struck out with the pen. Rodericke, in the next line, may have been a drama on "Roderick the great," who divided Wales, and who is mentioned in "Thameseidos," 1600, by E. W., Lib. 2.

July 31. 1601.

Rd from Mr Henslowe, by me, Willm Plaistowe, to the use of my Mr, Mr Edmond Tylney, Mr of hir Maties Revells, for one monthes paye, due unto him the daie and yeare above written, the some of 3li. I saye........................ } iijli

p mei, WILLM PLAYSTOWE.

Received of Mr Hinchlo, the xxixth of Agust, iijli, for this last moneths pay for the Fortune.[1]

ROBERT HASSARD.

Duke player } The j and twentie daie of septtember a thousand six hounderd borrowed of Mr Hinchlowe, in Redie monie, the som of fortie shillings, to be paid the twentie daie of october next follenge the date her of: in witnes her of I set my hand.

JOHN DUKE.[2]

Sowld unto Richard Bradshawe, player, the 15 of Desembr 1600, j pownd and ij owences of cooper lace, to be payd at his retorne agayne to London next after the datte herof: some of xiiijs; and for the aknowlegement of this the sayd Bradshaw hath herunto seat his hand ... } xiiijs

RICHARD BRADSHAWE

Wittnes E. ALLEYN.

[1] If this entry be taken as of the 29 August 1601, it will shew that the Fortune theatre was then open, and had been open for at least a month. The indenture with Street, the carpenter, under which it was constructed, bears date on the 8th Jan., 1599-1600. *Vide* Hist. of Engl. Dram. Poetry and the Stage, iii., 302. Perhaps Henslowe was required to pay £3 for each of the theatres, as long as he continued the use of the Rose as well as the Fortune.

[2] Duke never attained eminence in the profession. This entry is entirely written by him, and it is the first time his name has occurred.

| | |
|---|---|
| Lent more unto Richard Bradshawe, player, the 29 of aprell 1601, in money, to be payd at his next Retorne to London, the some of ........ | v[s] |

June 13[th] 1601

| | |
|---|---|
| Borrowed of M[r] Phillip Hinsloe, by me, Anthonie Wadeson, the sum of xx[s], in earnest of a booke cald the henorable lyfe of the Humorous Earle of Gloster, with his conquest of Portugall .............. .......................... | xx[s] |

ANT. WADESON.[1]

Wittnes THOMAS DOWNTON.

*The earlle of nothengames players deattes, as* (1600) *foloweth:*

| | |
|---|---|
| Lent at the apoyntment of Samwell Rowley,[2] and thomas towne, unto M[r] Ranckens, and M[r] Hathwaye, this 26 of Janewarye 1600, in earneste of a Boocke called ——, wherein is Skogen and Skelton, the some of .............. | xxx[s] |
| Lent unto W[m] Harton and J. Daye, at the apoyntment of Samwell Rowly, the 29 of Janewary 1600, in earnest of a Boocke called the second pte of the blinde beager of bednowle grene, with the end of Strowde,[3] the some of | xxxx[s] |

[1] The signature and the whole entry are Wadeson's writing. Downton witnessed the payment in his own hand.

[2] These entries are continued from p. 175.

[3] Malone miscalls this piece "the second part of Thomas Strowde," adding a conjecture in a note, that it was the same play as the Blind Beggar of Bethnall Green. (Shaksp. by Bosw., iii., 324.) There can be no doubt from this entry, which Malone overlooked, that it was a sequel to that drama. Thomas Strowd is a principal character in the play as it was printed in 1659. See note 1, p. 171.

| | |
|---|---|
| Lent unto Mr Hathwaye and Mr Rancken, upon a boocke wherein is Skogen and Skelton, at the apoyntment of Samwell Rowley, the 5 of febreary 1600, some of ........................ | xxs |
| Lent unto Mr Ranckens, the 8 of febreary 1600, in earneste .............. ........................ | ijs |
| Lent unto Wm Harton and John Daye, in earneste of a Boocke called the 2 pt of Thome Strowde,[1] the 10 daye of febreary 1600, some of | xxxs |
| Lent unto Mr Hathewaye, the 25 of febreary 1600, for a Boocke wherein is Skelton and skogen, at the apoyntment of Samwell Rowlye, in pte of payment, the some of ................. | xxxxs |

SAMUELL ROWLYE.[2]

| | |
|---|---|
| Lent unto the companye, the 6 of march 1600, to pay Mr Threeheren and his wiffe, and Mr haies screvener, some of .................... | xxvijs vjd |
| The companye dothe owe unto me, for my boye Jemes bristoes wages, frome the 3 of aprell 1600, unto the xv of febreary 1600 next, after the ratte of iijs a weeke, some ................. | vjli ixs |
| Layd owt for the companye, from the 14 of aguste 1600, at severall tymes, as may apere ....................... ..... 51li 19s 06d | |
| Pd unto Mr Ranckens and Mr Hathwaye, at the apoyntment of the companye, the 8 of marche 1600, in full payment of a Boocke wherein is skogen and skelton, some of ...... ..... ........ | xviijs |
| Pd at the apoyntment of Samell Rowley, unto John Daye and Wm harton, for a boocke called the second pte of thome strowd, the 10 of marche 1600, the some of.................... | xxxs |

[1] Meaning the second part of the Blind Beggar of Bethnal Green.

[2] This actor-author's own signature: he seems to have been only an actor at this date.

| | | |
|---|---|---|
| Lent unto Mr hathwaye and Mr Rankens,[1] the 24 of marche 1600, in earneste of a Boocke called conqueste of Spayne, some of— at the apoyntment of Samewell Rowly......... | | xs |
| Layd owte at the apoyntment of Samwell Rowlye, unto harey chettell, in pte of payment for a Boocke called Al is not gowld that glesters,[2] the laste of marche 1601, some of.............. | | xxxxs |
| Lent unto John Daye and Wm Haughton, the 4 of aprell 1601, in earneste of a playe called the conqueste of the weste enges,[3] at the apoyntment of Samwell Rowlye, the some of | | xxxxs |
| Lent unto Mr Hathwaye and Mr Ranckens, the 4 of Aprell 1601, in earneste of a playe called the conqueste of Spayne, the some of ......... | | vs |
| Pd unto Harey chettell, the 6 of aprell 1601, in full payment of a Boocke called al is not gould that glysters, at the apoyntment of Samwell Rowley, some of.............................. .. | iiijli | |
| Lent unto Mr Hathwaye and Mr Rankens, the xj of aprell, in earneste of a boocke called the conqueste of spayne, by John a Gant, some... | | xxs |
| Lent unto Mr Smyth and Wm Hawghton, the xj of Aprell 1601, in earnest of a Boocke called the conquest of the west enges, at the apoyntment of Samwell Rowlye, the some of......... | | xxs |

[1] Malone misread the name of Rankens, *Hawkins*, (Shakspeare by Boswell, iii., 325.) The full title of the play, as appears by other memoranda, was "The Conquest of Spain by John of Gaunt."

[2] Malone erroneously assigns to Samuel Rowley a share in the authorship of this play. Rowley was only the actor at whose instance the money was paid, and "All is not gold that glisters" seems to have been the sole work of Chettle.

[3] We find by other entries that Wentworth Smith was concerned with Day and Haughton in writing "The Conquest of the West Indies."

| | |
|---|---|
| Lent unto Mr Hathwaye and Mr Ranckens, the 16 of aprell 1601, in pte payment for a Boocke called the conquest of Spayne, some of ...... | iiijs |
| Lent unto Jubey, the 18 of aprell 1601, to lend unto Thomas Deckers and harey chettell, in earneste of a boocke called Kinge Sebastiane of Portingalle, the some of .............. | xxs |
| Lent unto the company, the 20 of Aprell 1601, to bye a blacke satten dublette, the some of... | xvjs |
| Lent Mr Ranckens and Mr Hathwaye........... | iiijs |
| Dd unto the littell tayller, the 27 of aprell 1601, for the yousse of the companye, to bye a sutte of lace for the 2 pte of Strowde, the some of | xxxs |
| Pd unto John Daye, at the apoyntment of the companye, 1601, after the playinge of the 2 pte of Strowde,[1] the some of ................ | xs |
| Dd unto the littell tayller, at the apoyntment of the companye, the 2 of maye 1601, to bye divers thinges for the playe of the blind begger of elexsandria.[2] | |
| Lent Wm Haughton, in earneste of the playe called the conqueste of the weste enges, the 2 of maye 1601, the some of...................... | vs |
| Pd unto John Daye and Wm Hawghton, in fulle payment of a playe called the 2 pte of Strowde, the 5 of maye 1601, some, at the apoyntment of Samwell Rowlye ............................ | xs |

[1] Probably these ten shillings were paid to Day as a gratuity, over and above the price of the play, after the successful performance of "the Second Part of the Blind Beggar of Bethnall Green." Only the date of the year is here given, and we shall see presently another memorandum of a final payment for the play, dated 5th May 1601.

[2] This must have been a revival of Chapman's play, which, as we have seen, p. 64, was first acted on the 12 February 1595, and printed in 1598.

| | | |
|---|---|---|
| Dd unto Radford, the littell tayller, the 5 of maye 1601, at the apoyntment of the Companye, to bye dyvers thinges for the playe of the blinde begger of Elexsandrea, the some of | | xxxx$^{s}$ |
| Layd owt for the company, to geatte the boye into the ospetalle, which was hurte at the Fortewne[1] .................................... | | x$^{s}$ |
| Lent unto the littell tayller, the 8 of maye 1601, at the apoyntment of the company, to bye thinges for the blinde beggar of elexsandrea, some ............................................ | | x$^{s}$ |
| Pd unto the coper lace man, at the apoyntment of the companye, the 8 of maye 1601, for coper lace, the some of ...... .................... | | v$^{s}$ |
| Pd unto M$^{r}$ Heath, merser, the 13 of maye 1601, at the apoyntment of the companye, for ther deat in pt, the some of tenne powndes, I saye | x$^{li}$ | |
| Lent unto the companye, the 16 of maye 1601, to paye unto Thomas Deckers and Harye chettell, in pte of payment of a playe called Kynge Sebastion of portingall,[2] the some of | | xxxx$^{s}$ |
| Lent unto Robart Shawe and M$^{r}$ Jube, the 19 of maye 1601, to bye divers thinges for the Jewe of malta,[3] the some of .................... | v$^{li}$ | |
| Lent unto the littell tayller, the same daye, for more thinges for the Jewe of malta, some of | | x$^{s}$ |

[1] i.e., The Fortune theatre, where performances at this date were taking place, as well perhaps as at the Rose, or the Fortune would not have been specified.

[2] In 1601 was published "The strangest Adventure that ever happened." It is by A. Munday, and relates to the history of Don Sebastian, and was doubtless the foundation of this play.

[3] Of course a revival of Marlowe's play, in the representation of which Edward Alleyn was so famous as the hero. The first mention of the Jew of Malta in this MS. is on 26 Feb. 1591. See p. 21.

| | |
|---|---|
| Lent unto W$^{m}$ Hawghton, the 20 of maye 1601, in earneste of the vj yemon of the weaste,[1] the some of...Lent more unto W$^{m}$ Hawghton ... | x$^{s}$ v$^{s}$ |
| Lent unto John Daye, the 21 of maye 1601, in earneste of a Boocke called the West enges, the some of— at the apoy̆ntment of Samwell Rowley ...... | xx$^{s}$ |
| Lent unto John Daye, at the apoyntment of Samwell Rowley, the 21 of maye 1601 in earnest of a Boocke called the 3 pte of Thome Strowde,[2] the some of ........................ | x$^{s}$ |
| Pd at the apoyntment of E. Alleyn, the 22 of may 1601, unto Thomas Deckers, in fulle payment of a boocke called Kynge Sebastian of Portyngall, the some of........................ | iij$^{li}$ |
| Pd unto the coper lace man for iij score ownce of coper lace, at x$^{d}$ an ownce, for the manes gowne and a sewte for the blind begger of elexsandria, the some of ..................... | iij$^{li}$ xiij$^{s}$ 4$^{d}$ |
| Lent at the apoyntment of Samwell Rowlye, the 4 daye of June 1601, unto John Daye, in pt of payment of a Boocke called the vj yemon of the weaste, the some of ........................ | xxxx$^{s}$ |

[1] Founded upon Deloney's "Thomas of Reading, or the six worthy Yeomen of the West," which had been printed only a short time before: the earliest extant notice of it is in Kempe's "Nine Days Wonder," 1600, 4to., but no impression seems to be now known of so old a date. Kempe there calls Deloney "the great ballad maker......chronicler of the memorable lives of the Six Yeomen of the West," &c. The memorandum of the *5s.* lent to Haughton was a subsequent interlineation.

[2] We have before had what was called "the end of Strowde," (p. 183) but as the character was popular, the dramatist seems to have thought that he could still make something more of him, and therefore wrote (or undertook to write) a *third* part of "The Blind Beggar of Bethnall Green."

| | |
|---|---|
| Pd unto M[r] Richard Hethe, sylckman, the 5 of June 1601, at the apoyntment of the companye, and for theyer deate, the some of forten powndes and fyften shellenges and sevenpence, in fulle payemente of the some of 24[li] xv[s] vij[d]: pd by me, Phillipe Henslow, some of ........................................ | xiiij[li] 15[s] 7[d] |
| Lent unto Samwell Rowlye 1601, to paye unto harye Chettell, for writtinge the Boocke of carnalle Wolseye lyfe,[1] the 5 of June, some of | xx[s] |
| Pd unto the coper lace man, the 6 of June 1601, at the apoyntment of the companye, for ther dete for coper lace, the some of sixe powndes, in pte of payment, I saye pd .................... | vj[li] |
| Pd at the apoyntment of Samwell Rowlye, unto W[m] Hawghton, in pte of payment of a boocke called the vj yemon of the weste, the 6 of June 1601, the some of ........................ | xv[s] |
| Lent unto Samwell Rowlye, the 8 of June 1601, to paye unto W[m] Howghton, in fulle payment of a boocke called the vj yemen of the weste, the some of.................................... | xxx[s] |

[1] "Carnalle Wolseye lyfe" of course means Cardinal Wolsey's life. Malone (Shaksp. by Bosw., iii., 325) "suspected" that this play (which he only calls "Cardinal Wolsey," and which is generally so entitled by Henslowe) was not written by H. Chettle, because the commentator only saw a subsequent entry for "altering" the play: here we find it stated that it was *written* by him, and, according to a subsequent memorandum, dated 14 July 1601, he received 40*s*. "in full payment" for "the Book of Carnowlle Wollsey." This play was, in all probability, anterior to Shakespeare's Henry the Eighth, which, at least in the form in which it has come down to us, could not have been produced before James I. came to the throne. See Collier's Shakespeare, v. 495. It will be seen by various memoranda hereafter, that the expenditure on bringing out "Cardinal Wolsey's Life" was unusually great.

| | |
|---|---|
| Lent at the apoyntment of Thomas Downton, the 13 of June 1601, unto Antony Wadeson, in earneste of a Boocke called the life of the humeros earlle of Gloster, and his conquest of portingalle, some of 20$^s$, as may apere[1] ...... | xx$^s$ |
| Rd of M$^r$ E. Alleyn, the 4 of maye 1601, the some of twenty eyght powndes and ten shellenges, which he receved at the Corte, for ther cort monye, for playinge ther at cryssmas, which was dewe unto the earlle of nothingames players, and I receved yt in pt of a more some, I say Rd[2] ........................................ | xxviij$^{li}$ x$^s$ |
| Lent unto M$^r$ Paschall, the 28 of Desembr 1599, upon the lickinge of his horse, the some of fyftie and five shillinges, which horse I licked not, so he is to paye me agayne my ........... | lv$^s$ |

Be it knowne unto all men by this presentes, that I, Williame Birde, being one of the earlle of nothingam players, dothe aknowlege my seallfe to owe and stand firmly indeatted unto phillipp Henslow, of the parishe of Sent Saveors in sothwarke, gentellman, the some of twenty and three powndes of good and lawfulle monye of Ingland to be payd unto the sayd phillipp or his ears, exseqetors, adminestrators or asynes, at suche tymes as he the sayd Phillipp or his asynes shall thinck

[1] This is followed by entries of two loans to Arthur Langworth, of Ringmer, Sussex, of £206 and £10, the first of which was paid to him by Henslowe on the 7th December 1594, and the last by Mrs. Alleyn on the 9th June 1595.

[2] The next entry relates to the payment of £26 10*s*. 0*d*., for the company to a Mr. Trehern, on a bond, but it is incomplete, as half the page has been cut away. On the following page are two notes of loans of 10*s*. and 50*s*. to Arthur Langworth, one dated 20th and the other 29th June 1604. The transactions out of which these several payments grew are not stated.

mette and convenient; and for which monye, well and trewlye to be payd, I bind me my ers, exsetors, adminestrators and asynes by this presence: in wittnes wherof I have her unto seatte my hand, even the 11 daye of Julye 1601.

W. BIRDE.[1]

| | |
|---|---|
| Rd in pte of paymente, the 29 of octobr 1601, of this bill above written, of W^m^ Birde, the some of ........................................... | xxv^s^ |
| Dd backe agayne, to W^m^ Birde of this........... | xx^s^ |

Md that the 12th daye of marche 1602, Wm Bird hath paid to me Phillipp Hinslowe, the some of xviijli xs, in pte of paiement of the saied debte of xxiijli, soe that there restes due by him to me perticulerlie, this daie, iiijli xs as the remaynder of this debte, and another debte of vjli or theareabouts uppon a bond. And he is cleere of all debtes and demaundes except theis debtes, and suche stocke and covenauntes as I maie clayme and challendge of him by reason of his conjunction with the companie.

PHILLIPPE HENSLOWE.

Witnes me Wm HARRIS.[2]

Be it knowen unto all men by thes presentes, that I George Chapman of London, gentleman, doe owe unto Mr Phillip Henshlowe, of the parishe of St Saviours, gentleman, the some of xli xs of lawfull money of England. In witnesse whereof I have hereunto sett my hand, this xxiiijth of octobr 1598.

GEO. CHAPMAN.[3]

[1] The signature only was written by Birde: the body of the acknowledgment, with its strange variety of orthography, was by Henslowe's scribe.

[2] This memorandum was drawn up by Harris, the scrivener, and signed by Henslowe.

[3] The signature only is in the handwriting of Chapman.

Be it knowne unto all men by thes presentes, that I William Paschall, on of her mãtes gentlemen Sewers, doe owe unto M$^{r}$ Phillip Henshlowe, of the parishe of S$^{t}$ Saviours, gentleman, the sume of v$^{li}$ of lawfull mony of England. In witnesse wheareof I have here unto sett my hand, this xiiij$^{th}$ of June 1599: to be payed upon the iiij of July nexte.

WILLIAM PASCHALL.

wittnes ED. ALLEYN.

Receyved by me William Paschall, at the apoyntement of my lord Chamberlen, at the hands of M$^{r}$ Phillip Henselow the sum of ten poundes, in part of twenty,[1] upon the xxviij day of marche 1600.

WILLIAM PASCHALL.

| | |
|---|---|
| Lent unto frances Henslow, to descharge hime seallfe owt of the whitte Lion,[2] from a hatmacker in barmsey streete, abowt his horsse which was stolen from hime, and he sewed my kynsman at the syes for hime, and to macke and end betwext he payde hime fyve pownd which I lent hime, I saye .............. | v$^{li}$ |
| Lent unto frances Henslow, the same tyme, to geve unto the knyghtes mane, which sewed them for robinge of his master, three pownds and sex shellynges and eyght pence, and promesed hime iij$^{li}$ more, which Saverey must paye his parte. I say ........................ | iij$^{li}$ vj$^{s}$ 8$^{d}$ |

[1] In what way this £20 became due to the Lord Chamberlain does not appear. This and the previous entry are in the handwriting of Paschall, witnessed by Ed. Alleyn in his own signature.

[2] See an account of the White Lion prison, Southwark, in Stow's Survey by Thoms, p. 153. It had been an inn, and was not used as a jail until about forty years before Stow wrote in 1598.

| | | |
|---|---|---|
| Layd owt[1] at the apoyntment of my sonne and the companye unto harey cheattell for the altrynge of the booke of carnowlle Wollsey, the 28 of June 1601 ............................................ | | xx^s |
| Lent unto the companye, the 1 of Julye 1601, to bye divers thinges for the vj yemen of the weaste, the some of fortye shellenges ........ | | xxxx^s |
| Pd unto the coper lace man, the j of Julye 1601 for coper lace, the some of....................... | | vj^s |
| Lent unto the littell tayller, at the apoyntment of the [companye], the 2 of Julye 1601, to bye divers thinges for the vj yemen of the weste, some of ........................................ | | xx^s |
| Pd unto the coper lace man, the 2 of Julye 1601, at the apoyntment of the companye, for coper lace for the vj yemen of the weaste, some...... | | ix^s |
| Pd at the apoyntment of the company, the 3 of Julye 1601, to the coper lace man for owld deats, the some of ................................ | iiij^li | |
| Pd at the apoyntment of the company, the 3 of Julye 1601, unto the coper lace man, for lace for the vj yemen of the weaste, some of —— Umfrey Jeffes sewte[2] ........................... | | vj^s |
| Lent unto John Daye and W^m Hawghton, at the apoyntmente of Robarte shawe, in earneste of a Boocke called fryer Rushe, and the prowde womon,[3] the some of —— the 4 daye of Julye ............................................... | | xx^s |

[1] These payments are resumed after an interval of three leaves: Henslowe in a note calls it *six* leaves, but he probably meant pages. This is the memorandum to which Malone refers respecting Chettle's connexion with the play of Cardinal Wolsey.

[3] i.e., The copper lace was for the *suit* worn by Humphrey Jeffes.

[3] Malone (Shakesp. by Boswell, iii., 325) calls this play merely "The proud Woman of Antwerp," whereas it appears that the piece was at

| | |
|---|---|
| Lent unto Robarte shawe, the 14 of Julye 1601, to paye unto Harey cheattell, for the Booke of Carnowlle Wollsey, in fulle payment, the some of | xxxx$^{s}$ |
| Pd unto the coper lace man, for coper lace, for the vj yemen of the west, the 4 of July 1601, the some of —— 10 a ownce, 36 onces......... | vj$^{s}$ |
| Lent unto Robart shawe, the 6 of Julye 1601, to paye unto the tayller for mackynge of Umfrey Jeaffes sewt in the vj yemen, the some of...... | xviij$^{s}$ |
| Pd at the apoyntment of Robarte shawe, the 6 of Julye 1601, unto the littell tayller, for mackynge of sewtes for the vj yemen, the some of | xxij$^{s}$ |
| Pd unto the coper lace man, the 10 of Julye 1601, at the apoyntment of the companye, in fulle payment, the some of........................... | lij$^{s}$ x$^{d}$ |

The wholle deat was xij$^{li}$ ij$^{s}$ x$^{d}$.

| | |
|---|---|
| Lent unto Robarte shawe, the 14 of Julye 1601, to geve unto W$^{m}$ hawghton and John Daye, in earneste of a Boocke called the prowde womon of Anwarpe and frier Rushe, the some of........................................ | xxx$^{s}$ |

Lent H. Chettell j$^{s}$. Lent H. Chettell ij$^{s}$.[1]

| | |
|---|---|
| Lent unto W$^{m}$ Hawghton, the 18 of Julye 1601, in pte payment of the 3 pt of Thome Strowde ........................................ | x$^{s}$ |
| Lent more, the same time, unto John Daye, in earnest of a Boocke called the 3 pt of Thome strowdė, some of.................................. | v$^{s}$ |

least in part founded upon the very popular tract of "The History of Friar Rush." The earliest known edition of it is dated 1620, but we may be quite confident that it had been printed many years before. (See Bridgewater Catalogue, p. 272.) As it has reached us, there is nothing in it relating to any proud woman of Antwerp, which was most likely engrafted upon it by the dramatists.

[1] These small advances to Chettle are crowded into the margin.

Lent John Daye ij$^{s}$. Lent John Daye ij$^{s}$.[1]

| | | |
|---|---|---|
| Lent unto the companye, the 17 of July 1601, to geve unto Harey chettell for the Boocke of the Carnowlle Woolsey, to pay unto M$^{r}$ Bromfield,[2] the some of ................................ | | xx$^{s}$ |
| Lent unto the companye, the 23 of Julye 1601, to paye for viij pownde of coper lace, the some of ........................................... | | xxiiij$^{s}$ |
| Lent unto Antony Wasone, at the apoyntment of[3] a boocke called the onerable lyfe of the hewmerus Earlle of Gloster, some of........... | | x$^{s}$ |
| Lent unto Samwell Rowley, 1601, the 25 of Julye, to lend unto John Daye, and W$^{m}$ Hawghton, in pt of payment of a boocke called the thirde pt of Thome Strowde, the some of.............. | | 40$^{s}$ |
| Lent unto Samwell Rowley, the 30 of Julye 1601, to paye unto John Daye and W$^{m}$ Hawghton, in fulle payment of a Boocke called the third pt of thome Strowde, the some of ........................................... | iij$^{li}$ | v$^{s}$ |
| Lent unto John Daye, the same time, in earnest of a Boocke called the 2 pte of Thome Dowghe,[4] the some of.......................................... | | x$^{s}$ |

[1] Also inserted in the margin.

[2] Bromfield was a mercer and dealer in cloth, who supplied the company, and is mentioned again afterwards.

[3] The words "the company for" have been accidentally omitted in this entry to Antony Wadeson: the title of the play has occurred before on p. 190, when Wadeson was paid 20*s.* "in earnest" for it, and when it is first noticed as in progress.

[4] We have heard nothing of any *first* part of Tom Dough. It is very likely that, like Tom Strowd, Tom Dough gave the name to the play in which he was a principal character, but no such drama is extant. Henslowe omitted the title at first, and inserted it afterwards, partly in a blank he had left, and partly by interlineation.

| | |
|---|---|
| Layd owt at the apoyntment of the companye, the 2 of aguste 1601, for aparell for Machewmet,[1] the some of .......... | x$^s$ iiij$^d$ |
| Layd owt at the apoyntment of the company, toward ther supper, to M$^r$ Mason,[2] at the quenes head, the some of ——, the 3 of aguste .......... | xx$^s$ |
| Pd at the apoyntment of the company, for mackynge of divers thinges for Mahewmett, unto Dover the tayller .......... | xij$^s$ |
| Pd at the apoyntment of the company, unto W$^m$ Whitte, for mackynge of crownes and other thinges for Mahewmett, the 4 of aguste 1601, the some of .......... | l$^s$ |
| Lent unto Samwell Rowley, the 5 of aguste 1601, to lend in pte payment, unto John Daye and W$^m$ Hawghton, of a Boocke called the weaste enges,[3] some of .......... | x$^s$ |
| Lent unto Robart shawe, the 7 of aguste 1601, to bye divers thinges, lange cottes, for the playe of Carnowld Wollsey,[4] the some of...... | xxx$^s$ |
| Lent the same tyme unto the littell tayller, for the same playe of Carnowlle Wollsey, some of .......... | vij$^s$ |

[1] Probably a mere revival of an older play, previously mentioned on p. 39. No author was paid for making additions to or alterations in it, unless a memorandum on p. 198, dated 22 Aug. 1601, of a payment of 40*s*. to Edward Alleyn, were for improvements he introduced.

[2] Mr. Mason might be the dramatic author who wrote a tragedy called "The Turke," printed in 1610, and entered two years earlier at Stationers' Hall; but it is more likely that Mason was the tavern-keeper at the Queen's Head.

[3] Doubtless the same play previously called the Conquest of the West Indies.

[4] The "long coats" for the play of Cardinal Wolsey are interlined.

| | | |
|---|---|---|
| Bowght of Mr Stonne, merser, the 10 of aguste 1601, ij pylle vellvet of carnardyn at xx$^{s}$ v$^{d}$, and sattenes at xij$^{s}$, and taffeties at xij$^{s}$ vj$^{d}$, which I layd owt for the company, for the playe of carnowll Wollsey,[1] some is ......... | xxj$^{li}$ | |
| Layd owt more for the playe of Carnowlle wollsey, for tynsell and tyffeny, and lynynge and other thinges, the same tyme, dd unto Jewby, the some of ..... ........................................ | iij$^{li}$ | x$^{s}$ |
| Pd unto the coper lace man for whit coper syllver lace, the same tyme, the some of ...... | | v$^{s}$ vj$^{d}$ |
| Lent unto Robart Shawe, the 11 of aguste 1601, to bye cottes for the play of carnowlle Wollsey, the some of........................................ | | xx$^{s}$ |
| Lent unto Wm Hawghton and John Daye, the 11 of aguste 1601, in pt payment of the playe called the west Enges, some of ................ | | xx$^{s}$ |
| Lent unto Robart shawe, the 12 of aguste 1601, to bye divers thinges for the playe of carnowlle wollsey, the some of .................... | | xx$^{s}$ |
| Lent unto the littell tayller, the 12 of aguste, to bye divers thinges for the playe of carnowlle Wollsey, at the apoyntment of my sonne,[2] the some of ........................................ | | x$^{s}$ |
| Layd owt at the apoyntment of the company, the 13 of aguste 1601, for ij tayllers billes and Wm Whittes bill, after the playe of carnowelle Wollsey,[3] the some of.............. | viij$^{li}$ | 4$^{s}$ |

[1] Henslowe seems to have gone to an extraordinary expense in getting up "Cardinal Wolsey." It is rarely that we meet with an item so large as this, itself more than £100 of our present money.

[2] i.e., Edward Alleyn, who probably acted the part of the Cardinal.

[3] Perhaps after the play of Cardinal Wolsey had been first acted. This entry may therefore shew that it was brought out prior to the 13th of August, 1601.

| | |
|---|---|
| Pd unto the tyerman, the 14 of aguste 1601, for mony which he layd owt to bye teffeny for the playe of carnowlle Wollsey, some of ...... | xiiij[d] |
| Lent unto Robart shawe, the 18 of aguste 1601, to pay unto harey chettell for his Booke of carnowlle Wollsey, [1] the some of .............. | xx[s] |
| Lent unto the companye, the 20 of aguste 1601, to bye a docters gowne, for the playe of carnowlle Wollsey, the some of ——, pd to Radford ........................................ | x[s] |
| Lent unto Robart shawe, the 21 of aguste 1601, for vellvett and mackynge of the docters gowne, in carnowlle Wollsey, the some of...... | xx[s] |
| Pd unto Edward Alleyn, at the apoyntment of the company, the 22 of aguste 1601, for the Boocke of Mahemett, the some of ........... | xxxx[s] |
| Lent unto Robart shaw, the 24 of aguste 1601, to lend unto harey chettell, in earneste called the j pt of carnall Wollsay, [2] the some of...... | xx[s] |

[1] If "Cardinal Wolsey" were brought out before 13th August 1601, Chettle was not paid in full for it until afterwards, which does not seem at all likely, considering his poverty; besides, according to other memoranda, Henslowe paid for the material and making of a doctor's gown subsequent to the production of the play.

[2] We may suspect an error here, and for "the j pt of carnall Wolsey" we ought perhaps to read "the 2 pt," which Chettle undertook in consequence of the success of his first part. On the other hand, it may refer to the play called "The Rising of Cardinal Wolsey," hereafter mentioned, in which Chettle and several other poets were concerned. It is certain that Henslowe's company produced two plays on the incidents of Wolsey's life, and that treating of his "rising" was posterior in point of composition: in a subsequent page, 204, it is called "the first part of Cardinal Wolsey," but Henslowe's memoranda are greatly confused, owing frequently to his ignorance of the titles of plays at the time he made his entries.

| | |
|---|---|
| Lent unto John Daye, the 26 of aguste 1601, in pt of payment of a boocke called the Weast enges, the some of ................................ | $x^s$ |
| Lent at the apoyntment of the company, the 27 of aguste 1601, unto Dover the tayller, to bye dyvers thinges for the 3 pte of Thome Strowde, the some of .. ................. ........ | $xxx^s$ |
| Lent unto the company, [1] the 29 of aguste 1601, to paye the Jewrey $xvj^s$, and the clarke of the syes $xj^s$ $viij^d$, and ower diner $viij^s$ $4^d$, some ... | $xxxvj^s$ |
| Lent unto the companye, the j of septembr, to lend John Daye, in pte of payment of a Boocke called the Weast enges, some of .............. | $x^s$ |
| Lent unto the company, the j of Septembr 1601, to bye blacke buckrome to macke a sewte for a fyer drack, in the 3 pt of thome Strowde,[2] the some of........................................... | $iij^s$ $vj^d$ |
| Lent unto the company, the 3 of septmbr 1601, to paye the tayller, Dover, for mackenge of divers thinges for the third pte of tome strowde, the some of ............................ | $l^s$ |
| Lent unto the company, the 3 of Septembr 1601, to paye unto John Daye and $W^m$ Hawghton, in pt of payment of a boocke called the 2 pte of thome Dowghe ................................. | $iij^{li}$ |

[1] Perhaps this entry has reference to the trial of Francis Henslowe, before mentioned on p. 192; but, if so, we do not see why the company should be charged with these expenses: it is also to be observed that, as well as we can gather from Henslowe's previous entry, the matter was settled without coming into court.

[2] A fire-drake was an artificial firework, and was sometimes used for a will o' the wisp; but in this memorandum it seems to have meant a fire-dragon, for which a suit of buckram was required. Those who wish to see more about fire-drakes of various kinds, may consult Malone's note to Henry VIII., A. v., sc. 3.

| | |
|---|---|
| Lent unto the company, the 3 of Septembr 1601, to paye unto the Mr of the Revelles for licensynge of the 3 pte of thome Strowde, and the remainder of Carnowlle Wollseye[1] .......... | xs |
| Lent unto the company, the 10 of Septembr 1601, which them sellfes must paye, for to paye unto Dover, the tayller, upon his bill for the 3 pt of thome Strowde, the some of ...... | xiijs 4d |
| Lent at the apoyntment of Robart Shawe, the 11 of Septembr 1601, to lend unto Wm Hawghton, in pt of payment of the 2 pt of Thome Dowghe, some of ...................... | xs |
| Pd at the apoyntment of the [companye], the 19 of septmbr 1601, for the playe of the wys man of Westchester,[2] unto my sonne, E. Alleyn, the some of...................... .............. | xxxxs |
| Layd owt for the company, the 21 of Septembr 1601, for ower meetynge at the tavern, wher we did eatte ower vensone,[3] the some of ...... | iijli xijs 9d |
| Pd at the apoyntment of the companye, 1601, the 23 of Septembr, unto Mr Bromfelld, for v yds of Roset brode clothe, the some of......... | xxxs |

For the 3 pt of thome Strowde

[1] This is rather a singular entry, showing that "Cardinal Wolsey" was licensed piecemeal by the Master of the Revels; as if he had not seen the whole of it at once, but that the company was in such haste to bring it out that had they sent it to him in portions. We must conclude, from the date, that the payment refers to what is called on p. 198 "the j pt of carnall Woollsay."

[2] This was a revival of the old play, often mentioned by Henslowe, and first produced 2 December 1594: see p. 45. Alleyn was probably paid 40*s*. for what he had done to render it fit for the purpose, by communicating some novelty to the performance.

[3] One of the patrons of the players had most likely presented the company with some venison: the feast was rather a costly one.

| | |
|---|---|
| Lent unto Samwell Rowley, the 24 of Septembr 1601, to paye unto Harey chettell, in pt of payment for a Boocke called the Orfenes tragedy,[1] some of ........................ | $x^s$ |
| Lent unto M^r Alleyn, the 25 of Septembr 1601, to lend unto Bengemen Johnson, upon his writtinge of his adicions in Geronymo,[2] the some of ........................ | $xxxx^s$ |
| Dd unto W^m Haughton, at the apoyntment of Samwell Rowlley, the 31 of septmbr 1601, in pt of payment of a boocke called the prowde womon of Anwarpe, the some of .............. | $x^s$ |
| Lent unto my sonne and W^m Jube, the 31 of septmbr 1601, to bye divers thinges, and sewttes and stockenes for the playe of the weaste enges, the som of .. .......... ......... | $x^{li}$ $x^s$ |
| Pd more the lace man, for coper lace, some ...... | $iij^s$ $ix^d$ |
| Pd more for coper lace for this playe ........... | $vij^s$ |
| Pd the tayllers bille, Radford and W^m Whittes bell, at the apoyntment of Robart Shawe and Jube, the 10 of octobr 1601, for the playe of the weaste enges, the some of ................. | $lvij^s$ |

[1] By a memorandum on p. 93 it appears that Chettle had been paid 10*s.* on account of the Orphan's Tragedy on 27 November, 1599.

[2] These additions were made not to the play called "The First Part of Jeronimo," but to "the Spanish Tragedy." Ben Jonson's additions, here spoken of, were printed in 1602 with "The Spanish Tragedy," which on the title-page is stated to be "newly corrected, amended, and enlarged, with new additions of the Painters part and others." They are reprinted in Dodsley's Old Plays, last edition, vol. iii., p. 97; but Gifford, and other biographers of Ben Jonson, have taken little notice of them, although singularly beautiful and highly characteristic of that great poet. The earliest known edition of "The Spanish Tragedy" is dated 1599, but it had been printed before, because on the title-page the "gross faults" in "the former impression" are mentioned.

| | |
|---|---|
| Lent unto Robarte shawe, to lend unto hary Chettell, and antonye Mondaye, and mihell Drayton, in earneste of a boocke called the Rissenge of carnowlle Wolsey,[1] the 10 of octobr. 1601 ........................................ | xxxx$^s$ |
| Lent at the apoyntment of Samwell Rowley, the 12 of octobr 1601, to M$^r$ Hathwaye and Wentworte Smyth, and W$^m$ Hawghton, in earneste of a playe called the vj clothers, the some of........................................ | xxxx$^s$ |
| Lent at the apoyntment of Samwell Rowley, the 22 of octobr 1601, unto M$^r$ Hathewaye and Wentworthe Smyth, and W$^m$ Hawghton, in pt of payment of a boocke called the vj clothers, some........................................ | iij$^{li}$ |
| Lent unto W$^m$ Jube, the 3 of novmbr 1601, to bye stamell clothe for a clocke for the Gwisse — Webster[2] ........................................ | iij$^{li}$ |

[1] This new play, "The Rising of Cardinal Wolsey," we may presume had its origin in the success of Chettle's "Cardinal Wolsey's Life" (generally called "Cardinal Wolsey" by Henslowe). We shall hereafter see that not merely Chettle, Monday, and Drayton, but Wentworth Smith were engaged upon "The Rising of Cardinal Wolsey," for the greater despatch in bringing it out, in order to take advantage of the popularity of the drama, to which, in fact, it was introductory.

[2] The name of Webster is interlined, perhaps in a different hand; but there is little doubt that this distinguished dramatist at this date either re-wrote, or made some extensive alterations and additions to, Marlowe's "Massacre at Paris:" in the next entry it is called by Henslowe, not "the Guise," as in the memorandum before us, but "the Massacre of France." In the dedication to his "Devil's Law Case," (as already stated in a note on p. 110) Webster mentions that he had written a play called "The Guise," which is most likely the very piece referred to by Henslowe. It might be an entirely new play upon the same historical event as that treated by Webster's great predecessor.

| | |
|---|---|
| Lent unto the company, to lend the littell tayller, to bye fusthen and lynynge for the clockes for the masaker of France, the some of ........... | xxx[s] |
| Lent unto Samelle Rowley and Robt Shawe, to paye unto M[r] Hathewaye, and M[r] Smyth, and W[m] Hawghton, for a boocke called the 2 pte of the vj clothyers ................................ | xxxx[s] |
| Lent unto the company, the 8 of novmbr 1601, to paye unto the littell tayller, upon his bell for mackynge of sewtes for the gwesse,[1] the some of ........................................... | xx[s] |
| Lent unto Samwell Rowley, by the apoyntment of the companye, the 9 of novmbr 1601, to paye unto W[m] Hawghton, for his boocke of the prowd womon of Anwarppe, the some of | xx[s] |
| Layd owt for the company, for the mending of hew Daves[2] tanye cotte, the some of ........ which was eatten with the Rattes | vij[s] vj[d] |
| Lent unto harey chettell, by the company, at the eagell and the childe,[3] in pt of payment of a Boocke called the Rissynge of carnell Wollsey, the some of, the 6 of novembr 1601........... | x[s] |
| Lent unto the companye, the 9 of novmbr 1601, to paye unto M[r] mondaye and Hary chettell, in pt of payment of a boocke called the Rissynge of carnowlle Wollsey, the some of ...... | x[s] |

[1] i.e., The Guise, or Massacre of France, Webster's drama.

[2] Hugh Davies, whose name has frequently occurred before, was a member of the company in some inferior capacity.

[3] Probably the sign of a public-house, or tavern; but it is to be recollected that Thomas Walkley, the publisher of the first edition of "Othello," lived at the sign of "the Eagle and Child," and he might be in treaty with Chettle for the printing of the play, although usually objected to by companies in the time of Shakespeare.

| | |
|---|---|
| Lent unto the company, the 12 of novmbr 1601, to paye unto Antony mondaye and harey Chettell, mihell Drayton and Smythe, in fulle paymente of the firste pt of carnowll Wollsey,[1] the some of ........................ | iij^li |
| Lent unto the companye, the 13 of novmbr 1601, to paye the littell tayllor, Radford, upon his bill for the Gwisse, the some of................ | xx^s |
| Lent at the apoyntment of the companye and my sonne, unto Hary Chettell, in earneste of a playe called to good to be trewe, or northern Man,[2] the some of — the 14 of novmbr 1601 | v^s |
| Pd at the apoyntment of the companye, unto my sonne, E. Alleyn, for a Boocke called Vortiger,[3] the 20 of novmbr 1601, the some of... | xxxx^s |
| Pd at the apoyntment of the companye, unto the littell tayller, in fulle payment of his Bille for the Gwisse, the 26 of novmbr 1601, some | xxiiij^s 6^d |
| Lent unto Samwell Rowlley, the 29 of novmbr 1601, to paye W^m Hawghton, in full paye-[ment] for his playe called the prowd Womon of anwarpe, the some of........................ | xx^s |
| Layd owt for the companye, to bye buckerom for a sewt for the playe of the Nutte,[4] to the littell tayller, the 4 of desembr 1601, the some of | v^s |

[1] Here we see "The Rising of Cardinal Wolsey" called the first part of Cardinal Wolsey. See also p. 198, note 2.

[2] Doubtless, a comedy upon the story of "the King and the poor Northern Man, or too good to be True." In other entries the play is called only "Too good to be True." An old poem on this subject was reprinted in 1841 by the Percy Society.

[3] A revival of a play first acted 4 Dec. 1596. (See p. 83.) Alleyn was paid 40*s*. for his trouble, &c.

[4] In all probability, a revival of the old play "Crack me this Nut." It was originally produced 5 Sep. 1595. See p. 56.

| | |
|---|---|
| Dd unto the littell tayller, to bye for the playe of hercollas,[1] the 14 of desembr 1601, the some of.......... .................................... | xx$^{s}$ |
| Pd unto the littell tayller, 18 of desembr 1601, for divers thinges for the playe of Hercolas, the some of............ ......................... | v$^{s}$ |
| Pd unto W$^{m}$ Borne, at the apoyntment of the company, the 20 of desembr 1601, in earnest of a Boocke called Judas, which Samewell Rowly and he is a writtinge[2] some of ........ | xx$^{s}$ |
| Pd at the apoyntment of the companye unto M$^{rs}$ Gosson,[3] for a head tyer, the 21 of desembr 1601, the some of...................... | xij$^{s}$ |
| Pd at the apoyntment of the companye, unto him at the eagell and chyld, for holberds,[4] the 21 of desembr 1601, the some of ................ | xviij$^{s}$ |
| Pd at the apoyntment of the companye, in fulle payment, for a Boocke called Judas, unto W$^{m}$ Borne and Samwelle Rowley, the 24 of desembr 1601, the some of...................... | v$^{li}$ |

[1] See pp. 51 and 53 respecting the first and second parts of Hercules performed on 7th and 28th May 1595. "The two parts of Hercules" are also mentioned on p. 123, but which of them was now revived, or whether it was a play compounded of both, and printed, in 1613, as Thomas Heywood's, under the title of "The Brazen Age," must be matter of conjecture.

[2] Here the name of *Judas*, or *Indes*, or *Indas*, again occurs, as on p. 171. It seems the earliest notice of Samuel Rowley as an author.

[3] There was a bookseller of the name of Henry Gosson, who published the first edition of Pericles, 1609. As it is rather an unusual name, perhaps this was his wife, and he might be some relation to Stephen Gosson, the early enemy of theatrical performances.

[4] This is the second mention of "the Eagle and Child." See p. 203. It is probable that the halberts here spoken of had been borrowed of the keeper of a tavern for the purpose of some play.

| | |
|---|---|
| Lent at the apoyntment of the companye, unto the lettell tayller, to [bye] taffty sasenet, to macke a payer of hosse for Nycke[1] to tumbell in before the quene, the 25 of desembr 1601, some of ........................................ | xiiijs |
| Pd unto Robart shaw, the 26 of desembr 1601, to descarge his Recknynge at the sonne, the some of ........................................ | xvijs 3d |
| Pd for the company, to Mr Hewettes, for mony which they borowed of him for to bye xj yardes of vellvett, the 1 of Janewary 1601, which Robarte shawe borowed, the some ...... | iijli ijs vjd |
| Pd at the apoyntment of the companye, unto the sylkdier, for dienge of the imbradered klocke, the 2 of Janewary 1601, the some of | xs |
| Lent unto Antony Jeffes, the 3 of Janewary 1601, to bye clothe for the playe of Judas, the some of........................................ | xxxs |
| Pd at the apoyntment of Robarte shawe and thomas Towne, unto Mr Hathwaye and Mr Smythe, in pte of payment of a boocke called to goode to be trewe,[2] the 6 of Janewary 1601, the some of........................................ | ls |

| | |
|---|---|
| Rd by me, Kenricke Williams, the 2d of July 1601, in full pament, the somme of 7li 3s 0d, in full pament of all Reckning, the some of... | 07li 3s 0jd |

I say Rd p me

KENRICKE WILLIAMS.[3]

[1] Of Nick, the tumbler, who exhibited before the queen at Christmas 1601, we do not hear elsewhere.

[2] We have already seen, p. 204, that Chettle also had a hand in this play, there called "Too good to be true or Northern Man."

[3] This memorandum is inserted by Kenrick Williams in the midst of theatrical details. See also p. 208.

| | |
|---|---|
| Pd at the apoyntment of E. Alleyn, the 6 of Janeway 1601, in pte of payment of a Boocke called the spaneshe fygge, the some of | $iij^{li}$ |
| Pd at the apoyntment of Robart shawe, the 7 of Janeway 1601, unto Hary Chettell and $M^r$ Hathwaye and $M^r$ Smythe, in fulle payment for a boocke called to good to be trewe, the some of .......................................... | $iij^{li}$ |
| Pd unto Thomas Deckers, at the apoyntment of the companye, for a prologe and a epiloge, for the playe of Ponesciones pillet,[1] the 12 of Janeway 1601, the some of..................... | $x^s$ |
| Lent unto Thomas Deckers, at the apoyntment of the companye, the 16 of Janeway 1601, toward the alterynge of Tasso,[2] the some of | $xx^s$ |
| Pd at the apoyntment of the companye, the 18 of Janeway 1601, unto E. Alleyn, for iij boockes which were played called the french Docter, the massaker of France, and the nutte,[3] the some of ............................. | $vj^{li}$ |
| Pd for x dossen of lace, to lace the harecolord clocke, the some of $x^s$, and vj dossen more, $vj^s$, some........................................... | $xvj^s$ |

[1] Pontius Pilate is, in all probability, what Henslowe means by "Ponesciones pillet." It was perhaps an old scriptural play, on the revival of which Dekker was employed to write a new prologue and epilogue. The performance of such a piece makes it more likely that the drama on which Rowley and Borne were engaged in the preceding month was "Judas," and not *Indas*.

[2] A revival, with alterations, of the old play of "Tasso's Melancholy," which was performed for the first time in 1594: see p. 39.

[3] Alleyn, we may conclude, was paid this money for his instrumentality in reviving and getting up these three plays, which had been long upon the stage. See pp. 30, 43, 56. On pp. 200, 204, we are told that he had been similarly employed on two other old dramas.

Rd by me, Kenricke Williams, the 2 of auguste 1600, of M[r] Alline, the some of twenty pound, in pt of pament of a more some. I say Rd ꝑ me ........................................ 020[li] 0[s] 0[d]

KENRICKE WILLIAMS.[1]

Rd by me, Kenricke Williams, the 20 of Auguste 1600, of Alline, the some of ten pound, in part payment of a more some. I say Rd ........................................ 010[li] 0[s] 0[d]

ꝑ me, KENRICKE WILLIAMS.

Rd by me, Kenricke Williams, the 3 of September 1600, in pt pament of a more some: I saye Rd the fife pound in pt ... ............. 05[li] 0[s] 0[d]

ꝑ me, KENRICKE WILLIAMS.

Rd by me, Kenricke Williams, the 20[th] of September 1600, of M[r] Henslowe, in pt pament, the some of ten poundes, in pte of more some. I say Rd .................................... 10[li] 0[s] 0[d]

KENRICKE WILLIAMS.

Rd by me, Kenricke Williams, the 10[th] of October 1600, of M[r] Henslowe, in pt pament, the some of ten pounds. I say Rd ꝑ me ... 10[li] 0[s] 0[d]

KENRICKE WILLIAMS.

[1] There is no heading to these items, ascending in the whole to £75 10*s*. 0*d*., and some of the amounts were paid by Alleyn, and others by Henslowe. The date, which is earlier than the previous dramatic entries, tends to show that the payments were made on account of the Fortune Theatre, then in a course of construction and preparation: they also immediately precede a detailed statement, which evidently relates to the Fortune. Kenrick Williams was perhaps a contractor for some part of the work, and his receipt in full has been inserted on p. 201, with the date of 2 July 1601: Peter Street (the contract with whom is preserved at Dulwich, and the particulars of which may be found in the Hist. of Engl. Dram. Poetry and the Stage, iii., 302) was the carpenter employed, and Williams may have been the bricklayer.

Rd by me, Kenricke Williams, the fyrste of november 1600, in pt of pament, the some of $x^{li}$. I saye Rd the same ........................ $10^{li}\ 0^{s}\ 0^{d}$

p̱ me, KENRICKE WILLIAMS.

Pd unto Kenricke Williamse, the 26 of novmbr 1600, in fulle payment of all Reckenengs, from the begynenge of the world unto the daye of the datte herof, the some of thertie shellinges[1] $xxx^{s}$

*What we owe abowt our Howsse,*[2] *as foloweth:* 1600.

Itm̃ from Dickensone, j lode of dubell quarters
Itm̃ frome Dickenson, hallfe a lode of syngell quarters
Itm̃ northumbeland cort, ij hundred of delles, at $xij^{li}\ v^{s}$
Itm̃ more from hime, j hunderd of delle at ...... $v^{li}\ x^{s}$
Itm̃ more from hime, ij hunder of furepowlles
Itm̃ more, fore clape bordes
Itm̃ from Dickenson, ij lode of dubell quarters
Itm̃ from Dickensone, j lode of dubell quarters
Itm̃ from Dickenson, j lode of Rafters
Itm̃ from northumberland cort, j hunderd of del-borde ............................................. $vj^{li}\ ij^{s}\ vj^{d}$
Itm̃ from northumberland cort, j hunderd of del-borde ............................ .................. $vj^{li}$
Itm̃ for one powle for the stayer casse
Itm̃ frome Dickenson, j lode of Rafters

[1] This last note is Henslowe's writing: the others are written and signed by Kenrick Williams. This memorandum does not agree with the receipt on p. 206 either in date or amount.

[2] "Our house" was unquestionably the Fortune Theatre, built by Henslowe and Alleyn. The "Northumberland Court" mentioned in the account (which is in Henslowe's handwriting) was no doubt a timber-yard there, the proprietor of which is not named.

Itm̃ frome Dickenson, j lode of dubell quarters

Itm̃ frome Dickenson, j lode of singell and dubell quarters

Itm̃ from Dickenson, j lode of dubell quarters

Itm̃ frome Dickenson, hallfe a lode of syngell quarters

Itm̃ from northumberland corte, j hunderd of delbordes ........................................... ... vj[li]

Itm̃ from Dickensone, j lode of duble quarters

Itm̃ from Northumberland corte, hallfe a hunderd of delbordes

Itm̃ from Dickenson, j lode of quarters

Itm̃ from Dickenson, halfe a lode of Rafters

Itm̃ from Dickenson, j lode of sorted quarters

Itm̃ more vj gystes

Itm̃ from northumberland corte, hallfe a hunderd of dealle .............................................. iiij[li] x[s]

Itm̃ from northumberland corte, hallfe a hunderd of dealle

Itm̃ from Dickensone, hallfe a lode of dubell quarters, hallfe a lode of sengell quarters, halfe a lod of gystes }

Itm̃ from northumberland corte, j quarter of lod of slyte dealles

Itm̃ from northumberland cort, j quarter of lode of slette dealles

Itm̃ from northumberland corte, j quarter of delbordes

Itm̃ from Dickenson, ij of aguste 1600, hallfe a lode of syngell quarters

Itm̃ from northumberland, xv furpowles and vj delbordes

Itm̃ from Dickenson, vj dubell and vj syngell quarters

Itm̃ from Dickenson, —— Inche bordes

Itm̃ from northumberland cort, vj furpowlls and viij delbordes

Itm̃ from M^r^ Dickenson, j quarter of a hunderd of syngell quarters }

Itm̃ from northumberland corte, xx delbordes and x slette dealles at }

Itm̃ from northumberland corte, vj dealles

Jemes Rosse, goyner, and Gorge Dixson, hath geven his worde for a Biche[1] of W^m^ Dixson, that she shalbe forthe cominge to serve the Quene when I shall send for her, and upon this promisse hath tacken of me a j^d^, on a asumsette to forfette v^li^ yf she be not browght when I shall send for her, and for the performance of v^li^ they have sett to their handes the 29 of septembr 1601.

JEMES + ROSSES marke.
GORGE + DIXSON.

Wittnes to the above written,
JOHN NOLFELLD.[2]

Mdm that M^r^ arture Langworth hath promysed, the 16 daye of maye 1595, to paye unto me, phillippe Henslow, the some of j hundreth powndes, for a howsse, and land, with goods, which he bargened with me with owt any condition, but absolutly to paye me so muche mony, and to take suche a surence as I have at this time: witnesses to this promes of payement.

E. ALLEYN. EDWARD + ALLENES wiffes marke.[3]

[1] This bitch was to "serve the Queen," by being employed in the bear and other baitings for the amusement of the Court.

[2] The whole is in Henslowe's scribe's handwriting, excepting merely the marks of Ross and Dixon.

[3] Hence we see that Mrs. Alleyn (formerly Joan Woodward) could not write: the signature of the other witness is that of Edward Alleyn

| | |
|---|---|
| Rd in pte of payment, the 3 of June 1595, the some of fiftie pownd. I saye Rd .............. | $50^{li}\ 0^{s}\ 0^{d}$ |
| Lent unto M$^{r}$ artur Lengworth, in Redey money, the x of June 1595, the some of tenne powndes, which was delyvered unto hime by the handes of my dawghter, Edwardes Allenes wiffe. I saye.................................... | $x^{li}$ |

*A noot what I have layd owte sence we went abowt ower new howsse*[1] *as foloweth.* 1600 :—

| | | |
|---|---|---|
| Pd for removinge the dunge with the carte | $x^{s}$ | |
| Pd for goinge at Grenwiche with Robart shawe | | $xviij^{d}$ |
| Pd for a bracke faste at that time with shawe | | $xij^{d}$ |
| Pd for drincke when we payd wages | | $v^{d}$ |
| Pd at the Rede crosse for brackfaste, when we sowght Strete | $ij^{s}$ | |
| Geven to the workmen to drincke | | $vj^{d}$ |
| Pd the waterman for goinge throwe Brige from blackfryers | | $iiij^{d}$ |
| Pd the 2 of June 1600, for stretes diner and myne | | $xij^{d}$ |
| Pd for goinge by water with the M$^{r}$ of the Revelles[2] | | $xij^{d}$ |

himself. The body of the memorandum is in the handwriting of Henslowe's scribe.

[1] "Our new House" was the Fortune Theatre, to which this account also relates. It consists of many more items than are here inserted, but most of them are mere repetitions of the cost of Henslowe's dinners with East and Street. Street, as we have stated, was the carpenter, and East was perhaps another contractor for a different part of the work. The Red Cross, at which they once breakfasted, was, no doubt, in Red Cross Street, very near the new theatre.

[2] This item seems to show that the Master of the Revels (possibly in his official capacity) surveyed the progress of the undertaking,

Pd for cominge by water, my sonne and I xviij[d]
Pd the 25 of June, for workmen and our sellfes diner xviij[d]
Pd for whipcorde and goinge by water vj[d]
Pd the 6 of Julye for diner for Peter, Easte and my sellfe [1] xviij[d]

Rd of M[r] Henslow, the 6 of maye 1601, for the usse of my M[r], Richard Walles, in pte of payment, the some of fyve powndes. I saye Rd by me ........................................ } v[li]

ROBERT CLYFTON.

Receaved by us, Ri. Hathway, Wentworth Smyth, and William Haughton, of M[r] Hinslye, the summe of forty shillinges, in earneste of the play called the second pte of the sixe clothyers.

RI. HATHWAY.
W. SMYTH.

Receyved of M[r] Hynchloe, the 9[th] of June, iij[li], which he is to paye for the monethes paye for the Fortune, [2] and due unto the M[r] of the Revelles.

ROBTE HASSARD.

going part of the way by water, or accompanied Henslowe to Greenwich. We shall presently meet with the first payment to him of his "months money," £3, for his sanction to performances at the Fortune.

[1] These entries for dinners, at prices varying from 11*d.* to 18*d.*, are continued daily until the 8th August, when the account terminates at the bottom of the page.

[2] There is no date of the year to this memorandum, but it was probably 9th June 1601: we have just seen, by previous accounts, that the Fortune Theatre was not finished on the 8th August 1600. Peter Street, East, and Henslowe, were engaged upon it up to that date.

Lent unto frances Henslow, to goyne with owld Garlland, and Symcockes, and Savery, when they played in the Duckes name[1] at ther laste goinge owt, the some of vij$^{li}$. I saye lent ............................ . ............... } vij$^{li}$

Received of M$^{r}$ Philip Hinchloes in earnest of the Booke of Shoare, now newly to be written for the Earle of Worcesters players at the Rose, of M$^{r}$ Hinchloes, xl$^{s}$. I say received.[2]

30 Die Januarij 1598.[3]

Receaved by mee, Thomas Dekker, of M$^{r}$ Phillip Hynchlow, the some of Three Powndes Ten shillings, to bee repayd unto Him or his Assignes upon the last of February next

[1] This entry perhaps belongs to the year 1604, and "the Duke" (under whose name Francis Henslowe and others went into the country) was most likely the Duke of Lennox. Vide Memoirs of Edward Alleyn, page 69. Savery has been already mentioned on p. 192, under not very advantageous circumstances.

[2] This undated and unsigned entry gives us information on two or three points. In the first place, it is in the handwriting of Chettle, who had "newly written" a play on the story of Jane Shore: next, it informs us that the Earl of Worcester's, and not the Earl of Nottingham's players, were in the occupation of the Rose Theatre. Of this company, Thomas Heywood, who had originally engaged with Henslowe, was a member, and upon the accession of James I. (as Heywood himself informs us in his "Nine Books concerning Women," 1624) this association became the players of Queen Anne, as the Earl of Nottingham's players became the theatrical servants of Prince Henry. When the Earl of Worcester's players were acting at the Rose, those of the Earl of Nottingham had removed to the Fortune, both houses being occupied at the same time. This memorandum must be anterior to the accession of James I.

[3] The body and subscription of this acknowledgment are in the handwriting of Dekker. Those of the witnesses also are original signatures.

ensuing: for payment whereof I bynd mee my Heyres, Executors, and Administrators.

THOMAS DEKKER.

Wittnes E. ALLEYN
SAMUELL ROWLYE.

| | |
|---|---|
| Rd of Mr Henslowe, the viijth of July 1602, for one months paye due the third of July, being this present month, the som of 3li, to the use of my Mr, Mr Edmond Tylney esquire: I say Rd the som of.............................. | iijli |

ꝑ mei WILL. PLAYSTOWE.

William Birde.

| | | |
|---|---|---|
| Rd the 30 of June 1601, in pt ...................... | xvijs | 8d |
| Rd the 4 of Julye 1601, in pt......................... | xiiijs | |

Pd him backe agayne this mony.

| | |
|---|---|
| Lent unto Wm Kempe, the 10 of marche 1602, in Redy monye twentye shellenges for his necesary usses, the some of[1].................... | xxs |

Robarte shawe.

| | | |
|---|---|---|
| Rd the 30 of June 1601, in pte ................ ... | xvijs | 8d |
| Rd the 4 of July 1601, in pte....................... | xiiijs | |
| Rd the 11 of Julye 1601, in pte .................... | xiijs | 4d |
| Rd the 18 of Julye 1601, in pte .................... | xvjs | |

[1] This is the earliest notice of Kempe in the MS.; but he must have belonged to the company under Henslowe and Alleyn, as early as 1592 (see p. 28): he afterwards joined the Lord Chamberlain's servants; then rejoined some of his old associates, as one of the players of the Earl of Worcester, and finally re-united himself with the company to which Shakespeare was attached. It seems probable that Henslowe and Alleyn held out inducements to Kempe, the most popular low comedian of his day, when they opened the Fortune.

| | | |
|---|---|---|
| Rd the 25 of July 1601, in pte .................... | xvj[s] | j[d] |
| Rd the j of aguste 1601, in pte .................... | v[s] | viij[d] |
| Rd the 8 of aguste 1601, in pte .................... | x[s] | vij[d] |
| Rd the 15 of aguste 1601, in pte.................... | xv[s] | iiij[d] |

*Begininge to Receve of thes meane ther privet deates,*[1] *which they owe unto me, acordinge to the dayes which foloweth:* 1601.

Richard Jonnes.

| | | |
|---|---|---|
| Rd the 30 of June 1601, in pte .................... | xvij[s] | 8[d] |
| Rd the 4 of Julye 1601, in pte .................... | xiiij[s] | |
| Rd the 11 of Julye 1601, in pte .................... | xiij[s] | 4[d] |
| Rd the 18 of Julye 1601, in pte .................... | xvj[s] | |
| Rd the 25 of Julye 1601, in pte .................... | xvj[s] | j[d] |
| Rd the j of aguste 1601, in pte .................... | v[s] | viij[d] |
| Rd the 8 of aguste 1601, in pte .................... | x[s] | vij[d] |
| Rd the 15 of aguste 1601, in pte.................... | xv[s] | iiij[d] |
| Rd the 22 of aguste 1601, in pte.................... | xv[s] | vj[d] |
| Rd the 29 of aguste 1601, in pte.................... | xx[s] | |

Thomas Downton.

| | | |
|---|---|---|
| Rd the 30 of June 1601, in pte[2].................... | xvij[s] | 8[d] |
| Rd the 4 of Julye 1601, in pt.................... | xiiij[s] | |
| Rd the 11 of Julye 1601, in pt .................... | xiij[s] | 4[d] |
| Rd the 18 of Julye 1601, in pt .................... | xvj[s] | |
| Rd the 25 of Julye 1601, in pt .................... | xvj[s] | j[d] |
| Rd the j of aguste 1601, in pt.................... | v[s] | viij[d] |
| Rd the 8 of aguste 1601, in pt .................... | x[s] | vij[d] |
| Rd the 15 of aguste 1601, in pt .................... | xv[s] | iiij[d] |
| Rd the 22 of aguste 1601, in pt .................... | xv[s] | vj[d] |

[1] Money advanced by Henslowe on the condition of weekly repayments, which he records. Such was probably the case with the preceding accounts, under the names of Birde and Shawe, although Birde occurs again just afterwards as Henslowe's debtor.

[2] This first entry of a payment is struck through with the pen.

| | | |
|---|---|---|
| Rd the 29 of aguste 1601, in pte.................... | xx$^{s}$ | |
| Rd the 5 of Septmbr 1601, in pt.................... | xiiij$^{s}$ | |

| | | |
|---|---|---|
| Lent W$^{m}$ Birde, alles Borne, the some of... | v$^{li}$ | |
| Rd in pte .............................................. | x$^{s}$ | |
| Rd in pte .............................................. | x$^{s}$ | |
| Rd in pte .............................................. | viij$^{s}$ | |
| Rd in pt the 18 of octobr 1601 .................... | iij$^{s}$ | 8$^{d}$ |
| Rd in pt the 25 of octobr 1601 .................... | ij$^{s}$ | 4$^{d}$ |
| Rd in pt the j of novmbr 1601 .................... | iij$^{s}$ | 4$^{d}$ |

| | | |
|---|---|---|
| Lent unto Mr. Jonnes, the 2 of octobr 1601, and Receved as folowethe—some........................ | xxxx$^{s}$ | |
| Rd in pte, the 3 of octobr 1601 .................... | v$^{s}$ | |
| Rd in pte the 11 of octobr 1601 .................... | viij$^{s}$ | |
| Rd in pte, the 18 of octobr 1601.................... | iij$^{s}$ | 8$^{d}$ |
| Rd in pte, the 25 of octobr 1601.................... | ij$^{s}$ | 4$^{d}$ |
| Rd in pte, the 1 of novmbr 1601.................... | iij$^{s}$ | 4$^{d}$ |
| Pd and quite.[1] | | |

| | |
|---|---|
| Pd the 21 of Janewary,[2] for xij oz of lace for Indies,[3] x$^{s}$, and pd to Spencer for twiste, ij$^{s}$ vj$^{d}$: pd for ij tiers, x$^{s}$, and pd for v oz and lacynge the sleves, v$^{s}$ vj$^{d}$, to E. Alleyn, the some of ........................................ | xxviij$^{s}$ |

[1] The whole sum borrowed by Jones seems to have been £2, out of which, according to this account, though Henslowe declared it to be "paid and quit," Jones had only returned £1 2*s*. 4*d*. In the preceding account Birde only paid £1 17*s*. 4*d*. out of the £5 borrowed. Perhaps the difference was made up in some unexplained way at the time the matter was closed; but Henslowe's accounts are generally too confused to bear nice examination.

[2] These items are continued from p. 207.

[3] "Indies" in this entry means probably what Henslowe has previously called (p. 196) "enges" and "weste enges."

| | |
|---|---|
| Lent unto Robart Shawe, the 21 of Janeway 1601, to geve unto harey cheattell, for mendinge of the Boocke called the prowde womon,[1] the some of.................................. | $x^s$ |
| Pd at the apoyntmente of E. Alleyn, for the companye, unto the coper lace man, for lace, the 25 of Janewary 1601, the some of......... | $xxxv^s$ |
| Pd at the apoyntmente of the companye, to Mrs Gosson, for a headtyer, the 7 of febreary 1601, the some of ............................... | $xij^s$ |

Totalles frome ther handes before in the yeare 1600, from the x of July, is $318^{li}$ $16^s$ $04^d$.[2]

JOHN SINGER
THOMAS DOWNTON
WILLIAM BYRD
EDWARD JUBY
THOMAS TOWNE
HUMPHREY JEFFS
ANTHONY JEFFS
SAMUELL ROWLEY
CHARLES MASSY.[3]

Frome ther handes to this place is $308^{li}$ $06^s$ $04^d$, dewe unto me, and with the three hundred of owld is $608^{li}$ $06^s$ $04^d$.

[1] This play has been already assigned to Day and Haughton in a memorandum dated 4th July 1601 (see p. 193); and we hear of it again on 29th Nov. 1601: (see p. 204.) Perhaps "Friar Rush and the proud Woman of Antwerp" had never yet been performed, and Chettle was employed to "mend" it even before it was represented.

[2] This addition appears, from what follows the names of the players, (all of them written by John Singer) to be incorrect, but the figures are much altered and blotted.

[3] That some importance was attached to the order in which the names of the members of the company stood may be judged from the circum-

| | |
|---|---|
| Lent unto the company, to geve unto M^r Jonnes and M^r Shaw, at ther goinge a waye,[1] fyftye powndes, which is not in this Recknynge: I saye........ ...................... ................ | 50^li |

*Begininge with a new Recknyng with my lord of nottingames men, the* 23 *daye of febreary* 1601, *as foloweth:*

| | |
|---|---|
| Itm pd unto my sonne E. Alleyn, which was after we had Reckneyd togeather, the company and I, which after our castying dew to my sonne owt of the gallery mony, the some of................................................ | xxvij^s vj^d |
| Lent unto harey cheattell, March 25, at the apoyntment [of] Thomas Dowton and my sonne, E. Alleyn, at the seallynge of H. Chettells band to write for them,[2] the some of ... | iij^li |
| Pd at the apoyntment of the companye, the 18 of aprell 1602, unto Charlles massey, for a playe Boocke called Malcolm kynge of Scottes,[3] the some of.................................. | v^li |

stance that John Singer, the celebrated comedian, originally placed himself third in the list, but his name was subsequently erased with a pen and crowded in before that of Thomas Downton.

[1] Perhaps "their going away" referred to some temporary secession or absence in the country, for Jones and Shaw certainly did not finally quit the company.

[2] According to this item, Henry Chettle had entered into a bond to write, we may suppose, exclusively for the Earl of Nottingham's players, and had received £3 for so doing.

[3] Massey is put down by Malone (iii., 326) as the writer of Malcolm King of Scots, but he could only have been employed by the author or authors to introduce it to the theatre. Massey was comparatively illiterate, as may be seen by the fragment of a letter from him to Alleyn, requesting a loan of £50: "Memoirs of Edward Alleyn," p. 109.

| | | |
|---|---|---|
| Pd at the apoyntment of my sonne, the 21 of aprelle 1602, for a scertes[1] of clothe of sylver, for a womons gowne, the some of .............. | | xxxx$^{s}$ |
| Lent unto Thomas Downton, the 27 of aprell 1602, to bye a sewt of motley for the Scotchman, for the playe called the Malcolm kynge of Scotes, the some of .......................... | | xxx$^{s}$ |
| Lent unto Thomas Downton, the 4 of maye 1602, to bye a Boocke of harye Cheattell and M$^{r}$ Smyth, called the Love partes frenship, the some of.................................... | vj$^{li}$ | |
| Lent at the apoyntment of Samewell Rowlye, unto John Daye, the 4 of maye 1602, in earneste of a play called Bristo tragedi,[2] as may apere, the some of .......................... | | xx$^{s}$ |
| written by hime sellfe. | | |
| Lent unto the companye, the 5 of maye 1602, to geve unto antoney monday and thomas Deckers, in earnest of a Boocke called Jeffte,[3] as may apeare, the some of .................... | v$^{li}$ | |
| Lent unto Thomas Downton, the 15 of maye 1602, to pay Harey Chettell for the mendynge of the fyrste pte of carnowlle Wollsey, the some of .......................................... | | xx$^{s}$ |
| Lent unto Thomas Downton, the 16 of maye 1602, to geve harey cheattell, in earneste of a playe called Tobyas, the some of ............... | | xx$^{s}$ |

[1] A *scertes* perhaps means "a skirts" of cloth of silver.

[2] This was probably the play printed anonymously in 1605, under the title of "The fair Maid of Bristol." It has been assigned to Day on the authority of the above entry.

[3] This name is spelt differently, but (if it mean Jephthah, as it most likely does) never rightly spelt by Henslowe or his scribe. The ballad of "Jephthah Judge of Israel," quoted in "Hamlet," is well known: see Percy's Reliques, i., 193, edit 1812.

| | |
|---|---|
| Layd owt for the companye, the 16 of maye 1602, for to bye a dublett and a payer of venesyons of clothe of sylver wraght with read sylke, the some of fower pownd and ten shellinges, I saye .............................. | iiij$^{li}$ x$^{s}$ |
| Layd owt for the company, when they Read the playe of Jeffa, for wine at the tavern, dd unto Thomas Downton .............................. | ij$^{s}$ |
| Lent unto Thomas Downton, the 18 maij, to bye maskyng antycke sewtes, for the 2 pte of carnowlle Woolsey, the some of .............. | iij$^{li}$ v$^{s}$ |
| Lent unto Thomas Downton, the 20 of maij 1602, to bye a grene sewt and womon sleves, the some of —, for Wollseye .................... | l$^{s}$ |
| Lent unto the companye, the 22 of maij 1602, to geve unto Antoney Monday and Mihell Drayton, Webester, Mydelton and the Rest, in earneste of a Boocke called sesers Falle,[1] the some of........................................ | v$^{li}$ |
| Pd unto John Daye, at the apoyntment of W$^{m}$ Jube and the Reste of the companye, for a Boocke called Bristo tragedi, the 23 of maij 1602, the some of .............................. | xxxx$^{s}$ |

written by hime sellfe

| | |
|---|---|
| Lent unto Thomas Downton, the 27 of maij 1602, to bye W$^{m}$ someres[2] cotte and other thinges, for the 2 pte of Wollsey, the some of | iij$^{li}$ |

[1] Malone passed over this important entry without notice: it shews that in May 1602 four poets, who are named (viz. Monday, Drayton, Webster, and Middleton), and some others not named, were engaged in writing a play upon the subject of the Fall of Cæsar. See Collier's Shakespeare, vii., 4, where it is contended that the Julius Cæsar of our great dramatist was written in 1603.

[2] A coat for Will Sommers, the celebrated and favourite jester of Henry VIII.

| | | |
|---|---|---|
| Dd at the apoyntment of Thomas towne, the 28 of maye 1602, unto John Daye, in fulle payment for his playe, written by hime selffe,[1] called Bristo tragedie, the some of ........... | | xxxx^s |
| Lent unto Thomas Downton, the 29 of maye 1602, to bye Rebatoes and other thinges for the 2 pte of carnowlle Wollsey, the some of | | xxv^s |
| Lent unto Thomas Downton, the 29 of maye 1602, to paye Thomas Dickers, Drayton, Mydellton, and Webester, and Mondaye, in fulle paymente for ther playe called too harpes,[2] the some of ................ ........... | iij^li | |
| Lent unto Thomas Downton, the 31 of maye 1602, to paye unto the coper lace[man], in pt of payment, the some of ................. ..... | | xx^s |
| Lent unto Thomas Downton, the 31 of maye 1602, to bye a sewt for ther playe called love partes frenshippe ................................ | | l^s |
| Lent unto Thomas Downton, the 2 of June 1602, to paye unto the coper lace man, in fulle payment for the lace for the 2 pt of Wollsey ................................ ........... | | xxvj^s |
| Lent unto Thomas Downton, the 2 of June 1602, to geve harey cheattell, upon his Boocke of Tobyas, the some of ............... ......... | | xx^s |
| Lent unto Thomas Downton, the 8 of maye 1602,[3] to bye cottes for the playe of Jeffa, the some of........................................ | vj^li | |

[1] The meaning of the words "written by himself" is most likely that Day alone was the author of it, without any coadjutors.

[2] Malone calls this piece "the Two Harpies," and that may be the correct title of it. In the original entry it is difficult to ascertain whether Henslowe's scribe wrote "too hapes," "too hopes," or "too harpes."

[3] This date seems erroneously given as 8th May 1602. The place it occupies shews that it ought to be the 8th June 1602.

| | | |
|---|---|---|
| Lent unto Thomas Downton, the 12 of June 1602, to bye Rebatoes and other thinges for the playe of Jeffa, the some of .................. | iiij$^{li}$ | |
| Lent unto bengemy Johnsone, at the apoyntment of E. Alleyn and W$^{m}$ Birde, the 24 of June 1602, in earneste of a boocke called Richard crockbacke, and for new adicyons for Jeronymo,[1] the some of........................ | x$^{li}$ | |
| Pd at the apoynt of Thomas Downton, unto the tayller for mackynge of sewtes for Jeffa, the 25 of June 1602, some of ............. ... | | xxx$^{s}$ |
| Lent unto Thomas Downton, the 26 of June 1602, to paye unto harey Chettell, in pte of payment for a Boocke called tobyas, the some of .......................................... | iij$^{li}$ | |
| Lent unto Thomas Downton, the 27 of June 1602, to paye unto Harey chettell, in fulle payment of his Boocke called tobias, the some of .................................. ........... | | xx$^{s}$ |
| Lent unto the company, 1602, the 27 of June, to paye unto hime which made ther propertyes for Jeffa, the some of ................. | | xxv$^{s}$ |
| Lent unto Thomas Downton, the 5 of Julye 1602, to paye the cuter[2] for the playe of Jeffa, the some of .............................. | | xxij$^{s}$ |

[1] See Malone's Shaksp. by Boswell, iii., 335, where this entry, (in which the words "unto bengemy Johnsone" are interlined) with some slight variations, is quoted. The play was clearly on the events of the reign of Richard III. The "new additions to Jeronymo" were probably some scenes in the Spanish Tragedy beyond those which were entered on p. 201 as paid for before: there they are called merely "additions," but here "*new* additions" are spoken of.

[2] Who or what was "the *cuter* for the play of Jeffa" it is not easy to conjecture: the sum is too considerable, or we might suppose it to be payment to the man who played the executioner. A *cutter* was a well-

| | |
|---|---|
| Lent unto Thomas Downton, the 7 of Julye 1602, to geve unto Harye chettell, in earneste of a tragedy called a Danyshe tragedye, the some of ........................................ | xx^s |
| Lent unto Thomas Downton, the 9 of July 1602, to lend unto Antony the poyete, in earneste of a comody called the Widowes cherme,[1] the some of ........................................ | x^s |
| Pd at the apoyntment of E. Alleyn, the 16 day of July 1602, to M^r Stonnes man, for a payer of crymson satten venysions, with a strype of gowld lace, the some of[2] ...................... | xxx^s |
| Lent unto Thomas Downton and Edward Jewbe, to geve unto Thomas Dickers, in earneste of a comody called a medyson for a curste wiffe, 19 of July 1602.................................. | xxxx^s |
| Lent unto H. chettel, v^s.[3] | |
| Lent unto Samwell Rowley and Edwarde Jewbe, to paye for the Booke of Samson, the 29 of Julye 1602, the some of ........... .......... | vj^li |

known character, and Heywood was paid for writing the part of *cutting* Dick; but if introduced into the tragedy of Jephthah, the actor would hardly have been paid separately.

[1] "Antony the poyete" was either Anthony Munday, or Anthony Wadeson; most likely the latter, as Anthony Munday was better known. Malone suggests, without any apparent ground, that this comedy, "the Widow's Charm," was the play afterwards printed, and called "the Puritan Widow." He means of course "the Puritan, or the Widow of Watling Street," which came out in 4to in 1607, with the initials W. S. on the title-page, and was included in Shakespeare's Works, edit. 1664, folio.

[2] This entry (like some others) has a large cross against it in the margin, as if it had been erased, but the word *steate* (probably meant for *stet*) has been written over it. The same remark will apply to two subsequent entries on the same page.

[3] Inserted in the margin of the MS.

| | | |
|---|---|---|
| Lent unto Thomas Downton, the 31 of July 1602, to paye unto Thomas Dickers, in pte of payment of his comodey called a medyssen for a curste wiffe,[1] the some of................. | | xxxx$^{s}$ |
| Pd unto my sone, E. A., for ij boocke called Phillipe of Spayne and Longshanckes,[2] the 8 of aguste 1602, the some of ................. | iiij$^{li}$ | |
| Lent unto Antoney the poyet, in pt of payment of a comedy called widowes Charme, the 26 of aguste 1602, the some of ..................... | | v$^{s}$ |
| Lent unto W$^{m}$ Birde and W$^{m}$ Jube, the 2 of Septembr 1602, to paye unto Antoney the poyet, in pte of payment of a comodey called A widowes Charme, the some of .............. | | x$^{s}$ |
| Lent unto W$^{m}$ Birde, and Thomas Towne, and Edward Jube, the 8 of Septembr 1602, to paye unto W$^{m}$ Hawghton for a playe called Cartwryght,[3] the some of........................ | | l$^{s}$ |
| Lent unto Umfrey Jeaffes, the 9 of Septembr 1602, in pte payment to M$^{r}$ Robensone for a tragedie called Femelanco,[4] the some of ...... | iij$^{li}$ | |

[1] This "Medicine for a Curst Wife" was probably some new version of the "Taming of a Shrew," which preceded Shakespeare's comedy, and which has been reprinted by the Shakespeare Society from the *unique* copy of 1594, in the library of the Duke of Devonshire.

[2] Two old plays, we may presume, in the revival of which E. Alleyn had been instrumental. Longshanks had been brought out in 1595 (see p. 55); but of Philip of Spain we know nothing—excepting that he is introduced into Lust's Dominion, a play long erroneously assigned to Marlowe.

[3] Founded upon a tragical incident of the time: Cartwright murdered a Mr. Storr, a clergyman, and a tract containing the facts was published with the date of 1603, and is extant.

[4] This dramatist is heard of again afterwards: it appears that he was assisted by H. Chettle in the composition of Femelanco. There was a

| | | |
|---|---|---|
| Lent unto Edward Jube, the 10 of Septembr, to macke ij sewtes a licke for the playe of Mortymore,[1] the some of................................ | $vj^{li}$ | |
| More for the same sewtes at the playhowse ...... | | $xviij^{s}$ |
| Lent unto Antony the poet, the 11 of septembr 1602, in pte of payment of a comody called the widowes charme, the some of .............. | | $v^{s}$ |
| Lent unto Thomas Downton, the 15 of Septmbr 1602, to paye unto Harey chettell, in pte of payment for his tragedie of femelanco, the some of........................................ | | $x^{s}$ |
| Lent unto the company, 1602, to paye the billes for tayllors and others for the new playe of the earlle of Harford,[2] the some of .............. | | $xxxij^{s}$ |
| Pd at the apoyntment of Thomas Downton, to harey chettell, in full payment of his tragedie called Femelanco, some of........................ | | $l^{s}$ |
| Pd unto Samwell Rowley, the 27 of septmbr 1602, for his playe of Jhosua,[3] in fulle payment, the some of ................................. | $vij^{li}$ | |

player of the name of Robson in the company in 1597 (see p. 259); and two persons of the name of Robinson, Richard and William, were also on the stage: Richard Robinson is enumerated in the folio of 1623 as one of "the principal actors in all these plays." On the authority of Wright's *Historia Histrionica*, 1699, it has been stated that he was killed by Gen. Harrison in 1645 at the storming of the Basing House.

[1] Ben Jonson left behind him the fragment of a drama on the Fall of Mortimer, which is supposed to have been one of his later efforts; but it may possibly have been the "play" here mentioned, of which Malone takes no sort of notice.

[2] This anonymous piece of "the Earl of Hertford," or *Harford*, as Henslowe spells it, is not mentioned by Malone.

[3] This was a considerable sum for Rowley's Joshua (probably founded upon Scripture history); but perhaps he was paid also for his services as an actor in preparing it for the stage.

| | | |
|---|---|---|
| Pd unto my sonne, E. Alleyn, at the apoyntment of the company, for his boocke of Tambercam,[1] the 2 of octobr 1602, the some of | | $xxxx^{s}$ |
| Pd at the apoynt[ment] of $W^{m}$ [Edw] Jube, the 21 of octobr 1602, unto $M^{r}$ Medelton, in pte of payment for his playe called Chester tragedie,[2] the some of.................................... | $iiij^{li}$ | |
| Pd unto my sonne, E. Alleyn, the 22 of octobr 1602, at the apoyntment of the company, for a grogren clocke, ij velvet gerkens, and ij dublets, and ij hed tyers, j payer of hosse, the some of[3]........................................ | $xx^{li}$ | |
| Lent unto my sonne, E. Alleyn, the 3 of novmbr 1602, to geve unto Thomas Deckers, for mendinge of the playe of Tasso, the some of ...... | | $xxxx^{s}$ |
| Lent unto Edward Jube, the 8 of novmbr 1602, to geve unto John Daye, in earneste of a boocke called Mery as may be,[4] for the corte, the some of ........................................ | | $xxxx^{s}$ |

[1] "The plott of the first part of Tamer Cam," taken from the original formerly preserved at Dulwich College, is to be seen in Malone's Shaksp. by Boswell, iii., 356. There was a new play called Tambercame produced in May 1596 (vide p. 68), and in June of the same year, the *first* and *second* parts of the same piece are registered by Henslowe as having been performed, the second part for the first time, although a "second part of Tambercame" had been acted on 28th April 1592 (pp. 25, 74). The confusion may arise from revivals having been sometimes treated by Henslowe as new plays.

[2] Malone conjectured, without the slightest reason, that this play was "probably the Mayor of Queenborough." In a later entry, this "Chester Tragedy" is called "Randall Earl of Chester." "Femelanco" had been first written by Henslowe, and corrected by Singer, the actor.

[3] This memorandum is crossed out in the MS.

[4] Wentworth Smith and Richard Hathwaye were partners with Day in this comedy of "As Merry as may be," which they wrote for the

| | |
|---|---|
| Lent unto Edward Jube, the 9 of novmbr 1602, to paye unto M$^{r}$ Mydelton, in fulle paymente of his playe called Randowlle earlle of Chester, the some of..... ................................ | xxxx$^{s}$ |
| Lent unto Thomas Downton, the 17 of novmbr 1602, to paye unto John Daye and M$^{r}$ Smyth, and hathwaye, in fulle paymente for a Boocke called as merey as be, the some of.............. | vj$^{li}$ |
| Lent unto the companye, the 22 of novmbr 1602, to paye unto W$^{m}$ Birde and Samwell Rowley, for ther adicyones in Docter Fostes,[1] the some of ............................................ | iiij$^{li}$ |
| Lent unto Edward Jube, the 2 of desembr 1602, to paye unto Antoney Monday, in fulle payement for a playe called the seeat at tenes,[2] some is ............................................ | iiij$^{li}$ |
| Lent unto W$^{m}$ Birde, the 4 of desembr 1602, to paye unto Thomas Deckers, in pte of payment for Tasso, the some of .................... | xx$^{s}$ |
| Lent unto Thomas Downton, the 14 of desembr 1602, to paye unto M$^{r}$ Mydelton for a prologe and epeloge for the playe of Bacon[3] for the corte, the some of ......................... | v$^{s}$ |

Court, and for which they obtained, as appears by this entry, 40*s*., and subsequently £6 more. A blank was left for the name of the piece, which was subsequently filled in by Day.

[1] Marlowe's "Faustus," which at this date was revived with additions by Birde and Rowley.

[2] The true title was "The Set at Tennis." See p. 47, note 1, respecting the play called "The Set at Maw."

[3] Greene's "Friar Bacon," which was revived for the Court with a new prologue and epilogue by Middleton, of which Malone takes no notice. Mr. Dyce did not consult Henslowe's Diary, and was therefore not acquainted with this and some other interesting particulars relating to Middleton and his works.

| | |
|---|---|
| Pd at the apoyntment of the company, the 18 of desembr, unto M$^{r}$ Stone, merser, in fulle payment of all Recknynges, to this daye, as may aper by his quitance, the some of ............... | viij$^{li}$ xviij$^{s}$ |
| Lent unto Thomas Downton, the 17 of desembr 1602, to paye unto harey chettell, in earneste of a playe called London florenten,[1] the some of | x$^{s}$ |
| Pd at the apoyntment of the company, the 20 of desembr 1602, unto Thomas Hewode, in pt for his playe called london Florentyne, the some of ........................................ | xxxx$^{s}$ |
| Lent unto Thomas Downton, the 22 of desembr 1602, to paye unto Harey chettell, in fulle payment for his play called the London florentyn, the some ........................................ | iij$^{li}$ |

Caste up my acowntes[2] to this place, now at cryssmas 1602, all Recknenges abated, and they owe unto me, with fyftie pownde which I lent them to geve Jones and Shawe, ........................................ 226$^{li}$ 16$^{s}$ 8$^{d}$

| | |
|---|---|
| Lent unto Thomas Downton, the 29 of desembr 1602, to paye unto harey chettell for a prologe and epyloge for the corte, the some of ... | v$^{s}$ |
| Lent unto Thomas Downton, the 29 of desembr 1602, to geve unto Harey Chettle, in pte of paymente for a tragedie called Hawghman,[3] the some of........................................ | v$^{s}$ |

[1] It appears by the item immediately following, that Thomas Heywood was partner with Chettle in writing this play called "the London Florentine."

[2] The summing-up of the debt of the company is crowded in at the foot of a page, and in the midst of the entries.

[3] "Hoffman," no doubt the tragedy here meant, was printed anonymously in 1631: it has many merits.

| | |
|---|---|
| Pd for the company, the 7 of Janewary 1602, unto Thomas Hawode, in fulle payment for his playe called the London florantyn, the some of ........................................ | xx[s] |
| Pd at the apoyntment of the company, 1602, the 13 of Janewarye, unto John' Synger, for his playe called Syngers Vollentarye,[1] the some of ........................................ | v[li] |
| Ld owt at the apoyntment of Thomas Hewode, in earneste of a playe called Like quits Like,[2] unto Mr Harey chettell and thomas Hewode, the 14 of Janewary 1602, some of ...... ..... | xxxx[s] |
| Layd owt for the companye, the 10 of desembr 1602, unto Robarte Shawe, for a boocke of the 4 sonnes of Amon, the some of ........... | xl[s] |
| Lent unto Jube, the 1 of marche 1602, to geve unto John Daye and Hathwaye, in earneste of a playe called the bosste of billengesgate,[3] the some of........................................ | xxxx[s] |

[1] John Singer, the celebrated comic actor, was the reputed author of this piece before noticed on p. 6. Henslowe calls it "a play," and the sum paid for it (£5) may show that it was more than that brief species of entertainment technically called "a jig," which seems to have consisted of singing, recitation, and dancing, by actors who usually filled the parts of clowns in the theatres. A work by Singer in verse, printed in 1600, is extant, of which no notice has ever been taken.

[2] It is just possible that this may have been a play on the same story as Measure for Measure, near the end of which this line occurs—

*Like doth quit like*, and Measure still for Measure.

The success of Measure for Measure at this date might have produced the rival play. As has often been the case, the title of the piece was clumsily filled in by Henslowe after he made the entry.

[3] Day and Hathwaye, according to another memorandum by Henslowe, had either one or more coadjutors in this Boast of Billingsgate.

| | |
|---|---|
| Lent the 7 of marche 1602, in pt of paymente for the playe called the Bosste of bellingsgate, unto John Daye and Hathwaye, the some of | xxxx^s |
| Lent unto Edward Jube, the 7 of marche 1602, to geve unto Charles Masseye, in earneste of a playe called the sedge of Doncerke, with Alleyn the pyrete,[1] the some of ............. | xxxx^s |
| Pd at the apoyntment of the companye, the 7 of marche 1602, unto M^r Bromfelde, for the playe which harey chettell layd unto hime to pane[2] for ........................................ | xx^s |
| Pd the 12 of marche 1602, for the companye, unto John Daye and his felowe poetes, in fulle paymente for his playe called the boste of Belleingesgate, the some of .......... ...... | xxxx^s |
| Pd at the apoyntment of Thomas Dowton, the 12 of marche 1602, unto harey chettell, in earneste of the 2 pte of the florentyne,[3] the some of ........................ ................ | xx^s |

Some is vj^li Some upon band 211^li 9^s 0^d
188^li 11^s 6^d

400^li 0^s 6^d

ttottalles ...... 193^li 10^s. 06^d besydes the 50 which M Jonnes and Robart Shawe hade } Besydes the band which they owe unto me as maye apere by band and boocke, the some as foloweth dew.

[1] Massy must have been instrumental in procuring this play for Henslowe's theatre, not in writing it: see p. 219, note 3. Malone mentions "the Siege of Dunkirk," iii., 328, but omits "Alleyn the Pirate."

[2] Another proof of the distresses of Chettle, who had "laid" a play "to pawn" with Mr. Bromfield, the mercer, for 20*s*.

[3] No doubt the second part of a play before mentioned on p. 229, "The London Florentine." Malone concludes that Heywood assisted

Ther resteth dew unto me to this daye, beinge the v daye of Maye 1603, when we leafte of playe now at the Kynges cominge,[1] all Recknynges abated, the some of a hundred fowerscore and sevntene powndes and thirtene shellynges and fowerpence: I saye dew .......................... 197li 13s. 4d

The fyftye powndes which Jonnes and Shawe had at ther goinge a way not reconed.[2]

Layd owt for facynge of a blake grogren clocke, with taffytye .................................... } ixs

Lent unto the company, to geve unto Thomas Deckers and Middelton, in earneste of ther playe Called the pasyent man and the onest hore, the some of — 1604[3] .................. } vli

ttotalles from there hands[4] is 194li 10s 06d

Caste up all the acowntes from the begininge of the world

Chettle in the second part, as well as in the first, and though it is likely, there is no evidence of the fact.

[1] This memorandum shews that two days before the arrival of James I. at the Charter House on the 7th May, Henslowe's company had ceased to perform; most likely by order from the Lord Chamberlain.

[2] Henslowe is far from clear, and it is not easy to make his calculations here tally with his former statement on p. 229.

[3] Malone notices this entry, but by an obvious error assigns the date of March 1602-3 to it, when 1604 is very distinctly written at the end of it. (See Shaksp. by Bosw., iii., 328). It is upon this authority that Middleton has been assigned a share in the composition of the play, which was printed in 1604 under the following title:—"The Honest Whore, with the Humours of the Patient Man and the Longing Wife." Together with the second part, it may be found in vol. iii., of Dodsley's Old Plays. The Rev. Mr. Dyce knew nothing of Henslowe's memorandum but what he found stated by Malone, and therefore necessarily fell into Malone's error.

[4] i.e., From where the players had entered their names in the book.

untell this daye, beinge the 14 daye of marche 1604, by Thomas Dowghton and Edward Jube, for the company of the Prynces men,[1] and I, Phillipe Henslow; so ther reastethe dew unto me, P. Henslow, the some of xxiiij$^{li}$,[2] all Reconynges consernynge the company in stocke generall descarged, and my sealfe descarged to them of al deates.

Lent unto John Ockey, the 4 of febreary 1601, in Redye monye, the some of ——

Memorandum, that I, John Ockeye, doe owe, and ame in deatted unto Phillippe Henslow and E. Alleyn the some of fyve pownde, which I borrowed of them in monye, and to be payd agayne at the saylle of ther starce:[3] in wittnes whereof I have herto sette my hand, the 4 of febreary 1601.

The marke of + JOHN OCKEY.

Wittnes to this,
NYCOLAS + DAME.

Memorandum, that I, Robert Shaa, have receaved of M$^r$ Phillip Henshlowe, the some of forty shellinges, upon a booke called the fower sones of Aymon, which booke, if it be not played by the company of the Fortune, nor noe other company by my leave, I doe then bynd my selfe by theis presentes to repay the sayd some of forty shillinges upon the delivery of my booke att Christmas next, which shall be in the yeare of

[1] After the accession of James I., the Earl of Nottingham's players became "the Princes men," i.e., the players of Prince Henry.

[2] On the 5th May 1603, the company owed Henslowe £197 13*s*. 4*d*., and by the 14th March following the whole debt appears to have been paid off, with the exception of £24.

[3] By "starce" we are to understand *starch;* and it will be seen hereafter that Henslowe, Alleyn, and Ockey, or Ockley, entered into a speculation with Nicholas Dame in the manufacture of starch.

our Lord god 1603, and in the xlvj^th^ yeare of the Raigne of the queene.[1]

ꝑ me, ROBT. SHAA.

*Menses Jenewary* 20, *A° Re. Elizabeth xl*, 1597.

Richard Connesbey, one of the ordenary gentlmen ushers, asketh the allowance for hime sealfe and a grome of the chamber and a grome of the wardropp, for making redey and attending of the cowntis of Darbe, debitie for the Quenes Ma^tie^ at the Crystenyng of my lord Winsers chillde att is howsse in London, by the space of two dayes: wherefore they praye to be allowed for ther botheyer and other charges two and frowe, and to be rated and payed them by the Tresorer of her Ma^tie^ most honorable chamber.[2]

| | |
|---|---|
| Lent, the 12 of marche 1602, unto Thomas Blackwode, when he ride into the contrey with his company to playe, in Redy mony, the some of .......................................... | x^s^ |
| Lent unto John Lowyn, the 12 of marche 1602,[3] when he went into the contrey with his company to playe, in Redy mony, the some of .......................................... | v^s^ |

[1] This was a prospective entry, and "the Queen" did not live until Christmas 1603, as it was presumed she would have done when the note was written by Robert Shaw, or Shaa.

[2] This claim is writtten the length-way of the page, and after two leaves which are left blank. It seems likely that there were dramatic performances at Lord Windsor's on the christening of his child, when Lady Derby was deputy for the Queen. How this memorandum found its way into Henslowe's book does not appear; but perhaps he used it as a precedent for the form in which he might send in some claim of his own.

[3] This seems to be the earliest notice, in Henslowe's Diary, of an actor who afterwards obtained a high reputation.

*Quinto die Maij* 1602.

Bee it knowne unto all men by theis presents, that wee, Anthony Mundy and Thom̃s Dekker, doe owe unto Phillip Hynchley, gent, the somme of five powndes of lawfull mony of England, to bee payd unto him, his executors or assignes, uppon the x^th^ of June next ensuing the date hereof. In wittnes hereof hereunto wee have sett our handes: dated the day and yere above written.[1]

| | |
|---|---|
| Lent unto Thomas Hewode, the 1 of Septembr, to bye hime a payer of sylke garters, the some of .......... | ij^s^ vj^d^ |
| Lent unto Richard Perckens, the 4 of septmbr 1602,[2] to bye thinges for Thomas Hewode playe, and to lend unto Dick Syferweste to ride downe to his felowes, some of .......... | xv^s^ |
| Lent unto Rychard Perckyns, the 12 of marche 1602, when he rid with the company to playe in the contrey, in Redey monye, the some of | x^s^ |

Memorandom, that the 25 of June 1603, I talked with Mr. Pope,[3] at the scryveners shope wher he liffe, consernynge

[1] The signatures to this acknowledgment have been cut away. The entry is in Dekker's handwriting.

[2] Richard Perkins afterwards became an actor of first-rate eminence, and, prior to 1633, sustained Alleyn's famous part of Barabas, in the Jew of Malta. (See Dodsley's Old Plays, viii., 248.) The present is the earliest mention of him. Whether "Dick Syferweste" were a real or a nick-name cannot perhaps be determined, but we do not hear of him elsewhere.

[3] No doubt Thomas Pope, the celebrated comic performer in Shakespeare's plays, who, according to Malone (Shaksp. by Bosw., iii., 198,) "died before 1600," but who in fact made his will on 22d July 1603, a month after the date of the above memorandum by Henslowe. (Chalmers' Suppl. Apology, 162.) Pope was therefore interested in the Rose

the tackynge of the Leace of the Littell Roose, and he showed me a wrytynge betwext the pareshe and hime seallfe, which was to paye twenty pownd a yeare Rent, and to bestowe a hundred marckes upon billdinge, which I sayd I wold rather pulle downe the playhowse then I wold do so, and he beade me do, and sayd he gave me leave and wold beare me owt, for yt wasse in hime to do yt.

*Lent unto my Lorde of Worsters players*[1] *as foloweth, begynynge the* 17 *daye of aguste* 1602.

| | |
|---|---|
| Lent unto the companye, the 17 of aguste 1602, to paye unto Thomas Deckers, for new adicyons in Owldcaselle,[2] the some of ............. | xxxx$^{s}$ |
| Lent unto John Dewcke, the 18 of aguste 1602, to bye Rebatose and fardingalls, the some of ............................................ | xxxx$^{s}$ |
| Lent unto Thomas Blackwode and John Dewcke, to bye tafetie and other stuffe to macke ij wemens gownes, the 19 of aguste 1602, the some of ............................................ | ix$^{li}$ |
| Layd owt for the company, at the mermayd, when we wearo at owre agrement,[3] the 21 of aguste 1602, toward our super, the some of... | ix$^{s}$ |

(here called *the Little Rose*) as well as in the Globe and Curtain theatres. This is a new point in Pope's history.

[1] The players of the Earl of Worcester became the theatrical servants of Queen Anne on the accession of James I. See p. 214, and Hist. Engl. Dram. Poetry and the Stage, i., 350.

[2] The first part of Sir John Oldcastle having been printed in 1600, these additions may have belonged to a second part of the same play, which has not survived.

[3] This agreement no doubt related to the advances Henslowe was to make to the Earl of Worcester's players, to which these and many following items refer. Henslowe paid for the treat at the Mermaid.

| | |
|---|---|
| Lent unto Wm Kempe, the 22 of aguste 1602, to bye buckram to macke a payer of gyents hosse,[1] the some of ..... ...................... | vs |
| Lent unto John Ducke and John Thayer, the 21 of aguste 1602, to bye a sewt for owld castell, and a sewt and a dublet of satten, the some of ......................................... | xijli |
| Lent unto John Ducke, to paye for the Turcke head, and ij wemens gownes mackinge, and fresh water for Owld castell, and the merser bill, and harey chettell, in earneste of a tragedie called —,[2] the 24 of aguste 1602 ...... | 3li xs |
| Layd owt for the companye, the 25 of aguste 1602, for a clocke of chamllett lined with crymson tafetie, pincked, the some of ......... | iiijli |
| Lent unto John Ducke, the 27 of aguste 1602, to paye the merser for layce for the clocke ... | xiiijs |
| Layd owt more for the company, in pte of paymente for a booke called Medsen for a curste wiffe, some of —, unto thomas Deckers ...... | xs |
| Lent unto John Ducke, the 28 of aguste 1602, to paye unto Xpofer Bestone[3] for a manes gowne of branshed vellvet, and a dublett for the some of...................................... | vjli |

[1] This and other entries, anterior and subsequent (see p. 215) of money paid to William Kempe shew that at this date he did not belong to the company to which Shakespeare was attached, but was one of the Earl of Worcester's players, with whom Henslowe was connected. We are nowhere informed in what drama these giants, for which hose were required, were introduced, but formerly, as we have seen, giants figured in the play of "Brute."

[2] A blank is left for the name of the tragedy. Freshwater (as appears afterwards) was the name of a person.

[3] This seems to be the earliest entry in which the name of Christopher Beeston (often afterwards mentioned in the history of the stage) occurs.

Lent unto John Ducke, the 28 of aguste 1602, to paye unto the tayller for stufe and mackynge of ij wemens gownes, the some of ...... xxxiiij$^{s}$

Pd at the apoyntment of the company, the 1 of septmbr 1602, in pte of payment for a comody called a medysen for a curste wiffe, to thomas Deckers, some of.................................. iiij$^{li}$

Pd at the apoyntment of the company, the 2 of septmbr 1602, in fulle payment for a comodey called a Medysen for a curste wiffe, to thomas Deckers,[1] the some of........... ................ xxx$^{s}$

Lent unto the company, the 3 of septembr 1602, to bye a sewte for W$^{m}$ Kempe, the some of ............................................ xxx$^{s}$

Layd owt for the company, the 3 of septmbr 1602, to bye iiij lances for the comody of Thomas Hewodes and Mr. Smythes,[2] some of viij$^{s}$

Layd owt for the company, the 4 of septmbr 1602, to bye a flage of sylke, the some of ... xxvj$^{s}$ 8$^{d}$

[1] This sum of 30*s.*, with the £4 in the preceding entry, £2 on 31st July, and 10*s.* which Dekker received on the 27th August, made up the sum total of £8 for the play of "a Medicine for a Curst Wife." On the 27th September, Dekker was paid 10*s.* "over and above his price" for the "Medicine for a Curst Wife," owing perhaps to its great success when acted.

[2] We may conjecture that these "four lances" were for the apprentices in the play of "the Four Prentices of London," printed in 1615 (and no doubt earlier, though no earlier edition is now known) in the name of Thomas Heywood, although from this memorandum it seems that Wentworth Smith was also concerned in the authorship of it. On the title-page of the edition of the play in 1615, the four Prentises are represented in a woodcut with their four lances, and in Beaumont and Fletcher's "Knight of the Burning Pestle," Act iv. sc. 2, one of the characters says, "Read the play of the Four Prentices of London, where they toss their pikes so."

| | |
|---|---|
| Pd at the apoyntment of the company, the 4 of septmbr 1602, unto Thomas Hewod and M^r^ Smyth, in fulle payment for a Boocke called alberte galles,[1] some of........................ | vj^li^ |
| Pd unto your tyerman, for mackinge of W^m^ Kempes sewt and the boyes, the 4 of septmbr 1602, some of........................................ | viij^s^ 8^d^ |
| Lent unto John Thare, the 7 of septmbr 1602, to give unto Thomas Dickers for his adicions in owld castell, the some of .................... | x^s^ |
| Lent unto harey chettell, the 7 of septmbr 1602, at the apoyntment to lend in earenest of a boocke called Robin hoodfellowe,[2] some of ... | x^s^ |
| Lent unto John Thare, the 8 of septmbr 1602, to geve unto harey cheattell, the some of...... | x^s^ |
| Lent unto harey chettell, the 9 of septmbr 1602, in pte of payment of a playe called Robin goodfellowe, some of ............................ | x^s^ |
| Lent unto John Thare, the 10 of septmbr 1602, to paye unto the merser in pt for sylke for Robes, the some of................................ | lvj^s^ iiij^d^ |

[1] The reader in this instance, as in many others, must exercise his ingenuity in discovering the true name of this play, for which possibly the lances and silk flag were required. Can the subject have been Albertus Wallenstein, on which Glapthorne wrote a play printed in 1634? The first name *Alberte* has been altered by the apparent insertion of the letter *r*, Henslowe having first written it *Albete.*

[2] "Robin hoodfellowe" in this memorandum certainly means "Robin Goodfellow," and in a subsequent entry the play is so called. The word "tragedie" originally followed "in earenest of a," but it was struck out when Henslowe found that it was not a piece of that description. In the other entry regarding the same production, the word "tragedie" was erased and "playe" written over it. No doubt this was done at a subsequent time, as the ink in which the correction is written is of a different colour. Malone takes no notice of these remarkable entries.

Lent unto Thomas blackwode, the 19 of septmbr 1602, to paye unto Robarte Shawe, the some of .......................................... $\text{xvj}^{s}$

Lent unto the companye, the 20 of septmbr 1602, to paye unto $\text{M}^{r}$ Smythe, in pte of payment of a Boocke called marshalle Oserecke,[1] some of .......................................... $\text{iij}^{li}$

Pd unto Thomas Hewode, the 20 of septmbr 1602, for the new adicyons of cuttyng Dicke,[2] some of .......................................... $\text{xx}^{s}$

Lent unto John Thare, the 21 of septmbr 1602, to paye for targates, the some of .............. $\text{xx}^{s}$

Lent unto John Ducke, the 25 of septmbr 1602, to bye a blacke sewt of satten for the playe of Burone,[3] the some of.......................... $\text{v}^{li}$

Pd unto Thomas Deckers, the 27 of septmbr 1602, over and above his price of his boocke called a medysen for a curste wiffe, some of... $\text{x}^{s}$

Pd unto Thomas Hewode, the 30 of septmbr 1602, in fulle payment for his boocke of Oserecke, the some of ......................... $\text{iij}^{li}$

Lent unto John Thare, the 30 of septmbr 1602, to paye unto the armerer for targattes, in full payment, the some of.......................... $\text{xx}^{s}$

[1] By a subsequent memorandum it appears that Heywood joined Wentworth Smith in the production of "Marshal Osrick."

[2] Cutting Dick was possibly a new character introduced by Heywood into some known play: see also p. 224.

[3] In the Hist. of Engl. Dram. Poetry and the Stage, iii., 95, it is suggested that this entry and others may refer to Chapman's "Byron's Conspiracy and Tragedy," printed in 1608, but this is questionable on a comparison of dates. See Collier's Shakespeare, i., ccix, where it is shown that Chapman's two plays have not reached us as they were originally written, in consequence of the remonstrance of the French Ambassador against certain incidents in them.

| | |
|---|---|
| Pd at the apoyntment of the companye, the j of octobr 1602, to Mr Smythe, in pte of payment for a tragedie called the ij Brothers,[1] the some of ........ | xxxxs |
| Pd unto my sonne E. Alleyn, at the apoyntment of the companye, for his Boocke of Tambercame, the 2 of octobr 1602, the some of[2] ........ | xxxxs |
| Layd owt at the apoyntmente of the companye, to macke a scafowld and bare[3] for the playe of Berowne, and carpenters wages .............. | xiijs |
| Lent at the apoyntment of John Ducke, in earneste of a playe called ——, the some of ——, 3 of octobr 1602, to Mr Mydellton ... | xxs |
| Pd for poleyes and workmanshipp for to hange Absolome[4] ........ | xiiijd |
| Pd at the apoyntment of John Ducke, unto Mr smythe, in pte of payment of his Boocke called the ij brothers tragedie, the 11 of octobr 1602, the some of ........ | xxxxs |
| Pd unto Underell, at the apoyntemente of the company for wages which they owght hime, the 11 of octobr 1602, the some of ........... | xs |
| Pd at the apoyntmente of John Ducke, to Mr Smythe, in fulle payment of his Boocke called the ij brothers, the 15 of octobr 1602, the some of ........ | xxxxs |

[1] Malone names this tragedy "The Three Brothers," (Shaksp. by Boswell, iii., 337.) Elsewhere Henslowe several times over calls it "the ij Brothers tragedie." "The Three Brothers" is however afterwards mentioned, and may have been the same piece.

[2] This item respecting Tambercam is erased in the MS.

[3] i.e., Probably, a *scaffold* and *bar*.

[4] No scriptural play on the story of Absalom is mentioned by Malone in his quotations from Henslowe's Diary.

| | |
|---|---|
| Lent unto John Thare, the 15 of octobr 1602, to geve unto harey chettell, Thomas Deckers, Thomas Hewode, and M^r Smyth, and M^r Webster, in earneste of a playe called Ladey Jane,[1] the some of............ | l^s |
| Lent at the apoyntment of the company, to the tyerman, to bye sowtedge to macke devells sewtes for the new playe of the ij brothers tragedie, the some of............ | viij^s |
| Lent at the apoyntment of the company, unto the tyerman, to bye saye for the playe of the ij brothers, to macke a wiches gowne, the some of............ | 18^s |
| Lent unto Thomas Hewode, the 21 of octobr 1602, to paye unto M^r Dickers, chettell, Smythe, Webester and Hewode, in fulle payment of ther playe of ladye Jane, the some of............ | v^li x^s |
| Pd unto E. Alleyn, the 22 of octobr 1602, at the apoyntment of the company, for a grogren clocke, ij velvet gerkens, ij dubbletes, ij hedtyres, the some of[2]............ | xx^li |
| Pd for bordes, and quarters, and naylles, for to macke a tabell and coffen for the playe of the iij brothers,[3] the 22 of octobr 1602, some of... | xij^s iij^d |
| Lent unto John Thare, the 23 of octobr 1602, to paye unto the paynter of the propertyes for the playe of the iij brothers, the some of... | xx^s |

[1] Malone enters this play, which he naturally supposes to be upon the story of Lady Jane Grey, under the date of Nov. 1602, whereas it clearly belongs to the month of October.

[2] This entry, having been previously inserted (p. 227), is erased with the pen.

[3] Here we find notice of the play called the Three Brothers: if it be an error, it is several times repeated.

| | |
|---|---|
| Pd unto the tyerman, for mackynge of the devells sute, and sperethes,[1] and for the witche, for the playe of the iij brothers, the 23 of octobr 1602, some of .................... | x$^{s}$ ix$^{d}$ |
| Pd unto Xpofer Beston, the 26 of octobr 1602, in pte of paymente for the Jerkyn which the company had of hime, the some of ........... | xx$^{s}$ |
| Lent unto John Ducke, the 27 of octobr 1602, to geve unto Thomas Deckers, in earneste of the 2 pt of Ladye Jane,[2] the some of ......... | v$^{s}$ |
| Lent unto Thomas Hewode and John Webster, the 2 of novmbr 1602, in earneste of a playe called Cyrssmas comes but once a yeare,[3] the some of .................................................. | iij$^{li}$ |
| Pd for vj yardes of tynsell for the companye, the 2 of novmbr 1602, the some of ........... | iij$^{s}$ |
| Pd at the apoyntment of the companye, the 3 of novmbr 1602, unto the tayller, for the mackynge of the sewte of Oserocke, the some of.................................................... | xxvj$^{s}$ |
| Layd owt for the companye, the 6 of novmbr 1602, for xiiij ownces of coper lace, the some of.................................................... | ix$^{s}$ 4$^{d}$ |
| More, the same tyme, vj ownces and ½ of coper lace ........... ........................................ | iiij$^{s}$ 4$^{d}$ |

[1] By "sperethes" Henslowe probably meant *spirits* attending upon the devil and the witch. This memorandum certainly looks as if the Two Brothers and the Three Brothers were the same piece; for on the preceding page we have had "devil's suits" and "a witch's gown" introduced as required for the *Two* Brothers.

[2] Lady Jane appears to have been finished on 21st Oct. 1602, and by the 27th, Dekker had begun a second part to the same play.

[3] Malone assigns "Christmas comes but once a year" to Dekker alone, whereas it is evident, from this and other memoranda, that he was associated in it with Heywood, Webster, and Chettle.

| | |
|---|---|
| Lent unto John Dewcke, the 6 of novmbr 1602, for to macke a sewt of satten of ——, for the playe of the overthrowe of Rebelles,[1] the some of .......................................... | v li |
| Pd at the apoyntment of the company, the 12 of novmbr 1602, unto the coper lace man, in pt of payment for his lace...................... | xx s |
| Pd at the apoyntment of John Lowen,[2] the 12 of novmbr 1602, unto Mr Smyth, the some of............................................... | x s |
| Pd at the apoyntment of John Lowen, the 12 of novmbr 1602, unto harey Chettell, the some of ............ ............................. | iij s |
| Lent unto John Dewcke, the 23 of novmbr 1602, to paye unto harye chettell and Thomas Deckers, in pte of paymente of a playe called Crysmas comes but once a yeare, the some of...................................... .......... | xxxx s |
| Pd at the apoyntment of John Ducke, the 24 of novmbr 1602, to Mr hathwaye, in earneste of a playe called blacke Doge of Newgate,[3] the some of ........................................ | xxxx s |
| Pd unto Thomas Hewode, the 24 of novmbr 1602, in pte of payment of his playe called the blinde eates many a flye, the some of...... | iij li |

[1] There is no entry to show by whom the Overthrow of Rebels was written. It is in fact not mentioned again, and very possibly it was not performed, judging from Henslowe's silence, and the questionable and temporary nature of the title.

[2] At this date John Lowen was therefore a member of the company of the Earl of Worcester's players: he became one of "the principal actors" in Shakespeare's plays afterwards.

[3] The words "blacke Doge of Newgate" are interlined above "John Dayes comody," which are struck through: the same is the case when the play is next mentioned.

| | |
|---|---|
| Pd at the apoyntment of Thomas Hawode, the 26 of novmbr 1602, to harey chettell, in fulle paymente of a playe called Cryssmas comes but once a yeare, the some of ................. | xxxx[s] |
| Lent unto Xpofer beston and Robart Palante, the 26 of Novmbr 1602, to pay unto John Daye, M[r] Smythe, M[r] hathwaye, and the other poet,[1] in pte of payment of the playe called the blacke Dogge of newgate, the some of | xxxx[s] |
| Bowght for the company, of Robart shawe, the 6 of desembr 1602, iiij clothe clockes layd with coper lace, for iiij[li] a clocke, and for my forberance of my mony, to alowe me v[s] upon every clocke,[2] some is ........................ | xvij[li] |
| Layd owt for the companye, the 9 of novmbr[3] 1602, to bye ij calleco sewtes and ij buckram sewtes, for the playe of Cryssmas comes but once a yeare, the some of ...................... | xxxviij[s] 8[d] |
| Sowld unto the companye, the 9 of desembr 1602, ij peces of cangable taffetie, to macke a womones gowne and a robe, for the playe of crysmas comes but once a year, some of ...... | iiij[li] x[s] |

[1] The "other poet" who assisted Day, Smith, and Hathway, in writing the Black Dog of Newgate is not known, as he is not elsewhere mentioned by Henslowe. Luke Hutton, who was executed in 1598, wrote a tract under the title of "The Blacke Dogge of Newgate," which was again printed in 1638. (See the Bridgewater Catalogue, p. 149.) The present entry contains, we believe, the earliest mention of Robert Pallant as an actor: he afterwards acquired considerable celebrity; and from a document in "The Alleyn Papers," p. 52, we may conclude that he was tenant to the founder of Dulwich College.

[2] The company being indebted to Henslowe, the latter appears to take the opportunity of adding *5s.* each to the price of four clokes by way of interest, for forbearance of his money.

[3] *November* seems miswritten for *December* in this entry.

| | |
|---|---|
| Lent unto the companye, the 15 of desembr 1602, to paye unto Thomas Hewode, in pte of paymente for his playe called the Blinde eates many a fley, the some of ........... ..... | xxx[s] |
| Pd at the apoyntment of John Dewcke, the 18 of desembr 1602, unto ij tayllers for mackyn of gowns and thinges for them; j, xx[s], the other, xix[s], the some ........................... | xxxix[s] |
| Pd at the apoyntment of the companye, the 20 of desembr 1602, unto M[r] hathwaye, M[r] Smythe, and John Daye, and the other poyet in fulle payment for a playe called the blacke Dogge of Newgat, some of ....... ........... | xxxx[s] |
| Lent unto John thare, the j of Janewary 1602, to geve unto M[rs] Calle for ij corenets for hed tyers for the corte,[1] the some of .............. | x[s] |
| Lent unto the companye, the 7 of Janewary 1602, to paye unto M[r] Hawode, in fulle paymente for his playe of the Blinde eates many a flye, the some of .............................. | xxx[s] |
| Lent unto Crystofer beston and John Ducke, the 7 of Jeneware 1602, to geve unto M[r] Hathwaye and M[r] smythe, in earneste of a playe called unfortunate Generall, frenshe hestory,[2] the some of........................... | xxx[s] |
| Lent unto John Dewcke, the 10 of Janewary 1602, to bye lame skenes,[3] for the blacke dogge of newgate, the some of ................ | x[s] |

[1] The company had been called upon to perform at Court, and these coronets were for a play then represented.

[2] Henslowe left a blank here for the words "Unfortunate General," and filled it up afterwards. Malone miscalls it "the Fortunate General:" Shaksp. by Bosw., iii., 328.

[3] There is another entry, farther on, for "a canvas suit and skins" for the Black Dog of Newgate.

| | |
|---|---|
| Pd at the apoyntment of the companye, the 10 of Janewarye 1602, unto M^r^ hathwaye and M^r^ Smythe, in pte of paymente for ther playe called unfortunate Generalle, the frenshe hestorey, the some of......... | xxx^s^ |
| Layd owt for the companye, the 10 of Janewary 1602, to bye coper lace, x ownces, at 10^d^ and ownce, the some of ......... | viij^s^ 4^d^ |
| Pd at the apoyntment of thomas Hewod, the 14 of Janewary 1602, in earneste of a Playe called ——, unto harey chettell and Thomas hewod, the some of......... | xxxx^s^ |
| Pd for the company, the 16 of Janewarye 1602, unto the tayller in the borowghe, which they owght unto hime, the some of ......... | xviij^s^ |
| Pd for the company, the 16 of Janewary 1602, unto the coper lace man in pte of paymente for coper lace, the some of......... | xxxx^s^ |
| Pd more for the company, the 16 of Janewary 1602, unto goodman Freshwater, for a canves sewte and skenes for the blacke Doge of newgate......... | xij^s^ |
| Pd at the apoyntment of the companye, the 16 of Janewarye 1602, unto M^r^ hathwaye, M^r^ smythe, and John Daye, in pte of payment for ther boocke called unfortunat generall, frenshe hestorey, some of ......... | 40^s^ |
| Pd at the apoyntment of John Ducke and the company, the 19 of Janewary 1602, unto M^r^ Hathwaye, and M^r^ Smyth, and John Daye, and the other poyet,[1] in fulle paymente for ther playe called unfortunat Generall, the frenshe hestorey, some of ......... | xxxx^s^ |

[1] "The other poet" is not named, and Malone assigned the play to Smith, Day, and Hathway.

Lent unto John Lewen and Cattarnes, the 24 of Janewary 1602, to by a sytysen cotte and sleves for the playe of the unfortunat Jenerall, the some of.................................. l$^{s}$

Pd at the apoyntment of the companye, the 24 of Janewary 1602, unto the coper lace man, in pte of paymente, the some of .............. xx$^{s}$

Lent unto John Lewen, upon John Duckes noote of his hande, the 29 of Janewarye 1602, to geve in earneste of the second pte of the boocke called the blacke Dooge of newgate, unto M$^{r}$ hathwaye and John Daye, and Mr. Smythe, and the other poete,[1] the some of. ............ iij$^{li}$

Pd at the apoyntment of John Ducke, the 3 of febreary 1602, unto M$^{r}$ Hathwaye, M$^{r}$ Smythe, John Daye, and the other poet, in fulle payment for the boocke called the second pte of the blacke Dooge, the some of ................ iiij$^{li}$

Pd at the apoyntment of the companye, the 4 of febreary 1602, unto the tayller for vellvet and satten for the womon gowne of blacke vellvet, with the other lynenges belonging to yt, the some of .......................................... xxij$^{s}$

Pd unto Thomas hewode, the 5 of febreary 1602, for a womones gowne of blacke vellvett, for the playe of a womon Kylld with Kyndnes,[2] some of ...................................... vj$^{li}$ 13$^{s}$

Pd unto the coper lace man, in pte of payment, the 7 of febreary 1602, for the companye, the some of ........................ ..... ........... xx$^{s}$

[1] The same dramatists who had produced the *first* part of the Black Dog of Newgate. In this instance, as in the case of the first part, Henslowe did not know the name of their coadjutor.

[2] Printed in 1607, and again in 1617 with the author's name on the title-page. It is inserted in vol. vii. of Dodsley's Old Plays.

| | | |
|---|---|---|
| Pd at the apoyntment of the company, the 12 of febreary 1602, unto Thomas Heywood, in pt of payment for his playe called A womon kylled with Kyndnes, the some of ........... | iij[li] | |
| Pd unto the tyerman for the companye, 1602, to bye viij yrdes and a halfe of blacke satten, at xij[s] a yrde, to macke a sewt for the 2 pte of the blacke Dogge, the some of, the 15 of feb. | v[li] | ij[s] |
| Pd at the apoyntment of the companye, the 16 of febreary 1602, unto the coper lace man, in pte of payment, the some of .................... | | xx[s] |
| Lent unto Thomas blackewode, the 21 of febreary 1602, to geve unto the 4 poetes, in earnest of ther adicyons,[1] for the 2 pte of the blacke doge, the some of .............................. | | x[s] |
| Lent unto Thomas blackwode, the 24 of febreary 1602, to geve unto the 4 poetes, in pte of paymente for ther adycyons in the 2 pte of the blacke Doge .................................. | | x[s] |
| Lent unto John Dewcke, the 26 of febreary 1602, to paye the poetes, in fulle payment for ther adycyones for the 2 pte of the blacke Doge, the some of .............................. | | xx[s] |
| Pd unto the coper lace man, the 4 of marche 1602, in pte of payment, the some of......... | | xx[s] |
| Pd at the apoyntment of the company, the 6 of marche 1602, unto Thomas Hewode, in fulle payment for his playe called a womon Kyld with Kyndnes, the some of .................... | iij[li] | |

[1] Preceding entries show that the authors of the Second Part of the Black Dog of Newgate had already received £8 for their play. By this and the two next memoranda it appears that they were paid £2 more for their additions, so that the play cost £10. Perhaps it had been acted between 3 Feb. and 21 Feb. 1602, and was found to require some improvements in the shape of additions.

| | |
|---|---|
| Pd at the apoyntment of Thomas blackewod and John Lewen, the 7 of marche 1602, unto M[r] Smythe, in earnest of and Etalleyon tragedie,[1] the some of ........................................ | xxxx[s] |
| Pd at the apoyntment of Thomas Blackewod, the 7 of marche 1602, unto the tayller which made the blacke satten sewt for the woman Kyld with Kyndnes, the some of .............. | x[s] |
| Pd at the apoyntment of John Lowine, the 12 of marche 1602, unto M[r] Smythe, in fulle payment for his tragedie called the Etallyan tragedie, the some of ............................ | iiij[li] |
| Pd for the companye, the 16 of marche 1602, unto the mercers man, Puleston, for his M[r] John Willett deate, the some of eighte powndes and x[s], which they owght hime for satten, and charges in the clynke for arestynge John Ducke :[2] I say, as may apere .. ............... | viij[li] x[s] |

Some is 140[li] 1[s] 00[d]

Memd., that the fulle some of all the deatbtes, which we owe unto M[r] Henslow to this xvj of marche 1603, cometh to juste the some of 140[li] 1[s] 00[d], which some of 140[li] 01[s] 0[d] we whosse names are here under wrytten do aknowledge ower dew deatte, and promysse trewe payment.

THOMAS BLACKWOD.[3]

[1] By "And Etalleyon tragedie" Henslowe or his scribe of course meant "an Italian tragedy." Malone says (iii., 328) that John Day was concerned with Smith in the authorship of it, but his name does not occur in the entries.

[2] It should seem by this item that John Duke, as one of the leaders of the company, had been arrested at the suit of Willett, the silk-mercer, and had been thrown into prison.

[3] This is the only name subscribed, but three leaves, originally following in the MS., have been cut away, and possibly the signatures of

Pd the coper lace man is to be payd .............. iiij^li

Pd more the coper lace, the some of .............. vj^li iiij^s

*In the name of god, Amen.*

*Begininge to playe agayne by the Kynges licence, and layd owt sense for my Lord of Worsters men, as foloweth,* 1603, 9 *of maye.*[1]

Lent at the apoyntment of Thomas hewod and John Ducke, unto harey Chettell and John Daye, in earneste of a playe wherein Shores wiffe[2] is writen, the some of[3] .................. xxxx^s

the other members of the company were upon one of them, in acknowledgment of the debt to Henslowe of £140 1*s*. 0*d*. This, however, is the less likely, because the entries to the copper-lace man immediately follow the name of Thomas Blackwood, and possibly Henslowe could not persuade the company at large to admit and subscribe to the correctness of his claim.

[1] This is the heading of a new account, but it only consists of a single item, and it is not continued in any other part of the MS. It looks as if Henslowe had made no farther advances to the Earl of Worcester's players in consequence of the non-adjustment of his claim to £140 1*s*. 0*d*. If the date of this account be correct, "the King's licence" was granted to the Earl of Worcester's players before it was conceded by James I. to his own company. The patent to L. Fletcher, Shakespeare, Burbage, and others, bears date on the 17th May 1603. Vide Hist. Engl. Dram. Poetry and the Stage, i., 348.

[2] Malone calls this play "Jane Shore," whereas it was only a play in which Shore's wife was a character. Shore's wife is introduced into Heywood's "Edward the Fourth," 1600, and this piece by Chettle and Day was no doubt on the same portion of history: "Edward the Fourth," a play in two parts, has been reprinted by the Shakespeare Society from the earliest edition.

[3] After two leaves, which are left blank in the MS., we come to an account headed "A juste note what I have lent unto Edmond Henslow,

| | |
|---|---|
| Sowld unto Mr Arthur Langworth, the howsse which my brother dwelte in after the decease of my syster Margery, his wiffe, with the trashe therin for the some of.................... | 80li |

iiij score powndes, wittnes E. ALLEYN.[1]

Rd of Mr Thomas Chaloner, upon a band[2] ........... 100li

in mony, and layd owt in the be hallfe of his iij cheldren as foloweth, 1593." In this account, which fills more than two closely written pages, P. Henslowe calls Edmond Henslowe his brother; and hence it appears that a William Henslowe was at one time in the service of the Lord Chamberlain, not as a player, but as one of his lordship's domestic establishment, and that Edmond was dead before the account was made out. P. Henslowe speaks of William Henslowe also as his brother.

[1] This, like many others, is merely a memorandum that Edward Alleyn was present at the transaction. The signature is not his handwriting.

[2] After this memorandum we come to another account, entitled, "Layd owt at several tymes for John Henslow, the sonne of Edmond Henslowe, as foloweth, 1596." This is for clothes, and subsequently money for the purchase of a boat, and for expenses when, in 1605, John Henslowe wished to buy "the King's waterman's place." Nevertheless, in 1604 it appears from another account that P. Henslowe was at law with John Henslowe respecting the will of Edmond Henslowe. The last particular in these family matters bears date in 1609. Some of the items shew that the Henslowes had property at East Grinstead. The entries at this end of the MS. here cease, and we come to a number of blank leaves, reserved apparently for memoranda which were never inserted.

*A not what Edward Allen hath layd owt, as foloweth:*[1]

| | | |
|---|---|---|
| Itm̃ pd for ij thowsen and halfe of bryckes | xxvij$^{s}$ | vj$^{d}$ |
| Itm̃ pd for a mantell tre | | xij$^{d}$ |
| Itm̃ pd for a lode of bryckes | vj$^{s}$ | vj$^{d}$ |
| Itm̃ pd unto R. laberer for iiij dayes | iij$^{s}$ | 6$^{d}$ |
| Itm̃ pd unto Gryges man John, the 24 of novmbr 1592 | xxxx$^{s}$ | |
| Itm̃ pd unto the glaser, the 24 of novmbr 1592 | xx$^{s}$ | |
| Itm̃ pd for ij lode of sande | ij$^{s}$ | |
| Itm̃ pd for bryngen the dele bordes by water | | xviij$^{d}$ |
| Itm̃ pd unto the Joyner for his worke | vj$^{s}$ | |

*The Acownte of suche Carges as hathe bene layd owt abowt Edward alenes howsse, as foloweth.* 1592.

Nov. 4, 1592.

| | | | |
|---|---|---|---|
| Itm̃ pd unto John Gryges, in pt | v$^{li}$ | | |
| Itm̃ pd unto the smyth, for Iorne bares for the windo | | v$^{s}$ | |
| Itm̃ pd the plomer for 4. 1. 22 of lead at j$^{d}$ qr. ℔ | | l$^{s}$ | |
| Itm̃ pd for vj payer of sheates and a coverlet | v$^{li}$ | | |
| Itm̃ pd the lyme man, the 23 of desembr 1593 | | xxiiij$^{s}$ | |
| Itm̃ pd the naylle man at the fryingpane, the 19 Jenewary 1593 | | lj$^{s}$ | |
| Itm̃ pd unto the gardener for diginge the garden | | | xvj$^{d}$ |
| Itm̃ pd the nayllman the 29 of Februeary 1594 | | vj$^{s}$ | viij$^{d}$ |
| Itm̃ pd for the leasse to Robartes | xxij$^{li}$ | | |
| Itm̃ pd for makinge the writtinges | | v$^{s}$ | |

[1] This account commences at the other end of the MS., to which we now turn for the succeeding particulars, which seem to relate to the repair, &c., of Alleyn's dwelling-house just after his marriage with Joan Woodward on the 22nd October, 1592. See p. 3.

| | | |
|---|---|---|
| Itm̃ pd to Edward Allen, the 5 of July, in money .......................... .................... | $\mathrm{x^{li}}$ | |
| Edward Allen had of me russett to make him a clocke .............................................. | | $\mathrm{xij^{s}}$ |
| Itm̃ pd unto Edward Allen, the 9 of septembr 1594, money ....................................... | $\mathrm{xx^{li}}$ | |
| Itm̃ pd unto Francis Hensley, for a Keverynge | | $\mathrm{xviij^{s}}$ |
| Itm̃ sowld unto my sonne a fetherbed for ...... | | $\mathrm{xxx^{s}}$ |
| Itm̃ pd unto $\mathrm{M^r}$ Langworth, for my sonne ...... | $\mathrm{xxvij^{li}}$ | $\mathrm{x^{s}}$ |
| Itm̃ pd unto $\mathrm{M^r}$ Langworth, the same time ... | | $\mathrm{x^{s}}$ |
| Itm̃ pd for makinge of writinges for my sones pte ......................................................... | | $\mathrm{xx^{s}}$ |
| Itm̃ pd unto $\mathrm{M^r}$ Langworth, in fulle payment | $\mathrm{xxxj^{li}}$ | |
| Itm̃ pd toward the beringe of Ardnold ......... | $\mathrm{ij^{li}}$ | $\mathrm{x^{s}}$ |
| Itm̃ pd hime in exchange of his clocke for satin and a clocke of mine .......................... | | $\mathrm{l^{s}}$ |
| Itm̃ torned over from the tayllor to my sonne | | $\mathrm{xx^{s}}$ |
| Itm̃ lent unto my sone, edward Alen, to leand unto edward Dutton,[1] the 14 of marche 1597, the some of ... .............. .................... | $\mathrm{iij^{li}}$ | |
| Itm̃ lent unto my sonne, edward Alen, to lend unto John Synger and Thomas Towne, when they went into the contrey—some ......... | | $\mathrm{xxxx^{s}}$ |

| | | | |
|---|---|---|---|
| Owinge unto my sonne[2] .......................... | 045 | 18 | 00 |
| My sonne owes me .................................. | 060 | 00 | 00 |
| And ................ ................................ | 100 | 00 | 00 |
| And ................................................. | 002 | 10 | 00 |
| Lent $\mathrm{M^r}$ Langworth ....................... ..... | 002 | 00 | 00 |
| For $\mathrm{M^r}$ Fuller ...... ................ .......... | 001 | 02 | 00 |

[1] Most likely an actor: there were players of the names of Lawrence and John Dutton, who were at the head of one of the Queen's companies in 1590. See Cunningham's Revels' Accounts, xxxii.

[2] These memoranda are on the page of the MS. opposite to the preceding account: they have no dates.

| | | | |
|---|---|---|---|
| Lent M$^r$ Langworth at my Lordes ............ | 0 | 02 | 06 |
| Lent M$^r$ Langworth ............................ | 024 | 00 | 00 |
| Lent M$^r$ Langworth in the Marshallsea ...... | 003 | 00 | 00 |

Itm̃ layd owt for edward Alleyn, the 9 of June 1597, for to descarge hime of his preve sealle,[1] the some of........................................ } xx$^s$

Itm̃ pd unto the clarke of the senette[2] for my sonne, Edward Alleyn, for alowenge of the pattyne ........................ .................. } xx$^s$

Lent unto edward Dutton, the 18 of July 1597, in redey money, to be payd me with in one forth nyghte agayne ............................ } xx$^s$

Wittnes E. ALLEYN and
M$^{rs}$ GRYGES.

Lent hime more in money——[3]

Itm̃ lent unto my sonne, edward allen, for Synger ... xx$^s$

Itm̃ lent unto my sonne, to bye a gowne for his wiffe xxxx$^s$

Itm̃ lent unto my sonne, for to geve the tayller ...... xxxx$^s$

Lent unto Bengemen Johnson, player, the 28 of July 1597,[4] in Redey mony, the some of fower powndes, to be payd yt agayne when so ever ether I, or any for me, demand yt: I saye } iiij$^{li}$

Wittnes E. ALLEYN and JOHN SYNGER.[5]

[1] This was perhaps a Privy Seal, granting Alleyn some privilege or appointment, but of what nature is nowhere stated.

[2] i.e., The Clerk of the Signet at the Privy Seal-office: "the pattyne" means *the patent*, for making out which the Privy Seal had been issued.

[3] No sum is placed opposite this item.

[4] Malone, who quotes this entry (iii., 333), misdates it the 22d of July 1597, and the words "or any for me" he misread "*or my sonne*," putting "Edw. Alleyn" within brackets.

[5] These are not original signatures. At this date Ben Jonson was probably an actor in Henslowe's company.

| | |
|---|---|
| Receved of my sonne for John Synger, in pte of payment ........................................ | x^s |
| Lent Bengemyne Johnson, the 5 of Jeneware 1597, in Redy mony, the some of.............. | v^s |

Memdum, that the 27 of Jeuley 1597 I heayred Thomas Hearne [1] with ij pence, for to searve me ij yeares in the qualetie of playenge, for fyve shellynges a weacke for one yeare, and vj^s viij^d for the other yeare, which he hath covenanted hime seallffe to searve me, and not to departe frome my companey tyll this ij yeares be eanded.—Wittnes to this,

JOHN SYNGER
JEAMES DONSTON
THOMAS TOWNE.[2]

| | |
|---|---|
| Lent unto John Synger, the 25 of July 1597, in Redy money, to be payd me within one fortnyght next after the date herof........ ..... ... | xx^s |
| Lent more, the 9 of aguste 1597, Redy money | x^s |

Wittnes E. ALLEYN.

*Lent unto Richard Alleyn,*[3] *at severalle tymes, in Redey money, as foloweth, this yeare* 1597.

| | |
|---|---|
| Lent hime, the 27 of maye 1597 ........ ........... | v^s |
| Lent hime, the 19 of June 1597 ..................... | v^s |

[1] Thomas Hearne thus became a "hireling," or "hired man," attached to Henslowe's company at *5s.* a week for the first year, and *6s. 8d.* a week for the second year: Stephen Gosson, in his "Schoole of Abuse," 1579 (Shaksp. Soc. reprint, p. 29), informs us that the "hyerlings" of his day were paid six shillings per week.

[2] These names were subscribed by Henslowe.

[3] Whether Richard Alleyn were any, and what, relation to Edward Alleyn does not distinctly appear. On the 25th March 1598 he became

Lent hime, the 4 of July 1597 ........................ vj[d]
Lent hime, the 23 of July 1597 .................... xij[d]
Lent hime, the i of aguste 1597 .................... xij[d]
Lent hime, upon a payre of sylke stockens .... .... xiij[s]
Payd for the dienge of them sylke stockens ......... xvj[d]

Lent to John Helle, the clowne,[1] the 3 of aguste 1597, in Redy money, the some of ... x[s]

At that tyme I bownd hime by ane a sumsett of ij[d] to contenew with me at my howsse in playinge tylle Shrafte tyde next after the date above written; yf not to forfytte unto me forti powndes. Wittneses to the same,

E. ALLEYN, JOHN SYNGER, JEAMES DONSTALL,
EDWARD JUBEY, SAMEWELL ROWLEY.[2]

Mem̃dum, that the 6 of aguste 1597, I bownd Richard Jones[3] by and a sumsett of ij[d], to continew and playe with the companye of my lord Admeralles players, frome michelmase next after the daye abowe written untell the eand and tearme of iij yeares emediatly folowinge, and to playe in my howsse only known by the name of the Rosse, and in no other howsse about London publicke; and yf restraynte be granted, then to go for the tyme into the contrey, and after to

one of the "hirelings" of Henslowe's company. By another entry it appears that he was dead in 1602, and had left a widow.

[1] Of "John Helle, the clown," we hear nowhere else: possibly Helle was a *nick*-name.

[2] These are not the signatures of the players, who were present at the agreement.

[3] Perhaps the son of the Richard Jones who, on the 3d January 1588-9, sold to Edward Alleyn his theatrical property for £37 10*s*. 0*d*. Vide "Memoirs of Edward Alleyn," pp. 4., 198. In "The Alleyn Papers," p. 19, is inserted a letter to Edward Alleyn from Richard Jones, who was then about to embark for the continent on an acting expedition: it has no date.

retorne agayne to London: yf he breacke this a sumsett then to forfett unto me for the same a hundreth markes of laful money of Ingland. Wittnes to this,

E. ALLEYN and JOHN MIDELTON.[1]

More over, Richard Jones at that tyme hath tacken one other ij^d of me, upon asumsett to forfet unto me one hundreth markes, yf one Robart Shaw[2] do not playe with my lordes admeralles men, as he hath covenanted before in every thinge and time to the other.

Wittnes E. ALLEYN, JOHN MIDELLTON.

Mdom, that the 10 of aguste 1597, W^m Borne[3] came and ofered hime sealfe to come and playe with my lord Admeralles men at my howsse, called by the name of the Rosse, setewate one the banck, after this order folowinge: he hath receved of me iij^d upon, and a sumsette to forfette unto me a hundrethe marckes of lafull money of Ingland, yf he do not performe thes thinges folowinge; that is, presently after libertie beinge granted for playinge, to come and to playe with my lord Admeralles men at my howsse aforsayd, and not in any other howsse publicke abowt London, for the space of iij yeares, beginynge imediatly after this Restraynt is recaled by the lordes of the cownsell, which Restraynt is by the means of

[1] Possibly related to Thomas Middleton, the dramatist. It is to be presumed perhaps that John Middleton was an actor from the company in which his name is found.

[2] Robert Shaw (whose name has frequently occurred) seems to have bound himself in the first instance to Richard Jones, and Richard Jones therefore undertook for him to Henslowe.

[3] The name of this actor, who was known as William Borne, or Birde (he always subscribed the latter) will be familiar to the reader. It does not appear by this "memorandum" that he was to be paid wages, but he engaged himself to play only at Henslowe's theatre, the Rose, as soon as the "restraint" occasioned by the performance of Nash's "Isle of Dogs" had been recalled. Henslowe seems to have taken advantage of the interval to strengthen his company.

playinge the Ieylle of Dooges:[1] yf he do not, then he forfettes this asumset afore, or ells not. Wittnes to this

E. ALLEYN and ROBSONE.[2]

Mdom, that the 6 of octobr 1597, Thomas Dowton came and bownd hime seallfe unto me in xxxx[li], in a sumesett, by the receving of iij[d] of me before wittnes: the covenant is this, that he shold, frome the daye above written untell Shraftid next come ij yeares, to playe in my howsse, and in no other abowte London publickely: yf he do, with owt my consent, to forfett unto me this some of money above written. Wittnes to this

E. ALLEYN    ROBARTE SHAWE.
W[m] BORNE    JOHN SYNGER
DICKE JONNES.[3]

Bowght my boye, Jeames Brystow, of William Augusten, player, the 18 of desembr 1597, for viij[li] [4]

Memd. that this 25 of marche 1598, Richard Alleyne[5] came and bownde hime seallfe unto me for ij yeares, in and a sumsette as a hiered servant, with ij syngell pence and to contenew frome the daye above written unto the eand and tearme of ij yeares: yf he do not performe this covenant, then he to

[1] Respecting Nash's play, the Isle of Dogs, see also pp. 94, 98.

[2] This is the memorandum referred to on p. 225 note 4, regarding Robson, who is not, however, to be confounded with Robinson.

[3] In all these instances the names of the witnesses were added by Henslowe.

[4] By other entries inserted on p. 149, &c., it appears that Henslowe let out his boy, James Bristow, to the company, and charged wages for him. We do not recollect elsewhere to have met with the name of William Augustine or Augusten as a player.

[5] Henslowe, as appears on p. 256, had lent money to Richard Alleyn in 1597, before he thus bound himself as a hireling to act with no other company.

forfette for the breach of yt fortye powndes, and wittnes to this

Wm Borne
Thomas Downton
Gabrell Spencer
Robart Shawe
Richard Jonnes

Md. that this 25 of marche 1598, Thomas Hawoode[1] came and hiered hime seallfe with me as a covenante searvante for ij yeares, by the Recevinge of ij syngell pence, acordinge to the statute of winchester, and to begine at the daye above written, and not to playe any wher publicke abowt London not whille thes ij yeares be exspired, but in my howsse: yf he do, then he dothe forfette unto me, by the Recevinge of thes ijd, fortie powndes, and wittnes to this

| | |
|---|---|
| Antony Monday[2] | Wm Borne |
| Gabrell Spencer | Thoms Dowton |
| Robart Shawe | Richard Jonnes |
| Richard Alleyn. | |

Mdm that this 16 of novembr 1599, I hired, as my covenente servantes, Charles Massey and Samewell Rowley, for a yeare, and as much as to Shraftide, begenynge at the daye above written, after the statute of winchester, with ij syngell pence; and for them they have covenanted with me to playe in my howes, and in no other howsse dewringe the thime publecke, but in mine: yf they dooe, withowt my consent, for yf they dooe, to forfett unto me xxxxli a pece. Wittnes thomas Dowton, Robart shawe, Wm Borne, Jubey, Richard Jonnes.

[1] We have had notices of Heywood, and of his connexion with Henslowe, anterior to this date when he hired himself as a covenant-servant. See p. 78, &c.

[2] Henslowe's writing: the original signature of Anthony Monday nowhere occurs in the MS. in its present state.

| | |
|---|---|
| Lent hime,[1] the 9 of aguste 1598, to geve the atorney Ceachen, for the bande which he hade in his hande, the some of ........................ | viij$^{s}$ iiij$^{d}$ |
| Layd owt for hime the same time to M$^{r}$ Ceatchen, and Receved his bande frome hime, some of.................................................... | l$^{s}$ |
| Lent unto M$^{rs}$ Alleyn, widow,[2] the 18 of septembr 1602, in Redy monye, the some of...... | xxxx$^{s}$ |
| Lent unto M$^{rs}$ Alleyn, widow, the 19 of septembr 1602, to fetche her mantell, and shette, and fascloth, from M$^{r}$ Colles, the some of ......... | v$^{li}$ x$^{s}$ |

This goodes be dd. backe agayne
and I Rd my monye, v$^{li}$ v$^{s}$.

Harey Porter tocke a somsete of me, Phillipe Henslowe, the 16 of Aprell 1599, upon this condition, that yf I would geve hime xij$^{d}$ at that instante, for that xij$^{d}$ he bownd hime seallfe unto me in x$^{li}$ of corant Inglishe mony, for this cawse to paye unto me the next daye folowinge all the money which he oweth unto me, or els to ferfette for that xij$^{d}$ tenn powndes; which deate wase unto me xxv$^{s}$, which he hath not payd acordinge to his bonde, and so hath forfetted unto me:[3] wittnes to this a sumsette

JOHN HASLETT, vater.
M$^{r}$ KYNGMAN, the elder.[4]

[1] i.e., Richard Alleyn. Preceding this item is a repetition of several entries of money advanced to the same performer.

[2] By this date, 18th Sept. 1602, Richard Alleyn was dead, and the "Mrs. Alleyn, widow," here mentioned was his relict.

[3] According to this statement, Henry Porter had forfeited £10 to Henslowe for failing to pay his debt of 25*s*. The signatures of Hazlett, the vaulter, and of Kyngman, are merely memoranda that they saw Porter receive the 12*d*.

[4] After about thirty leaves, some entire and others mutilated, (by having had parts, containing probably theatrical information and auto-

Itm̃, it is agreed betwixt us, Phillipe Henslow, E. Alleyn, John Ockley, free of the larymores, other wisse called the bit-makers, and nycolas Dame, starchemacker, as foloweth:

Itm̃ firste, that Phillipe Henslow and E. Alleyn is to previde a howsse for to macke starche in, and lickwisse to provide grownd to keppe hogges one, at ower owne charges; and the sayd John Ocklye and Nycolas Dame to paye unto us no Rente.

Secondlye, the sayd John ocklye and nycolas Dame is to provid at ther owne carges al fattes, and other vesselles what so ever, fitte for starche mackynge of starce, and when yt is mad and sowld the iij pte of the gayne to be unto the said P. H. and E. A. delyvered for ther pte.

Mr Hareys, I wold desyer you to macke a bande for me, which all the companye of the earlle of Nothingame players must stand bownd, for the payment to me——[1]

Mr Hares, I must paye xxli and ode mony to Mr Treheren, for the earlle of Nottingames players,[2] which they have borowed of hime upon ther bande; and for the payment therof they will geve me ther band generall to this efeacte, that I shall have ther corte mony, which they have dew unto them for playnge this crysmas afore the Quene, so sone as yt can be Receved by any of them, or ells by my sone, withowt frade.

graphs of poets and players, cut away) we come to a memorandum, which again shows that, at a date not here specified, Henslowe and Alleyn were engaged in a starch-manufactory. See also p. 233.

[1] This appears to be the commencement of an intended copy of a letter from Henslowe to Harris, the scrivener: no doubt, it related to what immediately follows.

[2] It does not appear in what relation Mr. Treheren stood with the Earl of Nottingham's players: Henslowe was to pay him £20 "and odd money," in return for which he was to have the court money

*A not of what I paye every yeare as foloweth,* 1602, *for Rente:—*

| | | | |
|---|---|---|---|
| Pd unto the Quene | xxvij[li] | 13[s] | 4[d] |
| Pd unto M[r] Ower | xiiij[li] | | |
| Pd unto S[t] mildreds | vij[li] | | |
| Pd unto the beshope | | ix[s] | |
| Pd unto windover | iij[li] | xij[s] | 4[d] |

*A note of alle my tenents and what they paye yearly, as foloweth, from the* 25 *of marche* 1602, *begining at our Ladye Daye.*[1]

| | | | |
|---|---|---|---|
| Roger Jonnes | | xl[s] | |
| M[r] Keayes his leace | | xl[s] | |
| M[r] Whotley | vj[li] | 13[s] | 4[d] |
| M[r] Williamsone | vj[li] | 13[s] | 4[d] |
| Goodman Pegette | iij[li] | | |
| Thomas Towne | iij[li] | | |
| Widowe Watsone | ix[li] | | |
| M[rs] Rockette | | xliij[s] | iiij[d] |
| M[r] Haryson, skner | | liij[s] | iiij[d] |
| Widow Spencer | iiij[li] | | |
| Edward Adyson | ix[li] | x[s] | |
| Gorge Tayller, owermaker | | liij[s] | iiij[d] |
| W[m] Tyghton | | xl[s] | |
| Robart Drewe | v[li] | vj[s] | 8[d] |

of the company, meaning the sum which had become due to them for performances before the Queen at Christmas. No date is given.

[1] Thomas Towne, in the ensuing list, was the actor in Henslowe's company. The "Widow Spencer" was in all probability the relict of Gabriel Spencer, whom Ben Jonson had killed in Hoxton Fields in Sept. 1598. There was a dramatic author of the name of Thomas Drew, or Drue, and perhaps Robert Drew was some relation to him. On p. 7, we have had *John* Taylor, oar-maker, mentioned under date of 8th April 1595: George Taylor might be his son.

*M$^r$ Malthowes Rentes,*[1] *as foloweth.* 1602:

| | | |
|---|---|---|
| W$^m$ Glover | | liij$^s$ iiij$^d$ |
| E. Alleyn | x$^{li}$ | |
| Simon Birde | | xxvj$^s$ 8$^d$ |
| W$^m$ Tyghton | | xxvj$^s$ 8$^d$ |

*The Rosse Rentes,*[2] *as foloweth:*

| | | |
|---|---|---|
| Ower tyerman | iij$^{li}$ | |
| Goody Seasy | | xl$^s$ |
| Goody Parson | | xxvj$^s$ 8$^d$ |
| Widow Underher | | xxx$^s$ |
| Goodman Thornes | | xl$^s$ |
| Goodman Richardson | | xl$^s$ |
| Goodman Balle | | xxvj$^s$ 8$^d$ |
| Goodman Flemynge | | xxx$^s$ |
| Goody glover | | xl$^s$ |
| Lytell howsse | vj$^{li}$ | |
| M$^{rs}$ Whitte | iij$^{li}$ | vj$^s$ |

*Windovers Rentes.*

| | | |
|---|---|---|
| Hew Daves | vj$^{li}$ | |
| M$^r$ Page | | xx$^s$ |

[1] Why these were called "Mr. Malthowes Rentes" does not appear: perhaps he collected them. Respecting Malthouse, see p. 107, *n* 2. E. Alleyn, whose name is in the list, resided in a house which Henslowe had either built or extensively repaired. He paid a higher rent than any body else in this or the other lists. William Tyghton seems to have rented two houses of Henslowe.

[2] These were most likely the rents of houses immediately connected with the Rose; and we may perhaps conclude, as was certainly the case with "our 'tireman," that the tenants were persons in some way employed about the theatre.

*M$^{r}$ Owers Rentes.*

| | |
|---|---|
| M$^{r}$ Juboy | vj$^{li}$ |

*The tenantes of Jemes Russelles Leace, as foloweth, begenynge at our Ladye Daye* 1602.

| | | |
|---|---|---|
| Harye Sparkes | ij$^{li}$ | |
| John Wade | ij$^{li}$ | x$^{s}$ |
| W$^{m}$ Smythe | ij$^{li}$ | x$^{s}$ |
| Robarte Mownte | ij$^{li}$ | x$^{s}$ |
| John Haynes | | xij$^{s}$ |
| John Wayshefelld | ij$^{li}$ | x$^{s}$ |
| Robarte Russell | ij$^{li}$ | x$^{s}$ |
| Mathew Hunte | ij$^{li}$ | |
| John Bande | ij$^{li}$ | |
| John Smythe | ij$^{li}$ | |
| Robart Washefellde | ij$^{li}$ | |
| Widowe Smythe | ij$^{li}$ | |
| Item iij shoppes | iiij$^{li}$ | x$^{s}$ |
| W$^{m}$ Corden | | xvj$^{s}$ |
| Jemes Russells howsse and yardes | xx$^{li}$ | |
| Robarte Mownte for a garden | j$^{li}$ | iiij$^{s}$ |

*The Bores Heade tenantes, as foloweth, begenynge at crystmase laste,* 1604.

| | | |
|---|---|---|
| Edward Rygmayden | x$^{li}$ | |
| Elizabeth Roosse | | xxvj$^{s}$ 8$^{d}$ |
| Lewes Easste | | xx$^{s}$ |
| Thomas Hardinge | | xxvj$^{s}$ 8$^{d}$ |
| Raffe Haynes | | xxxij$^{s}$ |
| Richard Sanders | | xxiiij$^{s}$ |
| Robarte Stockes | | xx$^{s}$ |
| Ellyn Foreste | | xxxx$^{s}$ |

| | |
|---|---|
| W^m Lowe | xx^s |
| Thomas Dawson | xx^s |
| John Strete | xx^s |
| Richard Homes | xx^s |
| Widow Saye | xx^s |
| Tege Lince | xxxx^s |

*A not of them of my tenantes which are to pay me Capones, and when, every year by ther leaces as foloweth,* 1604.

In a leace of widow Renowlls, to pay j capon at sentandrostyd
Good man Hichenson to paye at crystmas ij capones
M^r Mownt to paye at Shraftid ij capones
Thomas towne, to paye at Shraftid j capon
Goodman pigat to paye at Shraftid j capon
Goodman Hunte to pay at crystmas ij capones.

*Thes be my tenantes belonginge to the Bores head, one the other syde of the Leaffe, as foloweth, begynynge at crystmas last,* 1604, *al one rence.*[1]

| | |
|---|---|
| Simon Luttrell | xx^s |
| Harey Alleyn | xx^s |
| Thomas Lawsson | xx^s |
| Hamlet Bruther | xxiiij^s |
| John Malborne | xxvj^s 8^d |
| Sarey Brewer | xxx^s |
| Thomas Walborne | xxxx^s |
| John Hunte | l^s |
| John Hichenson | vij^li |

[1] What Henslowe meant by "al one rence" is not now intelligible: it cannot mean "all one *rent*," but possibly that the different rents were paid all at one date. This list is a continuation of an enumeration of his Boars-head tenants, which commences "on the other side of the leaf" in the MS.

Received of Mr Henslow, the xj[th] daye of aprill 1602, the some of ten poundes, dew to me at ower Lady abouff wrytten, for that quarter then dewe to me for Rent.[1]

JOHN DORINGTON.

Be it knowne unto all men by thes presentes, that I Charles Rose, servaunt to Mr Pullforde of Pawles Churchyarde, taylor in London, have bargained and soulde unto Phillip Henshlowe, of St Saviors in the county of Surrey, Gent., one dublett and a paire of rownd hose of cloath of gould, layd thicke with blacke silke lace, in open markett. In wittnes whereof, I the said Charles Rose have hereunto sett my hande this xxviij[th] of November 1598, in consideration of lviij[s] in currant Englishe money by me receaved the day and yeare above written.

By me CHARLES ROSSE.[2]

Wittnes ROBT. SHÀA.

*Decimo die Januarij, Anno Dni.* 1603.

Md, that I Francis Woodward do acknowledge my self to owe and to be indebtted unto Phillipp Henslowe, Citizen and

[1] From this entry, and other circumstances, (see p. 177) we may infer that Henslowe paid Sir John Dorington, Master of the Games, &c., (who wrote the memorandum) £80 per annum for the privilege of baiting bears, bulls, &c., at Paris Garden. It is followed by a number of pages which are either blank or filled with matter of no interest, medical recipes, "a good dryncke for the pestelence," "for the dropsey," &c.; and these are succeeded by seven pages respecting money advanced on pawns of various kinds, the dates being from 17 January 1593, to the 12th of April 1595. Philip Henslowe seems to have transacted this business himself, without the intervention of Francis Henslowe, who acted on previous occasions.

[2] The whole of this memorandum is in the handwriting of Charles Rose, or Rosse, for he spells his name differently in the body of the paper

Dier of London,[1] in the somme of tenn poundes of currant money, to be payd to the said Phillipp on the firste daye of February next comynge after the date hereof: for testimony hereof I have hereunto sette my hand.

ꝑ me, FRANCISCUM WODWARD.[2]

Wittnes my sonne,
E. Alleyn, and my dawther.

Lent unto Martyne Slawghter, the 22 of July 1604, the some of fyve powndes, to be payd me agayne the next moneth folowinge after the date, which mony was delyvered unto his wiffe, I saye lent ................................ } $v^{li}$

Wittnes E. ALLEYN.[3]

Lent unto M^r^ Freman, of Sussex, the 26 of novmbr 1604, to folowe his sewt in the Corte of Requestes ageanste M^r^ Bande, the some of twenty shellenges: I saye lent ................. } $xx^{s}$

Wittnes W^m^ HENSLOW.[4]

and in the subscription. "Robt. Shaa" was written by the actor, and no doubt the purchase was for the use of the company, which had occasion for additions to the wardrobe.

1 This entry, like another on p. 52, shows Philip Henslowe's original trade — that of a dyer — and hence, perhaps, his connexion with the starch business, in which he was joined (as in his other transactions) by Edward Alleyn.

2 Woodward, as we find elsewhere, was collector of the rents of Lord Montague; and was perhaps related by marriage to Henslowe, whose wife had been the widow Woodward.

3 Alleyn's name is only inserted as a memorandum: it is not his signature.

4 The MS. contains notices of William Henslowe as early as 1593; see p. 251, note 3. Philip Henslowe had a tenant of the name of John Bande, mentioned on p. 265.

Memd. that yt is agreed betwene M^r^ Robarte Weles, of Buxted in the Counte of Sussex, and M^r^ Phillip Hensly, of London, the xxiiij^th^ of maye, in the yere of our Lorde 1593, that the sayed Robarte Weles shall delyver unto the sayed Phillip Hensly, upon our Ladye daye nexte comeng after the date herof, on serten pece of Land, lyenge in Buxted, caled Locyers, quyetly withowte any troble by the sayed Robarte Weles.

ROBERT WELLES.[1]

*Rd at the Bergenden this yeare* 1608, *begining at Chrystmas holedayes, as foloweth:*

| | |
|---|---|
| Rd one mondaye, S^t^ Stevenes daye................. | iiij^li^ |
| Rd one tewesdaye, S^t^ Johns daye ................. | vj^li^ |
| Rd one Wensdaye, being Shilldermas daye .. ... | iij^li^ xiij^s^ |

*Rd at the Fortewne this yeare* 1608, *begenynge at Crystmas holedayes.*[2]

| | |
|---|---|
| Rd one S^t^ Stevenes daye.......................... | xxv^s^ |
| Rd one S^t^ Johnes daye .......................... | xxxxv^s^ |
| Rd one Chelldermas daye ...................... | xxxxiiij^s^ ix^d^ |

[1] This undertaking appears to have been written by some third person, and only signed by Wells: it serves to connect Henslowe still farther with the county of Sussex.

[2] With this brief account Henslowe's Diary abruptly concludes: by a comparison of it with the receipts, as given above, on the same days at "the Bear-garden," it appears that the latter was much the most profitable concern.

*tacken the* 10 *of Marche in the yeare* 1598.

Gone and loste.

Item, j orenge taney satten dublet, layd thycke with gowld lace.

Item, j blew tafetie sewt.

Item, j payr of carnatyon satten Venesyons, layd with gold lace.

Item, j longe-shanckes sewte.

Item, j Sponnes dublet pyncket.

Item, j Spanerds gyrcken.

Item, Harey the fyftes dublet.

Item, Harey the fyftes vellet gowne.

Item, j fryers gowne.

Item, j lyttell dublet for boye.

*The Enventary of the Clownes Sewtes and Hermetes Sewtes, w diever other sewtes, as followeth,* 1598 *the* 10 *of March.*

Item, j senetores gowne, j hoode, and 5 senetores capes.

Item, j sewtte for Nepton; Fierdrackes sewtes for Dobe.

Item, iiij genesareyes gownes, and iiij torchberers sewtes.

Item, iij payer of red strasers, and iij fares gowne of buckrome.

Item, iiij Herwodes cottes, and iij sogers cottes, and j green gown Maryan.

Item, vj grene cottes for Roben Hoode, and iiij knaves sewtes.

Item, ij payer of grene hosse, and Andersones sewte. j whitt shepen clocke.

Item, ij rosset cottes, and j black frese cotte, and iij prestes cottes.

Item, ij whitt shepherdes cottes, and ij Danes sewtes, and j payer of Danes hosse.

Item, The Mores lymes, and Hercolles lymes, and Will. Sommers sewtte.

Item, ij Orlates sewtes, hates and gorgetts, and vij anteckes cootes.

Item, Cathemer sewte, j payer of cloth whitte stockens, iiij Turckes hedes.

Item, iiij freyers gownes and iiij hoodes to them, and j fooles coate, cape, and babell, and branhowlttes bodeys, and merlen gowne and cape.

Item, ij black saye gownes, and ij cotton gownes, and j rede saye gowne.

Item, j mawe gowne of calleco for the quene, j carnowll hatte.

Item, j red sewt of cloth for pyge, layed with whitt lace.

Item, v payer of hosse for the clowne, and v gerkenes for them.

Item, iij payer of canvas hosse for asane, ij payer of black strocers.

Item, j yelow leather dublett for a clowne, j Whittcomes dublett poke.

Item, Eves bodeyes, j pedante trusser, and iij donnes hattes.

Item, j payer of yelow cotton sleves, j gostes sewt, and j gostes bodeyes.

Item, xviij copes and hattes, Verones sonnes hosse.

Item, iij trumpettes and a drum, and a trebel viall, a basse viall, a bandore, a sytteren, j anshente, j whitt hatte.

Item, j hatte for Robin Hoode, j hobihorse.

Item, v shertes, and j serpelowes, iiij ferdingalles.

Item, vj head-tiers, j fane iiij rebatos, ij gyrketruses.

Item, j longe sorde.

*The Enventary of all the aparell for my Lord Admiralles men, tacken the* 10 *of marche* 1598.—*Leaft above in the tier-house in the cheast.*

Item, My Lord Caffes gercken, & his hoosse.

Item, j payer of hosse for the Dowlfen.

Item, j murey lether gyrcken, & j white lether gercken.

Item, j black lether gearken, & Nabesathe sewte.

Item, j payer of hosse, & a gercken for Valteger.

Item, ij leather anteckes cottes with basses, for Fayeton.

Item, j payer of bodeyes for Alles Pearce.

*The Enventary tacken of all the properties for my Lord Admeralles men, the* 10 *of Marche* 1598.

Item, j rocke, j cage, j tombe, j Hell mought.

Item, j tome of Guido, j tome of Dido, j bedsteade.

Item, viij lances, j payer of stayers for Fayeton.

Item, ij stepells, & j chyme of belles, & j beacon.

Item, j hecfor for the playe of Faeton, the limes dead.

Item, j globe, & j golden scepter; iij clobes.

Item, ij marchepanes, & the sittie of Rome.

Item, j gowlden flece; ij rackets; j baye tree.

Item, j wooden hatchett; j lether hatchete.

Item, j wooden canepie; owld Mahemetes head.

Item, j lyone skin; j beares skyne; & Faetones lymes, & Faeton charete; & Argosse heade.

Item, Nepun forcke & garland.

Item, j crosers stafe; Kentes woden leage.

Item, Ierosses head, and raynbowe; j littell alter.

Item, viij viserdes; Tamberlyne brydell; j wooden matook.

Item, Cupedes bowe, and quiver; the clothe of the Sone and Mone.

Item, j bores heade & Serberosse iij heades.

Item, j Cadeseus; ij mose banckes, & j snake.

Item, ij fanes of feathers; Belendon stable; j tree of gowlden apelles; Tantelouse tre; jx eyorn targates.

Item, j copper targate, & xvij foyles.

Item, iiij wooden targates; j greve armer.

Item, j syne for Mother Readcap; j buckler.

Item, Mercures wings; Tasso picter; j helmet with a dragon; j shelde, with iij lyones; j elme bowle.

Item, j chayne of dragons; j gylte speare.

Item, ij coffenes; j bulles head; and j vylter.

Item, iij tymbrells; j dragon in fostes.

Item, j lyone; ij lyon heades; j great horse with his leages; j sack-bute.

Item, j whell and frame in the Sege of London.
Item, j paire of rowghte gloves.
Item, j poopes miter.
Item, iij Imperial crownes; j playne crowne.
Item, j gostes crown; j crown with a sone.
Item, j frame for the heading in Black Jone.
Item, j black dogge.
Item, j cauderm for the Jewe.

*The Enventorey of all the aparell of the Lord Admeralles men, taken the* 13*th of Marche* 1598, *as followeth:*

Item, j payer of whitte saten Vencsons cut with coper lace.
Item, j ash coller satten doublett, layed with gold lace.
Item, j peche coller satten doublett.
Item, j owld white satten dublette.
Item, j bleu tafitie sewtte.
Item, j Mores cotte.
Item, Pyges damask gowne.
Item, j black satten cotte.
Item, j harcoller tafitie sewte of pygges.
Item, j white tafitie sewte of pygges.
Item, Vartemar sewtte.
Item, j great pecholler dublet, with sylver lace.
Item, j white satten dublet pynckte.
Item, j owld white satten dublet pynckte.
Item, j payer of satten Venesyan satten ymbradered.
Item, j payer of French hosse, cloth of gowld.
Item, j payer of cloth of gowld hosse with sylver paines.
Item, j payer of cloth of sylver hosse with satten and sylver panes.
Item, Tamberlynes cotte, with coper lace.
Item, j read clock with white coper lace.
Item, j read clocke, with read coper lace.
Item, j shorte clocke of taney satten with sleves.
Item, j shorte clocke of black satten with sleves.
Item, Labesyas clocke with gowld buttenes.
Item, j payer of read cloth hosse of Venesyans, with sylver lace of corde.
Item, Valteger robe of rich tafitie.

Item, Junoes cotte.

Item, j hode for the wech.

Item, j read stamel clocke with whitte coper lace.

Item, j read stamel clocke with read coper lace.

Item, j cloth clocke of russete with coper lace, called Guydoes clocke.

Item, j short clocke of black velvet, with sleves faced with shagg.

Item, j short clocke of black vellet, faced with white fore.

Item, j manes gown, faced with whitte fore.

Item, Dobes cotte of cloth of sylver.

Item, j payer of pechecoler Venesyones uncut, with read coper lace.

Item, j read scarllet clocke with sylver buttones.

Item, j longe black velvet clock, layd with brod lace black.

Item, j black satten sewtte.

Item, j blacke velvet clocke, layd with twyst lace blacke.

Item, Perowes sewt, which W^m Sley were.

Item, j payer of pechcoler hosse with sylver corlled panes.

Item, j payer of black cloth of sylver hosse, drawne out with tused tafittie.

Item, Tamberlanes breches of crymson vellvet.

Item, j payer of sylk howse with panes of sylver corlled lace.

Item, j Faeytone sewte.

Item, Roben Hoodes sewtte.

Item, j payer of cloth of gowld hose with gowld corlle panes.

Item, j payer of rowne hosse buffe with gowld lace.

Item, j payer of mows coller Venesyans with R. brode gowld lace.

Item, j flame collerde dublet pynked.

Item j blacke satten dublet, layd thyck wyth blacke and gowld lace.

Item, j carnacyon dubled cutt, layd with gowld lace.

Item. j white satten dublet, faced with read tafetie.

Item, j grene gyrcken with sylver lace.

Item, j black gyrcken with sylver lace.

Item, j read gyrcken with sylver lace.

Item, j read Spanes dublett styched.

Item, j peche coller satten casse.

Item, Tassoes robe.

Item, j murey robe with sleves.

Item, j blewe robe with sleves.

Item, j oren taney robe with sleves.
Item, j pech collerd hallf robe.
Item, j lane robe with spangells.
Item, j white & orenge taney scarf, spangled.
Item, Dides robe.
Item, iij payer of basses.
Item, j white tafitie sherte with gowld frenge.
Item, the fryers trusse in Roben Hoode.
Item, j littell gacket for Pygge.
Item, j womanes gown of cloth of gowld.
Item, j orenge taney vellet gowe with sylver lace, for women.
Item, j black velvet gowne ymbradered with gowld lace.
Item, j yelowe satten gowne ymbradered with sylk & gowld lace, for women.
Item, j greve armer.
Item, Harye the v. velvet gowne.
Item, j payer of crymson satten Venysiones, layd with gowld lace.
Item, j blew tafitie sewte, layd with sylver lace.
Item, j Longeshankes seute.
Item, j orange coller satten dublett, layd with gowld lace.
Item, Harye the v. satten dublet, layd with gowld lace.
Item, j Spanes casse dublet of crymson pyncked.
Item, j Spanes gearcken layd with sylver lace.
Item, j wattshode tafitie dublet for a boye.
Item, ij payer of basses, j white, j blewe, of sasnet.
Item, j freyers gowne of graye.

*A Note of all suche bookes as belong to the Stocke, and such as I have bought since the 3d of March* 1598.

| | |
|---|---|
| Blacke Jonne. | Woman will have her will. |
| The Umers. | Welchmans price. |
| Hardicanewtes. | King Arthur, life and death. |
| Borbonne. | 1 p[t] of Hercules. |
| Sturgflaterey | 2 p[te] of Hercoles. |
| Brunhowlle. | Pethagores. |
| Cobler quen hive. | Focasse. |
| Frier Pendelton. | Elexsander and Lodwicke. |
| Alls Perce. | Blacke Battman. |

| | |
|---|---|
| Read Cappe. | 2 p. black Battman. |
| Roben Hode, 1. | 2 p[t] of Goodwine. |
| Roben Hode, 2. | Mad mans morris. |
| Phayeton. | Perce of Winchester. |
| Treangell cockowlls. | Vayvode. |
| Goodwine. | |

*A Note of all suche goodes as I have bought for the Companey of my Lord Admiralls men, sence the* 3 *of Aprell* 1598, *as followeth:*

| | *l.* | *s.* | *d.* |
|---|---|---|---|
| Bowght a damaske casock garded with velvett ........... | 0 | 18 | 0 |
| Bowght a payer of paned rownd hosse of cloth whiped with sylk, drawne out with tafitie ........................... Bowght j payer of long black wollen stockens .............. | 0 | 8 | 0 |
| Bowght j black satten dublett.............................. Bowght j payer of rownd howsse paned of vellevett......... | 4 | 15 | 0 |
| Bowght a robe for to goo invisibell ........................ Bowght a gown for Nembia .............................. | 3 | 10 | 0 |
| Bowght a dublett of whitt satten layd thicke with gowld lace, and a payer of rowne pandes hosse of cloth of sylver, the panes layd with gowld lace ........................ | 7 | 0 | 0 |
| Bowght of my sonne v sewtes................................ | 20 | 0 | 0 |
| Bowght of my sonne iiij sewtes ............................ | 17 | 0 | 0 |

# INDEX.

THE END.

FREDERICK SHOBERL, JUNIOR,
PRINTER TO HIS ROYAL HIGHNESS PRINCE ALBERT,
51, RUPERT STREET, HAYMARKET, LONDON.

# REPORT OF THE PROCEEDINGS

OF THE

## FOURTH ANNUAL MEETING OF THE MEMBERS

OF

# THE SHAKESPEARE SOCIETY,

## HELD ON THE 26TH APRIL, 1845,

AT THE ROOMS OF THE ROYAL SOCIETY OF LITERATURE, NO. 4, ST. MARTIN'S PLACE, TRAFALGAR SQUARE, LONDON.

---

## REPORT OF THE COUNCIL.

The Council, in presenting their Fourth Annual Report to the Society, have little more to do than congratulate the members on its continued success, and recapitulate the titles of the works issued in the course of the past year.

In compliance with a wish generally expressed, three extremely rare plays have been printed, affording considerable illustration of the drama of the period, and more particularly of the question of Shakespeare's obligation to his predecessors. The First Volume of a Miscellaneous Collection has also been issued, which, it is hoped, will be received as initiative of a series, that must prove very interesting and instructive, could Members of the Society and the possessors of rare documents be induced to contribute to it. It may be here stated that some papers of much interest have been most liberally furnished for the Volume now in progress; and it is hoped that this may induce others to aid in the establishment of a Miscellany worthy of the subject. The Council beg to reiterate their earnest anxiety to receive contributions from the Members generally.

The labour and research bestowed for the last hundred years on the illustration of our national poet, and his great contemporaries, prove the extreme difficulty there is in reproducing their works so as to give full expression and effect to their wonderful genius; and the reception afforded to all works on the subject, not only by those of their own country and language, but by the whole of Europe, establish also that the product of such labour and research, however necessarily slow in its progress and small in its results, is eagerly sought for and gratefully appreciated.

The amount of labour necessary to repair the inroads of time, and, by careful elucidation, to restore the full meaning of the ever-varying and universal allusions of such quick and prolific fancies as those of our early dramatists, can only be thoroughly understood by those who have had occasion to consult the vast quantity of material from which it must be acquired. This remark is made as some answer to those who expected that more directly illustrative works would have been able to be procured by antiquaries. The Society, however, has the satisfaction of seeing that the books issued by it have been universally appealed to by the numerous writers and commentators who, in reviews as well as separate works, have lately so largely availed themselves of the materials; thus proving the practical utility of the works selected.

The Council cannot too continually keep before the attention of lovers of old literature that it is only by extreme and patient perseverance that sufficient materials can be collected to entirely remove the obsoleteness and incrustations which the lapse of time and change of language and manners have wrought in these great writers. The experience of every day, however, convinces all classes of readers that no amount of labour can be misspent in elucidating that which in itself is so truly excellent.

One of the main purposes of the Society, as stated in its original prospectus and ever since kept closely in view, was to induce persons possessing old family papers to examine them, in the hope of finding something, if not directly elucidatory of Shakespeare, illustrative at least of our early drama and stage. This object has already, in part, been accomplished by the work last issued: a printed copy of one of our great dramatist's most popular historical plays, from a contemporary manuscript possibly anterior to the earliest of the printed editions. It has been preserved for ages among the domestic records of Sir Edward Dering, of Surrenden, Kent, Baronet; and the liberality of the possessor, in allowing it to be printed, cannot be too highly estimated, nor too often mentioned, as an example and an incentive to others who, thus encouraged, may unexpectedly discover that they have long had documents of a similar character in their care and custody.

The following six volumes have been printed and distributed during the year which closed 31 December, 1844:—

1. TARLTON'S JESTS, from the edition of 1611; and TARLTON'S NEWES OUT OF PURGATORY, from the earliest copy, preceded by a Life of that celebrated Comedian, and an Account of his Jigs and Merry Sayings. Edited by J. O. HALLIWELL, Esq., F.R.S., &c.

2. THE TRUE TRAGEDIE OF RICHARD THE THIRD, which preceded Shakespeare's Play. From a *unique* copy printed in 1594, 4to., in the library of his Grace the Duke of Devonshire. To which is added the Latin Play of RICHARDUS TERTIUS, by Dr. LEGGE, from the Manuscript in Emmanuel College, Cambridge. Edited by BARRON FIELD, Esq.

3. THE GHOST OF RICHARD THE THIRD, &c. Containing more of him than hath been heretofore shewed, either in Chrónicles, Plays, or Poems. By C. B., 4to., 1614; partly founded upon Shakespeare's Trágedy, and partly upon the Chronicles to which he resorted; and recommended by hitherto unknown Poems by Ben Jonson, George Chapman, W. Browne, George Wither, and Robert Daborne. With Introduction and notes by J. PAYNE COLLIER, Esq., F.S.A.

4. SIR THOMAS MORE: an unprinted Historical Play. From the original MS. (licensed for the stage by the Master of the Revels about

the year 1590) in the British Museum. Edited by the Rev. ALEXANDER DYCE.

5. Vol. I. of THE SHAKESPEARE SOCIETY'S PAPERS: being a Miscellany of Contributions illustrative of the Drama and Literature of the Shakespearean Era. To be continued as contributions are received.

6. THE TAMING OF A SHREW, which preceded Shakespeare's Comedy. From the *unique* copies of 1594 and 1596, 4to., in the collections of the Duke of Devonshire, and of Lord Francis Egerton, M.P. Edited by THOMAS AMYOT, Esq., F.R.S., Treas. S.A. &c. With a Fac-simile Title-page of the original edition.

The two following works have been issued since the commencement of the present year:—

1. ILLUSTRATIONS OF THE FAIRY MYTHOLOGY OF SHAKESPEARE, selected from rare books and manuscripts, exhibiting the old popular notions respecting fairies, and how far they have been adopted in the "Midsummer Night's Dream." By J. O. HALLIWELL, Esq., F.R.S., Hon. M.R.I.A., F.S.A., &c.

2. SHAKESPEARE'S PLAY OF KING HENRY THE FOURTH, printed from a Contemporary Manuscript. Edited by JAMES ORCHARD HALLIWELL, Esq., F.R.S., &c. With two fac-similes of the handwritings.

The following works are in the press, and will be issued as soon as completed:—

1. THE DIARY AND ACCOUNT-BOOK OF PHILIP HENSLOWE, between about the years 1590 and 1610, in which he entered his various Transactions relating to Plays, Players, and Dramatists. Edited (by permission of the Master, Warden, and Fellows of Dulwich College) by J. PAYNE COLLIER, Esq., F.S.A.

2. Vol. II. of THE SHAKESPEARE SOCIETY'S PAPERS.

3. THE CHESTER WHITSUN-PLAYS: a Collection of Early Dramatic Representations by the Incorporated Trades of Chester. Edited by THOMAS WRIGHT, Esq., F.S.A., Corresponding Member of the Institute of France, &c. In Two Parts. Part II.

The following works are under revision by the Editors:—

1. NOTICES OF SHAKESPEARE AND HIS WORKS, from the earliest period to the publication of the "Theatrum Poetarum," in 1675; with

memoranda drawn from other sources on his personal and literary history. By BOLTON CORNEY, Esq.

2. THE FAIR MAID OF THE EXCHANGE, with the Merry Humours and Pleasant Passages of the Cripple of Fanchurch: a Comedy, by THOMAS HEYWOOD. From the first edition, 1607: accompanied by the Play of FORTUNE BY LAND AND SEA, by Thomas Heywood and W. Rowley, from the edition of 1655. To be edited by BARRON FIELD, Esq.

3. A SELECTION FROM THE NOTES WRITTEN BY WILLIAM OLDYS, IN HIS COPY OF LANGBAINE'S LIVES OF THE DRAMATIC POETS, now in the British Museum. To be edited by PETER CUNNINGHAM, Esq.

4. A COLLECTION OF THE DOCUMENTS which have reference to the Events of Shakespeare's Life. The Will to be edited by Sir FREDERICK MADDEN, F.R S., F.S.A., Keeper of the MSS. in the British Museum, with Fac-similes of the Signatures. The Marriage Licence, transcripts from the Registers at Stratford-upon-Avon, and all the other Documents, to be edited by JOHN BRUCE, Esq., F.S.A.

5. FUNEBRIA FLORÆ. The Downfal of May-Games, &c.: an attack upon popular amusements. By THOMAS HALL, B.D. 1660, 4to. To be edited by W. B. D. D. TURNBULL, Esq., of Edinburgh, F.S.A., &c.

6. TWO MASQUES, by BEN JONSON, of which Copies in his own handwriting, unknown to all the Editors of Ben Jonson's works, are preserved among the Royal MSS. in the British Museum.

The following are the suggested publications, some of which have been accepted by the Council, and others still remain under consideration:—

1. AN ESSAY ON THE MADNESS OF SOME OF SHAKESPEARE'S PRINCIPAL CHARACTERS, illustrated by examples ancient and modern, with a view to show their peculiar characteristics, and exact truth to nature. By FORBES WINSLOW, Esq., M.D.

2. RALPH ROISTER DOYSTER, the oldest Comedy, and FERREX AND PORREX, the oldest Tragedy, properly so called, in our language: the one from the *unique* copy in the library of Eton College, and the other from the earliest edition in the collection of the Right Hon. Lord Francis Egerton, M.P. To be edited by W. D. COOPER, Esq., F.S.A.

3. THE JOURNAL OF A BARRISTER OF THE NAME OF MANNINGHAM, for the years 1600, 1601, and 1602; containing Anecdotes of Shakespeare, Ben Jonson, Marston, Spenser, Sir W. Raleigh, Sir John Davys, &c.

To be edited from the MS. in the British Museum, by THOMAS WRIGHT, Esq., F.S.A., Correspondent of the Institute of France, &c.

4. THE PASSIONATE SHEPHERD: a collection of poems by NICHOLAS BRETON. Written in imitation of poems in The Passionate Pilgrim of Shakespeare. From the only existing copy, 1604, 4to.

5. RICH'S FAREWELL TO MILITARY PROFESSION. From the *unique* copy of the first edition, in 1581, in the Bodleian Library, containing novels upon which were founded "Twelfth Night" and several dramas of the age of Shakespeare. To be edited by J. PAYNE COLLIER, Esq., F.S.A.

6. WHEN YOU SEE ME YOU KNOW ME, a historical play on events of the reign of Henry VIII. (perhaps anterior to that of Shakespeare) by Samuel Rowley. From the first edition in 1605, collated with the re-impression of 1632.

7. THE MIRROR OF MONSTERS: an attack upon theatrical performances in 1587. By WILLIAM RANKINS, who afterwards became a Dramatic Poet, and the author of Satires, &c., printed in 1596.

8. TRASLATIONS OF TWO ITALIAN COMEDIES, GL' INGANNI AND GL' INGANNATI, the plots of which bear a strong resemblance to Shakespeare's Twelfth Night. By GEORGE MACIRONE, Esq.

9. A COLLECTION OF BROADSIDES AND SHORT PIECES, PRINTED AND MANUSCRIPT, in prose and verse, relating to Authors, Plays, and Actors, during the Reigns of Elizabeth, James I., and Charles I.

10. A TRANSLATION OF ECHTERMEYER'S INTRODUCTION TO THE "QUELLEN DER SHAKESPEARE," containing an account of the sources of the Plots of Shakespeare's Plays.

11. A volume of the Names, Lives, and Characters of the Actors in the Plays of MARLOWE, GREENE, PEELE, SHAKESPEARE, LODGE, NASH, BEN JONSON, CHAPMAN, DEKKER, WEBSTER, HEYWOOD, MIDDLETON, MASSINGER, &c., alphabetically arranged.

12. PASQUIL'S JESTS, mixed with Mother Bunch's Merriments. Whereunto is added a dozen of Gulls. Pretty and pleasant to drive away the tediousness of a Winter's Evening. From the earliest edition of 1604, compared with several later impressions.

13. A ROYAL ARBOUR OF LOYAL POESIE, consisting of Poems and Songs, and including Dramatic Ballads founded upon Shakespeare's Much Ado About Nothing, Winter's Tale, Merchant of Venice, &c., as well as upon several other plays of the time.

14. DIE SCHÖNE SIDEA. An early German Drama, thought to be a

translation of an English Play, from which Shakespeare derived the plot of the Tempest. To be edited by WILLIAM J. THOMS, Esq., F.S.A., and to be followed by translations of three other German Plays, supposed to contain similar versions of Dramas on which Shakespeare founded Much Ado about Nothing, The Two Gentlemen of Verona, and Titus Andronicus.

15. AN ANSWER TO STEPHEN GOSSON'S SCHOOL OF ABUSE. By THOMAS LODGE. Printed about the year 1580.

16. The ALARUM AGAINST USURERS. By THOMAS LODGE, containing a farther reply to Stephen Gosson. From the edition of 1584, 4to., in the Bodleian Library.

17. A Volume of BALLADS UPON WHICH OLD PLAYS WERE FOUNDED, OR WHICH WERE FOUNDED UPON OLD PLAYS; including, of course, all those employed by Shakespeare, and many others in the Roxburghe Collection now deposited in the British Museum.

---

It is the annual duty of the Council to state publicly the great obligations of the Society to those gentlemen who have devoted much valuable time and labour to the editing of the various works; a service which is performed entirely gratuitously, and one which no merely pecuniary recompence could adequately remunerate.

It is also their grateful duty, as formerly, to express the obligations, not merely of the Society, but of all the admirers of our early dramatic poetry, to the noblemen and gentlemen who have afforded important facilities by the loan of, or means of consulting, works only to be found in the libraries of the wealthy, or in the possession of those who are curious in the literature of the time of Shakespeare.

The Society has also to express their sense of the kindness and liberality of the Master, Wardens, and Fellows of Dulwich College, in allowing their valuable and interesting Manuscript of Henslowe's Diary to remain so long in the hands of the Society. The Council are happy to state that this work, so important to the history of the drama, has been nearly completed for publication, and will be the next work placed in the hands of the Members.

*By order of the Council,*

CONYNGHAM, *President.*
F. G. TOMLINS, *Secretary.*

# REPORT OF THE AUDITORS.

We, the Auditors appointed to audit the Receipts and Expenditure of the Shakespeare Society, certify that the Treasurer has exhibited to us his Accounts from the 18th of April, 1844, to the 18th of April, 1845; that we have examined the same, together with the vouchers in support thereof, and find the whole Account correct and satisfactory.

And we further report that the following is a correct Abstract of the Receipts and Expenditure of the Society for the above period.

| RECEIPTS. | £ | s. | d. | EXPENDITURE. | £ | s. | d. |
|---|---|---|---|---|---|---|---|
| Balance in the hands of the Treasurer on the 18th of April, 1844, as per Report of Auditors . . . | 229 | 3 | 6 | To Mr. Shoberl, Jun., for Printing . . . . . . | 130 | 15 | 9 |
| New and Arrear Subscriptions for former years . | 278 | 0 | 0 | Mr. Stevens, for Miscellaneous Printing . . . | 28 | 10 | 0 |
| Subscriptions for the Current year. . . . . . | 270 | 0 | 0 | Bonsor and Co., for Paper | 87 | 3 | 0 |
| Balance in the hands of the Secretary . . . . . | 10 | 10 | 2 | Westley and Clarke, for Binding . . . . . . | 79 | 12 | 0 |
| | | | | Transcripts . . . . . | 34 | 9 | 6 |
| | | | | To the Secretary . . . | 52 | 10 | 0 |
| | | | | To the Royal Society of Literature, for One Year's use of their Council Room to 15th December, 1844 | 12 | 0 | 0 |
| | | | | To Mr. Rodd, the Society's Agent, for the delivery of Books, &c. . . . . . | 25 | 8 | 0 |
| | | | | To the Secretary, for Advertisements, Postage, &c. . . . . . . . | 19 | 9 | 10 |
| | | | | Advertisement in the Quarterly Review . . . . | 5 | 0 | 0 |
| | | | | To Mr. Culliford, per centage on Arrear Subscriptions received by him . | 6 | 17 | 0 |
| | | | | Treasurer's Expenses and other Expenses incurred by Local Agents—including a Gratuity to the Doorkeeper of the Royal Society of Literature. . | 4 | 15 | 6 |
| | | | | | 486 | 10 | 7 |
| | | | | Balance in hand . . . . | 301 | 3 | 1 |
| | 787 | 13 | 8 | | 787 | 13 | 8 |

And we, the Auditors, have further to report that, over and above the present Balance of £301 3*s.* 1*d.*, there still remain outstanding certain subscriptions, amounting for the first year to the sum of £5, for the second year to the sum of £15, for the third year to the sum of £41, for the fourth year to the sum of £113, and for the present year to £308: in all £482.

We have further to report that the Society remains indebted in the following sums, properly payable out of last year's Subscription: to Mr. Shoberl for Printing, £82 15*s.* 9*d.*, and to Messrs. Bonsor and Co. for Paper supplied £50.

J. W. Allen.
Henry Robertson.
Lewis Pocock.

# ANNUAL MEETING, 26th APRIL, 1845.

---

The Report of the Council and the Report of the Auditors having been read, the following Resolutions were passed:—

RESOLUTION I. That the Report of the Council for the past year be received and printed, and that the thanks of the Society be given to the Council for their services.

RESOLUTION II. That the Report of the Auditors be received and printed, and that the thanks of the Society be given to them for their services.

RESOLUTION III. That the thanks of the Society be given to Sir Edward Dering, Bart., for the loan of the unique manuscript of Shakespeare's Henry Fourth.

RESOLUTION IV. That the thanks of the Society be given to the President, The Most Noble the Marquis of Conyngham, for his lordship's services to the Society.

RESOLUTION V. That the thanks of the Society be given to the Editors of the various books issued for the past year, viz., to Mr. James Orchard Halliwell, for the editions of "Tarlton's Jests," "Illustrations of Fairy Mythology," and Manuscript of Shakespeare's "Henry the Fourth;" to Mr. Barron Field, for the edition of "The True Tragedie. of Richard the Third," &c.; to Mr. Collier, for "The Ghost of Richard the Third;" to the Rev. Alexander Dyce, for the edition of "Sir Thomas More;" to Mr. Amyot, for the edition of "The Taming of *a* Shrew," &c.; and to the various Contributors to the Volume of the Society's Papers.

RESOLUTION VI. That the thanks of the Society be given to the Director, and Treasurer, and Secretary, for their services.

JOHN BRUCE, ESQ., F.S.A., BARRON FIELD, ESQ., JAMES HEYWOOD, ESQ., F.R.S., JOHN OXENFORD, ESQ., THOMAS WRIGHT, ESQ., F.S.A., retiring from the Council in compliance with Law IX., the vacancies were filled up by the unanimous election of

LIEUT.-GENERAL SIR ANDREW BARNARD, K.C.B.
BERIAH BOTFIELD, ESQ., M.P.
JOHN FORSTER, ESQ.
WILLIAM C. MACREADY, ESQ.
SAMUEL NAYLOR, ESQ.

and the remaining Members of the Council were re-elected.

The following Members were also elected Auditors for the year ending 26th of April, 1846.

THOMAS BREWER, ESQ.
J. GOUGH NICHOLS, ESQ., F.S.A.
THOMAS POWELL, ESQ.

FREDERICK SHOBERL, JUNIOR,
PRINTER TO HIS ROYAL HIGHNESS PRINCE ALBERT,
51, RUPERT STREET, HAYMARKET, LONDON.

754871

Printed in Great Britain by
Amazon.co.uk, Ltd.,
Marston Gate.